"My friend Rick Phillips is known for his careful exegesis, faithful exposition, theological insights, and pastoral concern. He beautifully blends these qualities in this excellent commentary on Psalms 73–106. This book should be close at hand for any preacher or teacher of the Word of God who wishes to understand the holy text and proclaim its inerrant truth."

—**Daniel L. Akin,** President, Professor, Preaching and Theology, Southeastern Baptist Theological Seminary

"The Psalms open the soul to expose the heights of worship and the depths of sorrow—sometimes in the same psalm. They are, as Calvin put it, 'an anatomy of all parts of the soul.' Both informative to the mind and encouraging to the soul, Richard Phillips's sermonic commentary leads the believer through valley and mountaintop to discover that wherever we are, our faithful God is there with us and will minister to our every need."

—**Joel R. Beeke,** President, Puritan Reformed Theological Seminary

"Phillips not only expounds the rich doctrinal teaching of the Psalms with clarity (a welcome resource for any pastor), but also captures something of the poignancy of the poetry that contributes so significantly to their message. With the warm pastoral insights that we've come to expect from him, Phillips consistently demonstrates how these songs and prayers find their fulfillment in Christ, the ultimate singer of the Psalms."

—**Stephen Coleman,** Assistant Professor, Old Testament and Biblical Languages, Westminster Theological Seminary

"Another commentary on the Psalms? Thankfully, yes! Rick Phillips not only has provided the church with an exceedingly readable and insightful commentary on Psalms 73–106, but has done so with the wisdom and thoughtfulness of a pastor who understands the struggles, hopes, fears, joys, sorrows, and temptations of believers. Dr. Phillips understands what Calvin meant when he wrote that the Psalms are an anatomy of all the parts of the soul. In this commentary there is a fine blend of careful reading, thoughtful exposition, and pointed application, as well as engaging illustrations that give weight to the exposition and applications. This is a commentary that preachers will want to study and Christians in general to read with the greatest profit."

—**Ian Hamilton,** Professor, Systematic and Historical Theology, Westminster Presbyterian Theological Seminary

"The Reformed Expository Commentaries are usually the first books I turn to when preparing sermons. I'm therefore delighted that this volume fills up one of the few remaining gaps in the series. Yet Rick Phillips also has the rare gift of writing commentaries in such a way that all Christians, not just preachers, can read them with great profit and pleasure."

—**David Murray,** Professor, Old Testament and Practical Theology, Puritan Reformed Theological Seminary

"Rick Phillips has now written a dozen or more commentaries in this series and has developed a reputation as one of the finest and most trustworthy expounders of Scripture alive today. Each volume has excelled in exegetical and homiletical skills possessed by only a very few preacher-scholars. This current volume, on book 3 of the Psalms (73–106), contains all the things that we have come to expect from Phillips: close attention to the text, judicious illustrations, and practical, relevant application. For those collecting the series, this is a no-brainer. For those who are discovering these volumes for the first time, this is a good place to start. Phillips will guide you to a better understanding of Scripture and ensure that your feet are kept firmly on the ground."

—**Derek W. H. Thomas,** Chancellor's Professor of Systematic and Pastoral Theology, Reformed Theological Seminary; Senior Minister, First Presbyterian Church (ARP), Columbia, South Carolina

Psalms 73–106

REFORMED EXPOSITORY COMMENTARY

A Series

Series Editors

Richard D. Phillips
Philip Graham Ryken

Testament Editors

Iain M. Duguid, Old Testament
Daniel M. Doriani, New Testament

Psalms 73–106

Richard D. Phillips

P&R
PUBLISHING
P.O. BOX 817 • PHILLIPSBURG • NEW JERSEY 08865-0817

Italics within Scripture quotations indicate emphasis added.

ISBN: 978-1-62995-658-9 (cloth)
ISBN: 978-1-62995-659-6 (ePub)
ISBN: 978-1-62995-660-2 (Mobi)

Printed in the United States of America

Library of Congress Cataloging-in-Publication Data

Names: Phillips, Richard D. (Richard Davis), 1960- author.
Title: Psalms 73-106 / Richard D. Phillips.
Description: Phillipsburg : P&R Publishing, 2020. | Series: Reformed expository commentaries | Includes bibliographical references and index. | Summary: "Even by the Psalms' high standards, the poems of Books 3 and 4 are extraordinary in their insight and inspiration-inspiring beloved hymns and offering remedies to life's fiercest struggles"-- Provided by publisher.
Identifiers: LCCN 2019046823 | ISBN 9781629956589 (cloth) | ISBN 9781629956596 (epub) | ISBN 9781629956602 (mobi)
Subjects: LCSH: Bible. Psalms, LXXIII-CVI--Commentaries.
Classification: LCC BS1430.53 .P4635 2020 | DDC 223/.207--dc23
LC record available at https://lccn.loc.gov/2019046823

To D. A. Carson
With thanks to God for your friendship,
visionary gospel leadership, and
superlative scholarship
and
to the Savior King,
for
"The LORD has made known his salvation;
he has revealed his righteousness in the
sight of the nations" (Ps. 98:2).

Contents

Series Introduction

In every generation there is a fresh need for the faithful exposition of God's Word in the church. At the same time, the church must constantly do the work of theology: reflecting on the teaching of Scripture, confessing its doctrines of the Christian faith, and applying them to contemporary culture. We believe that these two tasks—the expositional and the theological—are interdependent. Our doctrine must derive from the biblical text, and our understanding of any particular passage of Scripture must arise from the doctrine taught in Scripture as a whole.

We further believe that these interdependent tasks of biblical exposition and theological reflection are best undertaken in the church, and most specifically in the pulpits of the church. This is all the more true since the study of Scripture properly results in doxology and praxis—that is, in praise to God and practical application in the lives of believers. In pursuit of these ends, we are pleased to present the Reformed Expository Commentary as a fresh exposition of Scripture for our generation in the church. We hope and pray that pastors, teachers, Bible study leaders, and many others will find this series to be a faithful, inspiring, and useful resource for the study of God's infallible, inerrant Word.

The Reformed Expository Commentary has four fundamental commitments. First, these commentaries aim to be *biblical*, presenting a comprehensive exposition characterized by careful attention to the details of the text. They are not exegetical commentaries—commenting word by word or even verse by verse—but integrated expositions of whole passages of Scripture. Each commentary will thus present a sequential, systematic treatment of an entire book of the Bible, passage by passage. Second, these commentaries are unashamedly *doctrinal*. We are committed to the Westminster Confession of Faith and Catechisms as containing the system of doctrine taught in the Scriptures of the Old and New Testaments. Each volume will teach, promote, and defend the doctrines of the Reformed faith as they are found in the Bible. Third, these commentaries are *redemptive-historical* in their orientation. We believe in the unity of the Bible and its central message of salvation in Christ. We are thus committed to a Christ-centered view of the Old Testament, in which its characters, events, regulations, and institutions are properly understood as pointing us to Christ and his gospel, as well as giving us examples to follow in living by faith. Fourth, these commentaries are *practical*, applying the text of Scripture to contemporary challenges of life—both public and private—with appropriate illustrations.

The contributors to the Reformed Expository Commentary are all pastor-scholars. As pastor, each author will first present his expositions in the pulpit ministry of his church. This means that these commentaries are rooted in the teaching of Scripture to real people in the church. While aiming to be scholarly, these expositions are not academic. Our intent is to be faithful, clear, and helpful to Christians who possess various levels of biblical and theological training—as should be true in any effective pulpit ministry. Inevitably this means that some issues of academic interest will not be covered. Nevertheless, we aim to achieve a responsible level of scholarship, seeking to promote and model this for pastors and other teachers in the church. Significant exegetical and theological difficulties, along with such historical and cultural background as is relevant to the text, will be treated with care.

We strive for a high standard of enduring excellence. This begins with the selection of the authors, all of whom have proved to be outstanding communicators of God's Word. But this pursuit of excellence is also reflected in a disciplined editorial process. Each volume is edited by both a series editor and a testament editor. The testament editors, Iain Duguid for the Old Testament and Daniel Doriani for the New Testament, are accomplished pastors and respected scholars who have taught at the seminary level. Their job is to ensure that each volume is sufficiently conversant with up-to-date scholarship and is faithful and accurate in its exposition of the text. As series editors, we oversee each volume to ensure its overall quality—including excellence of writing, soundness of teaching, and usefulness in application. Working together as an editorial team, along with the publisher, we are devoted to ensuring that these are the best commentaries that our gifted authors can provide, so that the church will be served with trustworthy and exemplary expositions of God's Word.

It is our goal and prayer that the Reformed Expository Commentary will serve the church by renewing confidence in the clarity and power of Scripture and by upholding the great doctrinal heritage of the Reformed faith. We hope that pastors who read these commentaries will be encouraged in their own expository preaching ministry, which we believe to be the best and most biblical pattern for teaching God's Word in the church. We hope that lay teachers will find these commentaries among the most useful resources they rely on for understanding and presenting the text of the Bible. And we hope that the devotional quality of these studies of Scripture will instruct and inspire each Christian who reads them in joyful, obedient discipleship to Jesus Christ.

May the Lord bless all who read the Reformed Expository Commentary. We commit these volumes to the Lord Jesus Christ, praying that the Holy Spirit will use them for the instruction and edification of the church, with thanksgiving to God the Father for his unceasing faithfulness in building his church through the ministry of his Word.

Richard D. Phillips
Philip Graham Ryken
Series Editors

Preface

One evening in the fall of 1990, when I was in graduate school at the University of Pennsylvania, I wandered into an evening service at Tenth Presbyterian Church of Philadelphia. There, I encountered James Montgomery Boice in his pulpit for the first time. While Dr. Boice certainly impressed me, my heart was captured by the message of God's grace in Jesus Christ that he preached so ably. Soon, as a new convert, I was attending morning and evening services each week. Around this time, Boice began preaching the book of Psalms in his evening pulpit. I remember those sunset worship services as a golden time in my new Christian life, and it was then that I was first captivated by the Psalms.

After meeting my wife in the pews of Tenth Church, I gave her as a Christmas gift a copy of John Calvin's commentary on the Psalms. I warmly remember her tentative reaction: "A book by . . . John Calvin. Honey, how . . . nice." Perhaps out of her habitual kindness, Sharon began reading Calvin on the Psalms as part of her morning devotional routine. Before long, those studies became exceedingly precious to her, and she has often ascribed a deepening spirituality to what has become a lifelong love affair with the book of Psalms. A few years later, when I was teaching on the faculty of the United States Military Academy at West Point, we would sometimes spend our Sunday afternoons walking the redoubt trails above the Hudson River, reading and praying the Psalms together. This experience taught me the value of the Psalms as an aid to the struggle of prayer that many believers experience. To this day, I regularly conclude my morning devotions by praying to the Lord the lines of a psalm I have read, and I often recommend this practice to others as an impetus to God-centered prayer.

I recount this biographical information as just one example of the power of the Psalms in a Christian's life of faith and worship. Preaching from the

Psalms has been a rich spiritual experience for me and, I believe, a great pastoral resource for the ministry of my congregation. The Psalms touch on every facet of the human experience, from the highs to the lows, including frank honesty about the human condition with its indwelling sin. Towering above these realities is the sovereign God, whose justice and grace offer the remedy to the struggles of life.

Even by the high standards of the Psalms, the poems contained in books 3 and 4 of the Psalter are extraordinary in the insight and inspiration they provide. Starting with the Asaph collection in Psalms 73 to 83, we receive wisdom and understanding that compel us to repent and believe. Included in book 3 are more psalms from the sons of Korah, including the pilgrim song of Psalm 84 that so stirs all "those whose strength is in you, in whose heart are the highways to Zion" (Ps. 84:5). Book 4 begins with the memorable line from Moses, "from everlasting to everlasting you are God" (Ps. 90:2). This collection is elevated by the royal psalms from Psalms 93 to 99 and concludes with the two potent couplets of Psalms 103–104, celebrating God as Redeemer and Creator, and Psalms 105–106, exalting God's faithfulness to save and man's reliance on his grace.

It is not by chance that so many beloved hymns in the Reformation tradition are drawn from this section of the Psalms. We sing "He Leadeth Me: O Blessed Thought!" from Psalm 73; John Newton's "Glorious Things of Thee Are Spoken" from Psalm 87; Isaac Watts's "Our God, Our Help in Ages Past" from Psalm 90; "Joy to the World!" from Psalm 98; and finally, the many renditions of Psalm 103, including Henry F. Lyte's "Praise, My Soul, the King of Heaven." The message of these familiar hymns introduces the material of Psalms 73–106, as worship songs exalting the Lord as our heavenly hope and his royal Son, Jesus, as our sovereign Savior.

The material in this volume was first preached from the pulpit of Second Presbyterian Church, Greenville, South Carolina, from 2014 to 2017 (unlike Dr. Boice, I did not plow straight through the Psalms, but took breaks between the books). I give thanks to God for the enthusiasm of this beloved congregation for these sermons (as for all the rest of God's Word) and for the session's support of my ministry. Having already mentioned my wife Sharon's companionship in the journey of the Psalms, I thank her as well, together with our five children, for the burden of supporting the demanding schedule of my sermon preparation, pastoral ministry, and book writing.

Special thanks go to my friends Philip Ryken and Iain Duguid for their significant contributions through the editing process, together with the devoted staff of P&R Publishing.

This volume is dedicated to D. A. Carson in appreciation for his decades of exemplary scholarship and leadership to the worldwide cause of the gospel. Don Carson's personal encouragement has been a great blessing to me, and I have been honored to serve with him on the council of The Gospel Coalition. Finally, this preface must conclude with a word of praise for the sovereign King and Redeemer of whom glorious things are spoken in the book of Psalms. May these studies encourage many in a love for the Psalms and a help to those called to preach its wonderful message: for "the Lord has made known his salvation; he has revealed his righteousness in the sight of the nations" (Ps. 98:2).

Richard D. Phillips
Greenville, South Carolina

Psalms 73—89: Book 3 of the Psalter

My Portion Forever

1

Spiritual Recovery

Psalm 73

Whom have I in heaven but you? And there is nothing on earth that I desire besides you. My flesh and my heart may fail, but God is the strength of my heart and my portion forever. (Ps. 73:25–26)

Psalm 73 begins with a statement of simple truth: "Truly God is good to Israel, to those who are pure in heart" (v. 1). A parallelism is at work here, as is common in Hebrew poetry. "Those who are pure in heart" is a qualification or amplification of "Israel." God's true people are those whose hearts are turned to him, and to them God is good. This is, says Asaph, a simple truth. The rest of this psalm, however, is dedicated to showing how hard it is sometimes to believe and be content with knowing that God is good.

According to the superscription, the author of this psalm is Asaph, the Levite whom David placed in charge of the musical worship before the ark in Jerusalem (see 1 Chron. 16:5, 7). Asaph was a prominent figure and no doubt a deeply spiritual man. Despite these qualifications, his psalm records his descent into a discontentedness with God and his providence, and then a spiritual recovery that not only restored him but elevated him to one of the highest plateaus of spirituality in all the Old Testament.

The Problem of Discontentment

The English Puritan Jeremiah Burroughs understood Asaph's struggle. His 1648 spiritual classic, *The Rare Jewel of Christian Contentment*, offered a lengthy reflection on Paul's declaration in Philippians 4:11, "I have learned in whatever situation I am to be content." Burroughs defined *contentment* as "that sweet, inward, quiet, gracious frame of spirit, which freely submits to and delights in God's wise and fatherly disposal in every condition."[1] Another Puritan, Thomas Watson, also spoke helpfully about contentment: "We glorify God, by being contented in that state in which Providence has placed us. We give God the glory of his wisdom, when we rest satisfied with what he carves out to us."[2]

Most of us, however, find it hard to be content with the circumstances that God has given us. We are not often satisfied with God's provision in our lives. Really, though we seldom put it this way, it is God with whom we are dissatisfied. This is a curious phenomenon, since the Bible not only does not promise us sunny skies and clear sailing but, quite the opposite, clearly informs us that as God's people we will be beset with troubles. Peter writes, "Beloved, do not be surprised at the fiery trial when it comes upon you to test you, as though something strange were happening to you" (1 Peter 4:12). Because we are his children, God gives us trials to strengthen our character and draw us close to him. Since we have been told this, it is inconsistent for us to be discontented by circumstances of difficulty.

However unreasonable our discontentment is, the Bible shows that we have good company in our misery. The prophet Habakkuk climbed into his watchtower to await God's justification for the woes he was inflicting on Israel. The prophet Jeremiah was a distinguished complainer (see Jer. 20:7–18). Job, who had better grounds than we do for discontentment, exercised them vigorously. Here in Psalm 73 we have a great man like Asaph saying, "But as for me, my feet had almost stumbled, my steps had nearly slipped" (v. 2).

The first section of Psalm 73, from verses 2 to 15, records Asaph's descent into spiritual depression, beginning with envy toward the ungodly: "For I was envious of the arrogant" (Ps. 73:3).

1. Jeremiah Burroughs, *The Rare Jewel of Christian Contentment* (Edinburgh: Banner of Truth, 1964), 19.

2. Thomas Watson, *A Body of Divinity* (Edinburgh: Banner of Truth, 1958), 13.

Asaph marshals an impressive argument for his envy. He begins with two observations that cause him to resent God's rule of affairs. First, "I was envious of the arrogant when I saw the prosperity of the wicked" (Ps. 73:3). Second, the ungodly seem to lead happy and carefree lives: "For they have no pangs until death; their bodies are fat and sleek. They are not in trouble as others are; they are not stricken like the rest of mankind" (vv. 4–5).

These are observations that we also make, since we are likewise prone to resentment. Many times I have heard complaints from Christian women about immodest girls who were rewarded with a husband and children, with a house in the suburbs and all they ever wanted. Meanwhile, these godly but distressed women had refused to compromise sexually and men didn't want them. It happens, and it is galling. I know men who stuck by their moral principles at work—and what happened? They lost their jobs, got passed over for promotion, and suffered professionally and financially. What about the cheaters and connivers? They were rewarded. They now had the powerful positions, lush offices, and big salaries. "How is that right?" the believer asks. The Bible depicts this same reality. A godly man such as Joseph can be sold as a slave by his brothers, and his father believes the deception they schemed to cover it up. This is a world in which righteous Lazarus can become a cripple and live in misery outside the gates of a pompous rich man who cares nothing for him. Lazarus just lies there, dogs licking his sores, and then he dies. It is hard not to ask God what kind of world he is running, what kind of justice there is when this is happening. The answer is that ours is a cold and cruel world, broken and scarred by sin.

Things get worse, however. Asaph points out that the wicked exult in their villainy: "Therefore pride is their necklace; violence covers them as a garment. . . . They scoff and speak with malice; loftily they threaten oppression. . . . They say, 'How can God know? Is there knowledge in the Most High?'" (Ps. 73:6–11). The unrighteous laugh at the righteous; they mock their victims and boast in the face of God. Yet lightning never strikes them! Far from it—they win awards, they garner praise, and people fawn over them while the righteous are despised.

Imagine, for instance, someone who commits a terrible crime—perhaps assault or even murder—and then gets off on a technicality. Imagine how the victim feels, along with the victim's parents. Then the criminal boasts about it, taunting the victim. He writes a book, and it becomes a best-seller. He laughs about pitiful people who do good and trust in God. Is there anything more galling than that? Perhaps something like this has happened to you, and you are embittered by it, as Asaph was.

Asaph was undone by envy for the success of the wicked, and he was indignant over God's providential ordering. Today he would watch reality television shows and fume over the godless wealth that so many of them glamorize. He would tune in to the Hollywood award shows and seethe over the money and glamour of those who prance about in debauchery. By thinking this way, Asaph ended up blaming God and found himself in a spiritual abyss.

Asaph reaches rock bottom in Psalm 73:12–13: "Behold, these are the wicked; always at ease, they increase in riches. All in vain have I kept my heart clean and washed my hands in innocence." This is a terrible conclusion. Asaph finds himself saying: "It's not worth serving God. All my religion and faith is foolish if this is the way things are." This is the blasphemy that worldly people believe, but a pious man such as Asaph ought to know better. First came envy and indignation, then self-pity made its appearance, and finally he finds himself denying altogether the value of serving God. Now Asaph is the one mocking God; having envied the ungodly, he is molded into their image, attitude, and sinful speech.

Referring to this spiritual descent, the psalmist said, "My feet had *almost* stumbled, my steps had *nearly* slipped" (Ps. 73:2). It is important to see what it was that kept his foot from slipping completely. What was the foothold on which he found traction and from which he began to climb back up? He answers: "If I had said, 'I will speak thus,' I would have betrayed the generation of your children" (v. 15).

This assessment shows that Asaph realizes how ridiculous was his self-pitying attitude. Yet only concern for the influence he might have on others checks his free-fall. In this, he shows the value of being part of a Christian community. How often, when we are too stubborn or depressed to care about ourselves, our love for others reins us in and makes us speak and act in a godly manner. If we are ever thinking the way Asaph was, we should follow his example. He waited to report his feelings and thoughts until he had worked his way out of the difficulties and was able to say: "Truly God is good to Israel" (Ps. 73:1).

Four Steps to Spiritual Recovery

From the foothold of his spiritual concern for others, Asaph begins his climb back to a right attitude toward God. Psalm 73 records four steps in his spiritual recovery, which we should follow when we need to escape from self-pity or despair. The first appears in verses 16–17: "When I thought how to understand this, it seemed to me a wearisome task, until I went into the sanctuary of God."

Here, Asaph provides one of the keys to Christian stability and growth. When we are foundering, when we have lost our sense of balance and have started falling because of doubt or discouragement, or when we can no longer remember why we once were so safe and happy as Christians, what enables us to regain our position? The answer: "I went into the sanctuary of God" (Ps. 73:17). The psalmist went to church—in his case, into the tabernacle. What he encountered there brought a perspective that he had forgotten. He was confronted with a mighty, holy, and saving God, and that realization changed everything.

How important it is to come to the place of worship! When I encounter a Christian who has badly fallen, it is nearly always the case that he has ceased attending church or at least actively participating in the worship service. One of the reasons that we must be constant in worship in order to thrive as Christians lies in what we find there. Martyn Lloyd-Jones explains:

> People who neglect attendance at the house of God are not only being unscriptural—let me put it bluntly—they are fools. My experience in the ministry has taught me that those who are least regular in their attendance are the ones who are most troubled by problems and perplexities. . . . It is a very foolish Christian who does not attend the sanctuary of God as often as he possibly can.[3]

Lloyd-Jones emphasizes what worship does for us. Worship takes our eyes off ourselves—off the troubles and the confusing data that our minds are dealing with—and puts our eyes onto God. Only then do things come into proper focus. "I could make no sense of this," Asaph says. "I was miserable, confused, bitter. But I went into the sanctuary. I went before God.

3. D. Martyn Lloyd-Jones, *Faith Tried and Triumphant* (Grand Rapids: Baker, 1994), 109.

I stopped accusing him and arguing with him and simply came before him. When I saw him again, my problems began to resolve themselves. Everything looked different when I looked to the Lord."

Have you ever experienced this kind of new perspective in prayer? You come to God with your petty anger, self-pity, and self-absorbed attitude. As you start praying, you realize how ridiculous it all is. You become like Job, who had questioned God's wisdom. God then spoke to him from the whirlwind and revealed his majesty, demanding of Job: "Who is this that darkens counsel by words without knowledge?" (Job 38:2). An abashed Job could only reply, "I had heard of you by the hearing of the ear, but now my eye sees you; therefore I despise myself, and repent in dust and ashes" (42:5–6). How foolish we can be, how quick to self-pity and depression. For this very reason, we need to be diligent in our Bible reading, in our study of God's awesome attributes and his great saving works. We need to be regular in prayer. But especially, we must be often in the sanctuary, present with the people of God in worship. These are our only protection against ourselves, against our sin, folly, and weakness.

Coming into the sanctuary was the first step in Asaph's spiritual recovery. We, too, must come before God. Do not try to solve your problems apart from God, but take them into God's presence! In the sanctuary is where spiritual recovery begins.

Second, Psalm 73:17 tells the immediate effect of Asaph's return to God: "Then I discerned their end." When Asaph put his eyes onto God, his perspective became different. His horizons were enlarged. Specifically, he noticed something that he had forgotten in his angry descent, namely, the end that awaits the ungodly. He elaborates: "Truly you set them in slippery places; you make them fall to ruin. How they are destroyed in a moment, swept away utterly by terrors! Like a dream when one awakes, O Lord, when you rouse yourself, you despise them as phantoms" (vv. 8–20).

Asaph had forgotten about the final judgment, just as we often do. What a difference this makes in our assessment. The judgment of God! There is a judgment at the end of days! Therefore, though the wicked may be carefree and prosperous now (although this is hardly the case in every instance), though they may avoid punishment in this world, and though they may gloat in their violence and crime, there is a judgment that they cannot and will not escape. While the rich man in Jesus' parable may have been too self-absorbed to notice the sufferings of righteous Lazarus, the story of these two men did not end at death. The man of God who suffered in life was blessed in death, while the arrogant rich man suffered in torment for his sins. This is the perspective that Asaph regained: "Then I discerned their end."

Once, on an airplane, from a couple of rows behind me came a lively conversation between a middle-aged man and a young woman. The man's boisterous voice overspread several rows of the plane, and most of us gave up trying to read or sleep and settled in for the in-flight talk show. The man pontificated on any number of subjects. He debunked religion as a fraud. He extolled the virtues of his carefree, happy-go-lucky life. Having earlier spoken at length about his wife, he later asked the younger woman out for a date. I felt many things toward this man, but envy was not among them! Apart from the obvious folly of his pleasure-seeking lifestyle, there is the judgment of God to be faced! Being at enmity with God, the man was at peace with the world and with his sin. Of course such a person is carefree now! He is a child of this present evil age, with no struggle against the flesh, the world, and the devil. Meanwhile, the believer, having peace with God, has ceaseless conflict in this present life. But none of a Christian's struggles made me envy the man on the airplane. Unless he were to repent and turn to God in faith, how sure and sudden would be his fall into inescapable doom.

I thought this especially as the man laughingly recounted the many ailments arising from his smoking, drinking, and carousing, along with the daily round of medicines he confessed to needing to keep the party going. I remember this now because I was at that moment trying to read Psalm 73. There before me was verse 18: "Truly you set them in slippery places; you make them fall to ruin." On what a slippery slope the man pranced in his dancing shoes! Verse 20 asserts, "Like a dream when one awakes, O Lord, when you rouse yourself, you despise them as phantoms." Worldly and sinful happiness has no more security or substance than a dream that allures us in our sleep. So it is for all boastful sinners. Like Haman's situation in the book of Esther, the gallows that the ungodly erect will one day become the instrument of their own demise. Like a house built on a fault line, all happiness in sin rests on the brink of woe.

Do you realize this? Instead of envying, do you look on the mocking and arrogant unbelievers and pity them for their laughter? Do you mourn over the calamity of their sin? You should. Not being able to speak to the man on the airplane, I prayed for his soul, that God would wake him from his dreamy state before it was too late. Only from a perspective centered on God, from an understanding of life gained from the Bible, do we see things rightly. It is then simply impossible for us to envy the ungodly. Instead of complaining about our troubles, we become more fervent in prayer, more diligent in our witness, and more sober in our lives. "Fret not yourself because of evildoers; be not envious of wrongdoers!" writes David. "For they will soon fade like the grass and wither like the green herb" (Ps. 37:1–2).

The third step in Asaph's recovery came when he applied these insights to himself. Earlier, in his depressed state, he complained about how little he got for his righteousness. Now he realizes that everything he was thinking about other people is true of himself: "When my soul was embittered, when I was pricked in heart, I was brutish and ignorant; I was like a beast toward you" (Ps. 73:21–22). If the wicked were foolish and brute beasts before God, the same was no less true of Asaph in his accusations and discontentment.

Likewise, it is necessary for our spiritual well-being that we become aware of our own sin, guilt, and unworthiness. Earlier, I cited frequency in worship as a spiritual barometer. But here is another: if we are boastful and arrogant before God, we are surely far from him. C. S. Lewis put it this way:

> Whenever we find that our religious life is making us feel that we are good—above all, that we are better than someone else—I think we may be sure that we are being acted on, not by God, but by the devil. The real test of being in the presence of God is that you either forget about yourself altogether or see yourself as a small, dirty object.[4]

This attitude of self-abasement is not morbid self-loathing, but healthy realism about our sin in the presence of God's holiness. It is borne out in the Bible whenever people really are brought to see God. They see themselves as naked and dirty, like Adam and Eve after their sin, needing to be clothed in the righteousness of Christ. Or, like Peter, they respond to the awareness of God's presence in the way that Peter spoke when he perceived the deity of Jesus: "Depart from me, for I am a sinful man, O Lord" (Luke 5:8).

If you are disappointed with what God is providing for you, I assure you that you fail to appreciate your own sin and guilt. Therefore, we all should

4. C. S. Lewis, *Mere Christianity* (New York: Macmillan, 1958), 111.

pray for a fresh remembrance of our sin. "Blessed are the poor in spirit," Jesus taught, "for theirs is the kingdom of heaven" (Matt. 5:3).

The first step to recovery is to come before God in worship. Second, we must realize the end that awaits the ungodly, and then, third, also notice that this is precisely our own predicament. This leads to the fourth step of spiritual recovery, which is a fresh appreciation of the blessings we enjoy from the unmerited grace of God. When Asaph realizes that he himself is among the wicked, deserving judgment and destruction like the others, he remembers with joy the blessings that he previously despised: "Nevertheless, I am continually with you; you hold my right hand. You guide me with your counsel, and afterward you will receive me to glory" (Ps. 73:23–24). "How wonderful it is," he says in essence, "though I have been such a sinner, that God is nonetheless with me. He holds me in his hand; he guides me in this life. Despite all I have done and left undone, there is glory ahead into which God is taking me."

Asaph has arrived at the doctrine of salvation by grace alone: the Bible teaching that God has freely provided sinners a way for their salvation. God provides grace through faith in Jesus Christ. Each of us is a foolish, brutish beast before God. Our lives in sin are built on the fault line of a coming doom. But God sent his Son to save us: fulfilling the demands of his law on our behalf, weaving by his life a garment of righteousness for us to wear, and then bearing the punishment of our sins on the cross. Through faith alone, God offers us the benefits of Christ's great saving work: "Whoever believes in him shall not perish but have eternal life" (John 3:16 NIV).

This same doctrine that offered us salvation in the first place—salvation by grace alone—also preserves the Christian from discontentment. Why are you unhappy? Because you think you deserve something and aren't getting it. Yet in truth, the thing that you deserve and do not get is God's judgment for your sins. While deserving only judgment from God, you are instead receiving an inheritance of eternal life through Jesus Christ. Your great spiritual blessings were gained at an infinite cost to the God whom you are so prone to resent.

The psalmist realizes this gospel truth, and it leads him upward to recovery. God has saved us at the cost of his precious Son's blood! He now sends the Holy Spirit into our hearts that we might have fellowship with him. God has given the light of his Word to guide us and a sure hope of glory to await us. How can we complain? How can we harbor discontentment toward such a Savior? Whatever trials and disappointments we now endure, they come with a promise of glory ahead; in this light, we see sorrows as instruments that God is using to wean us from the idols of this world and draw our hearts to him.

My Portion Forever

It is remarkable that within this one psalm we find one of the lowest expressions of unbelief and one of the highest expressions of spiritual devotion. Having descended into the pit of depression, Asaph made a horrible statement, telling the same devilish lie that turned the first Paradise into a hell and that blinds so many people today. He said, in Psalm 73:13, that trusting God is vain. The nadir of unbelief is to say that God doesn't matter—or, worse, that God is the one we must escape if we want to be happy. Exactly opposed to this lie is the great truth that forms the apex of faith. We read it in verses 25–26, the glorious height to which Asaph now climbs. He proclaims that nothing else matters if only we have God. "Whom have I in heaven but you?" asks the psalmist. "And there is nothing on earth that I desire besides you. My flesh and my heart may fail, but God is the strength of my heart and my portion forever." Both these statements—one despising God and the other glorifying God—come from the same man in the same psalm; surely this proves the importance of a biblically shaped mind. The same man finds himself either in the pit or on the heights, either in hell or in heaven, all depending on the way he allows himself to think.

Verses 25 and 26 of Psalm 73 are so great that I am almost afraid that expounding them can only tarnish them. But it is safe to reflect that our present happiness cannot and will not be found in anything of this world—not in money, not in achievement, not in romance, not in pleasure. Only God can fill our hearts: "God is the strength of my heart and my portion forever." If we have him, we have all that we really need. How much more must this be true for our eternal destiny?

This much is certain—"my flesh and my heart may fail" (Ps. 73:26). Indeed, they certainly will. This body that I serve and feed and pamper is not a ship that will sail me safely into harbor. But in all that it lacks, in all that this whole world lacks, God abounds. "God is the strength of my heart and my portion forever." When I consider this, why would I place anything before my relationship to God? Why would I complain if I have him? God is what I really need, and all I really need.

Earlier, I mentioned Burroughs's book *The Rare Jewel of Christian Contentment*. Here is what Burroughs concludes, in line with this thought:

> It is not necessary for me to be rich, but it is necessary for me to make my peace with God; it is not necessary that I should live a pleasurable life in this world, but it is absolutely necessary that I should have pardon of my sin; it is not necessary that I should have honour and preferment, but it is necessary that I should have God as my portion, and have my part in Jesus Christ, it is necessary that my soul should be saved in the day of Jesus Christ. The other things are pretty fine indeed, and I should be glad if God would give me them, a fine house, and income, and clothes, and advancement for my wife and children: these are comfortable things, but they are not the necessary things; I may have these and yet perish for ever, but the other is absolutely necessary.[5]

This is quite clearly the position to which the psalmist has arrived. He concludes with a great realization and firm resolution: "For behold, those who are far from you shall perish; you put an end to everyone who is unfaithful to you. But for me it is good to be near God; I have made the Lord God my refuge, that I may tell of all your works" (Ps. 73:27–28).

This is what heaven is—to be with God—and it is something that we need not wait to enjoy. If we share Asaph's need to be near to the Lord, we will concern ourselves far less with the things of this world and far more with the things of God: faith, holiness, service to God, and our witness to the world. And in these things we will find not merely a present contentment, but a joy that will never end and a glory that will never fade away.

5. Burroughs, *Rare Jewel of Christian Contentment*, 92–93.

2

Why, O God?

Psalm 74

Yet God my King is from of old, working salvation in the midst of the earth. (Ps. 74:12)

Psalm 74 is a lament offered to God at one of the bitterest times in Israel's history. It is ascribed to Asaph, who was chief musician in the time of David. But since the psalm describes the burning of the temple, which occurred centuries later during Nebuchadnezzar's conquest of Jerusalem in 587 B.C., the author must have been a descendant of Asaph or a later holder of his office. Grieving for the fallen city and temple, and burdened even more for the eternal prospects of Israel, the psalmist cries an impassioned plea for God to remember and save his covenant people: "O God, why do you cast us off forever? . . . Remember your congregation, which you have purchased of old" (Ps. 74:1–2).

God's People May Suffer Greatly

This lament makes it clear that God's people may suffer greatly in this world. One kind of Christian attitude suggests that true believers need never worry about trouble. The Bible teaches otherwise, as does the experience of the church in the world. Peter advised the early Christians: "Beloved, do not be surprised at the fiery trial when it comes upon you to test you, as though something strange were happening to you" (1 Peter 4:12). The Old Testament believers likewise endured many ordeals, and Psalm 74 records one of the worst.

The first section of the psalm details the extent of this calamity. The author invites the Lord to take a tour with him around the ruins of the holy city: "Direct your steps to the perpetual ruins; the enemy has destroyed everything in the sanctuary!" (Ps. 74:3). He points out the battle standards of pagan armies in the city of God's dwelling, no doubt together with the emblems of their false gods: "Your foes have roared in the midst of your meeting place; they set up their own signs for signs" (v. 4). Verses 5 and 6 compare the enemy to axmen felling trees in the forest—"like those who swing axes in a forest of trees"—except that these men were hewing the gilded panels of the holy temple: "all its carved wood they broke down with hatchets and hammers." Moreover, the temple building itself was put to the torch. Jeremiah 52:13 records that Nebuchadnezzar "burned the house of the LORD, and the king's house and all the houses of Jerusalem." Asaph complains especially about the calamitous loss of Solomon's golden temple: "They set your sanctuary on fire; they profaned the dwelling place of your name, bringing it down to the ground" (Ps. 74:7). Summing up the enemy's destruction, he points out that their aim was nothing less than to make a final end of God's people: "They said to themselves, 'We will utterly subdue them'" (v. 8). It was with this genocidal intent that the Babylonians "burned all the meeting places of God in the land" (v. 8).

Christians should realize that while worldly people will generally show hostility (see John 15:18–20), there are times when the ungodly attain such unrestrained power that they seek to remove the godly once and for all. Later in Babylonia, where the remaining Jewish people were taken as captives, Haman the Agagite "sought to destroy all the Jews" (Esth. 3:6), as recorded in the book of Esther. For a more recent example, in the aftermath of the Protestant Reformation, Louis XIV attained unchallenged power in France, revoked the Edict of Nantes that had promised freedom of religion to the Huguenots, and unleashed a savage persecution that drove nearly all the Bible-believing Christians from the land. Similar attempts at eradicating the Christian witness are taking place now in lands where Muslim zealots are able to gain control, such as Sudan and Turkey.

Psalm 74 recognizes that the suffering of God's people takes place with the full knowledge of God. While the psalmist appeals to God to look at their affliction, it is not because he doubts God's awareness. In fact, verse 1 makes it clear that Jerusalem was destroyed because God deliberately withdrew his protection: "O God, why do you cast us off forever?" John Calvin writes that the psalmist was "convinced, that had not God been angry with them, the heathen nations would not have been permitted to take such license in injuring them."[1] The Bible makes it clear that Jerusalem fell and the temple was burned because of God's judgment on the idolatry of his people. If they were determined to worship false gods, then God punished them by sending them to the virtual center of idolatry, Babylon, where they could experience the kind of life that results from evil worship (Jer. 16:10–13). When Asaph complained that pagan standards had been set up in God's city, the Lord might have reminded him that the faithless people of Israel had set up similar idols there themselves.

It is not always the case, however, that suffering Christians are being afflicted by God's chastising hand. In many cases—we think, for example, of the French Huguenots or the courageous Christians under persecution today in the Middle East—their affliction results from their valiant refusal to renounce Christ and his gospel. In these cases, God is working through his people to advance his kingdom in ways that may be hard to understand at the time. Whether our suffering is due to God's judgment or simply for the cause of God's glory, believers must look to God and take our case to him, whether in repentance or with the kind of bewildered plea that we see in Psalm 74. Charles Spurgeon described this psalm as a model for afflicted Christians, offering the kind of prayer that God is faithful to answer: "We have here before us a model of pleading, a very rapture of prayer. It is humble, but very bold, eager, fervent, and effectual."[2]

At the heart of this plea is not merely a lament for the afflictions of God's people, but the panicked fear that it might always be this way. Asaph laments not only that God has abandoned Israel, but, as Psalm 74:1 indicates, that God would "cast us off forever." Verse 11 concludes the opening lament, asking the *why* question: "Why do you hold back your hand, your right

1. John Calvin, *Calvin's Commentaries*, 23 vols. (1848; repr., Grand Rapids: Baker, 2009), 5:161.

2. Charles Haddon Spurgeon, *The Treasury of David*, 3 vols. (Peabody, MA: Hendrickson, n.d.), 2a:273.

hand?" The preceding verse, however, asks the more urgent question of *when*: "How long, O God, is the foe to scoff? Is the enemy to revile your name forever?" (v. 10).

It seems that one reason the psalmist felt anxiety over the duration of Israel's disgrace was the lack of a sign from God: "We do not see our signs; there is no longer any prophet, and there is none among us who knows how long" (Ps. 74:9). The psalmist laments the absence of God's Word to the people: "there is no longer any prophet," and therefore "none among us who knows how long" (v. 9).

This is a remarkable statement given the prophecies of Jeremiah, who foretold not only the fall and destruction of Jerusalem but also the seventy-year duration of the Jews' captivity in Babylon (Jer. 25:11). But given the chaos of his times, we can understand why the psalmist was ignorant of this revelation. The same excuse cannot be made in our time. Most Christians own numerous Bibles, with various translations and study notes. Our problem—the reason we lack knowledge of God's purposes and plans and the hope that comes from them—is that we do not read our Bibles. Many Christians today refuse to attend a church where serious Bible teaching takes place, showing far more interest in social programs and entertainment instead. We do not give priority in our schedules to the study of God's Word or primacy in our churches to in-depth scriptural teaching.

If we want to live with hope and spiritual strength in troubling times, we will follow the example of the Huguenots who were persecuted by Louis XIV. The French king forbade the possession of Bibles or Psalters, so the Huguenots committed large portions of Scripture to memory, especially the Psalms. One group of Huguenot exiles marched into Geneva, Switzerland, where they had sought refuge, singing Psalm 74:1: "O God, why do you cast us off forever? Why does your anger smoke against the sheep of your pasture?" Three years later, when military victories permitted their return to their homes, they sang the same psalm's triumphant conclusion: "Arise, O God, defend your cause; remember how the foolish scoff at you all the day!" (v. 22).[3] If we will make it our chief concern to place God's Word into our minds and hearts, we will have a similar resolve in trying times and a lively hope for the future.

3. Rowland E. Prothero, *The Psalms in Human Life* (New York: Dutton, 1904), 217–18.

God's People May Hope in God's Salvation

In the final statement of the opening lament, the psalmist complains that God seems to have his hands in his pockets while his people are destroyed: "Why do you hold back your hand, your right hand? Take it from the fold of your garment and destroy them!" (Ps. 74:11). The second section of the psalm, verses 12–17, provides reasons why the psalmist is confident that God will answer and deliver his people. For all the frustration expressed in his lament, he shows us that Christians always have hope in God's salvation.

Important as it is to learn of God's plans in the Bible, it is even more important to learn of God himself and his great saving works. James Boice writes: "Earlier he had asked God to remember Israel; here he himself remembers God."[4] Remembering what God is like, what promises he has made, and how he has redeemed his people in the past is our chief source of hope in a dark and dangerous world. With this in mind, we see that Psalm 74:12 makes a statement of confidence in God that turns Psalm 74 from a bereaved lament into a confident prayer. Here is the turning point that lifts the lament into a bold appeal: "Yet God my King is from of old, working salvation in the midst of the earth."

This basic confidence in God's saving power is joined to three specific reasons why the psalmist can trust in God, even with Jerusalem in ruins, reasons that Christians today can share.

First, the psalm's opening verses recall *God's sovereign election* of his people for salvation. Israel is "the sheep of your pasture" and "your congregation, . . . the tribe of your heritage!" (Ps. 74:1–2). Even Mount Zion, the Temple Mount, could not be abandoned, since it was chosen by God as the place "where you have dwelt" (v. 2). True, the Israelites had broken their covenant with God by worshiping false gods and refusing to obey God's Word. But their place in God's salvation was secured by his grace, according to his sovereign choosing. Paul specifies that the true Israel has always been the Israel of faith (Rom. 2:28–29); thus, God's election of Israel is fulfilled in the Christ-believing church. But even in the Old Testament, believers could look to God's election and know that he would not forget his people.

4. James Montgomery Boice, *Psalms*, 3 vols. (Grand Rapids: Baker, 1996), 2:620.

Christians can take strong comfort in knowing that they were chosen by God, whose sovereign grace cannot fail. In his Good Shepherd discourse, Jesus stated: "I give them eternal life, and they will never perish, and no one will snatch them out of my hand. My Father, who has given them to me, is greater than all, and no one is able to snatch them out of the Father's hand" (John 10:28–29). Though believers may suffer greatly in this world, and while even true believers may grievously sin against God and come under his frowning discipline, those who trust in the Lord know that "he who began a good work in you will bring it to completion at the day of Jesus Christ" (Phil. 1:6).

A second reason to retain confidence in God is *his costly redemption* of Israel in former days. Psalm 74:2 identifies Israel as the congregation "which you have purchased of old, which you have redeemed." This statement likely refers to Israel's exodus from Egypt, when God redeemed his people from bondage and caused his angel of death to pass over their houses because of the blood of the lamb. This theme of redemption is probably expressed in the apocalyptic language of verses 13–14: "You divided the sea by your might; you broke the heads of the sea monsters on the waters. You crushed the heads of Leviathan; you gave him as food for the creatures of the wilderness." God divided the Red Sea waters to permit his people to pass through, before drowning the pursuing Egyptian army. When verse 15 says that God "split open springs and brooks [and] dried up ever-flowing streams," this refers to God's provision of water to Israel in the desert and his stopping up of the Jordan River so that his people could pass through. The reference to monsters and Leviathan is thought by scholars to symbolize God's defeat of mighty Pharaoh and the power of Satan that stood behind him.[5] Imagery similar to this is used in the book of Revelation to depict Christ's victory over the great red dragon, Satan (Rev. 12:1–9). The point is that the God who exerted such power in delivering his people from bondage in Egypt and brought them into the promised land would not suffer to see his people utterly destroyed by the Babylonians.

Christians look back on an even greater redemption in the atoning death of Jesus. If God has redeemed us with the blood of his own Son, is there any chance that he will leave us to be destroyed by the powers of darkness? Jesus

5. See Calvin, *Commentaries*, 5:174–75, as well as H. C. Leupold, *Exposition of the Psalms* (Columbus, OH: Wartburg Press, 1959), 538–39.

instituted the sacrament of the Lord's Supper so that his people would remember his death for their salvation; is there any chance that God will forget the great offering of his Son to redeem his flock? Spurgeon assures us that by remembering our redemption in Christ, believers gain a great hope amid our trials and a strong plea in our prayers to God: "Let us put him in remembrance, let us plead together. Can he desert his blood-bought and forsake his redeemed? Can election fail and eternal love cease to flow? Impossible. The woes of Calvary, and the covenant of which they are the seal, are the security of the saints."[6]

Third, the psalmist settles his hope on *God's almighty power* as Creator. Some scholars believe that the reference to God's subduing sea monsters and the great Leviathan is not to the exodus but to God's subduing the forces of chaos in his ordering of the world. The Babylonian creation myths speak of the sea monsters being subdued and Tiamat (a Leviathan parallel) being slain. The psalmist may be saying that Israel's God is the true Creator who has power over tumult and rebellion.[7] In any case, there is no doubt that Psalm 74:16–17 highlights God's power as the Creator who has subdued and ordered nature: "Yours is the day, yours also the night; you have established the heavenly lights and the sun. You have fixed all the boundaries of the earth; you have made summer and winter."

Psalm 121 encourages us that God is always able to help because he "made heaven and earth" (Ps. 121:1). Christians can likewise draw strength to know that the God to whom we pray is the Creator of all that is and who thus has more than enough power to save us from any foe. David Dickson writes: "As the Lord hath set bounds to the sea, bounds and borders to every kingdom, to summer's heat and to winter's cold: so can he do, and so hath he done, and so will he do unto all the troubles of his own [people], to all the rage, power, plots and purposes of their enemies."[8]

God's People Have Confidence in Prayer

Remembering God and considering his sovereign election, costly redemption, and almighty power have changed Psalm 74 from a desperate and

6. Spurgeon, *Treasury of David*, 2a:273.

7. See Joseph A. Alexander, *The Psalms Translated and Explained* (1873; repr., Grand Rapids: Baker, 1977), 315.

8. David Dickson, *A Commentary on the Psalms* (1653; repr., Edinburgh: Banner of Truth, 1995), 464.

confused plea to a confident, purposeful prayer. The final stanza, verses 18–23, presents five petitions that Christians today may equally offer to God. The reasons that the psalmist provides for God to decisively intervene will also provide us with strong reasons to call on the Lord for salvation in times of need.

First, the psalmist calls for the overthrow of evil for the sake of *God's honor*: "Remember this, O Lord, how the enemy scoffs, and a foolish people reviles your name" (Ps. 74:18). The Babylonians who boastfully paraded their standards on Mount Zion were an affront to Israel's God, offering a direct challenge to his glory. We are reminded of a similar appeal made by King Hezekiah when the Assyrian king Sennacherib besieged Jerusalem. On the instructions of the prophet Isaiah, Hezekiah went into the temple, spread before the Lord the mocking terms of surrender given to him by the Assyrian ambassador, and prayed for God's help:

> Incline your ear, O Lord, and hear; open your eyes, O Lord, and see; and hear all the words of Sennacherib, which he has sent to mock the living God. . . . So now, O Lord our God, save us from his hand, that all the kingdoms of the earth may know that you alone are the Lord. (Isa. 37:17–20)

God answered Hezekiah's prayer by sending the angel of the Lord to slay 185,000 soldiers of Sennacherib's army in a single night, saving his people and defending the honor of his own name. Christians may likewise pray for God to defend his honor against those who mock his Word and revile his people.

The psalmist's second petition is a plea to *God's mercy* for his weak and needy people: "Do not deliver the soul of your dove to the wild beasts; do not forget the life of your poor forever" (Ps. 74:19). The turtledove symbolizes the church's vulnerability and is "an expression of affectionate endearment."[9] H. C. Leupold writes: "to surrender His people like a gentle and harmless dove into the power of 'the wild beast' would be a heartless act that God could not become guilty of."[10] Similarly, the Gospels show how Jesus was moved with compassion for the needs of the sick, weak, and hungry. When we pray to God for compassion in his name, Christ appeals to the mercy of the Father. James 5:11 explains that by studying Scripture we

9. Alexander, *Psalms*, 317.
10. Leupold, *Exposition of the Psalms*, 540.

learn "the purpose of the Lord, how the Lord is compassionate and merciful." How eager God is to answer a plea to act in mercy for the weak!

Third, the psalmist appeals to *God's covenant promises*: "Have regard for the covenant, for the dark places of the land are full of the habitations of violence" (Ps. 74:20). God had pledged himself to uphold the throne of David forever (2 Sam. 7:16). The Old Testament covenants of Abraham, Moses, and David are ultimately fulfilled in Christ (see Gen. 12:1–3; Josh. 14:9; 2 Cor. 1:20), so that Christ's church can be certain that God will preserve her against the greatest of foes. The eternal covenant between the Father and Son declared that "everyone who looks on the Son and believes in him should have eternal life, and I will raise him up on the last day" (John 6:40). Spurgeon exclaims: "Here is the master-key—heaven's gate must open to this. God is not a man that he should lie; his covenant he will not break, nor alter the thing that hath gone forth out of his lips."[11] Christians may present to God his covenant promise to grant eternal life to all who believe, thus calling on God to preserve us from every spiritual foe.

The psalmist's fourth petition concerns *God's praise* when he saves people by his grace: "Let not the downtrodden turn back in shame; let the poor and needy praise your name" (Ps. 74:21). If believers humbled themselves and prayed to God for help but were denied, this would shame the worship of the Lord. By answering with help, God will instead gain praise from the hearts of those who trust his Word. Jesus said that the Father "is seeking" people who will worship him "in spirit and truth" (John 4:23). A desire for God's glory should always be present in our prayers, and when we seek God's aid for his own praise, we can be confident of his intervention from heaven.

The psalmist's fifth and final petition concerns *God's cause* in the world: "Arise, O God, defend your cause; remember how the foolish scoff at you all the day! Do not forget the clamor of your foes, the uproar of those who rise against you, which goes up continually!" (Ps. 74:22–23). God's cause is bound up with his gospel, with his church, and with faith in his Word. God is not ignorant as to the great clamor of his foes and the constant "uproar of those who rise against" him. Therefore, when the church is besieged, when biblical truth is despised, and when faith is persecuted, Christians may confidently appeal to God to strengthen the cause of his gospel and his church.

11. Spurgeon, *Treasury of David*, 2a:278.

Consider these five petitions whenever you find yourself praying to God in desperate need. You may be bold in asking God to defend his honor, show mercy, uphold his covenant, gain praise through grace, and uphold his cause in the world. Such God-centered, God-glorifying, and God-dependent intercession is a biblical model for praying to God with confidence and success.

God's People Have a Savior

Psalm 74 has shown that God's people can be greatly afflicted, yet have hope in God's salvation and confidence with God in prayer. One might therefore ask how this particular psalm was answered by God in Israel's history. Before answering, we must remember that God had committed to punish Israel through the exile in Babylon. Therefore, the psalmist's generation would suffer great humiliation, deprivation, and affliction in a far-off pagan land. As far as history was concerned, Nebuchadnezzar had succeeded in his aim to subdue and dominate the people of Israel permanently (Ps. 74:8). But the Bible shows that Nebuchadnezzar's intentions would in fact be frustrated by God's faithful intervention to save his people in answer to their prayers. God protected and prospered the Jews in Babylon, as the book of Esther records. When the prescribed seventy years had passed, God was faithful to arrange their restoration to Jerusalem, as told in the books of Ezra, Nehemiah, Haggai, and Zechariah. God defended his honor, had mercy on his afflicted people, kept his covenant, restored worship to his name, and advanced the cause of his salvation in the world. In short, Bible history shows that within a century God answered every prayer so boldly brought to him in Psalm 74.

I mentioned that the turning point of Psalm 74 is found in verse 12, where the psalmist states: "God my King is from of old, working salvation in the midst of the earth." The Christian who reads this verse in the original Hebrew text cannot fail to think of Jesus Christ. The reason for this is that the Hebrew word for "salvation" is a plural form of the word *yeshuah*. Asaph praised God for making *yeshuah*, salvation, in the earth. This happens to be the same name that God's angel told Joseph to give the virgin-born child of Mary: "You shall call his name Jesus," which in Hebrew is *Yeshuah*, "for he will save his people from their sins" (Matt. 1:21). Here is the ultimate answer to the cry of Psalm 74, "Why, O God?" God works salvation—*yeshuah*—in the earth by sending his Son, *Yeshuah*, Jesus Christ, to be the Savior who redeems his people from sin, death, and defeat.

Christian parents have all heard their children blurt out pat answers to unexpected Bible questions. A boy has let his mind wander and his parents ask him to explain what he had neglected to pay attention to. Often, not knowing what has been read, the child will wisely exclaim, "Jesus!," thinking this a likely answer. The child is right! For "Jesus" is the correct answer to virtually every question pertaining to God's saving work.

Every Christian can look to the cross and see God's gift of love that redeems us from sin and secures for us eternal life. Whatever troubles, failures, or defeats we are suffering—sometimes because of the fallen world and sometimes because of our own sin—Christians can find hope in Jesus. "God my King is from of old," every Christian may claim, sending Jesus as a Savior for the world (Ps. 74:12). Paul thus reasoned that the needy believer who possesses Christ by faith can be sure that God will never permit him or her to fail: "He who did not spare his own Son but gave him up for us all, how will he not also with him graciously give us all things?" (Rom. 8:32). Thus, even when we are "regarded as sheep to be slaughtered . . . we are more than conquerors through him who loved us" (vv. 36–37).

3

The Horn of Righteousness Lifted

Psalm 75

All the horns of the wicked I will cut off, but the horns of the righteous shall be lifted up. (Ps. 75:10)

One of the most important precepts for good worship is the *dialogical principle*. The idea is that a worship service is a meeting of God with his people so that there is a dialogue in the service. God calls his people to worship through his Word, and the people sing to his praise and pray for his presence. God speaks through the reading of Scripture, and the people respond by professing the faith and confessing their sins, seeking pardon. God speaks through the preached Word and God acts through the sacraments, and the people respond by singing to him and praying to him with thanks.

A good example of the dialogical principle of worship is Psalm 75. The psalm breaks into four sections. In verse 1, the people give praise to God with thanksgiving. In verses 2–5, God speaks, assuring his people of his care and warning the proud and ungodly. Verses 6–8 present the pastor's reflections on what God has said, and in verses 9–10 the people respond with a pledge to act on what God has declared.

Psalm 75 also continues the theme of God's judgment that began in Psalm 73. In Psalm 73, Asaph admitted his distress over the apparent success of the ungodly, until he returned to the sanctuary and remembered God's judgment. Psalm 74 is a plea for God to intervene against the wicked, concluding in confidence as the psalmist remembers the past deeds of the Lord. In Psalm 75, he has learned these lessons well. He no longer doubts or complains against God, but praises him from the opening verse. Psalm 75 reflects the psalmist's grateful realization that while events in the world are often troubling, "God nevertheless is near, his judgments are timely, and the wicked will eventually be punished in full for the evil they have done."[1]

We Give Thanks

In this spirit of faith, Psalm 75 begins on a positive note: "We give thanks to you, O God; we give thanks" (Ps. 75:1). When a congregation gathers for worship, one of its chief purposes is to thank God for his innumerable blessings. When Asaph came back to the temple in Psalm 73, recalling God's judgment on the wicked took away his envy and anger (Ps. 73:17). In Psalm 74, Asaph remembered God as the eternal King who works "salvation in the midst of the earth" (Ps. 74:12), and this insight restored his confidence in God to answer prayer. Now in Psalm 75, he returns to the worship service and has thanksgiving on his heart. True worship that is centered on God's self-revelation in the Bible will produce thankfulness that will go forth in our praise. Douglas Jones writes that while "complaint is the flag of ingratitude, . . . yet, by grace, God's redemption and creation ought to keep us in a perpetual state of thanks which bursts out in celebration at every opportunity."[2]

The particular cause for thanks in Psalm 75 is the awareness that God is near: "We give thanks to you, O God; we give thanks, for your name is near" (Ps. 75:1). God's name stands not only for his person but also for his covenant promises. He is present to be the God he declared himself to be to our fathers in the past. The psalmist praises God for being present in a way that his people can always rely on him.

1. James Montgomery Boice, *Psalms*, 3 vols. (Grand Rapids: Baker, 1996), 2:624.

2. Douglas Jones and Douglas Wilson, *Angels in the Architecture: A Protestant Vision for Middle Earth* (Moscow, ID: Canon Press, 1998), 80.

Psalm 75:1 specifies that God is present through the remembrance of his saving works. "We recount your wondrous deeds," the worshiping congregation sings. God had stretched out a mighty hand to help his people in past times of need—parting the Red Sea, empowering Gideon's little band against the Midianites, and sending David's stone to strike down the giant Goliath, to name a few instances—so that the people who worship can be thankful to God for the help that he will have for them, too.

One of the greatest blessings in times of trouble is to realize that God is near. A pastor will frequently be found at a hospital bed, or at a graveside, or in a home where tragedy has struck, and he can bring few more comforting messages than the promise that God is close to his people in need. This message is found throughout the Psalms, which makes sense because the Psalms speak to us in all the circumstances of life. When I think of the verses that I am most likely to read to the sick, broken, or grieving, they include passages that give assurance that God is near in his mercy and grace:

> The angel of the Lord encamps
> around those who fear him, and delivers them. . . .
> The Lord is near to the brokenhearted
> and saves the crushed in spirit. (Ps. 34:7, 18)

> The salvation of the righteous is from the Lord;
> he is their stronghold in the time of trouble.
> The Lord helps them and delivers them. (Ps. 37:39–40)

> I lift up my eyes to the hills.
> From where does my help come?
> My help comes from the Lord,
> who made heaven and earth. (Ps. 121:1–2)

Notice the emphasis in Psalm 75 on how we can know that God is near: through his Word. Willem VanGemeren writes: "In the remembrance and retelling of the history of salvation lies the comforting affirmation of God's closeness to his people."[3] But we should go further and say that we know not only that God is near, but that God is actually brought near through his

3. Willem A. VanGemeren, "Psalms," in *The Expositor's Bible Commentary*, ed. Frank E. Gaebelein (Grand Rapids: Zondervan, 1991), 5:491.

Word. The congregation thanks God because his name is near, and the way that this happens is this: "We recount your wondrous deeds" (Ps. 75:1). Thus, the way to have a thankful heart that worships God is to experience God's presence through his Word. Worship that thanks God centers on the preaching and teaching of the Holy Scriptures. Paul made this point in Romans 10:6–8, quoting Moses from Deuteronomy 30:12–14:

> "Do not say in your heart, 'Who will ascend into heaven?'" (that is, to bring Christ down) "or 'Who will descend into the abyss?'" (that is, to bring Christ up from the dead). But what does it say? "The word is near you, in your mouth and in your heart" (that is, the word of faith that we proclaim).

Paul's point is that we do not truly experience God's presence through ecstatic worship that seeks to bring heaven down or by spiritual exercises designed to work God's presence up. Instead, God is near to us as his Word is proclaimed by our lips and believed in our hearts. Are you conscious of God's nearness to you with the same saving power that he has shown to others before? You can know God's presence through his Word, with the result that you will be thankful to God as you worship him together with fellow believers.

A Message of Assurance and Warning

According to the dialogical principle of worship, the congregation interacts with God as he speaks to us in his Word. Psalm 75 follows this pattern as God responds to the praise of his people with a message given through the psalmist. He begins with a word of assurance to humble and needy believers.

This message of assurance reminds the people that despite all appearances, God remains always in charge so as to uphold his order in the world: "When the earth totters, and all its inhabitants, it is I who keep steady its pillars" (Ps. 75:3). This statement assumes that there are times when it seems as though the world is tottering and God's moral order is being overthrown so that wickedness is taking over. Some scholars suggest that Asaph may be referring to the Assyrian invasion under Sennacherib, which led to the siege of Jerusalem in 701 B.C. The psalm might equally refer to an internal rebellion such as that of David's son Absalom, the division of the Israelite kingdom in the time of Solomon's son Rehoboam, or the reign of wickedness and idolatry in the time of Queen Athaliah in the ninth century B.C. Whether the situation involves foreign invasion, internal revolt, government breakdown, or simply a time of moral and spiritual collapse, God's faithful people need to know that he is always sovereign over all. Although the foundations of society and culture seem to be shaking, God is keeping steady the pillars of his reign. Knowing this, God's people have reasons even in the worst of times to uphold their witness to God and his Word, calmly obey his commands, and be thankful when gathered in worship.

Psalm 75:3 might be taken as a defense of a doctrine known as *common grace*. This doctrine states that even outside of God's redemption of sinners through faith in his gospel, he is graciously working to prevent sin from taking over completely. It is by God's common grace that the unbelieving world exhibits certain virtues and that many things of beauty are preserved. Common grace is not saving grace, but its purpose is to hold an evil world together and provide resources for the advance of the gospel. For this reason, God's common grace is a cause for his people to praise him with thanks, rejoicing to know that God keeps steady the pillars of history to hold off complete collapse until Christ returns in glory.

The particular emphasis of Psalm 75, however, is that God upholds the world's moral order by judging the wicked in his own good time: "At the set time that I appoint I will judge with equity" (Ps. 75:2).

The list of outstanding evil powers brought down by God is impressive. Pharaoh heads the list, having boasted against God, "Who is the LORD, that I should obey his voice and let Israel go?" (Ex. 5:2). Nebuchadnezzar destroyed Jerusalem and then boasted about his home city: "Is not this great Babylon, which I have built by my mighty power as a royal residence and for the glory of my majesty?" (Dan. 4:30). Herod put to death the apostle James and allowed the people to worship him as God. More recently, Murdoch Campbell records Adolf Hitler as looking at a picture of himself riding proudly on a white horse, on which was written the opening statement of John's Gospel, "In the Beginning was the Word." Hitler then challenged Christ, declaring, "I am providence."[4] All these despots at one time seemed almost godlike in the triumph of their evil regimes. Yet each of them was brought

4. Quoted in Murdoch Campbell, *From Grace to Glory: Meditations on the Book of Psalms* (Edinburgh: Banner of Truth, 1970), 124.

low by God in his own time. Campbell writes: "Pharaoh and his hosts are swept to destruction; Nebuchadnezzar becomes a companion of 'the beasts of the field'; Herod is devoured by worms and Hitler becomes a suicide."[5]

God's eventual judgment provides Christians with the answer as to the upheavals of immorality and violence that seem to engulf the world today. America and the West are experiencing a devolution of morality, especially concerning sexuality and gender identity, that could hardly have been imagined just a few years ago. Legislatures and courts arrogantly overthrow thousands of years of moral judgment in demanding acceptance for homosexuality and the redefinition of marriage. Backed up by coercive government power, the sources of anarchy seem to be shaking the very pillars of moral authority. Yet to alarmed and bewildered Christians, God declares, "When the earth totters, . . . it is I who keep steady its pillars" (Ps. 75:3).

Whatever the morally reckless cultural despots may insist, God's creation order of male and female remains the fundamental category of human life. Those who rebel against God's order bring only chaos onto themselves instead of the wholesomeness that they pretend to achieve. However the state may define marriage, only the sexually compatible union of a committed man and woman can provide the basis for a stable family and society. The more a nation erases moral lines and induces chaos into human relations, the more breakdown and suffering it will experience. God warns, "At the set time that I appoint I will judge with equity" (Ps. 75:2). This rule holds for the bloodthirsty violence of Muslim jihadists in the Middle East, with their almost unbelievable cruelty toward Christians and even other Muslims. However relentless and formidable their terror may seem, God is able to make them collapse into their own ruin.

Because God is certain to judge, Psalm 75:4–5 adds a warning to the arrogant and evil: "I say to the boastful, 'Do not boast,' and to the wicked, 'Do not lift up your horn; do not lift up your horn on high, or speak with haughty neck.'" In the day of God's judgment, which is certain to come either within history or at history's end when Christ returns, the boasting of the wicked will stick in their throats; the upraised horns of their tyranny will be broken off. There is a God, he is not far off, and he is able to uphold the order that he created and ordained.

5. Campbell, *From Grace to Glory*, 124.

Psalm 75 helps us with a matter that vexes many tried believers: why does it take God so long to act in judgment? The Bible's answer is that God judges in a way and at the time that best accomplish his great purposes. One of God's great purposes is to save sinners who repent. He thus delays his judgments so as to give the gospel its full opportunity to save sinners like us. Paul writes that "God's kindness is meant to lead you to repentance" (Rom. 2:4), to which he adds a warning that we should not thus presume on God's patience but instead should repent so as to be saved while there is still time.

A second reason why God waits to bring judgment "is so evil might have time to work itself out or come to full fruition."[6] If God were to judge immediately, the way that we often desire, evil might not be displayed in its true colors and God's justice might often be misunderstood. God informs us that he delays so as to "judge with equity" (Ps. 75:2). God therefore told Abraham that his judgment on the wicked inhabitants of Canaan would wait until the fourth generation, "for the iniquity of the Amorites is not yet complete" (Gen. 15:16). But when the time of judgment arrives, God's victory is fully displayed. Thus God said to Pharaoh when it was time for that tyrant to fall: "for this purpose I have raised you up, to show you my power, so that my name may be proclaimed in all the earth" (Ex. 9:16).

God's message of final justice encourages Christians to go about the business of serving, obeying, and glorifying him. An example of this reasoning is shown in Isaiah chapter 3, in which God threatens Judah with complete moral and societal breakdown as a result of the people's idolatry. God foretold that their economy would collapse, that their military would fail, and that chaos would destroy the integrity of families. Isaiah 3 sadly describes the trajectory that America and the once-Christian West are following today (Isa. 3:1–9). What are the godly to do in such times? The answer is given in Isaiah 3:10, in which God told the prophet: "Tell the righteous that it shall be well with them, for they shall eat the fruit of their deeds."

Putting Down and Lifting Up

Beginning at verse 6, Psalm 75 turns to the preaching of its sermon, which every good worship service includes. In verses 2–5, God speaks, as seen by

6. Boice, *Psalms*, 2:627.

his use of the divine *I*. In verses 6–8 it is the psalmist who serves as preacher, offering reflections to the faithful based on the message that God had given in verses 2–5.

This homily presents a two-part message, the first part of which notes that every advancement or abasement comes from the Lord: "For not from the east or from the west and not from the wilderness comes lifting up, but it is God who executes judgment, putting down one and lifting up another" (Ps. 75:6–7).

The ancient Romans believed in the goddess Fortuna, who turned her great wheel to determine the fortunes of men and women. The Bible instead teaches that we live in the presence of a moral God who cares about our conduct and our relationship to him as people of either faith or unbelief. God controls history in the great affairs of the world and in the small affairs of every individual life, so we should look to him both for our circumstances and for the grace to trust in him and do his will.

When the psalmist says that we should look neither to the east or west nor from the wilderness (that is, the south) for lifting up, he warns us against relying on earthly powers of exaltation. "Lifting up" refers to an animal's raising its horn in strength and victory over others. John Calvin points out that our normal experience suggests the opposite of what the psalmist teaches, since "the majority of men who attain to the highest degrees of honour, owe their elevation either to their own policy and underhand dealing, or to popular favor and partiality, or to other means of an earthly kind."[7] In fact, however, this "does not happen by chance . . . [but] by the secret purpose of God."[8] God knows how to exalt the ungodly so as to more perfectly humble them, and God knows how to prepare the godly for high positions by training them in lowly places.

One application of this principle is that Christians should not crave positions that receive the attention or the praise of men. Jesus once said that someone invited to a feast should

> not sit down in a place of honor, lest someone more distinguished than you be invited by him, and he who invited you both will come and say to you, "Give your place to this person," and then you will begin with shame to take

7. John Calvin, *Calvin's Commentaries*, 23 vols. (1848; repr., Grand Rapids: Baker, 2009), 5:188.
8. Calvin, *Commentaries*, 5:188.

> the lowest place. But when you are invited, go and sit in the lowest place, so that when your host comes he may say to you, "Friend, move up higher." Then you will be honored in the presence of all who sit at table with you. (Luke 14:8–10)

Jesus' point was that we should allow God to determine the attention we get, the promotions we receive, and the opportunities he decides for us. God is the one who knows best how we can serve and what he intends for his people, and thus we should always serve gratefully wherever he assigns us, leaving our advancement to his will. Jesus concluded with the principle of which he himself was the greatest example: "For everyone who exalts himself will be humbled, and he who humbles himself will be exalted" (Luke 14:11). Jesus humbled himself by taking up the cross and was exalted by God in his glorious resurrection. Those who trust in him realize that the only honor that truly matters is that which comes from God, which he bestows most highly on his most humble servants.

The psalmist offers a second point to his sermon that is designed to put our priorities in the right place: "For in the hand of the Lord there is a cup with foaming wine, well mixed, and he pours out from it, and all the wicked of the earth shall drain it down to the dregs" (Ps. 75:8). Since we are all sinners, he argues, what really matters is not what other men and women think of us but how we stand before the judgment of the perfectly just and holy God.

The image, often repeated in the Bible, shows God as holding forth a cup "with foaming wine, well mixed" (Ps. 75:8). The description emphasizes the teeming dread within the cup, its red color depicting divine wrath. Charles Spurgeon comments that "it is blood for blood, foaming vengeance for foaming malice," adding, "The very color of divine wrath is terrible, what must the taste be?"[9]

The psalmist sees God as tilting his cup of wrath to the lips of the wicked on the day of his judgment, leaving them no choice but to drink it to the bottom: "he pours out from it, and all the wicked of the earth shall drain it down to the dregs" (Ps. 75:8). It is true that when God acts in history to judge a people, people of all kinds will feel the effects of the calamities that God has mixed. But it is only the wicked who drink the cup of God's wrath down to its dregs. Many godly people suffer injustice, trials, and sorrows of

9. Charles Haddon Spurgeon, *The Treasury of David*, 3 vols. (Peabody, MA: Hendrickson, n.d.), 1a:295.

all kinds, but when they get to the bottom God provides a sweet and wholesome drink of salvation life. But at the bottom of God's cup of wrath for the wicked are the bitter remains of his just retribution, leading to eternal condemnation and utter darkness. Psalm 75:8 chronicles the dreadful end of the wicked who refused to repent when God showed them patience and mercy, instead lifting their horn with arrogance in the face of God. When the day of judgment comes for such people, as Spurgeon writes, "The full cup must be quaffed, the wicked cannot refuse the terrible draught, for God himself pours it out for them and into them. Vain are their cries and entreaties. They could once defy him, but that hour is over, and the time to requite them is fully come."[10]

When we put verses 6–8 of Psalm 75 together, we see the point that the psalmist is making in light of God's message. Since God is the true and only Judge, we should not seek earthly preferment and advancement but should make the forgiveness of our sins our prime pursuit. How we stand with respect to God is always the chief matter in life! The Bible declares that there is, in fact, a way for sinners to escape the just judgment and fiery wrath of God, namely, through faith in the Savior whom God has sent, his Son, Jesus Christ. In the garden of Gethsemane, Jesus made it plain that he would himself drink the cup of wrath for all who rely on his saving work through a true and living faith. So dreadful was the thought of taking the wrath of God for our sins that Jesus asked the Father for another way of our salvation: "Father, if you are willing, remove this cup from me. Nevertheless, not my will, but yours, be done" (Luke 22:42). How terrible is the cup of wrath! Yet Jesus was willing to drink this cup for those who come to him confessing their sins and seeking salvation, granting us in its place the cup of blessing from God for eternal life.

Witnesses, Worshipers, and Workers

In the final two verses of Psalm 75, the congregation gives its *Amen* to the teaching of God and the psalmist, coupled with their resolute response: "But I will declare it forever; I will sing praises to the God of Jacob. All the horns of the wicked I will cut off, but the horns of the righteous shall be lifted up" (Ps. 75:9–10).

Here is a three-point agenda for responding to the message of God's

10. Spurgeon, *Treasury of David*, 1a:295.

sovereign judgment over men and history. First, the people resolve to "declare it forever" (Ps. 75:9). They will spread the news to others about the nearness of God both to save and to judge, to lift up and to cast down. This mirrors the calling of Christians today: our lives are not to be dedicated to self-advancement and the pursuit of earthly riches or power. If God decides to bless our work and elevate us to high positions or wealth, than we accept them as gifts to be used on his behalf. But our passionate calling is to declare to a world in darkness the light of God that has come through Jesus Christ.

Second, the congregation commits itself to a life of worship: "I will sing praises to the God of Jacob" (Ps. 75:9). By referring to the Lord as "the God of Jacob," the people remember the covenant promises he has fulfilled—promises for which we worship him as Lord. Our worship is therefore centered with joy on the covenant fulfillment that has come through Jesus Christ and the eternal life that God has provided for us through faith in him. Whatever our earthly circumstances, we have the privilege of praising a God of salvation, whose pledge secures for us the cup of blessing forever.

Finally, the people of God determine to live in line with God's judgments: "All the horns of the wicked I will cut off, but the horns of the righteous shall be lifted up" (Ps. 75:9–10). So far as we are able, we will follow God's lead in supporting truth and godliness, while doing our best to thwart the cause of evil. H. C. Leupold writes that the believer "will do what he can to check the influence of the wicked and to promote the success of the righteous."[11] This mandate will shape our private relationships as well as our civil participation in society, where Christians will be at the forefront in countering social ills such as abortion, racism, and other moral obscenities.

If God's presence is real, and if God will in his time judge all things in equity as he said, then surely Psalm 75 shows the way for believers to live. We live as witnesses, as worshipers, and as workers for righteousness. We believe and serve as those who have been saved by grace through the blood of God's own Son, Jesus, who secures our forgiveness before God's throne. In this way, whatever circumstances God ordains for our lives, we can anticipate an ending in joy. Jesus will declare: "Well done, good and faithful servant. . . . Enter into the joy of your master" (Matt. 25:21).

11. H. C. Leupold, *Exposition of the Psalms* (Columbus, OH: Wartburg Press, 1959), 547.

4

The Lion of Judah

Psalm 76

In Judah God is known; his name is great in Israel.
His abode has been established in Salem,
his dwelling place in Zion. (Ps. 76:1–2)

Psalm 76 completes a progression that began in Psalm 74. That earlier psalm responded to the great distress of God's people by first asking why God did not intervene and then by praying to him with confidence. Psalm 75 picked up that theme by praising God for the certainty that he will judge evil in due time. Psalm 76 now looks back on a significant instance when God did just that. God heard, intervened, and destroyed the enemies of his people. As a result, the psalmist desires both that God's own people would be faithful to him and that surrounding peoples would realize that the God of Israel is the true and only God.

This psalm does not state which occasion it has in mind for when God saved his people and destroyed their enemies. Candidates include the great victory won over the Ammonite stronghold at Rabbah (2 Sam. 12:26) in the time of King David. An even more notable victory was God's destruction of the vast Ammonite coalition that swept on Judah in the time of Jehoshaphat (2 Chron. 20:23). Greater still was the slaying of the Assyrian army of

185,000 soldiers under King Sennacherib, when the angel of the Lord struck them down in answer to Hezekiah's prayer (2 Kings 19:35). This last example is considered most likely by commentators, since many of the details noted in Psalm 76 seem to fit that occasion.

Since it celebrates God's delivering his people, Psalm 76 has often been remembered by Christians undergoing trials. Among many notable examples, this psalm was included in the thanksgiving services when England marked what she considered God's direct intervention in destroying the Spanish Armada in 1588. The Pilgrims who settled New England also looked to Psalm 76, taking the name of one of their main settlements, Salem, from verse 2: "His abode has been established in Salem." They understood the psalm's purpose, as summarized by John Calvin: "the continual care of God in defending the Church, which he has chosen, is here celebrated to encourage the faithful without any doubt or hesitation to glory in his protection."[1]

God Revealed

The initial point of Psalm 76 is that God has revealed himself to his people: "In Judah God is known; his name is great in Israel" (Ps. 76:1). This does not deny that other people outside Israel were aware of God, since the Bible makes it clear that all people learn of God through the creation (see Rom. 1:20). But the only people who really know God in his grace are the people who receive his Word and are gathered together in his name. This situation is what makes the church the most vitally important institution in the world: Christians alone, like Israel of old, know who God is and what he has planned for the world.

The reason that God is fully and truly known only in the church, as once he was only in Judah, is that God's ways can be known only as he chooses to reveal them. God has revealed himself through his Word, that is, through the prophets and apostles whose writings make up the Bible. In ancient times, different civilizations had differing religious ideas that consisted of the musings of their own imaginations. In general, they made and worshiped gods in their own image, reflecting their own values. The Israelites would have been no different if God had not chosen them in which to dwell and

1. John Calvin, *Calvin's Commentaries*, 23 vols. (1848; repr., Grand Rapids: Baker, 2009), 5:193.

if God had not revealed himself to them. God chose them not for any merit in themselves but because of his sovereign grace, by which he willed for this people to know him and reveal him to others (see Deut. 7:7–8). Not only the Scriptures, but also the tabernacle and the temple, the priests and their atoning sacrifices for sin, their feasts and institutions—all the life of Israel—were all designed to reveal God and lead people to faith. God said: "I will make you as a light for the nations, that my salvation may reach to the end of the earth" (Isa. 49:6).

Likewise, today the chief function of the church in its worship is to reveal God so that his glory may be known. An excellent question to ask about any local church is "What did you learn about God through its worship?" Today, many churches reveal far too little about God because their focus is on themselves or on the world and because they devote little attention to the teaching of Holy Scripture. A true church's glory is that God dwells there by his Spirit, through his Word, just as Psalm 76:2 celebrates that God's "abode has been established in Salem, his dwelling place in Zion." The proper response to God's presence is that he should be praised and that his glory should be made known.

What is true of the church is also to be true of the individual Christian. Not only are believers all called to tell others about God and the gospel of his salvation, but our lives are to be indwelt by God's Spirit so that others come to know him by looking at us. Jesus taught: "let your light shine before others, so that they may see your good works and give glory to your Father who is in heaven" (Matt. 5:16). Therefore, the same question we should ask about a church should also be asked about ourselves: do people who spend time with us learn anything about the grace and truth of Christ? If God is known by us and if he dwells in us through faith, then it should be the case that others learn of him through our lives.

The Bible teaches that God's supreme revelation of himself was through his Son, Jesus Christ. Jesus declared, "I and the Father are one" (John 10:30) and "Whoever has seen me has seen the Father" (14:9). These verses state not only that Jesus is like God but, more pointedly, that God is like Christ. Colossians 1:15 says: "He is the image of the invisible God." Hebrews 1:3 adds: "He is the radiance of the glory of God and the exact imprint of his nature." Therefore, the best way for a church or a Christian to reveal God and glorify him to the world is to be centered on the person and work of

Christ. The one who speaks often of Christ and whose heart relies most clearly on the gospel best knows God and makes his name great to others. Christ is so important to knowing God that the New Testament makes it clear that one cannot otherwise be saved: "there is salvation in no one else, for there is no other name under heaven given among men by which we must be saved" (Acts 4:12).

God Known in Power and Wrath

This psalm does not merely celebrate God's presence among his people so that they know and reveal him in a general way. The particular point is that God's people know him through his mighty works to overthrow their enemies and deliver them from distress. Verse 3 brings to the fore the idea of God as the mighty Deliverer: "There he broke the flashing arrows, the shield, the sword, and the weapons of war."

In our study of the Psalms, we do not normally take much notice of the word *selah*, which appears at the end of Psalm 76:3. This word was likely a musical notation, and though it gives clues to the structure of a psalm, it is not often clear why it appears where it does. Psalm 76 is an exception in this because the *selah* seems to clearly indicate that we should reflect and meditate on God's having overthrown the enemy by breaking his arrows, shield, and sword. Not only is God known in Jerusalem, but he especially revealed himself by overthrowing Israel's enemies in a supernatural way.

I mentioned that there are a number of potential candidates for the historical background to Psalm 76, but the destruction of the Assyrian army under Sennacherib in 701 B.C. is at least a good example of what Psalm 76 is talking about. That particular episode is considered most likely not only because of its prominence in the Old Testament but also because of many details in this psalm.

The defeat of Sennacherib is so important that its full story is recounted three different times in the Old Testament (2 Kings 18–19; 2 Chron. 32; Isa. 36–37). The story begins in Isaiah 7, when foolish King Ahaz invited the mighty Assyrian empire to come and intervene in Palestine so as to defend Jerusalem from its threatening neighbors. Ahaz failed to heed God's warnings not to enter into the idolatry necessary to this treaty, and he failed to realize that when the northern conquerors came, they would not want to leave.

When Ahaz's godly son Hezekiah came to the throne, he therefore had to throw off the yoke of Assyrian domination, the result of which was a massive invasion of the mighty Assyrian army. Second Kings 18 tells how the Assyrians overran all the strongholds of Judah and came to besiege Jerusalem. The king's herald, known as the Rabshekah, came forward to mock Hezekiah's faith in God, assuring him and his people that if they did not surrender, their city would be destroyed and their god would be carted off in disgrace. Following the advice of the prophet Isaiah, Hezekiah went into the temple on Mount Zion and threw himself before the Lord in prayer. He said: "O Lord our God, save us, please, from his hand, that all the kingdoms of the earth may know that you, O Lord, are God alone" (2 Kings 19:19). In response to Hezekiah's prayer, "the angel of the Lord went out and struck down 185,000 in the camp of the Assyrians" (v. 35), thus eradicating the threat to God's people and the affront to God's name.

A number of details cited in Psalm 76:3–7 appear to correspond to God's miraculous intervention in the days of Hezekiah. Verse 5 notes that the "stouthearted were stripped of their spoil; they sank into sleep; all the men of war were unable to use their hands." This well describes what happened when the angel of the Lord slew the sleeping army of Assyria. Second Kings 19:35 relates that "when the people arose early in the morning, behold, these were all dead bodies." The equipment of the enemy was easily lifted from their lifeless hands to become the spoil of God's people. Moreover, God's conquest took place by the mere word of his command, as Psalm 76:6 celebrates: "At your rebuke, O God of Jacob, both rider and horse lay stunned." Verse 7 summarizes, "But you, you are to be feared! Who can stand before you when once your anger is roused?" Benjamin B. Warfield writes:

> When [God] enters the field, all the machinery of conflict stops. The lightning-like arrows which fly from the bow cease in their courses; the shield and the sword fall helpless to the ground; the stoutest-hearted with their chariots and horses drop into the inactivity of death. For Jehovah is terrible. None can stand before Him when His wrath begins to burn but a little.[2]

Psalm 76:4 employs striking imagery to describe God's fierce power in destroying all enemies: "Glorious are you, more majestic than the mountains

2. Benjamin B. Warfield, *Faith & Life* (1916; repr., Edinburgh: Banner of Truth, 1974), 24.

full of prey." Mountains symbolize kingdoms, and "mountains full of prey" stands for earthly powers that use violence to destroy. The point is that God is even more deadly than these contemporary threats, just as he was able to slay the entire army of the savage Assyrians. This statement corresponds to the words used in verse 2 for God's "abode" and "dwelling place," which can be translated as "lair" and "den." Thus, God is seen as the Lion of Judah, who prowls to destroy any who dare threaten his territory. The Assyrians who approached Jerusalem thought they were facing a weak and poorly fortified city, but they had in fact stepped into a lair where the majestic God defended his people. The same danger is present at all times for those who would arrogantly assail the church. Charles Spurgeon writes: "In the spiritual conflicts of this and every age, the like will be seen; no weapon that is formed against the church shall prosper, and every tongue that rises against her in judgment she shall condemn."[3]

Moreover, while the glory of earthly despots may shine for a season, God is the truly radiant champion. The word translated as "glorious" in Psalm 76:4 means "shining." William Plumer notes: "Their glory fills a little part of this world; his fills heaven and earth. . . . Their glory is fleeting; his is eternal."[4] C. S. Lewis captured this idea of combining untamed power and radiant glory in his Narnia children's fantasy, when he introduced his Christ-figure, Aslan, as "huge, and shaggy, and bright."[5] Martin Luther speaks of Israel's Savior in a way that could be spoken of Lewis's Aslan: "The Almighty Warrior is our Captain. He holds in his hands the hearts and spirits of our enemies. Without arms or weapons of men, he can lay our adversaries prostrate in a moment."[6] God's overwhelming power was likewise the subject of Moses' song after God's parting of the Red Sea to permit Israel to escape, after which he drowned the chariots of Pharaoh in the waves:

> The LORD is my strength and my song,
> and he has become my salvation;
> this is my God, and I will praise him,
> my father's God, and I will exalt him.
> The LORD is a man of war. (Ex. 15:2–3)

3. Charles Haddon Spurgeon, *The Treasury of David*, 3 vols. (Peabody, MA: Hendrickson, n.d.), 2a:303.
4. William S. Plumer, *Psalms* (1867; repr., Edinburgh: Banner of Truth, 1975), 734.
5. C. S. Lewis, *The Magician's Nephew* (New York: Harper Collins, 1955), 110.
6. Quoted in Plumer, *Psalms*, 737.

Several statements in this depiction of God's victory are of particular importance to Christians today. The first is in Psalm 76:6, which says that it was at God's "rebuke" that the enemy chariots were overthrown. Notice that God achieves his victory by speaking his Word. A similar emphasis is given in Luke 4, where Jesus casts out a demon and cures Peter's mother-in-law, in both cases doing so by rebuking that which was evil (Luke 4:35, 39). God's Word has power to overthrow ungodly powers in this world, and therefore Christians must wage war primarily with the Word of God. This is all the more true when the church suffers outward persecution and intense affliction. Revelation 12:11 summarizes the triumph of believers in their spiritual warfare with Satan: "they have conquered him by the blood of the Lamb and by the word of their testimony." Paul made this same point emphatically, focusing the warfare of Christians not on earthly weaponry but on the mighty power of God's truth:

> For though we walk in the flesh, we are not waging war according to the flesh. For the weapons of our warfare are not of the flesh but have divine power to destroy strongholds. We destroy arguments and every lofty opinion raised against the knowledge of God, and take every thought captive to obey Christ. (2 Cor. 10:3–5)

Moreover, Psalm 76:2 states that God's abode was "established in Salem, his dwelling place in Zion." The term *dwelling place* naturally calls to mind the temple, where the glory of God resided. Verse 3 then states: "There he broke the flashing arrows, the shield, the sword, and the weapons of war." The point is that God's victory took place not so much on the battlefield as in the temple, the place of prayer where his people met with him. Hezekiah came to the temple and prayed to the Lord, and it was there, in effect, that the enemy arrows, shields, and swords were smashed. In this instance, as on virtually every other occasion when God revealed his saving might in protecting his people, the victory resulted from the prayers of God's people as God heard and acted in reply. Psalm 76 thus teaches that prayer, combined with the ministry of God's Word, gives victory to the cause of Christ in this world.

Lessons from the Knowledge of God

The psalmist wants God's name to be praised by his people for the great deliverance he achieved. He also wants the people to learn some vital lessons as they come to know God through the saving power that he has worked on their behalf. To this end, he notes three precepts in Psalm 76:7–10.

First, since God is so radiant in glory and mighty in power, he should be feared by all people: "But you, you are to be feared!" (Ps. 76:7). The God of the Bible, the God who has so often revealed his glory in saving his people, should be treated with reverence and respect. To fear the Lord means to hold him in proper regard, as the Lord and Judge who determines the fate of men. The psalmist continues: "Who can stand before you when once your anger is roused? From the heavens you uttered judgment; the earth feared and was still" (vv. 7–8). Since God is the almighty Judge, only a fool treats him lightly. The wise man or woman responds to the knowledge of God not only in love for his kindness and joy for his grace but also in reverent fear because of his greatness.

When the psalmist writes to God, "You, you are to be feared" (Ps. 76:7), this carries the idea that *only* God is to be feared. Thus, the fear of the Lord teaches us not to be afraid of men or powers in the world. Paul reasoned, "If God is for us, who can be against us?" (Rom. 8:31). Spurgeon comments: "The fear of man is a snare, but the fear of God is a great virtue, and has great power for good over the human mind."[7]

The second lesson follows from the first, namely, that we should trust God to be our Savior. Psalm 76:9 points out that "God arose to establish judgment, to save all the humble of the earth." Just as God is roused to anger by the evil and pride of rebellious mankind, he is also moved with mercy toward those who humbly rely on his grace. "Blessed are the meek," Jesus taught, "for they shall inherit the earth. Blessed are those who hunger and thirst for righteousness, for they shall be satisfied" (Matt. 5:5–6). Mary sang of this saving grace in her song that celebrated the birth of Christ:

> [God] has brought down the mighty from their thrones
>   and exalted those of humble estate;
> he has filled the hungry with good things,
>   and the rich he has sent away empty.
> He has helped his servant Israel,
>   in remembrance of his mercy,
> as he spoke to our fathers,
>   to Abraham and to his offspring forever. (Luke 1:52–55)

7. Spurgeon, *Treasury of David*, 2a:303.

God is not only just to condemn all evil, but also faithful to save those who seek him in faith. This being the case, Paul urges: "everyone who calls on the name of the Lord will be saved" (Rom. 10:13).

The final lesson is given in Psalm 76:10, which warns against the futility of all opposition to God: "Surely the wrath of man shall praise you." This famous statement makes the point that even the worst that man can do in opposition to God is made an occasion for the display of his glory. Christians can therefore know that the most violent and spiteful acts against them are governed by the sovereign will of God and ordered by his almighty power to achieve precisely the purposes that he intends. Warfield writes that "though Satan may rage about like a roaring lion seeking whom he may devour, yet he has a bit in his mouth and it is God who holds the reins."[8]

This doctrine is taught in Romans 8:28, where Paul asserts that "for those who love God all things work together for good, for those who are called according to his purpose." There are indeed many evil things, and Christians may truly suffer. But God overrules the worst that men can do so as to promote his own glory and the ultimate good of those who trust in him. In the end, it is his wrath that prevails and not the wrath of man in opposition to his rule. Psalm 76:10 states that "the remnant of wrath you will put on like a belt." When man has done his worst and spent his wrath against God, God then takes up his own wrath like a garment and wields it in power. J. J. Stewart Perowne writes: "All the wrath of men, every attempt that they make to defeat the will of God, does but turn to their own discomfiture, and His glory; and after all their efforts, He has a store, a residue, of wrath to pour out upon them as punishment."[9]

When Christ returns and his judgment seat is set in place, rebels against God will have no escape from his condemnation. Revelation 6:15–17 records the terror of the ungodly in the day of Christ's return: they "hid themselves in the caves and among the rocks of the mountains, calling to the mountains and rocks, 'Fall on us and hide us from the face of him who is seated on the throne, and from the wrath of the Lamb, for the great day of their wrath has come, and who can stand?'"

If there was ever an occasion when Psalm 76:10 was fulfilled, when the

8. Warfield, *Faith & Life*, 27.

9. J. J. Stewart Perowne, *The Book of Psalms*, 2 vols. (1878; repr., Grand Rapids: Zondervan, 1976), 2:44.

wrath of man brought praise to God, that was the day when Jesus, God's Son, died for our sins on the cross. How mankind raged, under the banner of Satan, as Jesus was rejected by the crowds, scourged and mocked by the soldiers, nailed to the cross, reviled by the religious leaders, and left to die under the hot Judean sun. How complete was the apparent triumph of man's wrath against God on that day! Yet it was God who gained the victory and his gospel that received the glory. Afterward, the apostle Peter explained how futile this opposition to God proved to be, since the death of Christ achieved God's glorious plan to save sinners who believe: "this Jesus, delivered up according to the definite plan and foreknowledge of God, you crucified and killed by the hands of lawless men. God raised him up, loosing the pangs of death, because it was not possible for him to be held by it" (Acts 2:23–24).

RESPONDING TO GOD

Psalm 76 concludes with two pointed applications. The first is directed to believers: "Make your vows to the LORD your God and perform them" (Ps. 76:11). In other words, the more that we come to know God and to realize all that he does in saving his people, the more motivated we should be to offer our lives to his praise. For this great salvation, we owe him our allegiance and love. This principle is summed up by the first of the Ten Commandments, given by God after his great victory in delivering Israel from slavery in Egypt: "I am the LORD your God, who brought you out of the land of Egypt, out of the house of slavery. You shall have no other gods before me" (Ex. 20:2–3). Spurgeon writes: "He keeps his promises, let not his people fail in theirs. He is their faithful God and deserves to have a faithful people."[10]

The second application is directed to those outside God's people, summoning them to come and give their homage to the Lord: "let all around him bring gifts to him who is to be feared" (Ps. 76:11). Are you able to say that the God of Psalm 76 is your God? Do you look to the cross of Christ and know that your sins were forgiven there? Do you face the prospect of death without fear because your Savior reigns both in life and beyond the grave? If not, then come to know God by taking up his revealed Word in

10. Spurgeon, *Treasury of David*, 2a:304.

the Bible. Become aware not only of his power and justice but also of his mercy and grace. Consider the Lord Jesus Christ, the mighty Lion of Judah and also the tender Lamb of Calvary's cross. Believe in the Lord Jesus, and you will be saved.

The psalm ends with words that make it imperative that you come to God now, since he is "to be feared, who cuts off the spirit of princes, who is to be feared by the kings of the earth" (Ps. 76:11–12). These words echo the conclusion of Psalm 2, which calls you to bow in faith and obedience to God's Son, Jesus, who is established by his Father to rule over heaven and earth, life and eternity:

> Now therefore, O kings, be wise;
>   be warned, O rulers of the earth.
> Serve the Lord with fear,
>   and rejoice with trembling.
> Kiss the Son,
>   lest he be angry, and you perish in the way,
>   for his wrath is quickly kindled.
> Blessed are all who take refuge in him. (Ps. 2:10–12)

5

Up from the Depths

Psalm 77

Then I said, "I will appeal to this, to the years of the right hand of the Most High." I will remember the deeds of the Lord; yes, I will remember your wonders of old. (Ps. 77:10–11)

There is debate regarding the identity of the Asaph who is cited as the author of Psalms 73–83. It might be possible to assume that this inscription refers to the chief singer of Israel who bore that name in the time of David, who is mentioned in 1 Chronicles 16:5–7. The problem is that these psalms seem to refer to events that occurred many lives later and that are separated from one another by many generations. Psalm 74, for instance, refers to the destruction of God's sanctuary, which is naturally taken to mean the fall of Jerusalem in 587 B.C. Psalm 76 is generally believed to praise God for his intervention to destroy the Assyrian army under King Sennacherib in 701 B.C. Given this context, it seems best to take "Asaph" to indicate not a specific individual but a line of musical servants, perhaps even a title for the music director serving Israel at any one time.

One argument in favor of taking Asaph to be a single individual, however, is that these psalms display characteristics that cause us to think we are getting to know him personally. Primary among these characteristics is spiritual candor. James Boice comments: "One thing you have to say about Asaph: He tells it like it is. . . . If he is unhappy or puzzled about what God is doing (or not doing) in the lives of his people, he says so. And he also describes his own state of mind—his doubts and struggles, his questions and his inability to find satisfying answers to life's great problems."[1] In this way, the Asaph psalms relieve Christians of any obligation to pretend that we always have our thoughts and feelings together. Through the example of Psalm 77, the Holy Spirit uses the spiritual struggles of the psalmist to connect with Christians who are experiencing similar anguish, while providing believers with a way up from the emotional and spiritual depths.

As with Psalm 76, this psalm can be neatly divided according to the musical annotation *selah*. There are four sections, which break down into two main headings. The first two stanzas of Psalm 77, from verses 1–9, chart his spiritual anguish. First he recounts his misery, and then he expresses his feelings of abandonment by God. In the second two stanzas, he turns from his inward feelings to his knowledge of God that comes through the record of his mighty deeds (Ps. 77:10–15), and then finally he extols the faithfulness of God that is revealed through the exodus of Israel and its miraculous passage through the Red Sea (vv. 16–20).

In the Day of Trouble

We do not know the cause of Asaph's trouble, although the commentators are not shy in speculating. Given that both Psalms 74 and 77 are prayers of lament and that Psalm 74 seems to respond to the destruction of Jerusalem after the Babylonian siege of 587 B.C., many scholars assume that this calamity prompted the gloom of Psalm 77. But Asaph's depression need not have been caused by national events. The cause might have been some personal disaster, in the way that people today are spiritually panicked by the sudden loss of a job, a personal betrayal, or a deadly diagnosis. Whatever the reason, Asaph wrote this psalm "in the day of my trouble." As a result, he languished in the night with his hand stretched out in supplication and his soul beyond the reach of consolation (Ps. 77:2).

One way in which this psalm helps us is by showing that depression is a part of life in this fallen world from which many, even the most godly people,

1. James Montgomery Boice, *Psalms*, 3 vols. (Grand Rapids: Baker, 1996), 2:637–38.

may suffer. For this reason, we should not treat depression as a sin in itself, or as a sign of some significant spiritual failure. Charles Spurgeon pointed out in his remarks on Psalm 77 that he had spent long nights in the same bed of affliction as Asaph. The great Baptist preacher was greatly afflicted during the later decades of his life with painful physical ills, including gout and migraine headaches. He writes: "Some of us know what it is, both physically and spiritually, to be compelled to use these words [of Asaph]; no respite has been afforded us by the silence of the night, our bed has been a rack to us, our body has been in torment, and our spirit in anguish. . . . Deep glens and lonely caves of soul depressions, my spirit knows full well your awful glooms!"[2] In these struggles, Spurgeon had fellowship with Jesus, who according to Hebrews 5:7 "offered up prayers and supplications, with loud cries and tears."

Often, Christians who spend their nights in despair give little sign of anguish during the day. Psalm 77 reminds us to care about the personal struggles of even eminent servants of Christ, as Asaph undoubtedly was, to be in prayer for friends who are suffering, and to reach out with personal expressions of love and support.

Asaph charts his depression in vivid language. His emotional pain assails him as soon as he enters his bed at night. As he writhes in sadness, he reaches out his hand for help that does not come: "in the night my hand is stretched out without wearying" (Ps. 77:2). The afflictions that bear upon him leave him inconsolable in spirit. When he turns his thoughts to God, he finds not comfort but distress: "When I remember God, I moan; when I meditate, my spirit faints" (v. 3). This sense of abandonment by God seems to be at the center of Asaph's despair, leading him to give himself over to weeping and desolation.

We can observe two things about Asaph in this condition, one of which is to his credit and the other of which is not. First, despite his depression and his sense of God's absence, he nonetheless seeks God out in prayer. He begins, "I cry aloud to God, aloud to God, and he will hear me" (Ps. 77:1). However distant God seems, Asaph knows that his prayers will reach God's ear. "In the day of my trouble," he states, "I seek the Lord" (v. 2).

This prayerful response provides a good example for us. J. J. Stewart

2. Charles Haddon Spurgeon, *The Treasury of David*, 3 vols. (Peabody, MA: Hendrickson, n.d.), 2a:312–13.

Perowne comments: "These verses show both the reality and earnestness of the prayer, and the strong faith of the Psalmist."[3] Trials have the effect of testing our spiritual condition, and the prayers of Asaph show that he has been born of God. Paul wrote in Romans 8:15 of the spirit of sonship that is the birthright of all believers: "you have received the Spirit of adoption as sons, by whom we cry, 'Abba! Father!'" Paul means that true believers respond to threats and alarm by praying almost instinctively. However poor our emotional state, a true believer's heart will call out as a child seeking the Father's protective care.

Do you pray to God in times of doubt and fear? Matthew Henry wrote: "Days of trouble must be days of prayer."[4] The trouble with some people is that their lack of a saving relationship with God leaves them unable to pray in times of trouble. They may ask believing friends to pray, but they cannot say with Asaph, "I seek the Lord" (Ps. 77:2). If you respond to trouble by praying to God, almost as a reflex action, then be encouraged that this reflex is the mark of one who truly belongs to God in saving faith. If you, like Asaph, pray and seek God, yet seem not to find his consolation, you must continue in prayer and faith. Henry notes that "especially when God seems to have withdrawn from us; we must seek him and seek till we find him."[5]

Asaph's prayer was a positive sign, until we realize that in these opening verses he does not actually pray! This may be part of his problem: he speaks of praying and seeking God but never actually addresses him. The word *you* is never employed in the first stanza, but is crowded out by a forest consisting of *me* and *I*. While he is crying to God and stretching out his anguished hand for divine help, his heart is all the while caught up wholly with its own misery. In the second stanza, Asaph does address God. But still, the first six verses contain twenty references to "me" and "I" compared to only six addresses to God. This is the genuine danger that people in depression experience: their pain and suffering become the only thing real to them, so that even when they are trying to pray, they are wholly overcome with their emotional anguish.

3. J. J. Stewart Perowne, *The Book of Psalms*, 2 vols. (1878; repr., Grand Rapids: Zondervan, 1976), 2:49.

4. Matthew Henry, *Commentary on the Whole Bible*, 6 vols (Peabody, MA: Hendrickson, n.d.), 3:431.

5. Henry, *Commentary*, 3:431.

Searching about God

The second stanza starts by showing that Asaph is indeed in danger of falling prey to self-pity. The first three verses tell us how he was feeling in himself. Now the second stanza, Psalm 77:4–9, tells us how he feels about God. The Lord is here addressed as the problem, not the solution. "You hold my eyelids open," Asaph complains. Biblically informed Christians sometimes reason this way: we know that God is sovereign over all things, so the problem must be God's attitude that is permitting our misery. In this bitter spirit Asaph can only utter an accusation to the Lord; otherwise, he relates, "I am so troubled that I cannot speak" (Ps. 77:4).

I mentioned that whatever is afflicting Asaph is magnified by his sense of abandonment by God in his trial. Now he adds another burden, comparing his present lamentable state to previous times when his heart was happy and singing: "I consider the days of old, the years long ago. I said, 'Let me remember my song in the night; let me meditate in my heart'" (Ps. 77:5–6). Grasping for some leverage on his heart, he tries to connect with those more joyful emotions from previous experiences. The result, however, is the opposite: the more he meditates on the past, the more he realizes that those days are gone, replaced by troubles that he could scarcely have anticipated in sunnier times. Perowne comments on this perceptively:

> Such recollections . . . may hush the storm of the soul, may give a man courage to say to himself, "Thou art His, He cannot forsake thee." But such recollections may also be made the very instruments of Satan's temptations, when the soul asks, "Why is it not always thus? And so falls into . . . sad and desponding thoughts.[6]

The issue, Asaph realizes, is not God but his perception of God: his experience with God is different from what it was in better times. His feelings about God are different. Does this mean that God is different? Has God changed, so that Asaph's former trust was misplaced? Asaph's heart turns to this issue in Psalm 77:6: "Then my spirit made a diligent search." Asaph is like the Persian king in the book of Esther, who, being unable to sleep, gave instructions for the royal records to be brought for him to read (Esth. 6:1).[7] Sleepless

6. Perowne, *Psalms*, 2:50.
7. William Gurnall, cited in Spurgeon, *Treasury of David*, 2a:321.

Asaph brings out his records of God in order to make search of the ultimate question: Is God who I thought he was? Here we may discern something of God's purpose in Asaph's depression, to lead him to a clearer knowledge of his character and works. Applying this situation to Christians, might this be the Lord's purpose in your trials? Ancient astronomers would sometime dig deep, narrow pits into the ground so that, looking upward, they might have a more brilliant sight of the heavenly stars. God sometimes puts us into pits with a similar motive: that we might see him in all the sufficiency of his divine being.

Turning back to Asaph, we find him not yet searching *for God*, but rather searching *about God*. The question is now not *how* to turn to the Lord but *whether* to trust him. Psalm 77:7–9 contains five rapid-fire questions through which the psalmist wonders whether God is still what Asaph once thought he was:

> Will the Lord spurn forever,
>   and never again be favorable?
> Has his steadfast love forever ceased?
>   Are his promises at an end for all time?
> Has God forgotten to be gracious?
>   Has he in anger shut up his compassion?

The sense of these questions is to wonder whether God is the same now as he had been before. His key concern is seen in the repeated use of *forever*. He feels abandoned by God: will he always be? He cannot sense God's mercy: has his steadfast love ceased forever? God's promises do not seem to be coming true for him: will that always be the case?

Questions such as these may seem irreverent or unbelieving, but that does not seem to be true of Asaph. Rather, he is simply wrestling with the difference between what he has believed and what he is now feeling. Which perspective is final: his sense of abandonment or God's saving grace?

We can understand Asaph's attitude better if we compare it to that of the prophet Habakkuk, who famously sat up in his watchtower, waiting for answers from God. In Habakkuk's case, God had informed him that the Babylonians were being sent to bring judgment on sinful Jerusalem. This perplexed the prophet, who could not reconcile how a holy God would permit the Babylonians, who were even worse sinners, to triumph over God's people (Hab. 1:12–13). Not finding an answer, Habakkuk resolved: "I will take my stand at my watchpost and station myself on the tower, and look out to see what he will say to me, and what I will answer concerning my complaint" (2:1). That action is similar to Asaph's resolve to make "a diligent search" (Ps. 77:6). Neither man has turned away *from* God but has turned *to* God, trying to make sense of the misery he is facing. That is exactly the right way to handle doubts and disagreements with God: to take them to him and await an answer. Habakkuk wrote: "If it seems slow, wait for it; it will surely come; it will not delay" (Hab. 2:3). This seems to be the spirit of Psalm 77: Asaph searches with the expectation of having his doubts cleared up.

Remembering God's Deeds

One of the lessons of Psalm 77 is that Asaph emerges from his depression because he simply does not give up. He starts out by trying to pray but finds it too difficult. He tries to cheer himself with memories of better times, but the opposite happens. Realizing that he needs to think rightly about God, he makes a search of the divine character. This is where his doggedness in pressing on is rewarded. Even though he begins this exercise with a bitter spirit, the search pulls his thoughts away from himself and onto God. After the opening sections, which were dominated by self-pitying references to his own misery, the final eight verses of Psalm 77 contain twenty-one references to God and none about himself. Walter Brueggemann has labeled this transition "the turn from self to God," and it is how Asaph recovers from the depths of despair.[8]

The specific way that Asaph turns from self to God is by opening the Scriptures. This turn to the Bible is suggested by Psalm 77:6, where he resolves to make "a diligent search." Where else would he seek answers about God than in God's Word? This assessment is confirmed in verses 10–11: "Then I said, 'I will appeal to this, to the years of the right hand of the Most High.' I will remember the deeds of the LORD; yes, I will remember your wonders of old." There is only one place to study God's deeds from of old, and that is in the Bible. Indeed, this is the purpose of the Bible: not merely

8. Walter Brueggemann, *The Psalms and the Life of Faith* (Minneapolis: Fortress, 1995), 258–67.

to give pious religious advice but to record the great saving acts of God in history and explain their significance to us. Paul spoke about the events of the Old Testament: "Now these things happened to them as an example, but they were written down for our instruction, on whom the end of the ages has come" (1 Cor. 10:11). Asaph likewise found the Scriptures to speak with relevance to his own struggles, as have countless other bewildered people who sought answers in the Bible and received light from God for their souls.

Psalm 77:10 is the key to the whole psalm and the decisive turning point for Asaph: "Then I said, 'I will appeal to this, to the years of the right hand of the Most High.'" The meaning is that the psalmist will reconcile his troubles by referring to the long record of God's saving deeds in history, as recorded in Scripture.[9] The expression is striking and beautiful: "the years of the right hand of the Most High." The idea is that a long record of mighty deeds establishes God's sovereign role as Savior of his people.

Psalm 77:11 makes Asaph's approach clear: "I will remember the deeds of the LORD; yes, I will remember your wonders of old." The point is that once the believer turns to the biblical record of God's great saving deeds, the arguments of unbelief and doubt begin to fall away. William Plumer writes: "Unbelief says, There is no hope, there is no help even in God. Faith says, When I sit in darkness the Lord shall be a light unto me."[10] This believing attitude is fed by "the years of the right hand of the Most High" (Ps. 77:10), as the long perspective of Bible history shows God's always returning to his seemingly forsaken people, God's wisely knowing when to withdraw and when to appear, and God's being graciously faithful in rescuing his people in their greatest need. William Gurnall thus compares the struggling Christian to the tracking hound that loses the scent of his prey and therefore "hunts backward and so recovers it, and [then] pursues his game with louder cry than ever."[11] In answer to Asaph's prior questions, the record of the Bible shows that God does not spurn his people forever but returns in favor (Zech. 1:3). As Jeremiah wrote, "The steadfast love of the LORD never ceases" (Lam. 3:22). God does not forget but always remembers his covenant and its mercy

9. The translation of this verse is uncertain. Another alternative is given by the NASB: "Then I said, 'It is my grief, That the right hand of the Most High has changed.'" While this interpretation is supported by commentators such as Calvin and Leupold, the context makes the ESV translation more likely.

10. William S. Plumer, *Psalms* (1867; repr., Edinburgh: Banner of Truth, 1975), 742.

11. Quoted in Spurgeon, *Treasury of David*, 2a:324.

(Luke 1:54–55). God never ceases to be gracious in his approach, but is slow to anger and swift to forgive (Ex. 34:6).

It should be pointed out that Asaph recovered these truths not by a brief and shallow reading of Scripture, but by diligent study and meditation. He recounts: “I will ponder all your work, and meditate on your mighty deeds” (Ps. 77:12). Christians who derive strong benefit from the Bible are those who labor in it. Whereas Habakkuk set his watchtower up over Jerusalem, Asaph set his over the Bible. We will do well to follow his example of zeal. Some Christians make a practice of setting passages of Scripture to memory, while others follow a disciplined plan of daily Bible reading. Through both diligent Bible study and the reading of wholesome Christian books, believers are given occasion to meditate on the attributes and achievements of God, strengthening their faith through this effort.

What, exactly, did Asaph receive from his search of Scripture? The answer is that he recovered a right view of God and his attributes. Psalm 19:10 asserts that God’s Word is more valuable than gold and sweeter than honey, and Asaph discovered this benefit primarily by regaining his knowledge of what God is like. Asaph needed faith to endure his trial, and his faith found a sure foothold in a recovered knowledge of God as he is revealed by his Word.

The psalmist highlights three things that he has relearned about God, beginning with his holiness: “Your way, O God, is holy” (Ps. 77:13). Properly speaking, God’s holiness is his transcendent majesty by which he is separate from sin and infinitely high above all things. The idea is that the Bible’s record of God’s works and deeds shows that his intentions are always holy and upright. Even when the believer faces terrible suffering and when doubts and griefs assail him, he can know that God’s intentions can be trusted. We may not understand why or what God is doing, but knowing his holy nature assures us that his intentions are aligned with who he is. God emphasized this in his letter to the Jews who were suffering exile in Babylon: “For I know the plans I have for you, declares the Lord, plans for welfare and not for evil, to give you a future and a hope” (Jer. 29:11).

Asaph further realized that God is great and almighty: “What god is great like our God? You are the God who works wonders; you have made known your might among the peoples” (Ps. 77:13–14). The false gods and idols are impotent, but the true God is omnipotent. He can stop the sun in the sky, part the waves of the sea, cause bread to fall from heaven, and crash down mighty towers by the sounding of trumpets. God is therefore not only upright in his ways but wholly able to cause his decrees to come to pass.

Finally, Asaph relearns in the Bible that God is compassionate in his care for his people: "You with your arm redeemed your people, the children of Jacob and Joseph" (Ps. 77:15). By naming Jacob and Joseph, the psalmist highlights the exodus from Egypt, in which God showed such concern in redeeming his nation. It is one thing if God is able, but not willing. But the God of the Bible is both fully able and always willing to save those who call on his name. This means that even the depression in which Asaph languished must have been permitted by God for purposes that Asaph can trust, since he is a caring God who intends for good to come even by means of the sorest trials.

Boice reflects on Asaph's tour through the biblical record of God's character and deeds: "This is practical theology of the best sort, for it reasons from the immutable character of God to God's purpose for his acts in history and takes comfort from such truths."[12] The lesson for those of us who suffer today, whether briefly or during long, bitter seasons, is that God is not the problem, so that we should turn away from him in unbelief or resentment, but God is always the answer to whom we should turn even with our doubts and our tears.

God's Way of Salvation

Asaph's study of the Bible seems to have particularly focused on the exodus of Israel from Egypt. He confirms this focus in the final stanza, writing about God's saving intervention to enable Israel to pass into safety through the parted waters of the Red Sea: "When the waters saw you, O God, when the waters saw you, they were afraid; indeed, the deep trembled. The clouds poured out water; the skies gave forth thunder; your arrows flashed on every side. The crash of your thunder was in the whirlwind; your lightnings lighted up the world; the earth trembled and shook" (Ps. 77:16–18).

The exodus was the greatest redemptive event of the Old Testament, and thus of Israel's experience up to the time when Asaph wrote. Not only did it prove God's mighty power to save his people, as God displayed his utter sovereignty over the creation, but it also provided critical lessons. One lesson is given in Psalm 77:19: "Your way was through the sea, your path through the great waters." The point is that Israel's salvation was achieved through the

12. Boice, *Psalms*, 2:642.

tribulations of this world, as the people's faith relied on God's power to save them. This is at least a partial explanation for the grief that Asaph was suffering: God has ordained that we would learn to trust him as he parts the waters of difficulty and distress with a supernatural salvation. Acts 14:22 teaches that "through many tribulations we must enter the kingdom of God," as God wisely teaches us lessons in grace and weans us from the world and from sin.

Moreover, Asaph observed that "your footprints were unseen" (Ps. 77:19). God was leading Israel even though he was not visibly present. God left no footprints in the seabed floor as the Israelites passed through the Red Sea, but the Lord was leading them all the same. We can be sure of the same as we seek his aid in trials and walk the path of faith in a difficult world.

Christians look back to a greater salvation event, the cross of Jesus Christ, which teaches us these lessons in even bolder strokes. If Asaph, trusting God and his Word, could conclude by affirming God as the faithful Shepherd in whom his people may trust, we can look to Jesus and conclude the same: "You led your people like a flock by the hand of Moses and Aaron" (Ps. 77:20). Since God has sent his own Son to redeem us by his blood, and since we know that Jesus reigns in heaven until he soon returns to deliver us from all trouble, we can trust him to be our Good Shepherd as well.

Indeed, we can do more than trust him with resentful hearts. We can rejoice in his salvation even in the midst of distress and dismay. This is what Habakkuk learned when he sought God's answer in his watchtower. The answers of faith changed his attitude and lifted his heart, so that he wrote words of hope that we can embrace through Jesus Christ:

> Though the fig tree should not blossom,
>   nor fruit be on the vines,
> the produce of the olive fail
>   and the fields yield no food,
> the flock be cut off from the fold
>   and there be no herd in the stalls,
> yet I will rejoice in the Lord;
>   I will take joy in the God of my salvation.
> God, the Lord, is my strength;
>   he makes my feet like the deer's;
>   he makes me tread on my high places. (Hab. 3:17–19)

6

The Wonders That He Has Done

Psalm 78:1–39

We will not hide them from their children, but tell to the coming generation the glorious deeds of the Lord, and his might, and the wonders that he has done. (Ps. 78:4)

The book of Judges records a tale of woe of the generations between Joshua's conquest and the kingship of David, during which Israel lived in spiritual weakness and foreign subjugation. The explanation for this deplorable situation is given in Judges 2:10: after Joshua's time, "there arose another generation after them who did not know the Lord or the work that he had done for Israel." An allusion to Judges is appropriate for our study of Psalm 78 for two reasons. One is that the evidence of the psalm suggests that it may have been written not long after the era of the judges. Another reason is that the psalm has the express intention of avoiding the situation that occurred in Judges. Psalm 78 serves to "tell to the coming generation the glorious deeds of the Lord, . . . so that they should set their hope in God" (Ps. 78:4, 7).

A Testimony to God

Asaph states that God has "established a testimony in Jacob and appointed a law in Israel," regarding passing on the knowledge of God's works (Ps. 78:5). This same approach was mandated in the Bible's earliest books. God told Moses that he had hardened Pharaoh's heart "that you may tell in the hearing of your son and of your grandson . . . , that you may know that I am the Lord" (Ex. 10:1–2). The retelling of God's mighty acts of redemption was the explicit purpose of the Passover, which Israel celebrated annually (Ex. 13:14–15). Deuteronomy 6:6–7 made this task of passing on the history of God's saving works a priority: "And these words that I command you today shall be on your heart. You shall teach them diligently to your children, and shall talk of them when you sit in your house, and when you walk by the way, and when you lie down, and when you rise." Israel's offspring were intended to know not only *what* they were supposed to do but *how* their worship and obedience related to God's saving works:

> When your son asks you in time to come, "What is the meaning of the testimonies and the statutes and the rules that the Lord our God has commanded you?" then you shall say to your son, "We were Pharaoh's slaves in Egypt. And the Lord brought us out of Egypt with a mighty hand." (Deut. 6:20–21)

This text makes the point that biblical religion—both Old and New Testament—is based on history, that is, the great saving works that God has done. Christianity does not consist merely of abstract beliefs, ethics, or even religion. Rather, Christianity proclaims what God has done for our salvation and life. The Old Testament proclaimed the exodus of Israel and all the great redemptive works that followed. The New Testament adds the life, death, and resurrection of Jesus Christ, God's Son and our Savior. It is not possible to be a Christian at all without knowing and believing what God has done in the coming of Jesus. It is virtually impossible to be a strong and thriving Christian without an intimate awareness of the Old Testament and its record of divine works that anticipated and eventuated in the coming of Christ.

Realizing this principle, Christians will see it as their duty to teach the Bible to the generations that follow. Speaking of what the "fathers have told us," the psalmist resolves, "We will not hide them from their children" (Ps. 78:3–4). Notice that he sees the young of his own time as "their children," the offspring of the fathers who came before. David Dickson writes: "The godly in every age ought to have the same care to transmit the word of truth to their posterity, which their ancestors had to transmit to them, and to pay the debt they owe to their faithful ancestors unto succeeding generations."[1]

In addition to redemptive history, we need teaching that explains the meaning and significance of Bible events. In other words, our faith relies on both history and doctrine. J. Gresham Machen pointed this out a century ago:

> From the beginning, the Christian gospel . . . consisted in an account of something that had happened. And from the beginning, the meaning of the happening was set forth; and when the meaning of the happening was set forth then there was Christian doctrine. "Christ died"—that is history; "Christ died for our sins"—that is doctrine. Without these two elements, joined in an absolutely indissoluble union, there is no Christianity.[2]

Psalm 78:2 pursues this same agenda, saying, "I will open my mouth in a parable; I will utter dark sayings from of old." The word for "parable" (Hebrew, *mashal*) has the general meaning of "riddle," which is why this verse is quoted in Matthew 13:35 as being fulfilled in the parables of Jesus. Psalm 78 is like Jesus' parables in that a story is told with a redemptive meaning. The emphasis in Psalm 78 is to ensure that events that might be misunderstood are clearly explained. It is important for us to understand the meaning of biblical events and the doctrines that arise from them, so that they do not remain "dark sayings" from the past. Paul wrote in the New Testament that the ancient events "took place as examples for us" and for our faith (1 Cor. 10:6), and this means that we must understand them biblically and practically.

In case we doubt the importance of passing on knowledge of Bible events and doctrines, and thus of serious Bible teaching in the church, Asaph works out four vital results. The first is so that coming generations will know "the glorious deeds of the LORD, and his might, and the wonders that he has done" (Ps. 78:4). This need for Bible knowledge is urgent in our generation. The comedian Jay Leno pointed out the ignorance of Americans about the Bible by asking people in his studio audience to name even one of the four Gospel writers in the New Testament. When no answer was

1. David Dickson, *A Commentary on the Psalms*, 2 vols. (1653; repr., Edinburgh: Banner of Truth, 1995), 2:3.

2. J. Gresham Machen, *Christianity and Liberalism* (Grand Rapids: Eerdmans, 1923), 27.

given, he asked for the names of the pop-music group The Beatles. Immediately, voices rang out, "Paul, John, George, and Ringo." The point is that our generation with vast cultural knowledge is plagued by vast ignorance of God and his work. This situation does not get much better even with professing Christians. In 1999, the Bible department at evangelical Wheaton College conducted surveys of the Bible knowledge of incoming freshmen. One-third could not identify Matthew as an apostle from a given list of names. A third could also not identify the book of Acts as containing the record of Paul's travels. One-half could not tell that the Christmas story is told in Matthew or that the Passover is recorded in Exodus.[3] Albert Mohler attributes this biblical ignorance to evangelical youth ministries, which "are asked to fix problems, provide entertainment, and keep kids busy." He asks, "How many local-church youth programs actually produce substantial Bible knowledge in young people?"[4] If Psalm 78 is taken seriously, ministries directed toward children and teenagers will be especially directed to teaching Bible knowledge and doctrine. In fact, as Asaph sees it, the task of conveying biblical truth to the young will not be relegated solely to the church but will be taken up as a primary calling of fathers and mothers in the home.

All Christians should desire to know the Lord's deeds because, as Asaph says, they are "glorious" and "wonders" that tell of his might to save (Ps. 78:4). The result of this knowledge is the second reason for teaching our children, "so that they should set their hope in God and not forget the works of God" (v. 7). It is because of our generation's ignorance of the wondrous deeds of God that we are spiritually weak, hoping in things of the world rather than hoping in God. Dickson writes: "The way to foster faith and hope in God, is to mark, consider, and keep in a sanctified memory, how God hath already confirmed his word by his works, and by pledges both of his power and purpose to perform what he hath said."[5]

A third important result of Bible knowledge is that we thus will "keep his commandments" (Ps. 78:7). Biblical doctrine is immensely practical, leading to a lifestyle of cheerfully obeying God's Word out of the great hope

3. Gary M. Burge, "The Greatest Story Never Read," *Christianity Today*, August 9, 1999, http://www.christianitytoday.com/ct/1999/august9/9t9045.html.

4. R. Albert Mohler, "The Scandal of Biblical Illiteracy: It's Our Problem," AlbertMohler.com, October 13, 2005, https://digital.library.sbts.edu/handle/10392/1921, accessed May 24, 2019.

5. Dickson, *Psalms*, 2:4.

that is born in his saving deeds. When we realize that God's law is the way of love—love for God and love for man—we will find it less onerous to refrain from hatred, lust, theft, false speech, and discontent.

Fourth, Asaph is concerned that by knowing the Bible, his readers will not forsake God and abandon the faith. This was a pressing problem among the Israelites, who were so often plagued with apostasy and idolatry. Asaph's burden was that "they should not be like their fathers, a stubborn and rebellious generation, a generation whose heart was not steadfast, whose spirit was not faithful to God" (Ps. 78:8). Some may object that God has promised to keep safe the salvation of all who have trusted in him. This is true, but the Bible's teaching of eternal security includes the necessity of our persevering in the faith and helping others to persevere. First Peter 1:5 combines these two truths, noting that we "*by God's power* are being guarded *through faith* for a salvation ready to be revealed in the last time." God's power is joined to our faith in safeguarding our souls for heaven. Realizing the necessity of our persevering in faith and the importance of Bible teaching to our faith, Matthew Henry writes: "Our great care must be to lodge our religion, that great deposit, pure and entire in the hands of those that succeed us."[6]

An Example of Spiritual Failure

The warning against falling away through ignorance of God and his works is illustrated by the failure of the tribe of Ephraim: "The Ephraimites, armed with the bow, turned back on the day of battle. They did not keep God's covenant, but refused to walk according to his law" (Ps. 78:9–10). Scholars debate the precise reference here. Some assert that Asaph is referring to the failure of Israel at the battle of Ebenezer (1 Sam. 4:1–11) when the army was largely led by the tribe of Ephraim, or that the psalm is obliquely referring to the division of Israel when the northern tribes broke away from Solomon's son Rehoboam (1 Kings 12). But a key to the psalmist's meaning is at the end, where he writes: "[God] rejected the tent of Joseph; he did not choose the tribe of Ephraim, but he chose the tribe of Judah, Mount Zion, which he loves" (Ps. 78:67–68). This is a clear reference to God's establishing his kingdom under David and Judah, rather than in the northern kingdom under Ephraimite leadership, and the passing of God's tabernacle from the

6. Matthew Henry, *Commentary on the Whole Bible*, 6 vols. (Peabody, MA: Hendrickson, n.d.), 3:434.

northern locale of Shiloh to Mount Zion at Jerusalem. The statements that Ephraim "turned back on the day of battle" and thus "did not keep God's covenant" may refer to the failure of this tribe, like the others that it led, to fulfill God's mandate to remove all the Canaanites from their portion of the promised land.

Most important to the psalmist's thought, Ephraim "forgot his works and the wonders that he had shown them" (Ps. 78:11). Verses 12–20 remind us of three great occasions when God's wondrous deeds revealed his salvation. The first was the breaking of Pharaoh's yoke so as to deliver Israel from bondage in Egypt: "In the sight of their fathers he performed wonders in the land of Egypt, in the fields of Zoan" (v. 12). By means of ten plagues strategically directed against the gods of Egypt, the Lord showed his power to Pharaoh. In the tenth plague, the angel of death slew the firstborn in every house not guarded by the blood of a lamb, as the Israelites were instructed. Remembering this deliverance, Ephraim should have realized the omnipotence of the Lord and his power to drive out the idol-worshiping Canaanites. How often it is precisely because we forget God's power that we give in to sin, failing to pray for his way of escape. Yet the Bible is replete with proofs that God can deliver us from temptation. By keeping in mind his "works and . . . wonders," we are helped to apply our faith in the fight against sin.

Next, Asaph recounts the great wonder of Israel's passage through the Red Sea: "He divided the sea and let them pass through it, and made the waters stand like a heap" (Ps. 78:13). The Israelites despaired when they saw the army of Pharaoh pursuing them with the sea at their back. Yet at God's command, "Moses stretched out his hand over the sea, and the Lord drove the sea back . . . , and the waters were divided" so that the people could pass through (Ex. 14:21–22).

Third, Asaph recalls the various ways by which God provided for Israel during its harrowing passage through the Sinai desert. God protected his people from the harsh elements: "In the daytime he led them with a cloud, and all the night with a fiery light" (Ps. 78:14). He further provided for their need of refreshing water: "He split rocks in the wilderness and gave them drink abundantly as from the deep. He made streams come out of the rock and caused waters to flow down like rivers" (vv. 15–16). Anyone who has traveled through a great desert can testify to the grave threat of the sun and the severe difficulty of finding water; this was especially so for the millions of Israelites who departed Egypt with Moses. God's provision shows his miraculous power over nature and also his caring concern to provide for his own. Israelites who remembered this episode would be encouraged in their faith so as to hope in God and obey his commands.

These great deeds of God were vital to Old Testament faith, just as they should continue to be for Christians. They were particularly useful in pointing Israel's hope forward to Jesus Christ, who would provide a greater fulfillment to all these wonders. Moses led Israel out of Pharaoh's Egypt, but Jesus Christ has broken the bond of Satan that held us in slavery to sin. The blood of the Passover Lamb was a type of the atoning blood of Christ for our sins (1 Cor. 5:7). Moreover, the Lord who stood up to mighty Pharaoh will take up the quarrel with those who persecute his people today. The Red Sea shows the pattern for our passing from spiritual death to life in Christ (1 Cor. 10:1–4). Dickson writes: "The Lord's bringing his people, both out of Egypt and out of the sea is a pledge of his power and purpose to bring his people through all hazards whatsoever, wherein others shall perish."[7] God's provision for Israel in the desert is a reminder of his pledge to care for all believers (see Phil. 4:19; Heb. 13:6). George Horne comments: "Thus is Christ present with his church, while she sojourns upon earth by his Word and his Spirit, guiding her steps enlightening her darkness, and mitigating her sorrows."[8]

As Asaph understood it, the great danger is that God's people would forget what he has done and fall back into unbelief. He saw this danger fulfilled in Ephraim and the other Israelites who "forgot his works and the wonders that he had shown them" (Ps. 78:11). As a result, they committed the great sins that are recorded in Exodus and Numbers. Psalm 78:17 recounts: "Yet they sinned still more against him, rebelling against the Most High in the desert." Numbers 16 records the attempt of Korah and Dathan to lead an insurrection against God's chosen leader, Moses, because of the difficulty of the journey. Psalm 78:18 notes that they "tested God in their heart by demanding the food they craved." The ideas of testing God and quarreling refer to how Israel was unsatisfied with God's mighty wonders

7. Dickson, *Psalms*, 2:8.

8. George Horne, *Commentary on the Psalms* (1771; repr., Audubon, NJ: Old Paths Publications, 1997), 331.

but demanded ever more signs of his faithfulness and power. In Exodus 17:1–5, we learn of how the people quarreled with Moses out of their fear for the lack of water and food: "Why did you bring us up out of Egypt, to kill us and our children and our livestock with thirst?" (Ex. 17:3). Moses had challenged them: "Why do you quarrel with me? Why do you test the Lord?" (v. 2). Psalm 78:19–20 recalls the people doubting, "Can God spread a table in the wilderness?" They admitted, "He struck the rock so that water gushed out and streams overflowed," but still demanded, "Can he also give bread or provide meat for his people?"

Jesus compared the ancient Israelites to unbelieving religious leaders in his day who would not believe in him. Declaring his death on the cross a sufficient sign to prove God's faithfulness forever, Jesus warned: "An evil and adulterous generation seeks for a sign, but no sign will be given to it except the sign of the prophet Jonah" (Matt. 12:39).

The psalmist is appalled at the practical unbelief among God's ancient people, despite such abundant testimonies that should have led them to trust in God with praise to his name. We should be more careful in condemning them, since we actually do worse in light of the greater revelation that we have received in Jesus Christ. Do we realize the foolish and sinful company we keep when we refuse to walk in God's way, demand that God do something more to gain our trust, or complain against God's providences? Charles Spurgeon reminds us of our need for both forgiveness and a new spirit from God:

> Alas, how have we also quarreled with our mercies, and querulously pined for some imaginary good, counting our actual enjoyments to be nothing because they did not happen to be exactly conformed to our foolish fancies. They who will not be content will speak against providence even when it daily loadeth them with benefits.[9]

A God to Remember

As we draw near to the middle of this long, historical psalm, we have been exhorted to teach the record of God's deeds and therefore to avoid the spiritual failures into which others have fallen. Having been exhorted not

9. Charles Haddon Spurgeon, *The Treasury of David*, 3 vols. (Peabody, MA: Hendrickson, n.d.), 2a:335.

to forget what God has done, we are reminded by Psalm 78:21–39 of things that we should always remember about God.

First, Bible history should cause us to remember that ours is a holy God whose wrath burns against sin. Psalm 78:21–22 tells of the Lord's reaction to the rebellion and testing of Israel: "Therefore, when the Lord heard, he was full of wrath; a fire was kindled against Jacob; his anger rose against Israel, because they did not believe in God and did not trust his saving power." Divine wrath is not petty, vindictive, or ignoble, as human anger so often is. Rather, as John Murray writes, God's wrath is "the holy revulsion of God's being against that which is the contradiction of His holiness."[10] J. I. Packer notes that wrath is "the *right* reaction of moral perfection in the Creator towards moral perversity in the creature."[11]

Asaph wanted the Israelites to remember specifically what happened when Israel rebelled against God. He seemed to note a specific episode when Israel "complained in the hearing of the Lord," and "his anger was kindled, and the fire of the Lord burned among them" (Num. 11:1). Numbers 16 records also that when Korah, Dathan, and Abiram rebelled against the Lord, leading 250 chiefs against Moses and Aaron, God struck them down by causing the earth to swallow them whole (16:32–33). Anyone who foolishly assumes that God will not respond angrily to high-handed wickedness would do well to remember what is recorded in the Bible! Psalm 78:21 says, "The Lord heard," just as God is aware of all sin, so that he is perfectly informed about the true state of all rebellion in order to send forth his perfect wrath.

Notice that the sin toward which God is particularly wrathful is unbelief: "because they did not believe in God and did not trust his saving power" (Ps. 78:22). This shows that a heart that rebels in unbelief and ingratitude to God is at the core of all wickedness. Dickson writes: "Misbelief is a more grievous sin than men esteem it; for it calleth God's truth, mercy, goodness, power, constancy, and all in question."[12] This is why Jesus responded to Satan's temptations in the desert, when the devil sought for Jesus to follow the Israelites in their sin, "Man shall not live by bread alone, but by every word that comes from the mouth of God" (Matt. 4:4). Notice, then,

10. Quoted in J. I. Packer, *Knowing God* (Downers Grove, IL: InterVarsity Press, 1979), 166.

11. Packer, *Knowing God,* 166.

12. Dickson, *Psalms*, 2:11.

how faith in God's Word causes us to trust his power. John Calvin comments:

> Faith, then, is the root of true piety. It teaches us to hope for, and to desire every blessing from God, and it frames us to yield obedience to him; while those who distrust him must necessarily be always murmuring and rebelling against him.[13]

The history of God's dealings with Israel reveal him to be not only a God of wrath, but also a God of grace. This truth is recounted in a summary of the episode in which God provided manna from heaven to feed his hungry people: "Yet he commanded the skies above and opened the doors of heaven, and he rained down on them manna to eat and gave them the grain of heaven" (Ps. 78:23–24).

God's saving grace is bestowed on the undeserving, and this was the case when he fed the rebellious Israelites. No sooner had the exodus generation passed through the Red Sea than they complained again about their hardships and longing to return to bondage. God graciously responded by causing bread to fall down out of heaven. Asaph says, "Men ate of the bread of the angels; he sent them food in abundance" (Ps. 78:25). Likewise, it was after the people complained in Numbers 11 that God caused the wind to shower quail on them to give them meat. Notice how Psalm 78 joins God's goodness to his power over nature to enable his grace to succeed: "He caused the east wind to blow in the heavens, and by his power he led out the south wind; he rained meat on them like dust, winged birds like the sand of the seas; he let them fall in the midst of their camp, all around their dwellings" (vv. 26–28).

God did not give poorly, but showered blessings on the Israelites. Asaph notes the wonder of it all: grain that fell from heaven and food that was provided at the hands of angels. We are thus reminded that while God is holy so that we should not rebel against him or face his wrath, he is also filled with grace so that those who trust him will receive, as Paul wrote, "far more abundantly than all that we ask or think, according to the power at work within us" (Eph. 3:20). God's gifts are freely given, marvelously worked, abundant in meeting our needs, and satisfying to our souls: "they ate and were well filled, for he gave them what they craved" (Ps. 78:29). Let us therefore remember the grace of God and trust him completely.

13. John Calvin, *Calvin's Commentaries*, 23 vols. (1848; repr., Grand Rapids: Baker, 2009), 6:245.

Sadly, these great blessings did not keep the former Israelites from unbelief and sin, which is why Psalm 78 wants us to learn the lesson from their failure. The stories mentioned in this psalm show not only that God is wrathful to sin and gracious to those in need, but also that he is faithful to his covenant both in fulfilling his warnings and in providing mercy according to his promises. Verses 30–33 recall how God fulfilled his judgments on the people who continued in unbelief: "while the food was still in their mouths, the anger of God rose against them, and he killed the strongest of them and laid low the young men of Israel. In spite of all this, they still sinned; despite his wonders, they did not believe. So he made their days vanish like a breath, and their years in terror." God had warned the Israelites not to disbelieve and rebel, and when they persisted he brought forth his threatened warnings. The generation of the exodus, which had seen such great wonders of the Lord, was required to wander forty years in the desert until the last of them had died! In this way, Psalm 78 shows that those who live in a worldly way and in unbelief will die under God's judgment, unless they repent and seek his mercy.

This covenant mercy, as God remembered his promises to save, is the theme on which the first half of the psalm concludes: "When he killed them, they sought him; they repented and sought God earnestly. They remembered that God was their rock, the Most High God their redeemer" (Ps. 78:34–35). Asaph notes that even this seeking was partly hypocritical and somewhat dishonest, since "their heart was not steadfast toward him; they were not faithful to his covenant" (v. 37). Even then, God was compassionate: "he . . . atoned for their iniquity and did not destroy them; he restrained his anger often and did not stir up all his wrath. He remembered that they were but flesh, a wind that passes and comes not again" (vv. 38–39).

This covenant mercy, in fulfillment of God's promises, is why there even was an Israel in Asaph's time and why there is a Christian church today. God understood the weakness of sinful human nature and showed compassion on those whom he promised to save. Far from merely winking at sin and tolerating evil, God did something more wonderful: he sent his Son to bear our sin and atone for our guilt. Asaph writes that God in his compassion "atoned for their iniquity and did not destroy them" (Ps. 78:38). By having his Son, Jesus, bear on the cross the penalty that our sins deserved, God propitiated his own wrath. Whereas Asaph rejoices that God "restrained his anger often and did not stir up all his wrath" (v. 38), the New Testament declares that God has put an end to the sins of those who believe by pouring out his wrath once for all at the cross. While God was patient with Israel, he has promised to do even more for you, if you will look to him in covenant faith. God promises in Christ to grant eternal salvation. He proclaims in Hebrews 8:12, "I will be merciful toward their iniquities, and I will remember their sins no more."

Demands My Life, My All

For the same reason that Psalm 78 urges its readers to know and pass on the record of God's saving deeds and their meaning, Jesus provided the sacrament of the Lord's Supper to his disciples before leaving to take up the cross. "Do this in remembrance of me," he declared (1 Cor. 11:24). In this way, Jesus points us back to the original exodus from Egypt, and its Passover meal, and then to the great event of all redemptive history: his death on the cross to atone for our sins. Speaking of this, Paul wrote: "Christ, our Passover lamb, has been sacrificed" (5:7).

The great point of the Bible, as it carries on the story of Psalm 78 and centers it on the coming of Christ, is that sinners must believe in the death of Jesus for their forgiveness and salvation. Do not forget that God is wrathful toward sin, but gracious in providing a Savior in his Son. And those of us who have read and learned the lessons of Scripture, who remember the wondrous things that God has done and have set our hope in God, should not forget the proper response in surrendering our entire lives to his glory. Isaac Watts explained the lessons that we are to learn from the history of Christ:

> When I survey the wondrous cross on which the Prince of glory died,
> My richest gain I count but loss, and pour contempt on all my pride. . . .
>
> Were the whole realm of nature mine, that were a present far too small;
> Love so amazing, so divine, demands my soul, my life, my all.[14]

14. Isaac Watts, "When I Survey the Wondrous Cross" (1707).

7

A Hymn to the Good Shepherd

Psalm 78:40–72

He chose David his servant and took him from the sheepfolds;
from following the nursing ewes he brought him
to shepherd Jacob his people. (Ps. 78:70–71)

There is a tendency among some Christians to want to avoid speaking anything negative. Ours is a positive religion, they emphasize, and we are called by God to proclaim good, not bad, news to the world. This approach seems both gracious and appealing, until we realize how unbiblical it is. As the Bible presents it, the Christian message is good news precisely because of the bad news it resolves. Indeed, without the bad news of God's judgment for sin, the good news of Christ and his salvation is cheapened so as to make little sense. In proclaiming the Christian gospel, evangelists must declare and explain the bad news of God's wrath on sin. By this means, the gospel not only is made relevant but is also illuminated. When we see the full problem of sin, Christ's saving works exceed our wildest imagining and highlight a grace that is truly amazing.

An example of the bad news making the good news relevant is found in Paul's teaching in Romans. There, Paul teaches in detail the salvation that comes through faith in Christ. He therefore starts his gospel exposition with the bad news of sin: "For the wrath of God is revealed from heaven against all ungodliness and unrighteousness of men" (Rom. 1:18). What a negative message! Yet Paul is explaining the best good news that humanity has ever heard, through the saving grace of Christ. Another example that uses the bad news of sin and human failure to glorify God's grace is seen in the second half of Psalm 78. Asaph will conclude this psalm by noting how God shepherded his people "and guided them with his skillful hand" (Ps. 78:72). This might not be seen as a remarkable statement, unless we have read the history that precedes it: a record of sin, folly, and rebellion against God. How can it be that a story that mainly consists of human failure and sin can end with lines of praise to God as our gracious Good Shepherd? Julia Johnston answers in her famous hymn:

> Marvelous grace of our loving Lord, grace that exceeds our sin and our guilt . . . .
>
> Grace, grace, God's grace, grace that will pardon and cleanse within;
> Grace, grace, God's grace, grace that is greater than all our sin.[1]

How Foolish Was Israel in Committing Sin

Asaph, the writer of Psalm 78, pointed out in the first thirty-nine verses how Israel had sinned against God during the exodus. In the second half of the psalm, he goes back over much the same ground. Verse 40 begins, "How often they rebelled against him in the wilderness and grieved him in the desert!"

Even Christians today who are willing to speak about sin and God's judgment still have a tendency to say as little as possible. Asaph takes the opposite approach. He is determined to detail extensively the awfulness of Israel's sin. Asaph is not merely applying a surface bandage on the sin habit of Israel (see Jer. 6:14). His purpose, rather, is to deliver the people with thoroughly changed hearts toward God. To this end, the first half of Psalm 78 detailed Israel's sin from the time of the exodus and Israel's journey through the wilderness. Having struck hammer blows on the nails of Israel's disobedience, Asaph

1. Julia H. Johnston, "Marvelous Grace of Our Loving Lord" (1910).

turns back over the same material to make the point of how foolish was Israel's sin.

Psalm 78:40–41 summarizes the basic facts as the psalmist returns to Israel's record of sin: "How often they rebelled against him in the wilderness and grieved him in the desert! They tested God again and again and provoked the Holy One of Israel." These two couplets pair Israel's actions with God's response. Over and over again during the exodus, Israel rebelled against God's Word as given through Moses. This "grieved" God, reminding us of how closely God's heart is knit together with his people and stricken by their disobedience. The description that Israel "tested God" is particularly poignant. The people made demands of God in order to prove his intentions, and then they limited by their unbelief what God should be allowed to do. This provoked the Lord, with the result that he caused the rebel nation to wander in the desert until the insolent generation died away. H. C. Leupold comments: "These were not trifling peccadillos; they were disastrous and devastating instances of deep iniquity."[2] In Psalm 81:13, the Lord bares his aggrieved heart over these foolish sins: "Oh, that my people would listen to me, that Israel would walk in my ways!"

How foolish it is to rebel in sin against a God whose heart is so loving and tender. But it was especially foolish of Israel to rebel against God in light of the saving works that he had performed, yet that the people quickly forgot. In Psalm 78:42–51, Asaph recounts God's delivering Israel from the bondage of Pharaoh in Egypt: "They did not remember his power or the day when he redeemed them from the foe, when he performed his signs in Egypt" (Ps. 78:42–43). Here again is the main theme of Psalm 78 in calling the Israelites to remember God's salvation and to teach his deeds to their children. James Boice applies this principle to Christians: "If we forget what it cost God to redeem us from our sins through Jesus' death, we will not long trust him in life's trials or love him enough to obey him in times of temptation."[3]

In recalling God's deliverance of Israel from Egypt, Asaph reminds his readers of the mighty plagues that broke the Egyptians' opposition to God's will. In Exodus 3:19–20, the Lord told Moses that "the king of Egypt will not let you go unless compelled by a mighty hand. So I will stretch out my

2. H. C. Leupold, *Exposition of the Psalms* (Columbus, OH: Wartburg Press, 1959), 569.
3. James Montgomery Boice, *Psalms*, 3 vols. (Grand Rapids: Baker, 1996), 2:649.

hand and strike Egypt with all the wonders that I will do in it; after that he will let you go." In Psalm 78:44–51, Asaph recounts six of the ten plagues with which God afflicted Egypt. First, he "turned their rivers to blood, so that they could not drink of their streams" (Ps. 78:44). Egypt worshiped the Nile, and God proved his power by corrupting it as a source of life. Second and third, God "sent among them swarms of flies, which devoured them, and frogs, which destroyed them" (v. 45). Fourth was a locust plague on their crops (v. 46), and fifth was hail to destroy their vines (v. 47) and livestock (v. 48). Each of these plagues was targeted at Egyptian idols and the sources of life in the land. Sixth, Asaph mentions God's harshest blow, when the angel of death "struck down every firstborn in Egypt" (v. 51). Incredibly, the very people who were delivered out of lifelong slavery by these mighty strokes forgot them when they were later faced with trials! Yet such is the folly of sin that it forgets the great works by which God has eternally proved his love. Marvin Tate writes that "Israel's behavior in the wilderness was characterized by a massive forgetfulness."[4] Likewise, the sins of Christians, especially when we complain against God and reject his commands, reflect a foolish forgetfulness of God's love in sending his Son to die for our sins.

The whole point of this section is that believers should trust God in light of what he has done for our salvation. Paul argues this point in a verse that should often occur to the minds of Christians: "He who did not spare his own Son but gave him up for us all, how will he not also with him graciously give us all things?" (Rom. 8:32). The point is that we have no need to test God and no basis to doubt his faithfulness, since he has already done more than we could ever imagine by securing our eternal salvation when Christ bore our sins on the cross. "How can you say that God loves me?" demands the sullen Christian, foolishly forgetting that God has already given the greatest proof imaginable through the blood of Jesus' cross.

Asaph makes a significant statement about not forgetting the Lord's redemption when he says that Israel "did not remember his power" in delivering the people from Egypt (Ps. 78:42). In the Hebrew, the word translated "power" literally means "hand." They did not remember God's *hand*, says Asaph, even though Pharaoh's own magicians cried out, "This is the finger of God" (Ex. 8:19). The plagues on Israel were not merely blasts from heaven sent by a distant God. Rather, God became personally involved in their

4. Marvin E. Tate, *Psalms 51–100*, Word Biblical Commentary 20 (Waco, TX: Word, 1990), 292.

plight, just as God is personally involved in the trials and challenges that each of his people faces today. In Psalm 34:17–18, David wrote: "When the righteous cry for help, the LORD hears and delivers them out of all their troubles. The LORD is near to the brokenhearted and saves the crushed in spirit." God's hand will reach out to you as well when you call on his name in time of need.

Not only is the Lord willing to help, reaching out his own hand, but he is also able to save because of his almighty power. Psalm 78:49 informs us of the angelic hosts that God employed in the final plague on Egypt: "He let loose on them his burning anger, wrath, indignation, and distress, a company of destroying angels." Armed with such supernatural resources, God is able to overcome any earthly threat to our salvation. The Bible's references to angels should never cause us to put our trust in these mighty servants but rather should fortify our confidence in the God who commands them. In Psalm 34:7, David tells us, "The angel of the LORD encamps around those who fear him, and delivers them."

With such divine power to remember, Eric Lane asks why the Israelites must "compromise with their enemies or make treaties, or call upon pagan fertility gods to provide," referring to the sins of the exodus generation.[5] Likewise, with even greater instances of salvation to remember in the work of Jesus Christ, how can Christians accuse God when troubles come or fail to honor him in our daily lives? The folly of sin is seen in those who forget the deeds of the Lord, just as true wisdom consists of trusting him with an obedient faith in every situation of life.

How Destructive Was Israel's Judgment for Sin

If Asaph wants his readers to see the folly of sin in Psalm 78:40–51, the next section highlights how destructive was Israel's judgment for sin. The psalm recounts Israel's abandoning God in idolatry, God's abandoning Israel in judgment, and the nation's utter ruin as a result of the loss of God's protection.

First, the psalmist showed how the people of Israel abandoned God even after he had graciously forgiven them and brought the nation safely into the promised land. Those familiar with the Bible recognize a description of the passage from the wilderness into the land of Canaan:

5. Eric Lane, *Psalms 1–89: The Lord Saves* (Ross-shire, Scotland: Christian Focus, 2006), 348.

Then he led out his people like sheep
  and guided them in the wilderness like a flock.
He led them in safety, so that they were not afraid,
  but the sea overwhelmed their enemies.
And he brought them to his holy land,
  to the mountain which his right hand had won.
He drove out nations before them;
  he apportioned them for a possession
  and settled the tribes of Israel in their tents. (Ps. 78:52–55)

The people responded by reveling in the bounty of their new home and turning completely away from God: "Yet they tested and rebelled against the Most High God and did not keep his testimonies, but turned away and acted treacherously like their fathers; they twisted like a deceitful bow" (Ps. 78:56–57). Because of her people's sinfulness, Israel was like a faulty bow that is never able to cause an arrow to strike the target. Like the generation before them, "they tested and rebelled against" God. In fact, they became ever worse: "For they provoked him to anger with their high places; they moved him to jealousy with their idols" (v. 58). Similar danger faces the church whenever it finds itself comfortably settled in the world. We often forget, as Hebrews 11:13 puts it, that we are "strangers and exiles on the earth." Whenever Christians set their hearts on the things of the world and look to its provision, we begin following the ways of the world and worshiping the world's idols, abandoning God and his Word.

Psalm 78:59–64 brings us through the book of Judges to the early chapters of 1 Samuel. God, being "provoked . . . to anger" by idolatry and sin, "was full of wrath, and he utterly rejected Israel" (Ps. 78:58–59). The episode in mind is Israel's falling to the Philistines in the battle of Ebenezer, when God "forsook his dwelling at Shiloh, the tent where he dwelt among mankind, and delivered his power to captivity, his glory to the hand of the foe" (vv. 60–61). Learning of a Philistine offensive, the sensual sons of Eli the high priest brought the ark of the covenant to the battle, thinking that this symbol of God's presence would be a magical weapon. To their great shock and dismay, not only did God give victory to the Philistines, but his holy ark was also captured by the enemies. First Samuel 4:10–11 records: "So the Philistines fought, and Israel was defeated, and they fled . . . . And the ark of God was captured." Asaph looks back on this event as God's separating his presence from the people, abandoning them because of their sin, utterly rejecting Israel and removing himself from the tabernacle at Shiloh. Charles Spurgeon notes: "It seemed to say that Jehovah would sooner dwell among his avowed adversaries than among so false a people as Israel; he would sooner bear the insults of Philistia than the treacheries of Ephraim."[6]

When God departs from his people because of sin, the result is always calamitous disaster, and so it was for Israel after the ark fell into Philistine hands. God "gave his people over to the sword and vented his wrath on his heritage" (Ps. 78:62). First Samuel 4:10 tells us that after Israel was defeated and its army fled, "there was a very great slaughter, for thirty thousand foot soldiers of Israel fell." Asaph speaks of this metaphorically, saying, "Fire devoured their young men, and their young women had no marriage song" (Ps. 78:63). Spurgeon writes: "The nation had failed in its solemn task of instructing the young in the fear of Jehovah, and it was a fitting judgment that the very production of a posterity should be endangered."[7] Moreover, "their priests fell by the sword, and their widows made no lamentation" (Ps. 78:64). This refers to what happened when news of the defeat came to Shiloh, telling of Israel's defeat and the death of Hophni and Phinehas. Eli the high priest fell from his seat, broke his neck, and died instantly (1 Sam. 4:18). Instead of observing the traditional rites of mourning, Phinehas's pregnant wife gave birth to a son, naming him "Ichabod," saying, "The glory has departed from Israel!" (v. 21).

We might look for many examples of this pattern taking place during church history, but most relevant is the history of the last hundred years in our nation. The America of 1900 was not perfect in godliness, yet most of the nation's institutions acknowledged the value and authority of God's Word. By 1920, however, led astray by the secular humanism of Darwinian evolution and corrupted by material prosperity and national success, the situation had fundamentally changed. Under the influence of European rationalism, most of the large Protestant denominations began abandoning their high view of the Bible and were teaching it as an error-filled, man-made book of merely human authority.

One leader who confronted this slide was J. Gresham Machen in the northern Presbyterian Church. When the denomination reorganized Princeton

6. Charles Haddon Spurgeon, *The Treasury of David*, 3 vols. (Peabody, MA: Hendrickson, n.d.), 2a:345.
7. Spurgeon, *Treasury of David*, 2a:345.

Theological Seminary's board of directors in order to permit liberal doctrine, Machen resigned in 1929 and formed Westminster Theological Seminary. In the 1930s, Machen fought against the denomination's missions agencies for permitting men and women who denied the gospel to serve in the field. Failing to bring reform, Machen launched his own missions agency, for which he was brought up on charges and expelled from the denomination in 1936. This was one prominent example of how the mainline denominations abandoned God's Word in the early half of the twentieth century.

What has resulted from America's abandonment of God? After rising to worldwide power in the 1940s, America has experienced decline in national well-being and social harmony. Exactly the kinds of judgment that fell on Israel in the days after the loss of the ark to the Philistines are occurring in America today. Abandoned by God, Israel experienced virtually complete destruction: military losses and slain youths, the failure of national religion, a declining prosperity, and the breakdown of families.

Calamity and destruction not only fall on nations when they abandon God, but also strike individuals who do likewise. To live under the judgment of God with your sins unforgiven is to suffer the burden of dissatisfaction even with the blessings of earthly life, together with a loss of meaning and peace. Isaiah 48:22 summarizes: "'There is no peace,' says the Lord, 'for the wicked.'"

How Gracious Is God in Delivering from Sin

If Psalm 78 had ended with the devastation of verse 64, it would have provided a suitable warning against sin, which has been shown to be both foolish and destructive. Yet the Bible goes beyond mere reasoning in urging us to be faithful to God. Therefore, Psalm 78 makes its most important point in the final section, which argues that God is gracious in delivering us from sin in such a way that surpasses any expectation, so that we should desire to serve him not only out of fear but even more so out of gratitude and love.

Asaph's narrative left off with Israel's defeat in battle with the Philistines, the destruction of their army, and the capture of the ark of the covenant. As always, God's saving grace began not with something his people did but with his own sovereign action. Asaph writes, "Then the Lord awoke as from sleep" (Ps. 78:65). This metaphor refers to God's rousing himself after apparent inactivity. Asaph then boldly describes God's offensive outburst in terms of a man who is made heroic by strong drink: "like a strong man shouting because of wine" (v. 65). Marvin Tate writes: "The imagery here is . . . that of the Divine Warrior who wakes from sleep to do battle once more for Israel."[8]

This description refers to how God seemed to awaken when his ark was held captive in the temple of the Philistine god Dagon. The Philistines looked on Israel's God as defeated, if not asleep. John Calvin explains: "when he exercises forbearance, and does not promptly execute his judgments, the interpretation which ignorant people put upon his conduct is, that he loiters in his manner like a man who is stupefied, and knows not how to proceed."[9] The Philistines learned their mistake when they discovered the statue of Dagon first fallen at the feet of the Lord's ark and then with its head and hands broken off, a symbol of conquest (1 Sam. 5:3–4). Then people started dying in great numbers from a plague (vv. 6–12), until the Philistines were so desperate to be rid of God's presence that they sent the ark back to Israel (6:1–12). God continued his offensive by raising up Samuel to lead Israel in victory over the Philistines, removing from his people the yoke that had come upon them by sin. Asaph writes: "And he put his adversaries to rout; he put them to everlasting shame" (Ps. 78:66).

God's victory over the Philistines took place without any aid from Israel. This reminds us that God does not require our help to conquer and achieve his aims. The episode of the ark's capture might have led some Israelites to conclude, with the enemy, that the Lord had failed. God's victory over the Philistines proved, however, that he had always possessed the power to achieve victory. The reason that Israel fell into disgrace was not God's failure but the people's own sin in turning from him. Likewise, the church today will avoid failure as we remain true to God's Word. We will not find God's strength failing, but are reminded of his sovereign might over every foe.

It was by grace alone that God returned his ark to Israel, having defeated her enemies. It was also by grace that under King David in the next generation he established his tabernacle on Mount Zion: "He rejected the tent of Joseph; he did not choose the tribe of Ephraim, but he chose the tribe of

8. Tate, *Psalms 51–100*, 294.

9. John Calvin, *Calvin's Commentaries*, 23 vols. (1848; repr., Grand Rapids: Baker, 2009), 6:274.

Judah, Mount Zion, which he loves. He built his sanctuary like the high heavens, like the earth, which he has founded forever" (Ps. 78:67–69).

God not only roused himself to deliver his people by grace, but also graciously came back to live among them. Should his presence not encourage us in repenting of our sin and turning back to God in faith? David did this after committing the most evil sins in his life, the seduction of Bathsheba and the betrayal of her faithful husband (2 Sam. 11). Crying out to God for forgiveness, David prayed, "Have mercy on me, O God, according to your steadfast love; according to your abundant mercy blot out my transgressions" (Ps. 51:1). While David would experience many severe temporal judgments, God did restore him. Then David prayed that God would resume his presence in David's life: "Create in me a clean heart, O God, and renew a right spirit within me. Cast me not away from your presence, and take not your Holy Spirit from me" (vv. 10–11). We may likewise call on God's grace to be forgiven and restored with his presence.

God's gracious deliverance of Israel was completed in the raising up of David to be a righteous king: "He chose David his servant and took him from the sheepfolds" (Ps. 78:70). Some of God's greatest mercies involve providing godly and effective leaders in the society and the church, and we should pray earnestly for this blessing.

David models three features of true spiritual leadership. First, he was humble in being raised up by God's grace: "He chose David his servant and took him from the sheepfolds" (Ps. 78:70). David did not advance himself by ambition but was called by God. Second, a leader should have demonstrated godly character in prior service. David was raised "from following the nursing ewes . . . to shepherd Jacob his people, Israel his inheritance" (v. 71). Spurgeon writes: "A shepherd of sheep he had been, and this was a fit school for a shepherd of men."[10] Third, David showed himself a true servant of God by both the godliness and the ability with which he ruled: "With upright heart he shepherded them and guided them with his skillful hand" (v. 72). Leaders who see themselves foremost as God's servants are most likely to rule righteously and do well in leading God's people.

Do you see Asaph's point? Look at how gracious God was in delivering Israel from sin! Let us respond in faithfulness to him! Christians look to the ark of the covenant and to David and see through them an even greater

10. Spurgeon, *Treasury of David*, 2a:346.

reason to love God in faithfulness. The ark of the covenant presented a picture of salvation by grace through the blood of Christ, especially on the Day of Atonement, when sacrificial blood was sprinkled on the ark's mercy seat. Here is the victory over our great enemies: Satan, sin, and death. Let us therefore draw near to God through the blood of Christ (Eph. 2:13).

David's kingship was especially given as a forerunner to the eternal reign of Christ the King. Following David, Jesus arose out of a humble setting with a conquering spirit, and fulfilled all righteousness in achieving God's saving work. Isaiah foretold: "He will tend his flock like a shepherd; he will gather the lambs in his arms; he will carry them in his bosom, and gently lead those that are with young" (Isa. 40:11). David Dickson thus writes that David "was but a shadow of the perfections of Christ in his government."[11] Jesus exceeds David in that as God's Son he lives and reigns forever. Therefore, "he is able to save to the uttermost those who draw near to God through him" (Heb. 7:25).

Jesus himself declared: "I am the good shepherd. The good shepherd lays down his life for the sheep. . . . I give them eternal life, and they will never perish, and no one will snatch them out of my hand" (John 10:11, 28). With what abounding grace has God delivered us from our sins through our Good Shepherd, Jesus, who died on the cross for our forgiveness! In David's place, Jesus is forever our righteous King. Seeing Jesus, as Asaph looked back to God's provision of King David, let us beware the folly of sin by remembering God's saving deeds, let us avoid the destruction of sin by remaining true to God, and let us rejoice in the surpassing grace of God in delivering us from our sins through Jesus Christ. As the psalmist urges later, in Psalm 81:16, if you would only walk in God's ways through faith, "he would feed you with the finest of the wheat, and with honey from the rock [he] would satisfy you."

11. David Dickson, *A Commentary on the Psalms* (1653; repr., Edinburgh: Banner of Truth, 1995), 29.

8

Help Us, O God

Psalm 79

Help us, O God of our salvation, for the glory of your name;
deliver us, and atone for our sins, for your name's sake!
(Ps. 79:9)

Psalm 79 is a classic psalm of lament, very much in the spirit of Psalm 74, which likewise grieved the destruction of Jerusalem. The main difference is that whereas Psalm 74 took God around in prayer to places where the city had been destroyed, the emphasis in Psalm 79 is on the people and their humiliation. While it is possible that Psalm 79 refers to a handful of different historical events, it is most likely that the psalmist wrote in light of the destruction of the covenant people in Nebuchadnezzar's overthrow of Jerusalem in 587 B.C. Verses 2–3 are quoted by the noncanonical book 1 Maccabees 7:17 in light of the occupation of Jerusalem during the reign of Antiochus Epiphanes in the third century B.C. This indicates that Psalm 79 is seen as a template for similar disasters. Indeed, to this day Psalm 79 is recited every Friday afternoon at the Wailing Wall in Jerusalem, as sorrowful Jews bemoan their final loss of the temple in A.D. 70.

It is interesting to wonder about the order of this collection of psalms attributed to Asaph in Psalms 73–83. The preceding psalm concludes with praise to God for providing David and his monarchy to lead the people (Ps. 78:70–72). Fast-forwarding four hundred years, we find that the sins of David's heirs caused God to remove from them all the blessings they had previously enjoyed, including God's house on Mount Zion (vv. 68–69). Thus, Psalm 79 stands as a monument to the calamity of sin, even as it ends with hope in the grace of a saving God.

An Outraged Plea

The psalm begins with an outraged plea that seeks for God to punish his people's enemies. "O God," the psalmist begins, unburdening his soul in the Lord's presence and trusting that God will care about the suffering of his nation.

Asaph's complaint details the sacrilege involved in the pagan destruction of the temple and degradation of Israel's people: "O God, the nations have come into your inheritance; they have defiled your holy temple; they have laid Jerusalem in ruins" (Ps. 79:1). The purpose of the temple was to communicate God's holiness to the earth. The nations are ungodly, and Asaph is outraged that they should trample God's inheritance and profane his holy temple.

Particularly on his mind, however, is the humiliation of God's people and the way in which this calamity reflects on the Lord. Not only were Israel's people slain in great numbers, but "they have given the bodies of your servants to the birds of the heavens for food, the flesh of your faithful to the beasts of the earth" (Ps. 79:2). Apparently the slain so outnumbered the living that the task of giving decent burials was too large to accomplish. Bones and corpses made the Lord's sanctuary unclean, and this is now the state of the entire city: "They have poured out their blood like water all around Jerusalem, and there was no one to bury them" (v. 3). The Babylonians, following standard ancient practice, dishonored their conquered foes by leaving them as carrion for birds and beasts. The psalmist is particularly grieved to note that the number of those defiled includes God's faithful servants, who were caught up in the debacle.

The psalm's reflection reminds us that God's people have always considered a proper burial to be a Christian duty. Recently, the practice of cremation has spread in our society, even among Christians. God's people have historically avoided this practice, however, instead showing honor to the body even in death. John Calvin states that God intends that "in the burial of men, there should be some testimony to the resurrection at the last day,"[1] and this is accomplished by burial of the body that Christ will summon from the grave before long.

It was not only the dead who were disgraced by Jerusalem's fall but also the living. The psalmist laments: "We have become a taunt to our neighbors, mocked and derided by those around us" (Ps. 79:4). Israel had long lived in pride for her covenant relationship with God, so now the surrounding peoples delighted to believe the nation abandoned by the Lord. Here, the cruelty of the world is seen not only in the bloodthirsty desire to slay and destroy, but also in the propensity to mock and taunt those who are brought low by calamity—especially the people of God.

Reflections on Prayer

The opening lament issues forth in pleas for God's intervention. From these petitions we may make useful observations regarding our own relationship to God in prayer.

First, believers in distress pray to God because we know that he is sovereign over all our affairs. Asaph responds to Jerusalem's calamity by calling out to God to relent of his chastisements: "How long, O Lord? Will you be angry forever? Will your jealousy burn like fire?" (Ps. 79:5). Notice that while the destruction was brought by foreign peoples, Asaph knows that it was God who struck Israel because of her idolatry and sin. Therefore, he does not pray as though God were ignorant of the situation or somehow uninvolved, but in his misery he prays for God to relent. In this case, it is clear that the psalmist knows that God is acting in punishment of his people. Perhaps he was aware of the prophecy given not long before in Jeremiah 7:33, when the weeping prophet foretold that "the dead bodies of this people will be food for the birds of the air, and for the beasts of the earth." This does not mean that outward calamities always indicate God's chastising displeasure, since believers suffer greatly for other reasons. But when our conscience afflicts us under trial with an awareness of high-handed sins that we have committed, then we should expect that God's hand is at work

1. John Calvin, *Calvin's Commentaries*, 23 vols. (1848; repr., Grand Rapids: Baker, 2009), 5:283.

and pray to his gracious heart to relent of his punishments. Knowing God's mercy, we may pray to him with anticipation of help. James Boice writes: "The hand of God often does seem heavy upon us, and his workings in our lives seem slow. But it is not forever! Remember that. And it will not be more than you can bear."[2] Since God is the one who has the mercy we need, we should pray our way through every calamity. William Plumer writes that "if we can bring our woes before God in prayer, we have done the best thing possible."[3]

Second, the ability to pray to God is a sign that all is not lost. The loss of God's temple building on Mount Zion seemed an irredeemable loss, because that was the place where Israel's intercessors had met with God. Yet with the temple destroyed, Asaph is still able to pray to the Lord, and this provides hope. The prophet Jonah learned the same lesson when he was cast overboard and swallowed by the great fish (Jonah 1:17). In that dark, watery grave, Jonah said: "I called out to the LORD, out of my distress, and he answered me; out of the belly of Sheol I cried, and you heard my voice" (2:2). Though he was in desperate straits, he prayed, "Yet you brought up my life from the pit" (v. 6). It is notable that Jonah prayed this before he had actually been delivered from inside the sea monster. His point was that simply by being able to exercise his faith in God through prayer, he was conscious of possessing God's salvation. When we pray to God in faith, we, too, receive proof of our salvation and enjoy a confident hope that God will deliver us in the end.

Third, Asaph's prayer raises questions about the propriety of Christians' praying for God's judgment and wrath on others. In Psalm 79:6, Asaph appeals to God: "Pour out your anger on the nations that do not know you, and on the kingdoms that do not call upon your name!" Embedded in this petition are two reasons for God to overthrow the wicked. First, they "do not know you" or "call upon your name." This might be thought of as an excuse for their ungodliness, but instead for Asaph it marks a willful and idolatrous neglect of the abundant evidence of God (see Rom. 1:19–21). The pagan nations that attacked Jerusalem deserved judgment for their unbelief and, as a second reason, for their violence against God's people: "For they have devoured Jacob and laid waste his habitation" (Ps. 79:7).

2. James Montgomery Boice, *Psalms*, 3 vols. (Grand Rapids: Baker, 1996), 2:656.
3. William S. Plumer, *Psalms* (1867; repr., Edinburgh: Banner of Truth, 1975), 765.

The question is raised whether Christians may pray in this same manner, seeking God to judge and condemn the wicked. Jesus taught: "You have heard that it was said, 'You shall love your neighbor and hate your enemy.' But I say to you, Love your enemies and pray for those who persecute you" (Matt. 5:43–44). Does this teaching bar Christians from praying for God to thwart the plans of evil deceivers and murderers? The answer is that we must discriminate between our prayers for individuals who harm us and our prayers for God to defend his gospel and the church. John Calvin writes:

> None may pray in this manner but those who have clothed themselves with a public character, and who, laying aside all personal considerations, have espoused, and are deeply interested in, the welfare of the whole Church.[4]

This means that we are to pray against evil, and even against those who pursue evil, while maintaining a spirit of grace toward our personal enemies. Christians above all others ought to have compassion on those in the grip of sin, even when sin is committed against us, remembering the Bible's teaching to "overcome evil with good" (Rom. 12:21). At the same time, we naturally pray for God to glorify his justice in judging those who will not believe and in protecting the gospel cause and its people. Therefore, Christians pray against evil, asking, as George Horne suggests, "that God, not to gratify any vindictive spirit of theirs, but to vindicate his own attributes, would break the teeth of the oppressor, and work a public and glorious salvation . . . ; at beholding which, the very adversaries themselves might possibly be converted."[5] In the face of those who not only revile God's church but also mock divine justice with their bloodthirsty violence, Christians pray for God's cause to be vindicated in judgment so that his name will be feared.

An application today might be made with respect to Christian opposition to the abortion industry. Christians of course pray that God would protect the unborn babies threatened with slaughter and for God to thwart plans to advance this evil, as well as to vindicate justice by judging those who will not repent. At the same time, Christians who plan and commit acts of violence against abortion clinics are guilty of sin against God, as

4. Calvin, *Commentaries*, 5:288.

5. George Horne, *Commentary on the Psalms* (1771; repr., Audubon, NJ: Old Paths Publications, 1997), 345.

are those who vindictively revile individuals involved in this bloody industry. Many of the greatest advances against abortion have come through expressions of Christian mercy and love for those involved in the sin. This includes the excellent Christian response of crisis pregnancy centers and the showing of love and compassion for individuals involved in performing abortions, remembering Jesus' compassion for us when we were sinning against him.

A Penitent Plea

One key to balancing our resentment against the ungodly is to keep our own sinfulness clearly in mind. Asaph realizes and admits that Jerusalem's destruction was caused not so much by the Babylonians as by the sin and idolatry of its own people, bringing God's chastising wrath. Surrounded by such devastation, he prays, "Do not remember against us our former iniquities; let your compassion come speedily to meet us, for we are brought very low" (Ps. 79:8).

Some commentators have taken the reference to "our former iniquities" to mean that the Jews blamed their ancestors for their troubles. It is more likely that the psalmist understands his own generation as having partaken in the habitual sins of the nation. When Asaph begs for God's compassion to "come speedily," he means that God should not take strict account of the people's sins, lest his chastisement last longer than Israel can survive. God's purpose in discipline is to bring his people to repentance and to bring us running back to him like the prodigal of Jesus' parable. Asaph realizes this as he pleads for the compassion of the Lord and professes the low state of the people. Far from pleading the supposed merits of Israel, he wisely accounts for the grace of God in appealing to his mercy alone. David Dickson writes that "a refuge is open to us in God's tender mercies who cannot destroy utterly a sinner fleeing to his mercy."[6]

Boice points out that Asaph's example should be a rule not only when Christians are particularly cast down but whenever we come to God in prayer: "Every true prayer should have within it a confession of the worshiper's sins. . . . This is because God is holy, and we are not. So if we are

6. David Dickson, *A Commentary on the Psalms* (1653; repr., Edinburgh: Banner of Truth, 1995), 2:34.

really praying to him, we will be aware of his holiness, and his holiness will convict us of our sinful state."[7]

In addition to confessing his sin and the sins of the people, Asaph improves his prayer further by appealing to the Lord as Savior: "Help us, O God of our salvation" (Ps. 79:9). Asaph is again like Jonah, who through prayer regained his awareness of God's grace, even in a place of despair. Jonah concluded, "Salvation belongs to the Lord!" (Jonah 2:9). It is God's nature to save penitent sinners who call on his name, and it glorifies him to be treated in this way. Thus Asaph adds "for the glory of your name" (Ps. 79:9). Dickson writes: "It is the glory of the Lord to forget sin, and when remission of sin is prayed according to God's promise, the Lord's glory is engaged."[8] The psalm continues: "deliver us, and atone for our sins, for your name's sake!" (Ps. 79:9). Charles Spurgeon writes:

> This is masterly pleading. No argument has such force as this. God's glory was tarnished in the eyes of the heathen by the defeat of his people, and the profanation of his temple; therefore, his distressed servants implore his aid, that his great name may no more be the scorn of blaspheming enemies.[9]

The covenant nation's well-being was bound up with the reputation of its God, and the nations either feared the Lord or despised him based on the apparent success of the people. With this in mind, Asaph pleads: "Why should the nations say, 'Where is their God?' Let the avenging of the outpoured blood of your servants be known among the nations before our eyes!" (Ps. 79:10). Rather than allow the nations to believe that Israel's God had been defeated, Asaph calls for God to educate them through displays of conquering might.

This prayer may be seen to have been answered, at least in part, through the faithful exploits of Daniel and his friends during their captivity in Babylon. Though completely disempowered in the weapons of the world, these faithful servants were successful in defying Nebuchadnezzar even from within the heart of his empire. On one infamous occasion, the Babylonian ruler set up a golden statue and required everyone to worship it. Only the Israelite youths refused to serve the gods of Babylon or treat the

7. Boice, *Psalms*, 2:657.
8. Dickson, *Psalms*, 2:35.
9. Charles Haddon Spurgeon, *The Treasury of David*, 3 vols. (Peabody, MA: Hendrickson, n.d.), 2a:378.

emperor's image as divine. When threatened to be cast into a fiery furnace, they still refused, defying the evil power of the king: "O Nebuchadnezzar, . . . our God whom we serve is able to deliver us from the burning fiery furnace, and he will deliver us out of your hand, O king" (Dan. 3:16–17). When they were thrown into a furnace so hot that their prison guards were consumed when casting them into the flames, the faithful Jews were delivered by the kind of supernatural intervention that Asaph was seeking. Nebuchadnezzar exclaimed to his aides: "Did we not cast three men bound into the fire? . . . But I see four men unbound, walking in the midst of the fire, and they are not hurt; and the appearance of the fourth is like a son of the gods" (vv. 24–25). As a result, the same Babylonian conqueror who had despoiled Jerusalem in Asaph's time gave praise and glory to Israel's God:

> Blessed be the God of Shadrach, Meshach, and Abednego, who has sent his angel and delivered his servants, who trusted in him, and set aside the king's command, and yielded up their bodies rather than serve and worship any god except their own God. (Dan. 3:28)

God delivered the Israelites after the destruction of Jerusalem not by immediately restoring their city but rather by empowering their faith in a land of idols. It is as a great a miracle for God to strengthen his people's faith in the midst of trials as it is to remove the trials altogether. Indeed, if Jerusalem was Asaph's concern, God's chief concern was the faith of his people. Realizing this priority urges Christians to pray in their trials for God's will to be done. For when God simply causes Christians today to defy the spirit of a wicked age through faith in the gospel, a mighty conquest is won that displays God's glory in the world. "This is the victory that has overcome the world," the apostle John wrote—"our faith" (1 John 5:4).

The key issue in God's concern was Israel's need to truly repent of sin. Asaph understood that sin was at the heart of the nation's travail and sought to repent on behalf of his generation. But the lesson had not yet been sufficiently learned. The time for repentance would come more than a generation later, when the elderly Daniel realized that the seventy-year period foretold for Israel's captivity was coming to an end (Jer. 25:10–11). Daniel took up the penitent plea of Psalm 79 and sought from God the mercy that resulted in the restoration of Jerusalem and its temple:

> O Lord, make your face to shine upon your sanctuary, which is desolate. . . . O Lord, hear; O Lord, forgive. O Lord, pay attention and act. Delay not, for your own sake, O my God, because your city and your people are called by your name. (Dan. 9:17–19)

Not only was sin the decisive issue for the ancient Jews, needing to be dealt with by God's mercy before his blessing could be restored, but sin is also the first issue that must be settled between us and God. St. Augustine realized this when he was deeply convicted for his sin but was not yet able to commit to Jesus Christ. In anguish, he prayed from Psalm 79, "Do not remember against us our former iniquities" (Ps. 79:8), bound in his guilt. It was immediately after this prayer that Augustine heard children singing a song with the words *Tolle lege! Tolle lege!*, meaning, "Take up and read! Take up and read!" He took up Paul's letter to the Romans and there found the forgiveness he needed in the grace of Jesus Christ. God's answer to Augustine was essentially the same answer that God had in response to Asaph's plea in Psalm 79: "all have sinned and fall short of the glory of God, and are justified by his grace as a gift, through the redemption that is in Christ Jesus" (Rom. 3:23–24).[10] Only when you have confessed your sin and found forgiveness in the blood of Christ will you have peace with God and receive the peace that your soul needs from God. The Scripture declares: "If we confess our sins, he is faithful and just to forgive us our sins and to cleanse us from all unrighteousness" (1 John 1:9).

A Grateful Plea

Psalm 79 presents an outraged plea and a penitent plea, concluding with a grateful plea that ends with praise for God's grace: "But we your people, the sheep of your pasture, will give thanks to you forever; from generation to generation we will recount your praise" (Ps. 79:13). How remarkable it is that a psalm that began in such anguish should end in such praise! The reason for this change of heart is that, having turned to God in prayer, Asaph remembered what God is like and found reasons not only to hope but also to praise the Lord from a grateful heart. He shows us that one of the greatest

10. Augustine, *Confessions*, trans. William Watts (Cambridge, MA: Harvard University Press, 1919), 8.12.

needs of Christians who are suffering most greatly is a renewed awareness of the great God that we serve and know.

For instance, the prayer of Psalm 79 indicates that even in a scene of horror and despair, Asaph remembers the *compassion* of the Lord: "let your compassion come speedily to meet us" (Ps. 79:8). In verse 11 he cries, "Let the groans of the prisoners come before you." Perhaps Asaph remembers an episode from earlier in Israel's history, when the nation was held in the torment of Egyptian slavery. The book of Exodus records that God heard the groans of his people in bondage as they cried to him: "Their cry for rescue from slavery came up to God. And God heard their groaning, and God remembered his covenant with Abraham, with Isaac, and with Jacob" (Ex. 2:23–24). If God had shown great compassion in the past and had remembered his covenant promises to save those who trusted him, then Asaph could not only hope in God's compassion but also praise him for it.

Second, the psalmist remembers the *power* of the Lord and gives him thanks for it as well: "according to your great power, preserve those doomed to die!" (Ps. 79:11). From Asaph's point of view, the bare survival of the nation seems unlikely apart from God's almighty intervention. Christians look back on the history that followed, learning in the Bible of a great multitude of saving acts by God. Most important was God's intervention in raising Jesus, Israel's true Messiah and Savior, from the grave after his crucifixion for our sins. Paul informed us that this same immeasurably great power is extended "toward us who believe," the same power "that he worked in Christ when he raised him from the dead" (Eph. 1:19–20). What reason we have to praise the God and Father of our risen Lord Jesus Christ, even amid afflictions and temptations, because of his saving power for us!

Third, Asaph remembers and praises the *justice* of the Lord, realizing that the wicked will not escape an eternal judgment unless they turn to God and repent. "Return sevenfold into the lap of our neighbors the taunts with which they have taunted you, O Lord!" Asaph prays (Ps. 79:12). "Sevenfold" restitution was a way of expressing God's full justice for the entirety of sin. In Psalm 73, the psalmist was aggrieved for the sins of the wicked, until he went into the sanctuary, where he remembered the teaching of God's Word and the coming judgment of those who do not repent. "Truly you set them in slippery places; you make them fall to ruin," Asaph exclaimed (73:18). Realizing the terrible end that will befall the wicked, Christians are overwhelmingly grateful just to be forgiven of our sins, and we remember to praise God for both his justice on sin and our forgiveness through faith in Christ.

Fourth, Asaph praises God for his *faithfulness*: "But we your people, the sheep of your pasture, will give thanks to you forever; from generation to generation we will recount your praise" (Ps. 79:13). Even with a broken city, a burned temple, and a graveyard of slain servants around him, the psalmist realizes that the church is the flock under the care of the Lord. Believers who suffer terribly in this life will have no such pains in the life to come, when the Good Shepherd has led all his flock into the house of the Lord forever. God will be faithful! Just as Jeremiah remembered God in Lamentations during the same disaster, Asaph finds praise for God in his faithful, covenant love: "The steadfast love of the Lord never ceases; his mercies never come to an end; they are new every morning; great is your faithfulness" (Lam. 3:22–23).

How Glorious the Day!

I mentioned that Psalm 79 is prayed every week at the Wailing Wall in Jerusalem, which is made of surviving stones from the original temple on Mount Zion that Nebuchadnezzar destroyed. In lamenting even today the very disaster for which Asaph prayed in Psalm 79 some 2,600 years ago, the Jews express awareness of the great loss they suffered. The full calamity of the lost temple is realized when we remember that there alone were the atoning sacrifices offered for the people's sin. Asaph's cry, "Atone for our sins!" (Ps. 79:9), raises a desperate question: How would sins be atoned for when the place of atonement had been destroyed?

In answering the prayer of Psalm 79, God showed his compassion, power, and faithfulness most gloriously in his provision of the cross of his Son, Jesus Christ. How tragic it is that Jews ask this question at the Wailing Wall today by praying Psalm 79, when in fact Asaph's answer was fully granted two thousand years ago when Jesus the Messiah made atonement for his people's sins. The apostle John rejoiced that "we have an advocate with the Father, Jesus Christ the righteous. He is the propitiation for our sins" (1 John 2:1–2).

If Asaph could look forward into history, not yet knowing how God would answer, and still conclude with thanks and praise for the faithful love of

God, how much more ought we who look back on the cross never forget the praise that God is due! From our perspective, we also look forward to Christ's return, when according to his Word God will give a final and consummate fulfillment to all his promises in a glory that will never end. Horne thus exults:

> How glorious will be the day, when triumphant over sin and sorrow, over everything that exalteth and opposeth itself, the church universal shall behold the adversary disarmed forever; while she herself, placed in pastures of joy, and led to the waters of eternal comfort, shall, from age to age, incessantly sing the praises of her great Shepherd and Bishop, her King, and her God![11]

11. Horne, *Psalms*, 346.

9

The Shining Face of God

Psalm 80

Restore us, O Lord God of hosts! Let your face shine, that we may be saved! (Ps. 80:19)

Benjamin Morgan Palmer tells of a friend who attended a series of evangelistic services. After several days, the man complained to Palmer that preachers "are the most contradictory men in the world." He explained, "Why yesterday, you said in your sermon that sinners were perfectly helpless in themselves—utterly unable to repent or to believe, and then turned square round and said that they would all be damned if they did not." Palmer's reply showed the master surgeon of souls that he was. "Well," he answered, "there is no use in our quarreling over this matter; either you can or you can not; if you can, all I have to say is that I hope you will just go and do it." This probe touched directly on the wound, as the friend replied, "I have been trying my best for three whole days, and cannot."[1]

This helpless situation is reflected in the prayer of the Asaphite writer of Psalm 80. Israel is suffering God's wrath for its idolatry and sin so that

1. C. N. Willborn, ed., *Selected Writings of Benjamin Morgan Palmer* (Edinburgh: Banner of Truth, 2014), 78–79.

salvation can happen only as the people return to God. The psalmist thus prays for Israel's return because he knows that only God can provide the grace for such repentance. Three times the psalm repeats the refrain of verse 3: "Restore us, O God; let your face shine, that we may be saved!" In seeking an answer, Psalm 80 presents some of the richest imagery of God found in all the Bible. It identifies God as the source of salvation's blessings, as the Judge who causes wrath in response to sin, and whose covenant grace is the hope of those who seek restoration to his care. Eric Lane describes Psalm 80 as "an appeal to God based on his pledged love to his people."[2] It is a theologically intense prayer that seeks to know God and remember his ways so as to persevere in the hope of salvation through faith.

Recalling God's Relationship

Psalm 80:1 calls on God by means of the imagery of the Lord as the Shepherd of his flock: "Give ear, O Shepherd of Israel, you who lead Joseph like a flock." This way of relating to God first appears in Genesis 48:15, where Jacob praised "the God who has been my shepherd all my life long to this day." The Israelites were herdsmen, so the thought of God as the Shepherd to his weak and needy sheep was both familiar and significant. David sang this way in Psalm 23: "The Lord is my shepherd; I shall not want. He makes me lie down in green pastures. He leads me beside still waters" (vv. 1–2). To pray to God as our Shepherd is to stress the intimate nature of our relationship, noting as well the difficulty of saving what James Boice describes as such "helpless, wayward, and even stupid animals."[3]

God's shepherding love came to full display when Jesus applied the imagery to himself: "I am the good shepherd. The good shepherd lays down his life for the sheep" (John 10:11). It is because God has taken this kind of interest in those who call on his name that we can pray with so much hope. If you can number yourself a member of Christ's flock through saving faith in him, you can pray to a Savior who has committed his divine will to your salvation.

Psalm 80:1 adds a second important image of God: "You who are enthroned upon the cherubim." This statement refers to the ark of the covenant, crowned

2. Eric Lane, *Psalms 1–89: The Lord Saves* (Ross-shire, Scotland: Christian Focus, 2006), 355.

3. James Montgomery Boice, *Psalms*, 3 vols. (Grand Rapids: Baker, 1996), 2:661.

with two golden images of mighty angels. The ark was the footstool of God on earth and the place where the Lord met with his servants. When Moses came before the ark to meet with God, he saw the overwhelming radiance of God's majesty. The psalmist thus calls on God to "shine forth" (v. 1), praying to God as a transcendent deity who is able to save. When we remember that the cherubim rested atop the "mercy seat," we remember as well God's willingness to forgive. The mercy seat is where the high priest sprinkled the atoning blood of the sacrificed goat on the Day of Atonement (Lev. 16:15). Thus, when God told Moses in Exodus 25:22, "There I will meet with you, and from above the mercy seat, from between the two cherubim that are on the ark of the testimony," he was promising saving grace through the atoning blood—blood that would ultimately be shed by Jesus Christ.

With these vivid images, Psalm 80 shows that biblical knowledge and theology are powerful to give consolation to believers who suffer. John Calvin writes, "The mercy-seat was a pledge of the presence of God, where he had promised to be near his people to hear their prayers."[4] Christians see the ark and the mercy seat as symbols pointing to the true fulfillment of the cross of Christ, and thus as tokens of God's salvation for those who pray to him in trusting faith. To pray "in Jesus' name" is for believers to approach God with a mighty confidence of saving grace.

Scholars are generally agreed that Psalm 80 calls on God in light of invasions that were ravaging the northern kingdom of Israel, probably in the years before the fall of Samaria in 722 B.C. Ephraim and Manasseh (Ps. 80:2) were the sons of Joseph who produced the two leading tribes of the northern kingdom. Benjamin is added as the other true brother of Joseph and as the tribe that marched with the other two during the exodus sojourn. Most likely, Asaph has in mind the devastations suffered by the house of Joseph during invasions by mighty Assyria. This was the view of the editors of the third-century B.C. Septuagint, the Greek translation of the Old Testament, who added the inscription, "A Psalm concerning the Assyrian."

If Psalm 80 does focus on the suffering of the northern kingdom and if it was written by a Jew of the southern kingdom, as the name *Asaph* suggests, then we have here an outstanding prayer of solidarity between one half of Israel for the sake of the other. A modern example would involve a Presbyterian's praying for the trials of Methodist churches, or a Baptist's

4. John Calvin, *Calvin's Commentaries*, 23 vols. (1848; repr., Grand Rapids: Baker, 2009), 6:297.

appealing to God on behalf of charismatics. Though the northern tribes were long estranged, Asaph wanted to pray for his neighbors as well as himself: "Stir up your might and come to save us!" he cries (Ps. 80:2). Then, in what becomes the refrain of this psalm, he prays: "Restore us, O God; let your face shine, that we may be saved!" (v. 3). The Aaronic blessing called for God's favor and protection, saying, "The Lord make his face to shine upon you and be gracious to you" (Num. 6:25). The psalmist echoes this benediction as he prays for God to turn his face toward his people and give them peace. If they were restored to a true and living faith, then God's favor would secure their salvation.

If the psalmist and his southern colleagues were so concerned about the fate of the northern kingdom, then they should also have exhorted their neighbors to return in faith to the Lord for salvation. We know that godly King Jehoshaphat attempted just this in the time of wicked King Ahab (2 Chron. 18). Asaph realized, however, that in addition to calling on sinners to repent, we should undertake the even more important work of prayer. David Dickson writes: "Conversion of people from their sin unto God, and leading them back from the misery drawn on by sin, is the work of God, which no man can work of himself in himself, or in others, till God begin, and enable to return, and lead them on in their turning."[5] Thus the psalmist pleads, "Restore us, O God" (Ps. 80:3).

How Long, O Lord?

The opening appeal is followed by a more detailed analysis and plea. Again, the psalmist realizes that the root problem lay in Israel's broken relationship with God. The result is that God has not been willing to answer Israel's prayers. Asaph thus pleads: "O Lord God of hosts, how long will you be angry with your people's prayers?" (Ps. 80:4).

Obviously, the psalmist has not given up on prayer, since he is still appealing to God. But he laments that God responded to previous prayers with apparent anger. There are several reasons why God may choose not to answer a prayer in the manner expected. For instance, he may want to strengthen our faith in the crucible of trials. Peter wrote that "you have been grieved

5. David Dickson, *A Commentary on the Psalms* (1653; repr., Edinburgh: Banner of Truth, 1995), 2:39.

by various trials, so that the tested genuineness of your faith—more precious than gold that perishes though it is tested by fire—may be found to result in praise and glory and honor at the revelation of Jesus Christ" (1 Peter 1:6–7). Another reason is that God often has a better way of answering our prayers—an answer for which we should wait in faith.

A third reason for unanswered prayer is that God may be chastising us for flagrant sin. An example of this is given in Malachi, when the priests of Israel complained because God was not answering their prayers. Why wasn't he listening to their petitions? "Because the Lord was witness between you and the wife of your youth, to whom you have been faithless, though she is your companion and your wife by covenant" (Mal. 2:14). The Israelite men had broken covenant with their wives, and yet they wondered why God did not fulfill his covenant with them! Peter gave a similar warning to Christian husbands, urging them to cherish their wives "so that your prayers may not be hindered" (1 Peter 3:7). Given this example, when we wonder why our lives are not flourishing spiritually, we should carefully consider our most basic Christian duties. Are husbands loving their wives? Are wives submitting themselves to the well-being of their husbands and children? Extending the principle further, are employers paying a fair wage to their workers, or are political leaders living before God in practical holiness?

Something similar to what Malachi describes seems to be happening in Psalm 80, but here the record of the Old Testament indicates that the problem was the worship of idols. In the service of the temple, prayer was represented by the burning of incense, which arose before God with a sweet aroma. As the psalmist sees it, however, the Lord has not responded with pleasure but with billows of wrathful smoke to smother both incense and prayer.

The idea of divine chastisement is strengthened in verses 5 and 6 of Psalm 80. God has "fed them with the bread of tears and given them tears to drink in full measure." When God has appointed daily sorrows as our divine provision, with no relief from remorse and lamentation, we may well feel that we have fallen under his displeasure. Added to this is strife with neighbors and mockery from enemies: "You make us an object of contention for our neighbors, and our enemies laugh among themselves." These statements prove the reality of divine chastisement and discipline that Christians may equally experience. O. Palmer Robertson comments: "Christian romantics imagine that God is like an indulgent father who never would lift his voice to speak in a way that would disturb his children."[6] David was this kind of father—he spoiled his sons by never rebuking them. First Kings 1:6 laments that he never said, "Why have you done thus and so?" The sad result was the ruin of his family and nation. In contrast, "God does not make the mistake of indulging his children."[7]

With so great a need of saving grace, the psalmist returns to his prior refrain: "Restore us, O God of hosts; let your face shine, that we may be saved!" (Ps. 80:7). Here is a verse that sufferers of all varieties may take as their own. The only difference from verse 3 is that instead of merely appealing to "God," he adds, "O God of hosts." The first instance, the Hebrew *Elohim*, calls on God as the Creator who has power to manage any earthly foe. By now addressing him as *Elohim Sabaot*, Asaph notes the legions of heavenly armies available to God's command. Robertson comments: "God's people are in distress. They need him to intervene in their lives. They are reeling under the chastenings of his hand. Their land has been devastated, and they are overpowered by their enemies. But they can hope in the God who has revealed his nature through his names."[8]

Recounting God's Investment

So far, Psalm 80 has noted God's covenant relationship with Israel as the Shepherd of his people and as the King who is "enthroned above the cherubim." Starting in verse 8, he takes a different tack, noting God's now-endangered investment in Israel. To this end, he employs another rich biblical image: "You brought a vine out of Egypt; you drove out the nations and planted it" (Ps. 80:8). Just as the imagery of God as Shepherd emphasizes the weakness of the sheep, so also a vine is a plant that can thrive only under careful tending, especially in a dry and dusty climate. George Horne notes that the vine is "wild and luxuriant, unless restrained by the pruning knife," but "capable of producing the most valuable fruit" when well managed, though it is, "if barren, the most unprofitable among trees, and fit only for

6. O. Palmer Robertson, *Psalms in Congregational Celebration* (Darlington, UK: Evangelical Press, 1995), 175.

7. Robertson, *Psalms in Congregational Celebration,* 175.

8. Robertson, *Psalms in Congregational Celebration,* 174.

the flames."[9] Israel is compared to a vine in Hosea 10:1, in Ezekiel 15, and most notably in Isaiah 5. In his Song of the Vineyard, Isaiah sang:

> My beloved had a vineyard
>   on a very fertile hill.
> He dug it and cleared it of stones,
>   and planted it with choice vines;
> he built a watchtower in the midst of it,
>   and hewed out a wine vat in it;
> and he looked for it to yield grapes. (Isa. 5:1–2)

Christians especially think of Jesus' *I am* statement in John 15: "Abide in me, and I in you. As the branch cannot bear fruit by itself, unless it abides in the vine, neither can you, unless you abide in me. I am the vine; you are the branches" (John 15:4–5).

Using this same imagery, the psalmist tells of God's rich investment in the planting of his people:

> You brought a vine out of Egypt;
>   you drove out the nations and planted it.
> You cleared the ground for it;
>   it took deep root and filled the land.
> The mountains were covered with its shade,
>   the mighty cedars with its branches.
> It sent out its branches to the sea
>   and its shoots to the River. (Ps. 80:8–11)

These verses tell the story of the exodus in three phases. Israel was *uprooted* from the hard soil of affliction where it was not able to bloom. The nation was then *planted* by God's power in a choice land, with the idolatrous occupants destroyed and removed. It then *prospered* there, reaching dimensions during the reign of Solomon that fulfilled God's promise for the nation to extend from the Mediterranean Sea to the Euphrates River (Deut. 11:24; 1 Kings 4:21).

Unfortunately, Israel's story did not move forward fruitfully. No sooner had Solomon died than the nation split into two halves, with the northern

9. George Horne, *Commentary on the Psalms* (1771; repr., Audubon, NJ: Old Paths Publications, 1997), 349.

kingdom abandoning its heritage of faith. The impact on the vine of Israel was tragic, as told by Isaiah: "he looked for it to yield grapes, but it yielded wild grapes," so God said, "I will remove its hedge, and it shall be devoured; I will break down its wall, and it shall be trampled down" (Isa. 5:2, 5). This is the very situation that Psalm 80 laments: "Why then have you broken down its walls, so that all who pass along the way pluck its fruit? The boar from the forest ravages it, and all that move in the field feed on it" (Ps. 80:12–13). This picture of destruction may be in response to the final overthrow of the northern kingdom when the Assyrians conquered Samaria in 722 B.C., although it could equally speak of the disastrous years that preceded this end.

Of course, the psalmist knew why all this had happened: God had judged his people for their infidelity in worshiping false gods. His argument, however, was that God had invested so much saving effort in his people that he should not allow his beloved vine to be ultimately despoiled. Christians in need of God's grace for repentance should plead on similar grounds. "I am sure of this," wrote Paul, "that he who began a good work in you will bring it to completion at the day of Jesus Christ" (Phil. 1:6; see also 1 Peter 1:5). In this light, Christians can and should respond to threats to their faith by praying for God to keep safe his own investment in our salvation.

God's Hand on the Son of Man

The final stanza begins with a renewed appeal for salvation and concludes with a final version of the psalm's refrain. In between, the psalmist provides one more potent argument that comes from the redeeming promises of God's Word.

The appeal calls for the Lord as "God of hosts" to "look down from heaven, and see; have regard for this vine, the stock that your right hand planted" (Ps. 80:14–15). Asaph's boldness reflects a knowledge of God's compassionate grace and is reflected in his imperatives: Turn! Look! See! Have regard! In light of the greater revelation of God's grace through Jesus Christ, Christians should have at least this much boldness when we pray. Robertson writes: "Considering the sacrifice Jesus Christ has made to clear the way, a timid approach would dishonor the effectiveness of his work."[10] Asaph's plea is simple and direct: "They have burned it with fire; they have cut it down; may

10. Robertson, *Psalms in Congregational Celebration*, 180.

they perish at the rebuke of your face!" (Ps. 80:16). God is able to overturn even these historic calamities, and the psalmist pleads that he would do it.

Psalm 80 has already proved to be one of the most theologically elevated poems of the Bible. In verses 15 and 17, however, pleas are made that raise it to an even higher pitch. In verse 15, the psalmist prays that God will have regard "for the son whom you made strong for yourself." In verse 17, he adds, "Let your hand be on the man of your right hand, the son of man whom you have made strong for yourself." The question is to whom he refers with these striking appeals.

One option is that the psalmist has the king of Israel in mind, since God established this northern line of royalty and appointed them for the leadership of the broken-off portions of the nation. The main argument in favor of this view is that the psalm seems to indicate a specific individual, and there is none more suitable than the vitally important king, whose faith or unbelief would determine the fate of the northern tribes. The king is "the man of your right hand" in that God had established him in authority. In such a position, he is viewed as "the son of man whom you have made strong for yourself!" (Ps. 80:17). The reliable scholar H. C. Leupold takes it this way, writing: "There seems to be no other feasible way of interpreting verse 17 than to think of it as being a prayer for the king that sits upon the throne of Israel."[11] Since Psalm 80 calls repeatedly for grace to repent, this view sees the psalmist as praying for God to turn the ungodly northern king back to him in faith.

A second view understands the psalmist to refer to the entirety of the nation, which has already been described as the vine of God's planting. Psalm 80:15 refers to "the stock that your right hand planted," which means the people, and "the son whom you made strong for yourself." The final clause is seen as introducing not a new person but another way of thinking about Israel. Exodus 4:22 described Israel as God's "firstborn son," and Hosea 11:1, written during the likely period of this psalm, says that God loved Israel and called it "my son." Calvin takes this view, seeing Israel (and, in our time, the Christian church) as "the man of your right hand, the son of man whom you have made strong for yourself" (Ps. 80:17). "Thus," writes Calvin, "by the Son of man is to be understood the people whom God had adopted to himself, that they might be as one man."[12]

11. H. C. Leupold, *Exposition of the Psalms* (Columbus, OH: Wartburg Press, 1959), 584.
12. Calvin, *Commentaries*, 6:308.

Most Christian expositors, however, view Psalm 80 as looking forward to the Messiah who was promised and would be the true Deliverer of his sin-afflicted people. In fact, this was the view of the Jewish rabbis in the centuries leading up to Christ. Charles Spurgeon summarizes: "There is no doubt here an outlook to the Messiah, for whom believing Jews had learned to look as the Savior in time of trouble."[13]

I believe that Spurgeon is right, for a number of reasons. Psalm 80:15 associates the son with "the stock that your right hand planted," and this parallels the teaching of Isaiah that the Messiah would be the branch "from the stump of Jesse," whose "roots shall bear fruit" (Isa. 11:1). Dickson writes: "There was a branch to come of the stock of Israel, for whose cause the nation of the Israelites could not be utterly forsaken and destroyed, and this was the Messiah, Christ Jesus . . . , of whose coming, because God had a special care that the stock should be . . . made strong till this branch came forth, the church of Israel might be confident not to be utterly cast off."[14]

Moreover, the expression "man of your right hand" (Ps. 80:17) does not fit any of the northern kings—all of whom turned away from the Lord—except in the most general sense of God's having appointed them. Only the promised Messiah would stand at God's right hand, both in the sense of his equality as God and in the sense of his appointment as true King. Finally, while "son of man" can be used in a general sense, it often has the special sense in the Old Testament of describing the coming Savior (Dan. 7:13). For Asaph to speak of "the son of man whom you have made strong for yourself" (Ps. 80:17) seems to clearly point to the unique Messiah whose coming would truly save God's people. To the extent that the psalm refers to the temporal king of Israel, this was partly as the representative of the coming Messiah, to whom God's people truly can point with a certainty of salvation.

In this way, Psalm 80 concludes with an appeal for God to send the promised Messiah and to strengthen him for his appointed work, so that his people may receive in him their promised salvation. This is precisely the way that Mary understood the coming birth of her son, Jesus Christ. Mary sang, "My soul magnifies the Lord, and my spirit rejoices in God my Savior . . . . He has helped his servant Israel, in remembrance of his mercy, as he spoke to our fathers, to Abraham and to his offspring forever" (Luke 1:46–55).

13. Charles Haddon Spurgeon, *The Treasury of David*, 3 vols. (Peabody, MA: Hendrickson, n.d.), 2a:391.
14. Dickson, *Psalms*, 2:45.

Pleading God's Promise

Having foreseen God's hand on the coming Messiah, Psalm 80 concludes with a return to its main theme: God's grace to empower the repentance of his people. "Then we shall not turn back from you," Asaph prays, adding: "give us life, and we will call upon your name!" (Ps. 80:18). The gift of a new, regenerate nature that will not turn away from faith in God is associated with the promised new covenant in Christ (see Jer. 31:33; Heb. 8:10). This is what sinners ultimately need: new life from God to turn to him and remain in faith. Only Jesus can provide this saving gift. He offers this very life to those who believe: "Truly, truly, I say to you, whoever hears my word and believes him who sent me has eternal life" (John 5:24).

This plea for saving life leads to a final version of the psalm's refrain: "Restore us, O Lord God of hosts! Let your face shine, that we may be saved!" (Ps. 80:19). What is added this time is the covenant name of the Lord, *Yahweh*, as it is appended to the name "God of hosts!" Asaph is asking for the covenant salvation in which alone there is hope, a salvation that finds fulfillment in the saving work of the Savior, Jesus Christ. Asaph's plea was not in vain, for the Lord of the covenant would fulfill all his promises in the coming of his Son. Jesus gave the answer to Asaph's plea when he instituted the Lord's Supper, saying, "This is my blood of the covenant, which is poured out for many for the forgiveness of sins" (Matt. 26:28).

In this light, Psalm 80 not only is one of the most theologically rich psalms but is also among the most redemptively astute. Israel's problem was not the Assyrian conquerors, but her sin that caused God's wrath to fall. The people's need, which only God could grant, was grace to turn in renewed faith to the Lord for salvation.

This grace is what Benjamin Morgan Palmer's friend discovered. He was frustrated that the preacher had taught from God's Word not only that the sinner is not able to turn to God, but also that he must perish unless he does. When he quarreled about this seeming contradiction, the preacher challenged him not to argue but to go ahead and turn his heart to the Savior. The man answered in anguish, "I have been trying my best for three whole days, and cannot." At this, Palmer said, "Ah, that puts a different face upon it; we will go, then, and tell the difficulty straight to God." The two men prayed in a simple, matter-of-fact way for God to answer the sinner's desperate problem by sending the grace of his Spirit to open his heart in the name of Jesus Christ. Having prayed in this way, Palmer left the man alone before God. He later wrote: "I left my friend, in his powerlessness, in the hands of God, as the only helper. In a short time he came through the struggle, rejoicing in the hope of eternal life."[15]

Similarly, Psalm 80 concludes with an appeal for the coming of Christ that was answered by God in due time. In good time, your prayer for God to save you will likewise be answered in grace. For as the New Testament declares, "Everyone who calls on the name of the Lord will be saved" (Rom. 10:13).

15. Willborn, *Selected Writings of Benjamin Morgan Palmer*, 79–80.

10

If Israel Would Listen

Psalm 81

Oh, that my people would listen to me, that Israel would walk in my ways! (Ps. 81:13)

According to a recent survey, Americans do not hold the organized church in high regard. Fifty-two percent stated that worship at home was a valid replacement for attending church. A majority did not think that the pulpit ministry of Bible preaching has authority for Christian living. Ninety-one percent answered that the church does not have authority to validate professions of Christian faith.[1] All these views are contrary to the plain teaching of the Bible, yet they reflect a tendency of thinking negatively about the church.

One reason for this antichurch attitude is that formal churches themselves have often opposed true Christianity. For example, when George Whitefield began preaching to massive crowds in 1737, at the beginning of what would be known to history as "The Great Awakening," his chief opponents were church officials. One biographer writes: "The parish churches generally at this date were sunk in nominal formal religion." Opposition to Whitefield's

1. Ligonier Ministries, *The State of Theology: Theological Awareness Benchmark Study* (Orlando, FL: Ligonier Ministries, 2014), 22.

preaching of the new birth and justification through faith "became so intense that churches of his own denomination were shut against him and he was forced to preach in the open air."[2]

An even more significant instance of the outward church's opposing God's work was the Jewish leaders' rejection of Jesus Christ. Jesus rebuked them, declaring: "But woe to you, scribes and Pharisees, hypocrites! For you shut the kingdom of heaven in people's faces. For you neither enter yourselves nor allow those who would enter to go in" (Matt. 23:13). This problem is seen at various times in the Old Testament. Even when the Israelites gathered to offer worship to the Lord, they often did so with unfaithful hearts.

Psalm 81 shares this concern. It summons the people to celebrate the prescribed festivals, but reminds them that worship is valid only when offered in a spirit of grateful faith. The psalmist does more, however, than rebuke false worship. He presents a God who is eager to bless those who turn to him sincerely and whose heart laments the idolatry of his people. "Oh, that my people would listen to me, that Israel would walk in my ways!" he cries (Ps. 81:13). In this way, not only does Psalm 81 emphasize the importance of the church and its worship, but it urges the necessity of true faith and devotion in worship that pleases the Lord and is therefore blessed by him.

A Biblical Call to Worship

Psalm 81 begins with a call to fervent musical worship: "Sing aloud to God our strength; shout for joy to the God of Jacob! Raise a song; sound the tambourine, the sweet lyre with the harp" (Ps. 81:1–2). It is evident from this summons that despite the ritually intense nature of the religion led by Old Testament priests, their worship was to be participatory and active in the joyful engagement of praising God. John Calvin writes: "They were not to stand deaf and dumb at the tabernacle; . . . but they were . . . to cherish among themselves the unity of faith; to make an open profession of their piety; . . . to endeavor to join, with one accord, in praising God; and, in short, to continue steadfast in the sacred covenant by which God had adopted them to himself."[3] Old Testament scholar Franz Delitzsch points out that order is involved in this summons: verse 1 calls on the congregation to shout and sing,

2. Iain H. Murray, *Heroes* (Edinburgh: Banner of Truth, 2014), 52.

3. John Calvin, *Calvin's Commentaries*, 23 vols. (1848; repr., Grand Rapids: Baker, 2009), 5:311.

verse 2 encourages the Levites who were set apart for choral singing and playing instruments, and verse 3 summons the priests whose calling included blowing the *shophar*, the great ram horn that announced God's presence.[4]

In addition to exercising their lungs, the gathered people were called to exercise their faith. We see this in the summons to worship "the God of Jacob" (Ps. 81:1). Jacob was the father of the nation with which God entered into covenant for salvation. It was by means of the same covenant that his offspring were also God's people. They were thus to worship God by believing his promises and by remembering the great saving works by which God had fulfilled his covenant purposes. Christian worship likewise is a covenant meeting of God with his people. We worship God by trusting the promises of his Word, and we "shout for joy to the God of Jacob" by publicly professing what God has done by sending Jesus Christ, as in the Apostles' Creed or the Nicene Creed. Worship is thus a covenant meeting in spiritual communion with the God who gives us strength.

In addition to involving active praise and faith in God's covenant, biblical worship is animated by thanksgiving for God's blessings. This is the point of Psalm 81:5–7, which recounts what God did for Israel in the exodus from Egypt:

> He made it a decree in Joseph
> when he went out over the land of Egypt.
> I hear a language I had not known:
> "I relieved your shoulder of the burden;
> your hands were freed from the basket.
> In distress you called, and I delivered you;
> I answered you in the secret place of thunder;
> I tested you at the waters of Meribah." (Ps. 81:5–7)

Multiple phases of the exodus are noted here. First came "Joseph," as the Egyptians seem to have labeled the nation, as a man hearing "a language I had not known" (Ps. 81:5). Some think this refers to the Egyptian language, although others think it refers to the voice of God speaking from Mount Sinai about Israel's deliverance.[5] There is no doubt, however, what this deliverance

4. Franz Delitzsch, *Biblical Commentary on the Psalms*, trans. Francis Bolton, vol. 2 (Grand Rapids: Eerdmans, n.d.), 393.

5. See, for the former, Calvin, *Commentaries*, 5:312f.; for the latter, J. J. Stewart Perowne, *The Book of Psalms*, 2 vols. (1878; repr., Grand Rapids: Zondervan, 1976), 2:98.

meant: "I relieved your shoulder of the burden; your hands were freed from the basket" (v. 6). This verse refers to Israel's redemption from her hard labor in slavery. Verse 7 speaks of the exodus itself, including Israel's salvation from Egypt, God's voice speaking from the mountain, and the testing that took place during the first stages of the wilderness crossing.

This catalogue reveals God's sense of priorities in saving his people. While the people tended to care more about their physical well-being, God was interested in building up and strengthening their faith. These were things that Israel should be grateful for, just as Christians today should be thankful for the way in which God is working in our lives for salvation through faith. In his ministry to his disciples, Jesus was always preeminently concerned for their faith. "O you of little faith" (Matt. 8:26), he often exclaimed. When Jesus rejoiced, it was usually because of a strong or growing faith. He once praised a centurion, saying, "I tell you, not even in Israel have I found such faith" (Luke 7:9).

Psalm 81 summons Israel to its annual feasts, the point of which was to remember God's saving works with thanks. We see this connection to the feasts because of the language highlighting the lunar calendar and the changing of moons that signaled the feasts: "Blow the trumpet at the new moon, at the full moon, on our feast day" (Ps. 81:3). The three great feasts all looked back on the exodus: Passover, which recounted the angel of death passing over the homes covered by lamb's blood; Pentecost, also called the Feast of Weeks, at the first summer harvest; and the Feast of Tabernacles, or Booths, which commemorated the exodus sojourn in tents and celebrated the completed harvest (Lev. 23:1–44). These feasts all pointed forward to the saving work of Christ: Passover anticipated the blood of Jesus' cross as the true Lamb of God; Pentecost looked forward to the outpouring of the Holy Spirit on the church; and Tabernacles anticipated the final ingathering of all of Christ's people at his return. As the Israelites were to be thankful in remembering the exodus sojourn from Egypt to the promised land, Christians have even greater reasons to worship with grateful praise. Considering how Christ's deliverance so greatly exceeds that of Israel, George Horne writes: "Let us remember, that we have been eased of far heavier burdens, delivered from severer taskmasters, and freed from a baser drudgery; the intolerable load of sin, the cruel tyranny of Satan, the vile service and bitter bondage of [corrupt desires]."[6]

6. George Horne, *Commentary on the Psalms* (1771; repr., Audubon, NJ: Old Paths Publications, 1997), 353.

Before concluding the opening call to worship in Psalm 81, we should note that it presents worship not merely as a privilege but also as a duty: "For it is a statute for Israel, a rule of the God of Jacob" (Ps. 81:4). Whatever inward state Christians may find themselves in, we should look on gathered worship with the church as a sacred duty to which we are solemnly called. Indeed, Psalm 81 summons us prayerfully to prepare for worship, asking God to mold our hearts with the right attitudes of joy, reverent faith, and thanksgiving, in order that he might receive some measure of the praise he so greatly deserves. Matthew Henry summarizes:

> Praising God is not only a good thing, which we do well to do, but it is our indispensable duty, which we are obliged to do; it is at our peril if we neglect it; and in all religious exercises we must have . . . [this] warrant and rule: "This I do because God has commanded me."[7]

A SOLEMN REBUKE FOR IDOLATRY

On the occasion of Psalm 81, God summoned the people not only for worship but also to receive his solemn rebuke: "Hear, O my people, while I admonish you! O Israel, if you would but listen to me!" (Ps. 81:8). Here we are reminded that the most important organ of worship is our ears: in order to worship God rightly with our mouths, hands, and hearts, we must first listen to his Word in faith. Calvin observes that the summons of verse 8 "teaches us that true religious worship begins with obedience."[8]

The particular admonishment here concerned the great sin that was characteristic of Old Testament Israel: the sin of idolatry. "There shall be no strange god among you," the Lord commanded; "you shall not bow down to a foreign god" (Ps. 81:9). This rebuke echoed the very first commandment given to Israel at Mount Sinai: "You shall have no other gods before me" (Ex. 20:3). That God has the first commandment in view is made even more certain by the quotation of its preamble in Psalm 81:10: "I am the LORD your God, who brought you up out of the land of Egypt" (see Ex. 20:2).

In declaring himself as the true God of the exodus, the Lord was saying that he is the God revealed in the Bible. He is the God who redeems his

7. Matthew Henry, *Commentary on the Whole Bible*, 6 vols. (Peabody, MA: Hendrickson, n.d.), 3:448.
8. Calvin, *Commentaries*, 5:318.

people through Jesus Christ, which the exodus prefigured. There is no multiplicity of gods, one for every person's opinion or preference. This theological truth rules out the idea that the different religions are equally right. According to God speaking in Scripture, the gods of Buddhism, Islam, and Shintoism are false idols. There is only one true God: the saving God of Scripture. We worship him alone not only because of all that he has done, but also because this is the most basic commandment in his dealings with us.

The Israelites committed idolatry by actually bowing down to the idols of false gods and by participating in the debased rituals of pagan religions. Most people who commit idolatry today worship the false gods of secular humanism, rather than idols of wood and stone. The Puritan Thomas Watson wrote: "Some make a god of pleasure," doing this when they love experiences more than God. "Others make money their god. The covetous man worships the image of gold, therefore he is called an idolater. Eph. 5:5. . . . He makes the wedge of gold his hope; he makes money his creator, redeemer, and comforter." Watson adds, "Another makes a god of his child," by making one's offspring an object of praise and glory. Still others "make a god of their belly" (Phil. 3:19), seeking to expand their appetites. Watson concludes: "The apostle [John] names the wicked man's trinity, 'The lust of the flesh, the lust of the eye, and the pride of life'" (1 John 2:16).[9] It is remarkable that Watson wrote those lines in seventeenth-century England, showing that the idols of our age are endemic to fallen humanity. Secular humanism, it turns out, does not represent a new phase in human development!

These idolatries are seen not only in people but also in churches, when they deviate from God's Word in order to gain wealth, popularity, acceptance, or worldly power. Any of these blessings—pleasure, money, honors—may be granted by God as a byproduct of faithful worship and ministry, but apart from true faith they are idols, which he abhors.

The tragedy of those who worship idols is that false gods not only are condemned by God, but also fail to deliver the satisfaction they promise. In contrast, God declares: "Open your mouth wide, and I will fill it" (Ps. 81:10). God desires true worship not only for the honor of his own name but also because he is the only true fount of blessing. Therefore, individuals and churches that make it their first concern to obey God's Word do not lose out in any real sense. When we open our mouths in grateful worship, exalting

9. Thomas Watson, *A Body of Divinity* (Edinburgh: Banner of Truth, 1958), 106–7.

only the Lord, he fills our mouths with both earthly and eternal blessings. God will not be a debtor in the end to any of his people. Rather, by his grace those who honor him as Savior and Lord will be filled with all fullness from him (Eph. 3:19). Faithful Christians may have many troubles in this life and may seem to lack many worldly things. Yet Paul confidently declared that "my God will supply every need of yours according to his riches in glory in Christ Jesus" (Phil. 4:19).

A Fervent Appeal for Faith and Salvation

The final section of Psalm 81 turns in a positive direction as the Lord appeals to his people to return in saving faith. First, however, he puts his finger on Israel's chief problem: "But my people did not listen to my voice; Israel would not submit to me" (Ps. 81:11).

This statement marks a vital relationship between the problem and its cause, and between the heart and the ear. The people "did not" listen to him because they "would not" submit. The issue was their rebellious, sinful nature, which must first be overcome if people are to hold fast to the Lord. Henry writes: "All the wickedness of the wicked world is owing to the willfulness of the wicked will. The reason why people are not religious is because they will not be so."[10] This willful rebellion is fundamentally expressed in the rejection of God's Word. To be right with God, we must be willing to receive his Word obediently. The Hebrew of Psalm 81:11 is actually more blunt than the English translation. Not being willing to obey God's Word, "Israel was not willing to me." The hard-heartedness of unbelievers is personal in its rejection of God, and it involves personal offense to him.

How, then, should we respond when we realize that our hearts are unruly before the Lord? What do we do when sinful desires have taken root, or when we find ourselves little interested in prayer or worship? The answer is that we must turn obediently to God's Word, seeking the power for godliness that comes through the Scriptures. Hebrews 4:12 says that "the word of God is living and active, sharper than any two-edged sword, . . . discerning the thoughts and intentions of the heart." Psalm 19:7–8 extols the blessed influence of the Bible:

10. Henry, *Commentary*, 3:449.

The law of the LORD is perfect,
reviving the soul;
the testimony of the LORD is sure,
making wise the simple;
the precepts of the LORD are right,
rejoicing the heart;
the commandment of the LORD is pure,
enlightening the eyes.

What other resource has this kind of effect on our hearts and in our lives? Therefore, when a Christian feels his or her heart turning away in sin, unbelief, fear, or resentment, the believer should follow the logic of Psalm 81:11, making the heart willing by submitting it to God's Word.

If God's people will not take this remedy, then God has his own more painful solution: "So I gave them over to their stubborn hearts, to follow their own counsels" (Ps. 81:12). This is often God's judgment on rebellious people or nations: he gives us up to the very sins and idols that we have insisted on serving. J. J. Stewart Perowne refers to this as "the greatest and most fearful of all God's punishments."[11] It is terrible because it submits us to the calamities of our own folly, yet it is often needed to break our will so that God may remold it in true faith.

Historically, this "giving over" took a number of forms. In the book of Judges, each time God saved Israel, the people turned to false gods and sin. God's punishment took the form of foreign conquest and occupation, which produced such misery that the people eventually remembered to seek their God. Here, the psalmist may have the northern kingdom particularly in mind, especially in light of his earlier reference to Joseph, whose tribes led the northern kingdom. After their rebellion from the house of David, God gave over the rebellious tribes by placing them under one foolish and ungodly king after another.

The idea of God's giving over to sin is seen in the New Testament through Jesus' famous parable of the prodigal son. This faithless son demanded his share of his father's inheritance, which he squandered in riotous living in a distant land. The father in Jesus' parable sets a good though painful example for Christian parents when covenant children throw themselves into sinful

11. Perowne, *Psalms*, 2:99.

lifestyles. Many such parents are tempted to protect their children from the effects of their sin, sometimes providing ongoing funding for what they know will be the most ungodly behaviors. The father of Jesus' parable did otherwise: he let the prodigal son go his way, even though his heart longed for the son after he departed. Yet God had plans for the prodigal. Jesus taught that "when he had spent everything, a severe famine arose in that country, and he began to be in need" (Luke 15:14). The son hired himself out to a farmer to feed his pigs, longing in his hunger to have even the pigs' food to eat. This is what the same God did in the psalm: "So I gave them over to their stubborn hearts, to follow their own counsels" (Ps. 81:12). These were God's own people, so this action was not merely punishment but the painful ministry that hardened unbelief and sin often requires.

According to the apostle Paul, God gives over not only people but also whole societies. In Romans 1:21, Paul described cultural idolatry when people who knew better "did not honor him as God or give thanks to him, but they became futile in their thinking, and their foolish hearts were darkened." Since that statement so accurately describes post-Christian America, people often ask me whether I think God will ever judge our nation. According to Paul, God has already done so, by giving us over to the moral depravity we have sought. Paul specifically mentions perverse sexual desires and especially the spread of homosexual desire and practice:

> Therefore God gave them up in the lusts of their hearts to impurity, to the dishonoring of their bodies among themselves . . . . God gave them up to dishonorable passions. . . . The men . . . gave up natural relations with women and were consumed with passion for one another, men committing shameless acts with men and receiving in themselves the due penalty for their error. (Rom. 1:24–27)

The widespread societal championing of homosexuality, as is now happening in the once-Christian West, is so rare in history that we should suspect it as a form of divine judgment. Paul confirms that a society that intentionally rejects God's Word for sinful pleasure can expect to be given over to the service of idolatry in this way.

There is good news, however, in that the grace of God endures for those who turn from their misery back to him in faith. In this light, how remarkable is the exclamation from the heart of the very God who has just spoken of giving Israel over to sin: "Oh, that my people would listen to me, that Israel would walk in my ways!" (Ps. 81:13). Here is the heart of God for his people who turn away in sin and experience the chastisement that their restoration requires. It is the same heart that spoke with tears when Jesus looked over the city of Jerusalem that had rejected him and forfeited salvation: "O Jerusalem, Jerusalem . . . ! How often would I have gathered your children together as a hen gathers her brood under her wings, and you were not willing!" (Matt. 23:37).

Earlier, I mentioned the prodigal son of Jesus' parable, who rebelled against his father and had to suffer the consequences of his sin. That is a beloved parable because of the hope that it goes on to reveal. For eventually the prodigal came to his senses and remembered his father, as God wants all prodigal sons and daughters to do in their misery. Thinking only to return as a slave, the son made the journey home. Jesus continues:

> But while he was still a long way off, his father saw him and felt compassion, and ran and embraced him and kissed him. And the son said to him, "Father, I have sinned against heaven and before you. I am no longer worthy to be called your son." But the father said to his servants, "Bring quickly the best robe, and put it on him, and put a ring on his hand, and shoes on his feet. And bring the fattened calf and kill it, and let us eat and celebrate. For this my son was dead, and is alive again; he was lost, and is found." (Luke 15:20–24)

The father in the parable is God himself, who is so graciously eager for his people to repent and be restored that he pictures himself as running along the lane to meet his once-wayward son. Jesus taught: "Just so, I tell you, there is joy before the angels of God over one sinner who repents" (Luke 15:10). This is the same loving heart of God that is heard in Psalm 81:13: "Oh, that my people would listen to me, that Israel would walk in my ways!"

As Jesus' parable indicates, restoration to the Father brings not merely a removal of divine judgment but also God's loving provision of rich blessings. Psalm 81 concludes: "I would soon subdue their enemies and turn my hand against their foes. Those who hate the Lord would cringe toward him, and their fate would last forever. But he would feed you with the finest of the wheat, and with honey from the rock I would satisfy you" (Ps. 81:14–16). The Lord had in mind military success and material bounty as his loving gifts to the people restored by his grace. The promises reinforce the message given throughout the Old Testament, as summarized by Charles Spurgeon: "The Lord can do great things for an obedient people. When his people walk in the light of his countenance, and maintain unsullied holiness, the joy and consolation which he yields them are beyond conception. To them the joys of heaven have begun even upon earth."[12]

Turn and Be Saved!

Can it really be so simple? Do we just turn to the Lord and walk in his ways and then enjoy his protection and blessing? The answer of Psalm 81 is "Yes!" The great problem of life is simple: "my people did not listen to my voice; Israel would not submit to me" (Ps. 81:11). The solution is equally simple: "Oh, that my people would listen to me, that Israel would walk in my ways!" (v. 13).

In 1850, young Charles Spurgeon was forced by a snowstorm to seek shelter in a small chapel where a worship service was beginning. The regular minister could not attend, so one of the members—Spurgeon later recalled him as "a very thin looking man, a shoemaker, or tailor, or something of that sort"—went up to the pulpit to preach. Reading Isaiah 45:22 as his text, he read an appeal similar to that of Psalm 81: "Turn to me and be saved, all the ends of the earth! For I am God, and there is no other." Fixing his eyes on Spurgeon, he said, "Young man, you look very miserable." Spurgeon admitted to himself that it was true, since he was in deep conviction for his sin. "You look very miserable," the man said, "and you will always be miserable—miserable in life, and miserable in death—if you don't obey my text; but if you obey now, this moment, you will be saved." Lifting up his hands, he shouted at young Spurgeon: "Young man, look to Jesus Christ. Look! Look! Look! You have nothin' to do but to look and live!" Spurgeon later recalled:

> I saw at once the way of salvation. . . . I had been waiting to do fifty things, but when I heard that word, "Look!" What a charming word it seemed to me! Oh! I looked until I could almost have looked my eyes away. There and then the cloud was gone, the darkness had rolled away, and that moment I saw the sun; and I could have risen that instant, and sung with the most

12. Charles Haddon Spurgeon, *The Treasury of David*, 3 vols. (Peabody, MA: Hendrickson, n.d.), 2a:403.

> enthusiastic of them, of the precious blood of Christ and the simple faith which looks alone to Him.[13]

Psalm 81 confirms this teaching! Turn to God, listen to his voice, walk in his ways, and salvation's blessing will fall upon you.

13. Charles Haddon Spurgeon, *Autobiography: The Early Years, 1834–1859* (Edinburgh: Banner of Truth, 1962), 87–88.

11

God's Judgment of Judges

Psalm 82

I said, "You are gods, sons of the Most High, all of you;
nevertheless, like men you shall die, and
fall like any prince." (Ps. 82:6–7)

It is important for Christians to understand the role of civil government and the Christian's relationship to the state. A number of New Testament passages make important points on this topic. On one occasion, the Pharisees sought to trip up Jesus by asking whether the people should pay taxes to Caesar. Their idea was either to get Jesus in trouble with the people by endorsing the Romans or to get Jesus in trouble with the Romans by opposing taxes. Jesus, who mastered every situation he was ever in, simply asked for the coin used to pay the tax. When a denarius was brought to him, Jesus asked, "Whose likeness and inscription is this?" They answered that it was Caesar's. Jesus stated, "Therefore render to Caesar the things that are Caesar's, and to God the things that are God's" (Matt. 22:20–21). His point was that Christians have obligations both to God and to their appointed government rulers.

Not only does the Bible acknowledge the legitimacy of secular rulers, but it also states that God established them. Jesus made this point to Pontius

Pilate when the Roman governor asked, "Do you not know that I have authority to release you and authority to crucify you?" (John 19:10). Jesus' answer highlighted the priority of divine authority over human rule: "You would have no authority over me at all unless it had been given you from above" (v. 11).

Not only does the Bible acknowledge civil rule and place it under God's higher authority, but an episode in the book of Acts reveals that when the rules of man directly violate the Word of God, they are not to be obeyed at all. The situation was the hauling of Peter and John before the Jewish Sanhedrin, which forbade them to continue preaching about Jesus. Peter made it clear that the apostles would not obey the Jewish rulers: "Whether it is right in the sight of God to listen to you rather than to God, you must judge, for we cannot but speak of what we have seen and heard" (Acts 4:19–20).

The principle that human authority is both established and judged by God is the message of Psalm 82. The psalm begins with God's taking his seat in the presence of earthly rulers: "God has taken his place in the divine council; in the midst of the gods he holds judgment" (Ps. 82:1). O. Palmer Robertson summarizes the psalm's perspective: "God is the ultimate Judge. He will bring under the scrutiny of his judgmental review all decisions of humans who judge."[1] John Calvin adds: "That the potentates of this world may not arrogate to themselves more than belongs to them, the prophet here erects a throne for God, from which he judged them all, and represses their pride; a thing which is highly necessary."[2]

God's Appointment of Earthly Rulers

The first question in understanding Psalm 82 is to identify those referred to as "the gods" (Ps. 82:1). According to a number of scholars, this refers to the kind of spiritual principalities and powers that Paul mentions in Ephesians. The idea is that "the divine council" of verse 1 involves God's holding court with angelic rulers given authority over different parts of the world. The situation is compared to Job 1:6, where "the sons of God came to present themselves before the Lord." This language is similar to that of Psalm 82,

1. O. Palmer Robertson, *Psalms in Congregational Celebration* (Darlington, UK: Evangelical Press, 1995), 191.

2. John Calvin, *Calvin's Commentaries*, 23 vols. (1848; repr., Grand Rapids: Baker, 2009), 5:329.

which in verse 6 refers to its hearers as "gods, sons of the Most High." In Job 1:1, the assembly is a gathering of angelic leaders, since "Satan also came among them." Scholars thus argue that Psalm 82 depicts a similar gathering in which God holds court with angelic powers both good and evil, during which the Lord stands up to accuse the unjust. It is pointed out that the Old Testament occasionally uses the word *Elohim*, which normally refers to God the Creator, to speak of his angelic representatives (e.g., Ex. 15:11; Ps. 89:6). Daniel 10 speaks of both good and evil angels who have authority over nations, and under this view Psalm 82 involves a gathering of these divine powers. Advocates of this position assert that this best accounts for the ironic mood of Psalm 82:7, which states, "Like men you shall die, and fall like any prince."

There are some reasons to doubt this interpretation, however. For one thing, it is hard to see how God would place "the weak and the fatherless" (Ps. 82:3) into the hands of evil spiritual powers and expect them to receive any justice. Another problem is that verse 7 speaks of these rulers' dying, which does not seem possible for angelic beings. Most telling is the fact that the psalm was quoted by Jesus Christ in one of his disputes with the religious authorities, specifically with reference to the "gods" in verses 1 and 6. In John 10, Jesus had identified God as his own Father, prompting the religious leaders to threaten him with stoning. Jesus answered, "Is it not written in your Law, 'I said, you are gods'?" (John 10:34). This was a direct reference to Psalm 82. Jesus continued, "If he called them gods to whom the word of God came—and Scripture cannot be broken—do you say of him whom the Father consecrated and sent into the world, 'You are blaspheming,' because I said, 'I am the Son of God'?" (John 10:35–36). His point was that the Bible itself refers to human leaders as "gods" who exercise authority from God. Since the Bible itself sanctions the use of this word for men, why would the Jewish leaders accuse Jesus, of all people, for having the word apply to him?

For our purposes, Jesus' interpretation clarifies that Psalm 82 is referring to human leaders who were placed as judges and civil magistrates to govern God's people. But how can the name "gods" and "sons of the Most High" be given to mere humans?

The answer is that judges and magistrates rule on God's behalf, so that his name is upon them in the fulfillment of their duties. William Plumer writes, "They were invested with the character of representatives of God."[3] In this way, the human rulers are as gods to the people, who are required to give honor and obedience to them. Paul taught this principle in Romans 13:1–5: "For there is no authority except from God, and those that exist have been instituted by God. . . . Therefore one must be in subjection" to them. Thus, since human rulers derive their authority from God and stand in God's place with respect to those under them, the divine stamp on their authority is reflected by referring to them as godlike in terms of their office. This perspective is seen in the charge given by King Jehoshaphat to the rulers he appointed: "Consider what you do, for you judge not for man but for the Lord. He is with you in giving judgment" (2 Chron. 19:6).

God's Commission to Earthly Rulers

Since human rulers receive their authority from God, it is God's commission that defines their duties. In Psalm 82:3–4, God makes his expectations clear: "Give justice to the weak and the fatherless; maintain the right of the afflicted and the destitute. Rescue the weak and the needy; deliver them from the hand of the wicked." This charge is not meant to describe the only duties of civil leaders, but it is the sum of their calling. Plumer writes: "The mighty and the majority can protect themselves. The feeble and the minority need the defence of good laws and good rulers."[4] The role of justice in society is the protection of the weak and oppressed, and good rulers should have an eye especially on the care of the destitute. Michael Wilcock writes: "The cause of the weak and the rights of the poor are dear to [God's] heart, and should be to theirs also."[5]

Francis I of France was a godly king who was greatly loved for his honest rule. On one occasion, a woman knelt before him, pleading for justice. The king caused her to rise and stand, saying, "Woman, it is justice that I owe thee, and justice thou shalt have; if thou beg anything of me, let it be mercy."[6] His point was that justice is the duty of kings and judges to provide; unlike mercy, which must be begged, justice should be taken as a divinely given

3. William S. Plumer, *Psalms* (1867; repr., Edinburgh: Banner of Truth, 1975), 782.

4. Plumer, *Psalms,* 784.

5. Michael Wilcock, *The Message of Psalms 73–150* (Downers Grove, IL: InterVarsity Press, 2001), 40.

6. Quoted in Charles Haddon Spurgeon, *The Treasury of David,* 3 vols. (Peabody, MA: Hendrickson, n.d.), 2:414.

right. Psalm 82 urges that just and impartial government will protect the weak and honor God.

God's commission in Psalm 82 shows one way in which free-market capitalism differs from the biblical view of wealth and society. Christians often bemoan high taxes, but we should not resent government efforts directed toward caring for the poor and needy. The problem with many government programs for poverty and social need is that they often do more long-term harm than good. Christians may well oppose wrongheaded social schemes, but we should be at the forefront of those who are earnestly concerned for the needy and should urge our leaders to take steps to alleviate affliction, even if sacrifices are required on our part.

Since human rulers receive their authority from God and exercise a commission that he has given, it is only appropriate that they should acknowledge God in their public work and pray to him for guidance and help. Human rulers need the spiritual fruits of wisdom, courage, faithfulness, and love, all of which God provides through faith. Civil leaders should especially pay attention to God's Word to ensure that they are serving their divine Sovereign appropriately. George Washington thus wrote in his prayer journal: "Let my heart, therefore, gracious God, be so affected with the glory and majesty of Thine honor that I may not do mine own works, but wait on Thee."[7] This very attitude was prescribed by statute for the kings of Israel. When a new king ascended his throne, he was commanded to

> write for himself in a book a copy of this law, approved by the Levitical priests. And it shall be with him, and he shall read in it all the days of his life, that he may learn to fear the Lord his God by keeping all the words of this law and these statutes, and doing them, that his heart may not be lifted above his brothers, and that he may not turn aside from the commandment, . . . so that he may continue long in his kingdom, he and his children, in Israel. (Deut. 17:18–20)

The founding fathers of the United States of America expressed this attitude by having public officials sworn into office by placing their hands on the Bible and making oaths in God's presence. At the Constitutional Convention of 1787 in Philadelphia, Benjamin Franklin emphasized the

7. Quoted in Benjamin Hart, *Faith and Freedom: The Christian Roots of American Liberty* (San Bernardino, CA: Here's Life Publishers, 1988), 274.

importance of the point made by Psalm 82. Rising to speak, he appealed to the role played by reverence for God in the winning of independence and urged a continued need for the same:

> In the beginning of the contest with Britain, when we were sensible of danger, we had daily prayers in this room for the Divine protection. Our prayers, Sir, were heard, and they were graciously answered. All of us who were engaged in the struggle must have observed frequent instances of superintending Providence. To that kind Providence we owe this opportunity of consulting in peace on the means of establishing our future national felicity. And have we now forgotten this powerful Friend? Or do we imagine that we no longer need His assistance? I have lived for a long time (81 years), and the longer I live the more convincing proof I see of this truth, that God governs in the affairs of men. And if a sparrow cannot fall to the ground without His notice, is it probable that an empire can rise without His aid? We have been assured, Sir, in the sacred writings, that "Except the Lord build the house, they labour in vain that build it." . . . I therefore beg leave to move that, henceforth, prayers, imploring the assistance of Heaven and its blessing on our deliberations, be held in this assembly every morning before we proceed to business, and that one or more of the clergy of this city be requested to officiate in that service.[8]

God's Accusation against Unjust Rulers

It is the tragedy of recent years in America that Franklin's wisdom has been neglected and forgotten. The same problem occurred in Israel under the successors of King David and especially in the rebellious northern kingdom of Israel. Because of this failure to submit to divine authority, the rulers are brought under accusation in Psalm 82. The basic charge is given in verse 2: "How long will you judge unjustly and show partiality to the wicked?"

Before we look at the specific charge, the most important fact is God's judgment. God is the Ruler of the rulers and the Judge of the judges, just as Christ is hailed in Revelation 19:16: "King of kings and Lord of lords." Charles Spurgeon writes that human judges "are gods to other men, but he is God to them. . . . They must take care that they do not misuse the power entrusted to them, for the Judge of judges is in session among them."[9] This principle

8. Quoted in Rowland E. Prothero, *The Psalms in Human Life* (New York: Dutton, 1904), 231–32.
9. Spurgeon, *Treasury of David*, 2a:411.

holds not only for presidents, congressmen, and judges, but also for fathers who exercise God's authority over wives and children, pastors and elders in ruling the church, and business leaders who exercise authority over those in their employ.

Especially those who have become used to exercising earthly authority most need the warning of Psalm 82. It is common for human rulers to believe that authority is at their sole disposal and for their own purposes. This was the mistake of the despotic kings of Europe, who upheld their reigns on the principle of divine right. Psalm 82 warns such rulers to be humble before God and faithful in performing justice. Samuel Rutherford pointed to Psalm 82 in his historically influential study of biblical authority and rule, *Lex Rex*. He noted the duty of lower judges and officials to oppose higher rulers such as kings and presidents when and if they descended into violent tyranny.[10] Rutherford's argument provided the rationale for righteous rebellions such as the American Revolution, since he urged that lower officials owe their loyalty to God before the king and that they are responsible to God to protect the weak from tyranny.

The psalmist's specific charge is that Israel's rulers "judge unjustly and show partiality to the wicked" (Ps. 82:2). The people were left in desperate straits because the rulers and judges appointed to provide them with justice were exercising their power for evil. Micah 3:2 condemned such evil rulers: "you who hate the good and love the evil, who tear the skin from off my people and their flesh from off their bones." From the context of Psalm 82, it seems that people were being made destitute by greedy power brokers and that the judges were in their pocket. The oppressed looked to their civil leaders for support but found them conspiring with the wicked. Where our English version reads that they "show partiality to the wicked," the Hebrew text employs an idiom saying that they "lift the face of the wicked." The idea is that of unrighteous acquittal and the upholding of an unjust cause. These judges and rulers who were appointed as God's protectors of the weak and vulnerable have instead given their blessing to the evil wolves who were ravaging the sheep.

The Lord condemns not only what the false judges do but also what they have become: "They have neither knowledge nor understanding, they walk about in darkness; all the foundations of the earth are shaken" (Ps. 82:5). By means of the corrupting influence of power, they have lost the ability to

10. Samuel Rutherford, *Lex Rex*, 3.4, 20.1, quoted in Spurgeon, *Treasury of David*, 2a:415.

discern right from wrong. There is a warp in their judgment so that they have lost touch with obvious moral obligations. We see this today in government support of those who rake in millions by the slaughter of unborn children and the harmful advocacy of sexual promiscuity and gender confusion. There is not the slightest doubt about the moral status of these issues, but in the welter of polls, political contributions, and power politics, the rulers and their political consultants have lost "knowledge" and "understanding" of what is good, true, and wholesome. Instead, "they walk about in darkness." Their ignorance is accompanied by ineptitude and moral chaos. The consequence is upheaval and ruin: "all the foundations of the earth are shaken" (v. 5).

Here the Bible gives an accurate description of Western society in its current collapse. The advocates of what is misnamed the "progressive" cause are unfazed by the reality that children are no longer safe outdoors, families are in chaos, schools are ineffective, and civic virtues are in radical decline. David Dickson writes: "When justice and judgment-seats are corrupted, and judges do not mind justice in their places, then the pillars of that land or kingdom must stagger, and all matters go to ruin, or a perilous alteration."[11]

God's Judgment of Unjust Rulers

God is angered by the injustice and corruption of rulers who were established by him to bring blessing rather than bane. The severity of his judgment reflects the trust that has been betrayed and the significance to God of our faithfulness in public duties.

God's threatened punishment is laced with holy scorn: "I said, 'You are gods, sons of the Most High, all of you; nevertheless, like men you shall die, and fall like any prince'" (Ps. 82:6–7). Though rulers and judges are like gods to men, God is yet their God, and his severe judgment reflects his holy perfection. No matter how high a man may be raised in life, he is not so high but that God can cast him down in a moment. Moreover, even the most exalted of the world are just men. They will all be claimed by the grave and stand before the final judgment of God. August Tholuck thus wrote: "Death, which levels all men, is the most effective sermon for earthly rulers."[12]

11. David Dickson, *A Commentary on the Psalms* (1653; repr., Edinburgh: Banner of Truth, 1995), 2:62.

12. Quoted in Plumer, *Psalms*, 785.

High office and worldly power offer no protection against disease and corruption, and in many cases earthly power provokes poor health as much as it invites a violent death. The one assailant who can never be stopped is God, when the time comes for his judgment to strike the lords of earth. For this reason, many of the highest in rank often suffer the most grievous of falls and the most shameful of ends, for the same God who exalted them for his own service abases them in judgment. Thomas Hall writes: "Most of the Caesars fell by the hands of the people. If you be like tyrants in sin, expect to be like them in punishment."[13] God thus declares, "Like men you shall die, and fall like any prince" (Ps. 82:7).

Where we read, "Like men you shall die," the Hebrew text literally reads, "Like Adam you will die." The name *Adam* is the same word as that for *man*, so this may be taken as a reference either to our first parent or else to people generally. At the least, the verse reminds us of the example of our first father, who took it upon himself to sin against God, while acting as covenant head of the entire human race in the covenant of works. The result was death for him and all his descendants. Hebrews 9:27 warns that "it is appointed for man to die once, and after that comes judgment." Remembering Adam's fall and our own accountability to God should compel every sinner to come to the foot of Jesus' cross, there to confess his sin and gain forgiveness through Christ's blood.

Because God is the final Judge and the only infallibly faithful Savior, Christians should appeal to him against unjust rulers. Thus, the psalm concludes with an appeal for God to step forward and put his judgments into action: "Arise, O God, judge the earth; for you shall inherit all the nations!" (Ps. 82:8). When God's people are afflicted, we can always turn to him, knowing that he is both willing and able to protect and provide for his people. Matthew Henry writes: "There is a righteous God to whom we may have recourse, and on whom we may depend for the effectual relief of all that find themselves aggrieved by unjust judges."[14]

The language of Psalm 82:8 evokes the promise of Psalm 2, which informs us that it is the Messiah who will inherit the nations. God says to his Son: "Ask of me, and I will make the nations your heritage, and the ends of the earth your possession" (Ps. 2:8). According to the New Testament, Psalm 2

13. Quoted in Spurgeon, *Treasury of David*, 2:416–17.

14. Matthew Henry, *Commentary on the Whole Bible*, 6 vols. (Peabody, MA: Hendrickson, n.d.), 3:452.

was fulfilled in the resurrection of the crucified Jesus Christ from the grave. Psalm 2:7 declares, "The LORD said to me, 'You are my Son; today I have begotten you.'" Paul explains in Romans 1:4 that this public declaration of Christ's sonship took place at the resurrection: he "was declared to be the Son of God in power according to the Spirit of holiness by his resurrection from the dead, Jesus Christ our Lord."

With this connection in mind, we see that the Eastern Orthodox Church showed good judgment when it placed Psalm 82:8 in the liturgy of the church for the Saturday between Good Friday and Easter Sunday. After a Scripture reading concerning Christ's resurrection, the choir chants, "Like a call to the sleeping Christ: 'Arise, O Lord, Judge the earth, for Thou shalt have an inheritance among all the nations.'"[15] The resurrection of Christ is the assurance that the plea of Psalm 82 will be answered, that the unjust rulers of the earth will be cast down, and that our appeal to heaven for aid will be answered. As Mary sang concerning the birth of her child:

> He has shown strength with his arm;
> he has scattered the proud in the thoughts of their hearts;
> he has brought down the mighty from their thrones
> and exalted those of humble estate. (Luke 1:51–52)

Our Judgment in Christ

It is in light of verse 8's plea for God to intervene and judge that we best connect Psalm 82 back to John 10, where it is referenced by Jesus. He had revealed himself in word and deed as the true Messiah, the very Son of God and Savior of the world. The unjust rulers replied in unbelieving violence, threatening to put Jesus to death. Jesus appealed to Psalm 82's description of earthly rulers as "gods" and "sons of the Most High." If this language can be used of civil magistrates who serve in God's name, how much more can it be said of God's true Son, to whom the eternal sovereignty of all the world has been committed?

Since the final judgment will be made by Jesus Christ on the last day when he returns, the most important judgment that each of us can make now concerns our response to him. Jesus said, "I am the Son of God"—that

15. Liturgy for Great Saturday, Greek Orthodox Archdiocese of America.

is, the true Savior consecrated by the Father and sent into the world for our redemption (John 10:36). When each of us stands before his throne on the day when Psalm 82 is fully realized, the day of judgment, what will matter most is how we have responded to Jesus. Will you be unjust toward Jesus by denying his claim as Messiah? If so, then Psalm 82:7's warning is given to you: "like men you shall die, and fall." But if you humbly bow before Jesus, submitting the judgment of your faith to him for salvation, then the final plea of the psalm will bring your redemption: "Arise, O God, judge the earth; for you shall inherit all the nations!" (v. 8).

12

That They May Know

Psalm 83

O God, do not keep silence; do not hold your peace or be still, O God! For behold, your enemies make an uproar; those who hate you have raised their heads. (Ps. 83:1–2)

The book of Psalms is unique in biblical literature, not only because of its poetic content but also because of how the Psalter is organized. Traditionally gathered into five books, Psalms begins with forty-one poems attributed to King David on a wide variety of subjects. After the opening couplet of Psalms 42–43, book 2 introduces nine psalms attributed to the Sons of Korah, highlighting God's sovereign, mighty reign. Twenty-one more psalms from David conclude the second book with one from Solomon. Book 3 features the Asaph collection, eleven psalms focused on the theme of divine judgment, and more psalms from the Sons of Korah. Book 4 contains mainly anonymous psalms written for public worship. Book 5 includes the well-loved psalms of ascent (121–134) and many others focused on thanksgiving and praise.

The psalms attributed to Asaph describe events separated by centuries, so these poems were probably authored by the original Asaph and his successors in the office of chief singer (1 Chron. 16:5). Psalm 83 was possibly written by Jahaziel, a descendant of Asaph who served as a Levite under King Jehoshaphat (2 Chron. 20:14). Taken together, so far the Asaph collection has offered valuable insights on God as the Defender of his people and Judge of evil. Psalm 73 taught us not to envy the wicked, since we remember the condemnation they face. Psalm 74 reminded us that we pray to the Creator God, whose power is infinite to save and judge. Psalm 75 recalls that there is a cup of judgment for all the wicked to drink, while "the horns of the righteous shall be lifted up" (v. 10). Psalm 78 looked back on the great events of the exodus and David's reign, reminding us of God's past judgment on Israel's foes. This theme of looking to the biblical past for the hope of salvation lies at the heart of Psalm 83. The Asaphite writer is so certain of divine intervention that his concern shifts from desperation to a desire for God's glory. God's Word should produce the same transformation in our lives. The psalmist prays for judgment, "that they may know that you alone, whose name is the Lord, are the Most High over all the earth" (Ps. 83:18).

An Urgent Plea and Its Reason

Psalm 83 begins with yet another desperate plea for God's intervention: "O God, do not keep silence; do not hold your peace or be still, O God!" (Ps. 83:1). This cry gives the impression that God has allowed a dangerous situation to ripen and that his people are becoming desperate for him to act. The Bible often shows God as waiting to act in this way, as when the people of Israel stood with their backs to the Red Sea and the Egyptian chariots were bearing down, before God made a lane for them through the waters. John Calvin writes, "It is unquestionably our duty to wait patiently when God at any time delays his help; but, in condescension to our infirmity, he permits us to supplicate him to make haste."[1]

The Irishman Edmund Burke served in England's House of Commons in the late eighteenth century. While he wrote many influential essays and speeches, his most famous words are recorded only in the writings of others. Most notably, Burke said, "All that is necessary for evil to triumph is for good men to do nothing."[2] Psalm 83 reminds us that of all the things that good men may do in times of crisis, none is more important than prayer.

1. John Calvin, *Calvin's Commentaries*, 23 vols. (1848; repr., Grand Rapids: Baker, 2009), 5:339.
2. Quoted in James Montgomery Boice, *Psalms*, 3 vols. (Grand Rapids: Baker, 1996), 2:681.

When the forces of unbelief and ungodliness have united to drive out Christian faith, God's people cry to him: "O God, do not keep silence; do not hold your peace or be still, O God!" (Ps. 83:1).

Psalm 83 was written in a desperate time when evil seemed to triumph. The enemies of God's people had risen up, banded together, and conspired for the destruction of Israel. Verse 2 cries, "For behold, your enemies make an uproar; those who hate you have raised their heads." Unlike some psalms, which deal with evil in general, this psalm concerns a crisis in which the enemies of Israel have summoned their strength in a confident expectation of victory.

More than this, the wicked have laid "crafty plans" against God's people. This onslaught involved a clever and devious strategy against God's truth and the church. "They consult together against your treasured ones" (Ps. 83:3). Christians should not be surprised when a devious plan is hatched against them by the advocates of unbelief. Just as Satan is a deceiver, so also the enemies of the gospel delight in deceptive schemes against the truth.

In A.D. 302, the joint rulers of the Roman Empire, Diocletian and Galerius, met to discuss the growing political power of Christians. Diocletian initially favored moderation, but Galerius called for extermination. The two men consulted the oracle of Apollo, hearing back that the gods could not speak until "the just on earth," that is, the Christians, were eliminated. On this basis, plans were hatched. With no warning, the order was given on February 23, 303, the feast of the pagan god Terminalia, to burn the newly built Christian church in Nicomedia. The next day, Diocletian issued an edict calling for the burning of all churches and Scriptures, the removal of Christians from public office, and the abolition of Christian worship. He followed up with other edicts calling for the arrest of all clergy, a requirement that Christians offer sacrifices to pagan gods, and finally the torture and execution of the thousands of Christians who refused to worship idols. The church thus suffered under a cleverly concealed and orchestrated plan designed to eradicate Christianity from the empire.[3]

Christians today should not be surprised when secular and pagan forces engage in deceitful stratagems to wage war on the gospel. These strategies involve claims for tolerance while unbelievers are in the minority, leading

3. Philip Schaff, *History of the Christian Church*, 8 vols. (1858; repr., Peabody, MA: Hendrickson, 2002), 2:64–70.

to the most strident intolerance of Christianity when they hold the majority. These cunning plans involve a biased media, dishonest political candidates, and the misleading promotion of immoral behavior through entertainment and the arts.

It is important for us to note the aim of the enemies of the gospel, both in the time of the psalmist and today: "They say, 'Come, let us wipe them out as a nation'" (Ps. 83:4). The aim of the enemy plan is the extermination of the Christian faith and the elimination of the church. Most important is the removal of God's Word and its restraining influence against the reign of sin. It was precisely because God's people held forth the light of Holy Scripture that their enemies cried: "let the name of Israel be remembered no more!" (v. 4).

An Encircling Conspiracy

In addition to facing a cunning uprising of evil, Israel was beset with a staggering confederation of nations: "For they conspire with one accord; against you they make a covenant—the tents of Edom and the Ishmaelites, Moab and the Hagrites, Gebal and Ammon and Amalek, Philistia with the inhabitants of Tyre; Asshur also has joined them; they are the strong arm of the children of Lot" (Ps. 83:5–8).

This list starts with the Edomites, who were descendants of Jacob's brother Esau, as were the Amalekites, together with the Ishmaelites, who descended from Abraham's son by the servant Hagar. Perhaps related to them are the Hagrites, together with the unknown people of Gebal. Added in were the Moabites, who were the descendants of Abraham's nephew Lot, as were the Ammonites. All these confederates dwelt to the east or northeast of Israel. Other enemies were located to the west and northwest: the Philistines and the merchant city of Tyre. Last came the Assyrians, who would rise to such astonishing power in the eighth century B.C., but who at this time are cited as hired mercenaries: "the strong arm of the children of Lot" (Ps. 83:8). This concluding statement indicates that the confederation was led by the Moabites and Ammonites, who descended from Lot.

The confederation against Israel shows how opposition to God and his people will unite enemies who would otherwise have no mutual interest. William Plumer writes: "In opposing God's cause and people the wicked are ever unanimous."[4] The chief example is the unlikely alliance of the Jewish priests and the Roman governor Pontius Pilate in the crucifixion of Jesus. We see similarly unlikely unions today as social progressives in America show sympathy for and even make common cause with socially regressive Islamic groups. It is hard to see how one group that champions women's rights can so fervently join with a religion that so brutalizes women, until you realize that they have a shared cause in opposing Christianity and the Word of God.

The source of this unifying opposition to God can be seen in the same chapter that records the fall of Adam into sin. God cursed Satan, saying, "I will put enmity between you and the woman, and between your offspring and her offspring" (Gen. 3:15). As a result, all unbelieving peoples, under the dominion of the devil (see Eph. 2:1), share a hatred for the church, which is the godly offspring united to the Savior-Son, Jesus Christ. This history of enmity shows that while salvation does not run through mere bloodlines, hatred to God most certainly does.

A second feature of this conspiracy is how many of the tribes were related to the people of Israel. There ought to have been fellowship between these cousins, but instead their hatred was most bitter. Similarly, today we find that some of the most eager opponents of biblical Christianity are the children of missionaries and pastors. Those who have a fleshly but not a spiritual relationship to the church, and who have turned away to ungodliness, are often the most spiteful in attacking the gospel. Calvin writes that "it is, as it were, the destiny of the Church, not only to be assailed by external enemies, to suffer far greater trouble at the hands of false brethren."[5]

The question is raised as to when this confederation rose against Israel. The best historical answer is to associate this psalm with the mass assault in the time of Jehoshaphat, recorded in 2 Chronicles 20. There, the Moabites, Ammonites, and Edomites are listed (2 Chron. 20:1–2), although the other nations are not mentioned. It could be, however, that they sent smaller forces that either were hired or simply were not mentioned by the Chronicler. If this was the occasion, it is interesting that a descendant of Asaph named Jahaziel is listed as leading the singers in going forth before Israel's army (vv. 14–21). Psalm 83 might have been written for this crisis, in which God gave a victory by his mighty power to his singing and praying people.

4. William S. Plumer, *Psalms* (1867; repr., Edinburgh: Banner of Truth, 1975), 791.
5. Calvin, *Commentaries*, 5:345.

Another view holds that since the entirety of this confederation is never listed in Scripture, the psalm provides a poetic idealization of how God's people are often surrounded by hostile forces in the world. Applying the conspiracy of Psalm 83 as a general principle, George Horne comments: "The acts are changed, and the scenes are shifted; but the stage and the drama continue the same."[6]

Summing Up the Doctrine of Divine Judgment

The second half of Psalm 83 works out the kind of judgment that the psalmist seeks in answer to his prayer. Like other similar psalms, Psalm 83 is criticized as an "unedifying and tedious catalogue of bloody violence."[7] Such a description, however, fails to connect with the spirit of these prayers. H. C. Leupold writes: "On closer inspection it will be recognized that we have here a normal prayer of an endangered people, for which no apologies need be made."[8]

First, the psalmist prays for Israel's enemies to suffer *defeat*:

Do to them as you did to Midian,
  as to Sisera and Jabin at the river Kishon,
who were destroyed at En-dor,
  who became dung for the ground.
Make their nobles like Oreb and Zeeb,
  all their princes like Zebah and Zalmunna,
who said, "Let us take possession for ourselves of the pastures of God."
  (Ps. 83:9–12)

The psalmist is drawing from the earlier history of Israel as recorded in the book of Judges, pointing out what God had previously done and asking him again to judge and defeat Israel's foes. The first instance is the defeat of the Midianites by Gideon and his small band (Judg. 6–8). In those days, the Israelites were under total pagan domination. But God called Gideon to rally the Israelite militia. When thirty-two thousand gathered, the Lord

6. George Horne, *Commentary on the Psalms* (1771; repr., Audubon, NJ: Old Paths Publications, 1997), 360.

7. Unspecified source quoted in H. C. Leupold, *Exposition of the Psalms* (Columbus, OH: Wartburg Press, 1959), 597.

8. Leupold, *Exposition of the Psalms*, 597.

insisted that these were too many, even against a massively larger enemy host. All who were fearful were told to go home, reducing Gideon's band to ten thousand. This number was later reduced to a bare three hundred, which sneaked up on the Midianites, holding torches and blowing trumpets.

It thus was God who delivered the enemy to defeat by his own power (Judg. 7:15). After Gideon's three hundred had pursued Zebah and Zalmunna, also mentioned in verse 11, the total enemy number defeated was one hundred twenty thousand! The psalmist prays that a similar divine intervention would destroy the confederation assailing God's people. Just as it may have seemed ridiculous for Gideon to believe God's Word by going forth against so great a host with such paltry earthly power, so in the psalmist's crisis and in those we face today, those who trust and obey the Lord can be confident of ultimate success, no matter how strong the opposition seems.

Another example involves the defeat of the Canaanite generals Sisera and Jabin in Judges 4. Barak was sent by the prophetess Deborah to lead Israel against the mighty chariot forces of the enemy. After Barak's victory, Sisera was slain by an Israelite woman named Jael, who drove a tent peg through his temple as he slept, while Jabin was captured. Like the Midianite princes Oreb and Zeeb, who were slain by Gideon (Judg. 7:25; Ps. 83:11), Jael and Sisera show God's judgment on the leaders of conspiracies against his people. The Song of Deborah celebrates this general principle of divine judgment: "So may all your enemies perish, O Lord! But your friends be like the sun as he rises in his might" (Judg. 5:31).

When God judges his enemies by causing their defeat, the *destruction* they suffer is thorough. In addition to the two examples from Judges, the psalmist elaborates with examples from nature: "O my God, make them like whirling dust, like chaff before the wind. As fire consumes the forest, as the flame sets the mountains ablaze, so may you pursue them with your tempest and terrify them with your hurricane!" (Ps. 83:13–15). God drives chaff away by dust, consumes forests with fire, and terrifies with the storm of the hurricane. He therefore has ample power to scatter and destroy every foe of his people: "Such is the storm and tempest of God's indignation, which pursues and terrifies the sacrilegious and ungodly."[9]

God's judgment not only defeats and destroys those who persecute his people, but in the end will also bring them to *dishonor*: "Fill their faces with

9. Horne, *Psalms*, 361.

shame, that they may seek your name, O Lord. Let them be put to shame and dismayed forever; let them perish in disgrace" (Ps. 83:16–17). Rebellion against God begins in pride; Psalm 83 thus describes Israel's foes as those who "make an uproar" and "have raised their heads" (v. 2). God's judgment causes those same heads to hang in "shame and [dismay] forever" (v. 17). How much better it is to embrace the humility of Christ in this world, perhaps suffering scorn for the sake of the gospel, rather than to join in the proud rebellion of those who are destined to spend eternity in the confusion of disgrace.

Two Parting Lessons from the Asaph Psalms

Before we depart from Psalm 83 and from the entire collection of Asaphite psalms with their focus on divine judgment, there are two lessons for us to consider.

The first lesson is that the Lord and his people are so joined that to war against the church is to war against God. Psalm 83:2 says that God should intervene because "your enemies make an uproar, those who hate you." Verse 3 observes that the crafty plans were directed "against your people," who are then called "your treasured ones." Verse 5 warns that "against you they make a covenant." The Lord and his people are like a husband and his wife, so that to attack his bride is to raise God's defense and guarantee his wrath. Calvin writes: "It affords us no small ground of confidence that those who are our enemies are also God's enemies."[10] Zechariah 2:8 asserts that "he who touches you touches the apple of his eye." Jesus spoke in a similarly protective way when he confronted Saul on the Damascus road for persecuting his church: "Saul, Saul, why are you persecuting me?" (Acts 9:4). Thus, Christians under assault for their faith, whether on a national scale or individually at work, in school, or within a family, may pray to God, saying, "Lord, they are attacking your beloved!" Since God treasures his people, we can be sure that the gospel witness and eternal destiny of his church are safeguarded by his omnipotent and vigilant power.

It was with this privileged relationship in mind that when Jehoshaphat faced the mighty confederation that is perhaps identified in this psalm, a prophet was sent to him with words of assurance: "Do not be afraid and do

10. Calvin, *Commentaries*, 5:339.

not be dismayed at this great horde, for the battle is not yours but God's" (2 Chron. 20:15). In answer, not only did the Asaphite psalmist perhaps author Psalm 83, but the Levitical singers also led the army going forth, singing Psalm 118: "Give thanks to the LORD, for his steadfast love endures forever" (2 Chron. 20:21).

James Boice points out that the realization that attacks on believers are really attacks on God should shape our attitudes toward enemies and their judgment:

> If the evil is thought of as being against one's self, then the call is for revenge. But if it is thought of as being against God, then our response is to leave justice in God's hands and trust him for whatever he sees fit to do. And we can trust him! God is not indifferent! He himself says, "It is mine to avenge; I will repay" (Deut. 32:35; Rom. 12:19).[11]

The final lesson of Psalm 83 is perhaps the most important. It is a lesson that shows us not only *why* we should pray for God to judge evil, but *how* we should pray for divine judgment. Psalm 83 concludes with an emphasis on the glory of God that results when he rises to judge his foes with destruction and shame:

> Fill their faces with shame,
> that they may seek your name, O LORD.
> Let them be put to shame and dismayed forever;
> let them perish in disgrace,
> that they may know that you alone,
> whose name is the LORD,
> are the Most High over all the earth. (Ps. 83:16–18)

This prayer shows the nobility of spirit to which believers are called, even in the face of dire threats to their safety. We can understand, according to nature, how a threatened person may pray for the defeat and destruction of his assailant. But only grace can cause that same person to pray mainly for God's name to be known and his glory to be exalted.

There are two different ways in which we may see God glorified through his judgment of evil. The first is that by this means, God often persuades

11. Boice, *Psalms*, 2:686.

the wicked to repent, and thus judgment leads to their salvation. This seems to be the emphasis of Psalm 83:16, where the psalmist prays for the enemies' faces to be filled with shame, "that they may seek your name, O LORD." What a remarkable statement to conclude not only this imprecatory psalm but the entirety of the judgment psalms authored by Asaph! Here is God's grace in action, that injured and threatened believers should still concern themselves with the conversion of the ungodly. This was, of course, the very attitude in the heart of Jesus that led to our salvation from sin. J. J. Stewart Perowne writes: "The man who loves and fears Jehovah desires to see others, even his enemies, love and fear Him too."[12] Thus, while Christians pray for God to judge, we remember Jesus' petition on the cross for forgiveness (Luke 23:34), and we imitate Stephen's prayer when he suffered the first martyrdom of the church age: "Lord, do not hold this sin against them" (Acts 7:60). As Christians remember the saving aim of our Lord on the cross, and the dying witness of the first believers, the first prayers that we ought to offer in response to gospel-opposing evil are appeals to God's mercy for the conversion of sinners.

The second way that God is glorified in judgment is when his enemies, though still unrepentant, acknowledge him as the true and mighty God. Paul wrote that in the end, even as the wicked are destroyed in the final judgment, "every knee [will] bow, in heaven and on earth and under the earth, and every tongue confess that Jesus Christ is Lord, to the glory of God the Father" (Phil. 2:10–11). Plumer comments: "In the end there shall not be found a dog to move his tongue against him. All the earth shall keep silence before him, or break forth into hallelujahs at the mention of his name."[13]

Earlier, I mentioned Galerius, who persuaded the Roman Emperor Diocletian to unleash persecutions seeking to destroy the Christian church. In the Eastern provinces, where Galerius reigned, believers in Christ suffered the greatest torment and vast numbers of deaths. But they showed Galerius a resolve in their faith that he had never imagined. By 311, even Galerius gave up trying to destroy the church, admitting his failure. Though he had never repented and believed, when he became sick and began to die he summoned the Christians who had escaped his persecution to come and

12. J. J. Stewart Perowne, *The Book of Psalms*, 2 vols. (1878; repr., Grand Rapids: Zondervan, 1976), 2:114.

13. Plumer, *Psalms*, 792–93.

pray for him to their God.[14] In the midst of the judgment for which he faced the wrath of God, he yet gave testimony that Jesus Christ, "whose name is the LORD," is "the Most High over all the earth" (Ps. 83:18).

When God Was Silent

As Galerius sensed, the church survives against all foes because of the mediatorial kingship of her Savior, Jesus Christ. Jesus secures God's favor for the church, and thus God's saving help, together with judgment on her foes, by the perfect life and sin-atoning wounds that he bears perpetually for believers in heaven. It was only in his own case, as Jesus suffered on the cross, that a believer's cry failed to rouse God's gracious answer: "My God, my God, why have you forsaken me?" (Matt. 27:46). It was only while Jesus, God's Son, suffered the hatred of men, but more importantly the wrath of God toward our sins, that heaven neglected Psalm 83, God's holding his peace while the righteous suffered death. It was, however, by this means that God most faithfully answered the plea of this psalm for believers in Jesus, performing the great work that saved us from our greatest enemies: sin, judgment, and death. As Isaiah foretold: "he was pierced for our transgressions; he was crushed for our iniquities; upon him was the chastisement that brought us peace, and with his wounds we are healed" (Isa. 53:5).

This means that the first and great need of every person, all of us being sinners who deserve God's judgment, is to look to Jesus Christ in saving faith, confessing our sins and believing in his cleansing blood. If we do, we will no longer be the enemies of heaven. We will be the "treasured ones" of God (Ps. 83:3). Then, whatever dangers we may face in this world, Asaph's greatest statement of faith, recorded in the first of this collection of psalms, will be our experience as well: "My flesh and my heart may fail, but God is the strength of my heart and my portion forever" (73:26).

14. Schaff, *History of the Christian Church*, 2:71.

13

A Heart for God

Psalm 84

How lovely is your dwelling place, O Lord of hosts! My soul longs, yes, faints for the courts of the Lord; my heart and flesh sing for joy to the living God. (Ps. 84:1–2)

When he was a boy, the great Welsh preacher Martyn Lloyd-Jones was sent to live in a nearby town to attend secondary school. His poor circulation caused him to suffer miserably from the frigid temperatures there. "But," he later recalled, "I suffered at the same time from a far greater sickness, and a more painful one, which has remained with me all along life's path—and that was *hiraeth* . . . . It is difficult to define *hiraeth*, but to me it means the consciousness of man being out of his home area and all that which is dear to him."[1] This feeling of longing never left Lloyd-Jones. All through life he was conscious of not being in the place where he really belonged, a place suitable for him to dwell in perfect rest. Centuries earlier, St. Augustine had explained this feeling in terms of man's relationship to God, in the famous prayer from his *Confessions*: "Thou hast formed us for thyself, and our hearts are restless till they find rest in Thee."[2]

1. Quoted in Iain H. Murray, *D. Martyn Lloyd-Jones: The First Forty Years, 1899–1939* (Edinburgh: Banner of Truth, 1982), 23–24.

2. Augustine, *Confessions*, trans. William Watts (Cambridge, MA: Harvard University Press, 1919), 1.1.

In his many years of ministry, Lloyd-Jones came to learn that this problem was not merely his own. He writes:

> Man by nature, man without God, is restless. . . . Where can we find peace? Where can we find tranquility? Where can we find rest and peace of mind and of heart and of spirit? Where can we find the point where all is well and nothing troubles? Where is it? Man cannot find it, he is restless. Why? . . . Man, though he does not know it, was made by God, and he was made in such a way that he is dependent upon God. There is the highest thing in man which can only be satisfied by God. Nothing else can satisfy it.[3]

A Home in God

The soul's longing for home comes to perhaps its fullest expression in Psalm 84: "How lovely is your dwelling place, O Lord of hosts! My soul longs, yes, faints for the courts of the Lord; my heart and flesh sing for joy to the living God" (vv. 1–2). The heading states that this song was written by the sons of Korah, a clan of the tribe of Levi that served as custodians in the temple courts. It seems that the psalmist was forced to be away from the tabernacle—perhaps, as many commentators suggest, fleeing with David during Absalom's rebellion. Whatever the circumstances, it is a psalm of a heart longing not merely for the religious rituals of the temple but chiefly for the living God who dwelt in his house.

Psalm 84 is organized with three sections set apart by the annotation *selah*, a musical notation or pause. Each section is defined by a beatitude, a statement of blessing. In the first and third sections, the blessing is at the end; in the second section, it comes at the beginning. The first of these beatitudes occurs in verse 4, summarizing the psalm's first point: "Blessed are those who dwell in your house, ever singing your praise!" In his longing for God, this Levite extols the blessedness of those who have God as their home.

In fine poetic style, the psalmist expresses his envy for the birds that he remembers making their nests in the temple courtyards. He contrasts their experience to his own: "Even the sparrow finds a home, and the swallow a nest for herself, where she may lay her young, at your altars, O Lord of hosts, my King and my God" (Ps. 84:3).

3. D. Martyn Lloyd-Jones, *The Cross* (Wheaton, IL: Crossway, 1986), 181.

Have you ever noticed how easy it is for birds and animals to find a satisfying home in this world? The creatures are able to have their highest aspirations fulfilled in the things of this present life—food, shelter, companionship. You see a dog resting on a rug, a cat preening in the shade, or birds settled in the eaves of the temple courts. But not so man! The animals seem to attain a contentedness far beyond what humans can find in this world. Surely our restlessness is explained by our spiritual nature, which is suited only for a higher realm than this present existence.

This is why the Levite pines for God when he is separated from the temple. Far more than in our present age, the Old Testament believer relied on outward ceremonies: on the building and the ritual of the tabernacle and later of the temple. Left without these symbols and sacraments that brought him to God, especially the altar on which the atoning sacrifices were offered, the Levite's heart was bereft: "My soul longs, yes, faints for the courts of the Lord; my heart and flesh sing for joy to the living God" (Ps. 84:2). He, like us, has a God-shaped hole in his heart; he can be fulfilled only by the presence and worship of God.

How few realize this today. All of us are seeking a home. We seek rest and peace, belonging and contentment, satisfaction and joy. Yet ours is an age that seeks these things everywhere but in God. That is why ours is such a restless, dissatisfied generation, despite an unprecedented abundance of wealth and leisure.

Think about the man of the world and his restless progression through life. He seeks excitement in dancing and drinking, in thrills and in sex. But do these satisfy him? No! He finds no home in them, no peace, no fulfillment. So if he has any depth to him at all, he moves on. He pours himself into his job. He attains to wealth and buys a great house and a prestigious car, thinking that these will make him happy. But they do not. He takes on a challenge, perhaps to rise to the top of his company, or to climb a great mountain. But when he achieves it, he is still restless. This is why after legendary pro football quarterback Tom Brady had reached his goal of three Super Bowl championships, he lamented: "I reached my goal, my dream, my life. Me, I think, 'God, it's got to be more than this.'" The interviewer responded, "What's the answer?" Brady said, "I wish I knew. I wish I knew."[4]

4. CBS News interview, https://www.cbsnews.com/video/2019-super-bowl-tom-brady-on-winning-theres-got-to-be-more-than-this-60-minutes-archives/.

Like Brady, many a person turns from career to romance, or adopts a political cause, or even takes on religious airs. But it doesn't matter what it is: none of it is big enough for him. None of it satisfies the soul. He is still restless; with all that he has, there is no peace, no home for his spirit. Why? Because only God is big enough to fill the soul that he made for himself.

Only in God is a man or woman able to settle as a bird does in its nest with peace, satisfaction, and the great longing fulfilled because home has been found. Augustine was right: "Thou hast formed us for thyself, and our hearts are restless till they find rest in Thee."

This is one way of describing what it means to be a Christian. First, it means that through the blood of Christ you are forgiven of your sins. But this is not all there is, a sort of insurance policy against the great fire of the judgment to come. To be a Christian means to have found your home in God, your longing satisfied in knowing him and serving him, in worship and in living before his face, in crying, "How lovely is your dwelling place, O Lord of hosts!" (Ps. 84:1). The Christian has found his identity, his purpose, and his home, because he has found God and has been accepted by God in return.

Don't you find, if you have been a Christian for some time, that wherever you travel, you feel at home in a true church, where the gospel is preached and where there are people you have never met but who know and serve the Lord? You can be in a strange city, feeling awkward and out of place, but you go to where God's people are, and your heart is at rest. It is almost as though you were at home. Why? Because it really is God who is your home. In worship with God's people, you are brought to the courts of God, and there you receive the psalm's benediction: "Blessed are those who dwell in your house, ever singing your praise!" (Ps. 84:4).

The Pilgrim Heart

None of us has achieved our full entry into this rest. Having found God and entered into communion with him, we nonetheless continue seeking him. We become pilgrims journeying to the distant land that is our final home. It is important for us to realize this about our present lives: we have not yet arrived at home, even though our hearts dwell there already. Our home is not in this world but in the next; "our citizenship is in heaven," Paul reminds us (Phil. 3:20). This is the idea of the second section of Psalm 84, which begins, "Blessed are those whose strength is in you, in whose heart are the highways to Zion" (Ps. 84:5).

Undoubtedly, the exiled Levite thinks of the regular pilgrimages that led God's people to Jerusalem from every corner of the nation. Israel's religious calendar was organized around three great feasts, for which all the faithful were called to appear before God's temple. In his mind the psalmist sees streams of worshipers forming into rivers. He hears their songs in his heart. He knows well the renewed strength that comes to their legs as the city comes into sight over the hills. Blessed are they, he reflects, who seek after God.

This, too, is how the Bible depicts the Christian life. Our home is with God, and yet our homeland lies ahead. In his faithful pilgrimage, Abraham was the prototype for our lives of faith. The book of Hebrews' great description of him is meant to serve as a model for us all: "By faith he went to live in the land of promise, as in a foreign land, living in tents with Isaac and Jacob, heirs with him of the same promise. For he was looking forward to the city that has foundations, whose designer and builder is God" (Heb. 11:9–10).

The psalmist's point is that pilgrim believers are blessed, and in this section he shows why. First, Psalm 84:6 says, "As they go through the Valley of Baca they make it a place of springs; the early rain also covers it with pools." *Baca* means "weeping." Perhaps the psalmist had in mind a particular place along the trail that was especially difficult for travelers; he knows that the pilgrimage involves many hardships, and this was especially such a place.

When I was in the army, I was once stationed at a post that was very hilly and rugged. The road we marched to our training sites included two exceptionally difficult climbs. The soldiers named the first *Misery*, which when ascended led to the base of the second hill, named *Agony*. How well I remember Misery and Agony Hills! The psalmist likewise thinks of a place he knows, called *Baca*, the valley of tears or sorrow.

The fact is that the Christian life includes such places—places of bitter trials and hard testing. The apostle Peter emphasized this hardship in his first epistle: "For a little while you may have had to suffer grief in all kinds of trials. These have come so that the proven genuineness of your faith—of greater worth than gold, which perishes even though refined by fire—may result in praise, glory and honor when Jesus Christ is revealed" (1 Peter 1:6–7 NIV). God employs trials to test and to grow our faith.

The writer of Psalm 84 speaks similarly. He says that when those who seek God pass through the vale of tears, "they make it a place of springs" (v. 6). Notice that it is the pilgrims who cause this transformation through the strength they receive from God. "*They* make it a place of springs"—this points to the redemptive influence that Christians bring to the sorrows of this world because of our relationship with God.

Susan Hunt tells of a friend named Ruth who was converted to Christianity and soon revealed an intense desire to know God more intimately, for which she fervently prayed. Not long afterward, she was diagnosed with an aggressive form of Parkinson's disease. She acknowledged that this was a legitimate way for God to have answered her prayer. She explained, "This is not easy, . . . but God's Word holds me together in His hand. Now I know as a fact the truth of 2 Corinthians 12:9: 'My grace is sufficient for you, for my power is made perfect in weakness.'" At this point Ruth paused, and then added, "I suspect I will know this even more in the months to come." Over those months, as Ruth progressed from a cane to a walker, to a wheelchair, and finally to the bed on which she died, she gave constant testimony to a growing knowledge of God that made her Valley of Baca a place of springs. She found that God was faithful, in sending, as the psalmist writes, autumn rains that covered her with pools of blessing and comfort.[5]

Elizabeth Prentiss was another woman who experienced redemptive transformation in sorrow. In her case, her trials made her newly sensitive to the needs of others. In light of her ill health, her chronic insomnia, and the death of a child, her husband wrote: "Her faith never failed; she glorified God in the midst of it all; she thanked her Lord and Master for 'taking her in hand' . . . . What is especially noteworthy, her own suffering, instead of paralyzing, . . . active sympathy with the sorrows and trials of others, had just the contrary effect."[6] Out of her own tears came springs of mercy for others. To another woman who lost a child, Prentiss wrote, "My dear friend, don't let this great tragedy of sorrow fail to do everything for you. . . . The intent of sorrow is to toss us onto God's promises."[7]

5. Quoted in Susan Hunt, *The True Woman* (Wheaton, IL: Crossway, 1997), 88.
6. Quoted in Hunt, *True Woman*, 92.
7. Quoted in Hunt, *True Woman*, 92–93.

"Blessed are those . . . in whose heart are the highways to Zion," writes the psalmist (Ps. 84:5). "As they go through the Valley of Baca they make it a place of springs" (v. 6). This does not trivialize our trials and sorrows. Rather, it explains why only the pilgrim heart finds such blessing in a world like ours. It is not those who trudge along miserably who are blessed, but those who have the pilgrim spirit, who have the highway not merely under their feet but also within their hearts, whose passion is to press forward in the knowledge of God, to gain a greater possession of heavenly things, drawing nearer to a vision of God's shining city. This desire for God transforms sorrows into blessing, because in our sorrows God makes his love wonderful.

Psalm 84:7 contains a second reason why the pilgrim heart is blessed: "They go from strength to strength; each one appears before God in Zion." I want to apply this especially to the weary Christian, burdened by sins, who looks on the life of faith as a long and frustrating journey. You feel in the grips of sin and are discouraged by your weakness. If all depends on your strength, then I agree that the pilgrimage is without hope. But the psalmist says to God, "Blessed are those whose strength is in you" (v. 5). Therefore, you will be blessed if you undertake God's journey of faith. Why? Because your strength is not in you but in God, and as you trust in his promises and look to his Word, as you fix your eyes on the cross that says he loves you and has removed the barrier of your sin, you will "go from strength to strength" (v. 7), until at last you, like so many before you, will appear in God's heavenly courts. If you have a pilgrim heart, you will not only seek God, but also look to him to provide all that you need, to forgive you of sin, supply you with strength, lift you when you fall, and make perfect his power in your weakness. "Blessed are those whose strength is in you, in whose heart are the highways to Zion" (v. 5).

Lessons along the Way of Faith

Psalm 84 expresses a longing for God, because those who dwell in him and seek him with a pilgrim's heart are blessed. The third section concludes the psalm with a final beatitude that sums up the whole: "O LORD of hosts, blessed is the one who trusts in you!" (Ps. 84:12).

In the verses of this last section, the psalmist relates lessons he has learned along the pathway of faith. He begins with the importance of prayer: "O LORD God of hosts, hear my prayer; give ear, O God of Jacob!" (Ps. 84:8). By example, he shows that the pilgrim heart is strengthened by prayer, since those who seek God often turn their souls to him. They realize that God is near, that he looks on his children and is always ready to hear, answer, and help.

This specific prayer probably throws light on the psalmist's circumstances. He asks God to "look on the face of your anointed" (Ps. 84:9). Many scholars say that this is a reference to the king, perhaps even to David, with whom the Levite was in exile. This especially makes sense because the psalmist describes him as "our shield" (v. 9). This tells us that the exiled Levite was not alone. He was in company with the Lord's anointed, the king, to whom great promises were made by God.

The word *anointed* in Hebrew is *Messiah*; reading this, the Christian cannot help but think of Jesus Christ. Just as the psalmist drew comfort from David's company and was made sure of God's favor, so we look to the fellowship of Jesus Christ, in whose company we walk as his disciples. We pray confidently in his name: "Behold our shield, O God; look on the face of your anointed!" (Ps. 84:9). We know that whatever our circumstances, we are not alone. Jesus declares, "I will never leave you nor forsake you" (Heb. 13:5). Christ is the guarantee of God's covenant favor to us and the Good Shepherd of his flock.

Psalm 84:8–9 shows that faithful pilgrims have access to God in prayer and walk in company with God's Anointed, our Shield and King. Verse 10 adds a third lesson: "For a day in your courts is better than a thousand elsewhere. I would rather be a doorkeeper in the house of my God than dwell in the tents of wickedness." The psalmist has learned that the smallest godly honor is better than the greatest worldly acclaim; the least holy blessing is far sweeter than the best that can be found in the pleasures of unbelief and sin.

How slow we are to learn this lesson! Have you learned it? Or are you still ashamed of being identified with Christ and his people for fear that you will lose the esteem of the world? What a shame it is that the best of us know so little of the spirituality expressed in this psalm. We scarcely, if ever, rise to the heights of this psalmist's fervor: "How lovely is your dwelling place, O LORD of hosts! My soul longs, yes, faints for the courts of the LORD; my heart and flesh sing for joy to the living God" (Ps. 84:1–2).

This pure expression of devotion makes us realize what sin is really about. Sin is not just breaking a few rules. Sin is our failure to glory in God as the psalmist did. The world knows nothing of this adoration and gives God no glory. This is its great sin and condemnation. People say that they are "pretty good people," when in fact they are ingrates and rebels. Christians are not much better. Like the Pharisees, we clean up our act a little bit, we come to church, we do a few good deeds, and we think we have attained to God's standard. Yet all the while, our hearts never approach this kind of love for God. At a profound level, this is our sin—that we do not render to God the glory he deserves; we do not give him the first place in our lives. We do not pant for the living God, but more greatly esteem the pleasures and treasures of this dying world. How great, then, is our constant need of God's forgiving mercy—no less now than when we first believed—and also of the Spirit's regenerating power. May God grant that we, like the psalmist, might learn this lesson, esteeming one day in God's courts better than a thousand in the palaces of this wicked world.

This is the very grace that God provides to those who seek it. Psalm 84:11 adds, "For the Lord God is a sun and shield; the Lord bestows favor and honor. No good thing does he withhold from those who walk uprightly." This is the only time in the Bible that God is compared to the sun, no doubt because of the idea of pilgrimage. Knowing God is like walking under shining skies, a clear sun lighting your way and warming your heart. He is a sun and shield, providing blessing and protection.

Furthermore, "the Lord bestows favor and honor" (Ps. 84:11). This is, literally, "grace and glory." These are things that the world can never offer, blessings to which the worldly man never dares even to aspire. Nothing we do could ever earn it, but God gives grace to his pilgrim people. The forgiveness we need, the love for which we long, the strength without which we would fail—God gives grace to those who trust in him. What is more, he gives glory. While worldly men and women sell themselves for entertainment, or tawdry measures of success, riches, power, or fame—all of which are fleeting at best and often enslaving—God gives glory to those who seek him. In this life, he gives the increasing glory of a Christlike character; in the life to come, he will grant the ultimate glory, when we will see him face to face.

"No good thing does he withhold from those who walk uprightly" (Ps. 84:11). Yes, the Lord withholds many things, but none that are ultimately for our good. So it is for all who trust him with integrity and sincerity, with a faith that translates into action. If we earnestly seek to find our home in God, and though with faltering step are truly walking out from this world and into the next, we will receive the wise and loving care of Almighty God. Nothing that is for our good will he withhold.

For these reasons, with all that he has learned, the psalmist says, "O Lord of hosts, blessed is the one who trusts in you!" (Ps. 84:12). Have you learned something of this? If you put into practice such faith as you have, making your home in God and following him in the strength he gives, you, too, will learn and grow in this confident reliance on God.

"I Am the Way"

In the last meeting before his arrest and crucifixion, Jesus Christ spoke to his disciples about the life of pilgrimage. He told them that he was going ahead of them to God's house, to prepare a home for them if they would follow. When Thomas, already doubting, asked how they could know the way, Jesus replied, "I am the way, and the truth, and the life. No one comes to the Father except through me" (John 14:5–6).

In these words is found the answer to every question raised by Psalm 84: "I am the way." We have said that the only home suitable for the human soul is found in God. But how, you may ask, do I know God? How do I find him? How do I gain his acceptance? The answer is found in Jesus Christ. He is the Way. It is Jesus who reveals God to the world. It is Jesus whose blood takes away our sin and his righteousness that clothes us to stand in God's holy presence. It is Jesus who presents us as his people to make our home in the heavenly courts of God.

The same is true about the Christian life as a present pilgrimage. Jesus is the Way. We enter at his cross and finish in his resurrection. As his disciples and sheep, we can be sure of God's protection and help. The writer of Hebrews thus exhorts, "Let us run with endurance the race that is set before us, looking to Jesus, the founder and perfecter of our faith" (Heb. 12:1–2).

It is because of Jesus that those who trust in God are blessed. We find in him everything we need, but especially, as Psalm 84:11 says, he bestows "grace and glory" (KJV). This is our present—grace from God through the cross. And this is our future destiny in Christ—we will have glory through his resurrection. John teaches in his first epistle, "When he appears we shall be like him, because we shall see him as he is" (1 John 3:2).

Do you want to love God as this psalmist did? Jesus Christ is the Way. We love him because he first loved us. Our present with him is grace. He has removed the barrier of our sin so that we feel God's warmth like the sun and know his favor like yellow rays of light. Our future with him is glory. For all his troubles, Job praised God because of Christ. "I know that my Redeemer lives," he cried, "and at the last he will stand upon the earth. And after my skin has been thus destroyed, yet in my flesh I shall see God, whom I shall see for myself, and my eyes shall behold, and not another. My heart faints within me!" (Job 19:25–27).

If this does not make you long for God, then nothing ever will. But if grace truly is your present and glory is your future, because of Christ, and if you believe this as God's true and certain Word, then it will grow in your soul until your heart and your flesh cry out for God. From strength to strength, God's people advance toward his city. And as we draw close, as the vision grows brighter, our hearts, too, like that of this psalmist, are trained by God to exclaim, "How lovely is your dwelling place, O LORD of hosts! . . . Blessed is the one who trusts in you!" (Ps. 84:1, 12).

14

A Prayer for Renewal

Psalm 85

Restore us again, O God of our salvation, and put away your indignation toward us! (Ps. 85:4)

One of the high points of biblical spirituality occurs in the prayer of repentance by King David after his sin of adultery with Bathsheba. In Psalm 51, David prayed not only to be forgiven but also for spiritual revival and restoration:

> Create in me a clean heart, O God,
> and renew a right spirit within me.
> Cast me not away from your presence,
> and take not your Holy Spirit from me.
> Restore to me the joy of your salvation,
> and uphold me with a willing spirit. (Ps. 51:10–12)

This same longing is expressed in Psalm 85, with a desire for the entire nation's renewal. We are not told the occasion, but the evidence fits the years after God's people returned to Jerusalem from the Babylonian exile, which is at least an ideal illustration of the psalm's purpose.

The Jews first returned to their holy city in response to the decree of

Cyrus in 538 B.C. Soon after, the foundation of a new temple was laid, but work bogged down and the people became discouraged. The city was in ruins, while the people were vulnerable and insecure. The book of Haggai rebukes them for withholding their tithes, which resulted in poor harvests from the Lord. The prophet Zechariah was given visions of success to encourage them, and in the years after 520 B.C. the temple was completed. After this, they sought to rebuild the city walls. This work also bogged down, until Nehemiah arrived in 445 B.C. with new resources. We can see why this period reminds us of Psalm 85. The nation had been forgiven, but not yet fully restored.

What Israel experienced in Psalm 85 is paralleled in the experience of believers today. H. C. Leupold writes that "we have a psalm before us in which a very hopeful situation failed, and the people were driven to prayer that God might, nevertheless, bring their hopes to pass."[1]

Remembering God's Grace

Psalm 85 is a prayer for renewal, leading upward in four steps from discouragement to rejoicing. Such a prayer needs confidence even to begin. In his opening verses, the psalmist encourages himself to hope for blessing by *remembering God's grace*. He begins: "Lord, you were favorable to your land; you restored the fortunes of Jacob" (Ps. 85:1). This is exactly what happened in the restoration of Jerusalem after God had returned his people from exile in Babylon.

The way to be encouraged about God's grace in the future is to remember how gracious he has been in the past. The restoration of Jerusalem was a notable instance of God's grace for his people. Psalm 85:1 explains why the people were back in their city: the Lord had shown favor. The grace or favor of God is the source of all of salvation's blessings, and when we remember how gracious God has been in the past, we are emboldened in prayer to seek God's grace for present and future needs. John Calvin writes: "Nothing contributes more effectually to encourage us to come to the throne of grace, than the remembrance of God's former benefits."[2]

Every Christian who is facing troubles may look back to his or her own

1. H. C. Leupold, *Exposition of the Psalms* (Columbus, OH: Wartburg Press, 1959), 610.
2. John Calvin, *Calvin's Commentaries*, 23 vols. (1848; repr., Grand Rapids: Baker, 2009), 5:368.

conversion and be encouraged by God's grace. Paul reasoned that "he who began a good work in you will bring it to completion at the day of Jesus Christ" (Phil. 1:6). You may look further back to the cross of Christ, where God graciously gave his Son to pay the penalty for your sins. Romans 8:32 argues that God's past gift of his Son ensures that he will go on to give whatever we need to be saved: "He who did not spare his own Son but gave him up for us all, how will he not also with him graciously give us all things?"

Speaking of the cross of Christ, Psalm 85 specifically remembers God's favor in forgiving Israel's sins: "You forgave the iniquity of your people" (Ps. 85:2). This reminds us that those who realize their need of God's help must first deal with the problem of their sins. It is only those who are first forgiven and justified through faith in Christ who go on to receive God's merciful care. Yet how few people value the grace of forgiveness! Even believers often complain against God, forgetting the amazing grace of his forgiving us through the death of his Son. Unbelievers, not realizing the peril of God's judgment, may not even realize their need to be forgiven. James Boice writes: "The greatest of all mercies that we can receive from God is forgiveness of sins, and it is from this foundation that all other covenanted mercies flow."[3]

Hebrew poetry tends to make a statement and then amplify or clarify it in a parallel line. Here, God's way of forgiveness is helpfully explained: "you covered all their sin" (Ps. 85:2). This makes two great statements about forgiveness. The first is that God forgives our sins by covering them. This refers to the biblical doctrine of the atonement, whereby God covers our sins through the blood of a sacrifice. Old Testament priests sprinkled the blood of bulls and goats on the people to cover their sin. But the true atonement appeared when John the Baptist spied Jesus and cried: "Behold, the Lamb of God, who takes away the sin of the world!" (John 1:29).

Our sins, too, are covered by the spotless righteousness attained for us by Jesus in his own perfect obedience to God's law. Around the time when Psalm 85 was likely written, Zechariah saw a vision of Joshua the high priest, who was polluted by Israel's sins. The preincarnate Christ appeared and declared, "Behold, I have taken your iniquity away from you, and I will clothe you with pure vestments" (Zech. 3:4). The priest's filthy clothes were removed, and clean, righteous garments were given him to wear. David Dickson explains what God does to cover our sins: "The way of God's

3. James Montgomery Boice, *Psalms*, 3 vols. (Grand Rapids: Baker, 1996), 2:696.

forgiving sins is . . . covering them with the imputation of the righteousness of the Redeemer."[4]

The second great point made in Psalm 85:2 pertains to how many of our sins are forgiven when we trust in Jesus: "you covered all their sin." Charles Spurgeon writes: "All of it, every spot, and wrinkle, the veil of love has covered all. Sin has been divinely put out of sight."[5] This teaching is confirmed by 1 John 1:7 in the New Testament: "the blood of Jesus [God's] Son cleanses us from all sin."

Psalm 85:2 involves two theological terms that Christians should know: *atonement*, which is the covering of sin by the blood of Christ, and *imputation*, the clothing of believers with the righteousness of Christ. Verse 3 leads us to consider another essential term, *propitiation*: "You withdrew all your wrath; you turned from your hot anger." Jesus died for us not only to cover our sin but also to turn aside God's wrath. Since God's nature is love (1 John 4:7), once the offense of our sin is removed, so also is the entirety of God's anger toward us. Romans 8:1 assures us, "There is now no condemnation for those who are in Christ Jesus." There is nothing for anyone to dread in God once we have been forgiven of our sins through faith in Christ.

Notice that the psalmist gives all the glory to God for restoring Jerusalem. God is the subject of each sentence in Psalm 85:1–3, and we likewise owe the whole of our forgiveness to the grace of God alone. We have no reason to boast in ourselves as we look back on past salvation blessings, but we have every reason to boast in and praise God as we remember his prior grace.

Praying for God's Reviving

Having seen God's grace in forgiving Israel's sin, the psalmist moves to the second stage of Psalm 85, having been made bold in *praying for God's reviving*. This prayer, which is the heart of Psalm 85, occurs in verses 4–7. It begins: "Restore us again, O God of our salvation, and put away your indignation toward us!" (Ps. 85:4).

The psalmist's idea of restoration is that of turning back from sin and to God. The verb used in Psalm 85:4 for "restore" is in fact the primary Hebrew word for "turning" in repentance (*shuv*). The psalmist realized that even

4. David Dickson, *A Commentary on the Psalms* (1653; repr., Edinburgh: Banner of Truth, 1995), 2:77.

5. Charles Haddon Spurgeon, *The Treasury of David*, 3 vols. (Peabody, MA: Hendrickson, n.d.), 2a:450.

after the Israelites had returned to their land, they still needed to repent of their sins. Thus, the prophet Haggai rebuked them for withholding tithes, informing them that poor harvests were God's chastisement (Hag. 1:9–10). When Nehemiah came to Jerusalem, he found the people cruelly oppressing their poor neighbors and intermarrying with pagan neighbors, which had led prior generations into idolatry (Neh. 5:1–13; 13:23–27). These sins had to be repented of if the people were to enjoy God's blessing. The same need for repentance is true in the life of every Christian. Sinclair Ferguson explains: "Faith cannot exist where there is no repentance. . . . They are two sides of the same coin of belonging to Jesus."[6] The psalmist thus prays for God to turn the people, so that God's indignation would be put away (Ps. 85:4).

Notice, however, that the power to turn from sin must come from God; verse 4 marks our turning as an act of God. Repentance restores us to God from our sins by the grace of God at work within us. Therefore, just as the key to expelling darkness is to turn on a light, the key to repentance is to appeal to God's grace through Jesus Christ. Paul stated this truth in Titus 2:11–12: "the grace of God has appeared, bringing salvation for all people, training us to renounce ungodliness and worldly passions, and to live self-controlled, upright, and godly lives in the present age." Far from God's grace relieving Christians of the need to turn from sin, it supplies the power and instruction we need to become holy.

Once we realize that God provides us with the power to repent and be restored from the reign of sin, we will gladly pray to him just as the psalmist does. In Psalm 85:5, the psalmist seems almost frustrated with God for the people's failure to repent fully and thus to be released from chastisement: "Will you be angry with us forever? Will you prolong your anger to all generations?" The poet will not be satisfied until God has restored the people not merely geographically by returning them to Jerusalem but also spiritually by restoring them to faithfulness.

Moreover, the faithfulness that the psalmist desires does not merely involve changed behavior; he further seeks for God to renew the people inwardly: "Will you not revive us again, that your people may rejoice in you?" (Ps. 85:6). This was the high ground of David's prayer in Psalm 51: "Create in me a clean heart, O God, and renew a right spirit within me" (v. 10). Do you realize that such spiritual transformation is possible in your

6. Sinclair B. Ferguson, *The Grace of Repentance* (Wheaton, IL: Crossway, 2000), 17.

own life? It is possible for you not only to be outwardly led away from wrong and harmful behavior, but actually to have your mind and heart renewed in the purity of Christ. This is our calling in Christ, Paul said, "to be renewed in the spirit of your minds, and to put on the new self, created after the likeness of God in true righteousness and holiness" (Eph. 4:23–24).

Noting the primarily corporate nature of Psalm 85's appeal, Christians should pray as well for the revival of the church. Church history shows many instances when God poured out the Spirit in abundance and brought great masses of people to saving faith. But such revivals always begin in the church. Boice points out that revivals all arise from the bold preaching of God's Word. The first result of clear Bible teaching is that many people in the church realize that they are not saved. Then, when hearts are awakened to the peril of sin, many are saved through the clear preaching of the gospel. Together with their faith, they repent of their sins and the world takes notice of the church in a new way, so that even more people give an ear to God's Word, and by the power of God's Spirit they believe and are saved.[7]

An example of the revival for which we ought to pray occurred in Ulster, starting in 1856. An English woman named Mrs. Colville began visiting neighbors to speak of the new life that Jesus gives. After a few months, she left Ireland, thinking her witness had made no impact. Unknown to her, however, she had made a profound impression on James McQuilkin, a rough individual from a nearby town who heard her in a friend's home. After his conversion, McQuilkin began meeting for prayer with some new Christian friends, asking the Lord to bring revival to their churches and towns. Their prayer group grew, and more and more people came to faith in answer to their pleas to the Lord. Encouraged by these signs, a local pastor held a gathering where new believers could tell of their conversions. In March 1859, a large gathering was held at First Presbyterian Church of Ahoghill, after which believers spread out into the streets, preaching to masses of people. These and further events were later called the 1859 Ulster Revival, during which thousands of people came to faith in Jesus. It all began with a few faithful Christians who prayed and preached in the spirit of Psalm 85:6: "Will you not revive us again, that your people may rejoice in you?"[8]

7. Boice, *Psalms*, 2:698.

8. Gareth Burke, "1859—The Year of Grace," *Evangelical Presbyterian Magazine*, January–February 2009, 5–7.

One reason to desire and pray earnestly for spiritual renewal is given in Psalm 85:6: "that your people may rejoice in you." Here is the secret that so many people—even Christians—do not know about growing in sanctification. The secret is that holiness produces happiness in the Lord. This happiness comes from knowing more closely the love of God and drinking more deeply from the wells of his salvation. Thus, in verse 7 the psalmist prays: "Show us your steadfast love, O Lord, and grant us your salvation." The closer we get to the Lord in prayer and the more conformed we are to his holy character, the less we will complain and the more we will rejoice. Moreover, note that the people will "rejoice in you" (v. 6). The more we realize how deeply God loves us, the more our rejoicing will focus not on the gifts that he gives but on the Giver himself in his steadfast love and mercy. So if we want to experience greater happiness, the revival prayer of Psalm 85 presents an ideal starting place.

Waiting for God's Blessing

The psalmist has prayed for a restoration that involves repentance and the reviving of the people's spirits. It does not seem, however, that God has yet granted his request. It will likewise often happen to us that we pray for God to enable us to repent of sin and to revive our spirits in godliness, yet God leaves us for a while to continue wrestling with our troubles. The third step in our renewal therefore involves *waiting for God's blessing*. The psalmist writes: "Let me hear what God the Lord will speak" (Ps. 85:8).

The prophet Habakkuk was famous for sitting in his watchtower to await the Lord's answer to his question. God had promised to destroy Israel by means of the evil Babylonian army. The prophet could not understand how a holy God could allow people who were even more wicked than the Israelites to destroy their city. He wrote: "I will take my stand at my watchpost and station myself on the tower, and look out to see what he will say to me, and what I will answer concerning my complaint" (Hab. 2:1). It did not take long for God to come with a revelation explaining his further plans of salvation, so that the prophet was able to be content. Thus, he concluded with words suited for all who wait upon God: "the Lord is in his holy temple; let all the earth keep silence before him" (v. 20).

Psalm 85:8–9 makes four brief points about waiting on the Lord. The first is that we must wait confidently: "for he will speak peace to his people, to his saints." Even though God's reviving grace had not yet come, the psalmist was confident that it would. If he could take this attitude, those who belong to Christ can be even more sure that the future holds words of peace and blessing from God. If we are able to say the opening words of Psalm 23 through faith in Jesus, "The Lord is my shepherd," we can also be sure to experience its end: "I shall dwell in the house of the Lord forever." As the psalmist waited confidently for God's blessing, so must we.

Second, those who are waiting for God to help them must be sure not to fall backward: "but let them not turn back to folly" (Ps. 85:8). If God has enabled you to turn from one sin, do not fall back into it while you are waiting for deliverance from another! Do not return to bad habits while you are waiting for new grace! Just as a doctor will often allow a period of healing between rounds of medicine, God will sometimes give time for his various mercies to settle in our lives. The best way, then, for us to accelerate his grace is to fully consolidate the grace he has already given.

Third, we wait for God's blessing, knowing that it is sure to come soon: "Surely his salvation is near to those who fear him" (Ps. 85:9). How often in the Bible the outward circumstance of God's people remained desperate when in fact his deliverance was about to arrive. All they had to do was to believe a little while longer. God is more ready to bless us than we are ready to be blessed. Thus, for example, when Moses asked to see God's glory, he heard these words: "The Lord, the Lord, a God merciful and gracious, slow to anger, and abounding in steadfast love and faithfulness" (Ex. 34:6). As Micah 7:18 declares, God "delights in steadfast love," so we can be sure that his help is near.

Fourth, while we wait for God's blessing, our hearts should be set on his glory: "that glory may dwell in our land" (Ps. 85:9). The psalmist desired Israel to be restored so that the Lord's worship would resume in Jerusalem from gladdened hearts. Our chief aim, even in our own blessing and spiritual revival, should be that God would have the praise that his grace deserves from our lives. While we are waiting for more grace, we should be motivated by the greater glory of God, and not simply by our own desire for peace and prosperity.

Embracing God's Promises

Psalm 85 shows that a prayer for restoration remembers God's grace, asks for God's reviving, and waits for God's blessing. The psalm concludes with verses *embracing God's promises* in faith.

In Psalm 85:10–11, the psalmist paints a picture of gospel blessings surrounding the believer. He sees steadfast love and faithfulness shaking hands, righteousness and peace kissing, truth springing up from the earth, and righteousness smiling down from heaven. Spurgeon points out how all these attributes find their full expression in the person and work of Christ: "In him, the attributes of God unite in glad unanimity in the salvation of guilty men."[9] Calvin sees these verses as celebrating the reign of grace in the kingdom of Christ, showing "how bountifully God deals with his Church, after he is reconciled to her."[10]

The first couplet states that "Steadfast love and faithfulness meet" (Ps. 85:10). Or, as the more familiar King James Version puts it, with equal accuracy: "Mercy and truth are met together." This scene is heightened in the parallel line: "righteousness and peace kiss each other" (v. 10). The point in both lines is that attributes of God that had been at odds in our salvation are now brought together in peace. George Horne writes:

> These four divine attributes parted at the fall of Adam, and met again at the birth of Christ. Mercy was ever inclined to save man, and Peace could not be his enemy; but Truth exacted the performance of God's threat—"The soul that sinneth it shall die"—and Righteousness could not but give to every one his due.[11]

It is easy to see why this scene is understood as pointing forward to Christ, for it is only in him that this situation takes place in God's Word. Of all the world's religions, only Christianity sees God as showing mercy to sinners without violating his truth, and God's righteousness as entering into holy union with his peace toward transgressors. Horne states that only the Christian gospel "can satisfy the demands of all these claimants, and restore a union between them; which can show how God's word can be true, and his work just, and the sinner, notwithstanding, find mercy and obtain peace."[12]

We should note carefully where this progression begins, starting with the Hebrew noun *hesed*, which is translated as either "mercy" or "steadfast

9. Spurgeon, *Treasury of David*, 2a:453.

10. Calvin, *Commentaries*, 5:375.

11. George Horne, *Commentary on the Psalms* (1771; repr., Audubon, NJ: Old Paths Publications, 1997), 368–69.

12. Horne, *Psalms*, 369.

love." *Hesed* encompasses the covenant grace of God to save his people. This sovereign mercy, together with God's faithfulness to his promises, causes righteousness and peace to join at the cross of Jesus Christ. At Calvary, God fulfilled the demands of his justice down to the smallest detail as Jesus paid the penalty for all our sins; in this way, God's cause of peace triumphed for the salvation of sinners who believe. If we desire peace with God, we must first receive the righteousness offered by Christ at his cross, relying on the covenant mercy of God in fulfilling the gospel promises of Holy Scripture.

The second pair of attributes depicts the result of God's saving mercy in the church. First, "Faithfulness springs up from the ground," and then "righteousness looks down from the sky" (Ps. 85:11). This scene depicts what God does in the life of his people. God provides a harvest of truth to his people (the word translated as "faithfulness" more naturally means "truth"), and his righteousness shines down with divine favor on a people who are justified through faith in Christ. For this reason, Christians are to be faithful people who grow strong by God's truth. We remember Jesus' defiant words to Satan: "Man shall not live by bread alone, but by every word that comes from the mouth of God" (Matt. 4:4). Meanwhile, our hearts flourish in knowing that our sins are forgiven and that we stand acceptable in God's sight through the righteousness of Christ. Calvin writes that "righteousness is represented as looking down from heaven, because it is the free gift of God, and not acquired by the merit of works; and that it comes from heaven, because it is not to be found among men."[13]

In light of the gospel reconciliation depicted in Psalm 85:10–11, verse 12 then speaks of earthly blessings flowing from God: "Yes, the Lord will give what is good, and our land will yield its increase" (Ps. 85:12). Notice that earthly goods flow from God *after* spiritual life has been restored; God's concern for our spiritual revival always takes precedence over merely outward or earthly blessings.

Finally, the psalm concludes, "Righteousness will go before him and make his footsteps a way" (Ps. 85:13). This statement concludes the emphasis of this psalm when it comes to our restoration and renewal. The psalmist's chief concern is God's righteousness and our justification. Until sins are addressed, other matters must wait. The path of blessing is ever that which

13. Calvin, *Commentaries*, 5:376.

begins with justification through faith and then proceeds by obedience to God's law. Having been made right with God, and walking according to his Word, we may expect an abundance of every kind of blessing from the hand of a kind and lovely Redeemer, together with many trials for our good. In Christ we have all things—past forgiveness, present grace, and future glory—which is why the Old Testament provides so many signposts all pointing to him. Isaiah foretold his coming as the reign of peace: "Prepare the way of the Lord; make his paths straight" (Matt. 3:3).

Oliver Cromwell, the Lord Protector of England after its civil war, once spoke on Psalm 85 before Parliament. He said, "Yesterday I did read a psalm, which truly may not unbecome both me to tell you of and you to observe. It is the eighty-fifth Psalm; it is very instructive and significant; and though I do but a little touch upon it, I desire your perusal and pleasure."[14] Cromwell then expounded from the psalm an ideal society where the virtues of God's grace would shake hands and kiss. Historians would find this aspiration to be ironic, since Cromwell's reign is largely known for harshness and tyranny. The hopes expressed by the psalm find their fulfillment only in the kingdom of Jesus Christ. Yet in our lives, in our homes, and in his church, we may earnestly aspire to this lovely harmony of blessings, looking forward to the day when Jesus returns and these blessings will come to life forever in full color and abounding grace.

A Pattern for Our Prayer

In applying Psalm 85, we should chiefly observe the psalmist's refusal to settle for a low spiritual plane or a partial restoration of Israel. Calvin Beisner writes: "Just so, the Christian must not be satisfied with a partial work of God's grace in his life. Not justification only, but sanctification also must be the goal of the Christian life. That is, no Christian should be satisfied merely to be delivered from the penalty of sin; we must press on in prayer until God has delivered us also from sin's power."[15]

Christians know that while perfection will never be achieved in this life, our destiny is to bear the image of Christ's glory (1 Cor. 15:49). With this in mind, we must press on in prayer and faith. Moreover, Psalm 85 urges

14. Quoted in Rowland E. Prothero, *The Psalms in Human Life* (New York: Dutton, 1904), 259.
15. E. Calvin Beisner, *Psalms of Promise*, 2nd ed. (Phillipsburg, NJ: P&R Publishing, 1994), 194.

us to pray with vigor for those who do not know Christ. They have not even started the progression of this psalm: they have not received God's grace, their sins remain unforgiven, and God's wrath is not withdrawn from their souls. How can we claim to love our neighbors if we do not pray for their salvation?

Psalm 85 also calls us to pray for the spiritual vitality of the church. We see some Christians falling prey to sin and others suffering persecution, so we must pray for God's grace to strengthen both the tempted and the oppressed in faith. We see ministries struggling to bear fruit and divisions rending the Christian community. We should pray for God's mercy to establish truth and God's righteousness to bring peace and harmony. Above all, Psalm 85 urges us to long for Christ to be exalted in the hearts of his people and through our witness to be embraced by sinners who are still in the world. Just as the psalm concludes with the harmony of grace in the joyful setting of Christ's kingdom, so also is Jesus alone the only hope for the world. "Come to me," he says, "all who labor and are heavy laden, and I will give you rest. Take my yoke upon you, and learn from me, for I am gentle and lowly in heart, and you will find rest for your souls" (Matt. 11:28–29).

15

Abounding in Love

Psalm 86

But you, O Lord, are a God merciful and gracious, slow to anger and abounding in steadfast love and faithfulness. (Ps. 86:15)

Some of the experiences that were most beneficial to my Christian growth involved spending time with more seasoned Christians in prayer. Once when I was in seminary, I participated in a day of prayer in which I was assigned to a prayer group consisting of four Korean women and me. They insisted on deferring to me, so I prayed first. We were praying for missionaries, so I mentioned some vague generalities about people I knew who were somewhere on the mission field. Having allowed me to go first, the Korean ladies commenced the real praying! They prayed with great specificity and a keen interest. They gave names and specific needs: one missionary had an eye infection and needed medicine; another was praying for the soul of a hardened opponent to the gospel, whom the women named in prayer. I realized that whereas I performed prayer, these women relied on prayer as absolutely necessary for spiritual success and even survival. I have never forgotten their prayers and have since tried to exhibit a similar seriousness and zeal in my petitions.

Another memorable prayer time occurred before a theological conference where I was speaking. One of the other speakers was an older Scotsman who was famous for preaching with great eloquence and power. As the speakers gathered for prayer, I began by asking God to bless what we were going to do. Then the Scottish minister began, and I realized that above all else he was worshiping a great God with reverence and awe in his heart. His praying was brokenhearted, humble, and filled with gravity. I learned from that experience that in prayer we really are in the presence of the God of glory, might, and amazing grace.

Not all of us have opportunities to pray with mighty saints, whether they are famous preachers or obscure missionaries. But we all have access to the prayers of the Bible, from which we should learn great things about God and prayer. Psalm 86 is an example of an instructive prayer from a great man of God. It is the only psalm specifically ascribed to King David in the third section of the Psalter (Pss. 73–89). Like so many of David's other prayers, this psalm pleads from a frightened and wearied soul afflicted with many troubles. It is a great prayer, however, in the firm grasp with which David lays hold of God's mercy, grace, and love. "To you, O Lord, do I lift up my soul," David prays, "For great is your steadfast love toward me" (Ps. 86:4, 13).

The Humble Approach of a Sinner

David begins this psalm in a way that reminds us that we should always approach God humbly, as sinners needing grace. Jesus emphasized this in his famous parable of the Pharisee and the tax collector. "Two men went up into the temple to pray," Jesus said, "one a Pharisee and the other a tax collector." The Pharisee stood tall before the Lord, boasting of his goodness. But the tax collector, who freely admitted his sin, "would not even lift up his eyes to heaven, but beat his breast, saying, 'God, be merciful to me, a sinner!'" Jesus concluded that the humble tax collector "went down to his house justified, rather than the other" (Luke 18:10–14).

We might think it appropriate for a wicked tax collector to come humbly before God, but Psalm 86 shows the spiritually eminent King David praying in the same manner. "Incline your ear, O Lord, and answer me," he begins, "for I am poor and needy" (Ps. 86:1). No doubt David felt his need in light of the trials he was facing; possibly Psalm 86 was penned during one of the many times when he was fleeing danger from King Saul, or facing some other mortal danger. But when we consider the greatness of God in his all-sufficiency, we realize that we are always poor and needy. Our precious faith is upheld only by the sovereign grace of God, so we should always approach God in the spirit that David models in this psalm.

The godly person not only realizes our humble position before the Creator but also sees our neediness as a cause for confidence in prayer. David approaches God as the provider for the poor and helper of those in need. The Lord proclaims in Psalm 12:5, "Because the poor are plundered, because the needy groan, I will now arise." Moreover, Isaiah 57:15 identifies humility as the key to God's comforting presence: "For thus says the One who is high and lifted up, who inhabits eternity, whose name is Holy: 'I dwell in the high and holy place, and also with him who is of a contrite and lowly spirit, to revive the spirit of the lowly, and to revive the heart of the contrite.'" In this spirit, David connects his own need with the Lord's love for the humble and poor.

It may seem, however, that David abandons his humility in Psalm 86:2, since he prays: "Preserve my life, for I am godly; save your servant, who trusts in you—you are my God." The question is how we should interpret the word translated by the English Standard Version as "godly." The King James Version renders it as "holy," and the New International Version takes it as "faithful to you." Can David apply such terms to himself without being guilty of pride? The answer is yes, since David is simply categorizing himself as a sincere "servant" of the Lord, who has been committed to his cause. It is obvious that David is not trusting his own godliness, since he says that he "trusts in you—you are my God." Today, David might pray, "I have trusted in Christ." George Horne writes: "The Christian only pleads in this expression, his relation to Christ, as being a member of Christ's body, the church."[1] Yet by naming ourselves as believers and servants of Christ, we gain a great confidence before God in prayer.

David further approaches God as a sinner seeking grace: "Be gracious to me, O Lord, for to you do I cry all the day" (Ps. 86:3). In the same way, we must always come to God, realizing his perfect holiness and our own unworthiness. This is why Jesus taught us to pray "Forgive us our debts" as part

1. George Horne, *Commentary on the Psalms* (1771; repr., Audubon, NJ: Old Paths Publications, 1997), 371.

of the Christian's standard prayer (Matt. 6:12). It ought to be our regular practice to confess our sins to God, and to call on his grace whenever we approach him. First John 1:9 promises: "If we confess our sins, he is faithful and just to forgive us our sins and to cleanse us from all unrighteousness." We approach God, seeking grace, looking to the cross of Christ where our sins were forgiven. Like David, who relates that he cried this "all the day," Christians must place our constant reliance on the grace made available to us as sinners through the blood of Jesus. We remember how often Jesus prayed on earth for God to save his sinful people. How much more confident can we be that our prayers will be answered when we consider how Jesus still prays for us as our High Priest in heaven, presenting the merits of his blood for our acceptance.

In the first stanza of Psalm 86, David prays to God, citing reasons within himself: he is poor and lowly, he is a believing servant, and he appeals to God's saving grace. Verse 4 adds the final appeal based on David's commitment to seek his help only from God: "Gladden the soul of your servant, for to you, O Lord, do I lift up my soul." When we are not merely mouthing the words of a prayer but actually lifting up our souls to God, seeking peace, comfort, and joy, we can be confident that God will answer with expressions of his mercy.

An Expression of Faith and Praise

In the opening stanza of Psalm 86, David approaches God with appeals based on his own attitude and condition. The word *for* appears in each verse, pointing to various reasons within David. The second stanza makes its appeal based on truths that David professes concerning God. Verses 5–10 contain three *for*-statements, each of them pertaining to God. In this way, having come humbly before God, David now expresses his faith in God so as to give him praise. Our prayers should likewise declare to God our grounds of confidence in him as we spend time simply adoring the greatness and mercy of our wonderful God. To do this, however, we must first know God. Philip Ryken writes:

> You must have a theology before you can have a prayer life. Knowing the character of God precedes having intimacy with him through prayer. Too

> many prayers are superficial in their grasp of the character of God. Instead, they ought to be saturated with the praise of his glorious attributes.[2]

In Psalm 86:5, David calls God's attributes to mind with a sweeping statement of his covenant faithfulness in salvation: "For you, O Lord, are good and forgiving, abounding in steadfast love to all who call upon you." Here, David gets straight to the chief reasons why believers can have confidence in prayer: because of God's goodness, his readiness to forgive, and his loving mercy to all who are in the covenant of his salvation. Here, the chief encouragement in prayer is knowing the character of God. David has come to know God through his Word and through his experience as a believer. The better he knows God, the more certain he is of God's willingness to help him in his need. What an incentive this is for us to study the attributes of God—his divine characteristics as they are revealed in Holy Scripture—and to walk with God through faith so as to know him better!

David praises God for being *good*. Creation itself reveals the goodness of God: we live in a world where rain falls and the sun shines so that living things grow. God is especially good to his people. He delivered Israel from bondage in Egypt and placed its tribes in the promised land. He has provided us with his Word so that we can know the goodness of his heart. All these good blessings motivate us in prayer and give us a reason to praise him.

God is also *forgiving*. Many people are good personally but indignant toward the bad they see in other people. But God's goodness advances into grace toward sinners. In the Old Testament, David could think of numerous occasions when God forgave the sins of his people. In the New Testament, we learn of God's gift of his own Son, so great is his resolve to forgive the sins of those who call on him. So whereas our sins would counsel us to keep a distance from God, knowing that God is good and forgiving should draw us near.

Moreover, God is *faithful*. Here, David uses the great covenant word *hesed*, which encompasses the loving-kindness and sovereign mercy of God for all who come to him by the way that he has offered. This reminds us that we may approach God only by the way that he has given, namely, through faith in his Son. Everyone has a duty to pray to God as Creator, and his goodness is evident to all as a motivation. But forgiveness of sin and covenant mercy

2. Philip Graham Ryken, *Courage to Stand: Jeremiah's Battle Plan for Pagan Times* (Wheaton, IL: Crossway, 1998), 164.

are found only in the Savior that he has provided. Those who wish to pray to God with confidence must therefore approach him through faith in Jesus. We should ask non-Christians in their need, "Have you prayed to God about your trouble?," reminding them that he is good. But when they ask, "How do I know that my prayers are blessed by God?," we must point them to faith in Jesus. We must tell them in love: "God has provided a Savior to reconcile sinners to himself, and you must pray in Jesus' name, which means trusting his atoning death to reconcile you to God."

We may remind ourselves and others that, as Psalm 86:5 says, God "abound[s] in steadfast love" toward those who approach him in Christ. John Calvin writes that "his mercy is so great, as to render it impossible for him to reject any who implore his aid."[3] Charles Spurgeon encourages us:

> God does not dispense his mercy from a slender store which perchance may be so impoverished as to give out altogether, but out of a cornucopia he pours forth the infinite riches of his mercy; his goodness flows forth in abounding streams towards those who pray and in adoring worship make mention of his name.[4]

Psalm 86:6–7 follows on this statement by specifically applying it to the matter of prayer: "Give ear, O Lord, to my prayer; listen to my plea for grace. In the day of my trouble I call upon you, for you answer me." Because of the grace that David has seen in God, he knows that God will listen to his plea, and when he needs God to save him, the Lord will answer and deliver. This is the confidence that comes to men and women who have practiced prayer and gained experience with the Lord. As the Psalms bear testimony, David had great experience in prayer because he was often in need. This shows the value of the trials that God permits us to endure. Only by having needed God and having experienced his answer to prayers, often in unanticipated ways, do we gain this confidence that he certainly hears us so that we can count on him to act.

These thoughts lead David to praise the Lord as the only true God, giving him further reasons to be confident: "There is none like you among the gods, O Lord, nor are there any works like yours" (Ps. 86:8). David realizes

3. John Calvin, *Calvin's Commentaries*, 23 vols. (1848; repr., Grand Rapids: Baker, 2009), 5:383.

4. Charles Haddon Spurgeon, *The Treasury of David*, 3 vols. (Peabody, MA: Hendrickson, n.d.), 2a:464–65.

the tragedy of the vast practice of idolatry in his time, when great masses of people worshiped the hideous gods of the Nile and the sensual idols of the East. Praying and making sacrifices to these idols left their adherents without a true God to hear and answer. In contrast, David is a recipient of the true God's revelation in his Word, as are readers of the Bible today. He writes, "Nor are there any works like yours" (v. 8). Only the true God is the Creator of all things and the Redeemer of his people. The great saving acts in the Bible such as Israel's exodus from Egypt have no corollary in the annals of idolatry, just as they have no parallel in the vain expectations of modern secular humanism.

Moreover, David notes that not only *should* the nations worship Israel's God, but the day is coming when they all *will*: "All the nations you have made shall come and worship before you, O Lord, and shall glorify your name" (Ps. 86:9). This is a remarkable anticipation of the coming Messiah, whose gospel will spread throughout the world and whose return will cause every knee to bow and every tongue to "confess that Jesus Christ is Lord, to the glory of God the Father" (Phil. 2:10–11). The Old Testament Jews did not always realize that God would use their witness to bring Gentiles from all over the world to salvation. David not only knew this but praised God for it and made it a source of confidence in his prayers. As those who have learned of Jesus' coming in the Bible and experienced salvation through the zealous witness of his church, Christians today should be especially keen to take up David's spirit in bold petitions for the missionary advance of the gospel into every tribe, tongue, and people.

Today we see once-Christian nations turning back to idolatry and pagan evil, yet Christians know that this is not because of some deficiency in our God. Rather, we look to the Bible and see that in the end the people of Christ will gather from every land and stand victorious. John saw in Revelation 7:9–10 "a great multitude that no one could number, from every nation, from all tribes and peoples and languages, standing before the throne and before the Lamb, . . . crying out with a loud voice, 'Salvation belongs to our God who sits on the throne, and to the Lamb!'" The God who has ordained victory at the end of history is sure to act within history to preserve the life and witness of these same beloved people.

Psalm 86:5–7 emphasized that God is *willing* to save his people, being good, forgiving, and abounding in love. But verses 8–10 declare that God is also *able* to save his people. Verse 10 rejoices: "For you are great and do wondrous things; you alone are God." The God who could part the Red Sea for Israel to pass through, who could stop the sun in the sky to permit Joshua to pursue the Canaanites, and who sent his own Son to be born of a virgin womb and die for our sins on the cross is able to meet any earthly or spiritual need we might face. Seeing this glorious combination of goodness and greatness, of willingness and ability to save, strengthens the faith of God's people in prayer. John Calvin notes: "The contemplation of God's glory in his works is the true way of acquiring genuine godliness."[5]

An Earnest and Godly Plea

In a sense, Psalm 86:1–10 is preparatory for David's petition, which begins in verse 11. We can see by his first request that David's humble approach and praise for God's attributes have not been wasted: his humility and adoration have shaped the priorities of what he requests from God. We can imagine that when David began his prayer, he was consumed with fear of his enemies. Now, however, he is animated by dread of his own sins and by a longing to be conformed to God's will: "Teach me your way, O Lord, that I may walk in your truth" (Ps. 86:11).

We see this same priority on personal godliness in Jesus' teaching on prayer. Jesus instructed the disciples to pray to God as Father, to pray for God's name to be kept holy, and then to pray, "Your kingdom come, your will be done, on earth as it is in heaven" (Matt. 6:10). David has the same priority, knowing that his true and great need is to honor God in a holy life. Moreover, David is aware that he can lead a godly life only as God goes before him in his Word: "that I may walk in your truth" (Ps. 86:11). Now that he remembers the glory and the saving power of God, David is no longer so concerned by his relationship to enemies in the world but sees his fearful relationship to God as more significant. "Teach me your way, O Lord," he prays (v. 11). And David would have gladly continued to sing the hymn that takes up this refrain:

> Teach me thy way, O Lord; teach me thy way!
> Thy guiding grace afford; teach me thy way!

5. Calvin, *Commentaries*, 5:386.

Help me to walk aright, more by faith, less by sight;
Lead me with heav'nly light; teach me thy way![6]

The more conscious we are of the goodness and greatness of our God, the more this hymn will reflect our desires as well.

The second half of Psalm 86:11 makes an instructive statement: "unite my heart to fear your name." David is no longer as concerned about divisions in the land as he is about his own divided heart. He wants his whole heart to trust the Lord's promises and do the Lord's will. Thus, he prays for a single-minded purpose in giving reverence to God. The apostle James warns of the man who doubts God's Word and "is like a wave of the sea that is driven and tossed by the wind . . . ; he is a double-minded man, unstable in all his ways" (James 1:6, 8). James notes the deadly effects of such a heart when it comes to prayer: "For that person must not suppose that he will receive anything from the Lord" (v. 7). Similarly, Moses urged a united heart when he pronounced the great creed of ancient Israel: "Hear, O Israel: The Lord our God, the Lord is one. You shall love the Lord your God with all your heart and with all your soul and with all your might" (Deut. 6:4–5). Jesus urged this same God-centered priority when he taught: "seek first the kingdom of God and his righteousness, and all these things will be added to you" (Matt. 6:33). Having humbled himself before God and catalogued God's goodness and greatness, David makes the united heart praised by the prophets, by the apostles, and by our Lord Jesus his chief request in prayer.

It is inevitable that such a God-centered prayer would immediately add a petition for God to be glorified: "I give thanks to you, O Lord my God, with my whole heart, and I will glorify your name forever" (Ps. 86:12). David desires God's glory in light of God's salvation blessings to him: "For great is your steadfast love toward me; you have delivered my soul from the depths of Sheol" (v. 13). Israel's King shows us that the way to have a heart that desires to glorify God is to remember his grace in saving our souls.

On August 20, 1608, the French philologist Isaac Casaubon was headed to his Huguenot church with his wife. As their boat made its way down the River Seine, the Christian couple was singing the Psalms. Suddenly a barge struck them, casting his wife overboard. Plunging into the river, Casaubon saved her, and they later made their way to church. Once there, the congre-

6. B. Mansell Ramsey, "Teach Me Thy Way, O Lord" (1919).

gation began to sing, and the great scholar reached into his pocket for his Psalter, which had been his wife's present to him on their wedding day, only to discover that it had fallen out into the river. Casaubon stood there grieving his lost treasure while the congregation began to sing Psalm 86. He recovered only when he heard the congregation sing verse 13: "For great is your steadfast love toward me; you have delivered my soul from the depths of Sheol." Casaubon realized that after God had saved him from hell by the blood of Jesus Christ, he no longer had any reason to complain about any trial or loss suffered during this life. He had been delivered from the depths of hell—so, wet or dry, with or without his precious psalm book, he wanted to give praise to God.[7]

Only in verse 14 of Psalm 86 does David finally get around to the original prayer with which he seems to have begun: "O God, insolent men have risen up against me; a band of ruthless men seeks my life, and they do not set you before them." Notice that even here, David is outraged not merely over the danger that his enemies pose to his life but also over their ruthless nature and especially that they do not give God the honor that he is due. David is therefore bold to seek God's intervention: "Turn to me and be gracious to me; give your strength to your servant, and save the son of your maidservant" (v. 16). Here David mentions not only his own need as a servant of God but also God's care for his believing mother, who was also a faithful follower of the Lord. David is concerned at her grief if he is allowed to fall to vicious men. How confident he is, then, of God's intervening care, given the various interests that God has taken in his life.

The psalm ends with David's seeking a sign from the Lord, some encouragement to assure him that God has heard and his help is near: "Show me a sign of your favor, that those who hate me may see and be put to shame because you, Lord, have helped me and comforted me" (Ps. 86:17). When praying with distressed believers, I often pray for God to act in even a small way to encourage their wavering faith with assurances of his care. Christians have, of course, already received the greatest sign and assurance of favor possible, in God's gift of his Son to bear our sins on the cross. Horne writes: "On this sign the Christian looks with joy, as the great proof that God has 'helped him and comforted him.'"[8] In light of Christ's saving work, we know

7. Rowland E. Prothero, *The Psalms in Human Life* (New York: Dutton, 1904), 187.
8. Horne, *Psalms*, 376.

that our unconverted enemies will be brought to shame if they remain hardened when Christ returns.

The Great Issue in Prayer

I have mentioned the benefit of praying in person with eminent and experienced believers, and also the value of studying this prayer of David as a model for our own intercession. The psalmist provides us with good advice in coming humbly before God as sinners seeking grace and then in giving praise to God for his goodness and glory. We see the impact that this preparation has had on his petitions. By reflecting on what he knows about God's mercy, faithfulness, and grace, David has lifted himself up from a low spiritual state and now prays with power and great effect.

Still, the greatest lesson we see from David in this psalm, and the greatest lesson I have gained from praying with godly believers in person, is the awareness that prayer is a covenant meeting of God's people with their gracious and glorious Redeemer. If nothing else happens in prayer and if nothing else results from prayer, something of the greatest significance has occurred when we simply set our hearts before the Lord adoringly to contemplate his glory. We see the true and great issue of David's prayer in the statement of Psalm 86:15: "But you, O Lord, are a God merciful and gracious, slow to anger and abounding in steadfast love and faithfulness."

If it seems that we have heard these words before, this was God's answer to Moses when Israel's great leader made his greatest request: "Please show me your glory" (Ex. 33:18). This is the chief issue in prayer and the great desire that should be on our hearts: to commune in faith with the God of grace and to be made aware of his glory. God answered Moses' prayer by placing him in a cleft of the rock where he would be safe while the Lord passed by. There Moses heard these words: "The Lord, the Lord, a God merciful and gracious, slow to anger, and abounding in steadfast love and faithfulness" (34:6).

In every setting and every need, in face of the world and its false glories and temptations, our greatest need is to know the Lord. We know him through his Word, and this knowledge gives substance to our prayers. But God would have us know him in our hearts. And when we seek his face in prayer, God makes the affairs of earth fade into seeming insignificance, and the knowledge of his glory, as a God "merciful and gracious, slow to anger and abounding in steadfast love and faithfulness" (Ps. 86:15), is sufficient to meet our every need.

16

Glorious Things of Thee

Psalm 87

Glorious things of you are spoken, O city of God. (Ps. 87:3)

Old Testament Israel was geographically and culturally remote from the other nations. Jerusalem was nestled on the Judean mountains far inland from the coast and equally distant from any of the great rivers that tied together the ancient world. This isolation was reinforced by the many restrictions of the Mosaic law, which made it difficult for Jews to mingle with Gentiles. Over time, their mindset often hardened into hatred and contempt for outsiders.

Nonetheless, an important strand of prophecy foretold the streaming of peoples into Zion's temple to worship Israel's God. Micah 4:1 proclaims: "It shall come to pass in the latter days that the mountain of the house of the LORD shall be established as the highest of the mountains, and it shall be lifted up above the hills; and peoples shall flow to it." This prophecy, which finds a memorable expression in Psalm 87, is fulfilled in the church of Jesus Christ.

Psalm 87 contributes to this vision an anticipation that is almost unique in the Old Testament. It foretells not only that people from all over the world will worship the Bible's God, but also that they will come as children who have been born into God's family. When Jesus chided the scholar Nicodemus for not understanding the new birth, saying, "You must be born again" (John 3:7), he might easily have proved his teaching by reference to Psalm 87:5, in which the sons of distant nations are "born in her," that is, Mount Zion. O. Palmer Robertson comments: "'Being born in Zion' is the image used to depict the conversion of nations whose inhabitants become citizens of the heavenly kingdom that now is manifest on earth."[1]

The Church as the City of God

The Bible presents a number of important images for the people of God, including the idea that the church is a temple and also a body in which the Holy Spirit dwells. Psalm 87 employs two of the most important metaphors: the church as the city and the family of God. These two images provide the structure for this psalm, in which verses 1–3 celebrate the glory of God's holy city, Zion, and verses 4–6 declare the gathering of citizens from all nations to dwell in the city as God's family. The final verse depicts the people as singing and dancing for joy, ascribing praise to God for the abundant life he has given.

The psalm begins, "On the holy mount stands the city he founded" (Ps. 87:1). The importance of this image can be perceived at the end of the Bible, where the church is seen as a glorious, walled city, inside of which grows the tree of life, watered by streams of living water, and where God and the Lamb sit on their throne (Rev. 22:1–2). St. Augustine took up this imagery for his great study of redemptive history, *The City of God*. His theme verse was Psalm 87:3, "Glorious things of you are spoken, O city of God." Augustine made the point that history involves a contest between two rival city-states:

> Two societies have issued from two kinds of love. Worldly society has flowered from a selfish love which dared to despise even God, whereas the communion of saints is rooted in a love that is ready to trample on self. . . . The city of man seeks the praise of men, whereas the height of the glory for the other is to hear God in the witness of conscience. The one lifts up its head in its own boasting; the other says to God: "Thou art my glory, thou liftest up my head."[2]

1. O. Palmer Robertson, *Psalms in Congregational Celebration* (Darlington, UK: Evangelical Press, 1995), 221.

2. Augustine, *The City of God*, trans. Gerald G. Walsh et al. (New York: Doubleday, 1950), 14.28.321.

Augustine did not invent the idea of the city of God, nor did he take it merely from Psalm 87. The New Testament especially employs this thinking. In Philippians 3:20, Paul wrote that "our citizenship is in heaven." Whereas the earthly Jerusalem sat atop Mount Zion, the writer of Hebrews declares that believers have come to a heavenly city:

> You have come to Mount Zion and to the city of the living God, the heavenly Jerusalem, . . . and to the assembly of the firstborn who are enrolled in heaven, and to God, the judge of all, and to the spirits of the righteous made perfect, and to Jesus, the mediator of a new covenant, and to the sprinkled blood that speaks a better word than the blood of Abel. (Heb. 12:22–24)

This packed summary describes the city of God as enduring eternally on the high mountain where God dwells, a city filled with the heirs of God, who are both justified and sanctified, blessed by fellowship with God and Jesus, whose sprinkled blood ensures their salvation forever. In Psalm 87, similar blessings are highlighted for God's city. John Calvin writes: "What we are taught in this psalm may be summed up in this, That the Church of God far excels all the kingdoms and polities of the world, inasmuch as she is watched over, and protected by Him in all her interests, and placed under his government."[3]

The Song of the City

Michael Wilcock has labeled the two halves of Psalm 87 as the "Song of the City" and the "Song of the Citizens."[4] The song for the city is extolled in the opening section: "Glorious things of you are spoken, O city of God" (Ps. 87:3). This line inspired one of John Newton's best-loved hymns: "Glorious things of thee are spoken, Zion, city of our God."[5] There is scarcely an end of the glorious things that could be said of God's city. William Plumer catalogues the "glorious histories, glorious predictions, glorious songs, glorious doctrines, glorious laws, glorious ordinances of worship, glorious promises and privileges" that were attached to Zion.[6] Psalm 87 cites three

3. John Calvin, *Calvin's Commentaries*, 23 vols. (1848; repr., Grand Rapids: Baker, 2009), 5:393.
4. Michael Wilcock, *The Message of Psalms 73–150* (Downers Grove, IL: InterVarsity Press, 2001), 59.
5. John Newton, "Glorious Things of Thee Are Spoken" (1779).
6. William S. Plumer, *Psalms* (1867; repr., Edinburgh: Banner of Truth, 1975), 814.

glorious features of God's city: the holy mount on which it stands, its sovereign founding by God himself, and the particular love that God assigns to its gates.

Jerusalem was sited on Mount Zion in the hilly terrain of Judah. The Hebrew text identifies this in the plural, "mountains," probably reflecting the fact that Mount Zion was located amid a complex of hills. What made Zion special was not its prominence or height, neither of which was exceptional, but rather its holiness. It is the "holy mount" (Ps. 87:1). It was designated as holy by God's sovereign decree. Moses had told the Israelites to "seek the place that the Lord your God will choose out of all your tribes to put his name and make his habitation there" (Deut. 12:5). Mount Zion was holy not only by God's choosing it but also by the presence of his temple and its sacrifices there.

Zion's sanctification makes a point that we should remember. What makes anything holy—whether it is a person, place, or thing—is the presence of God in his holiness. We may call an ornate gathering place a sanctuary, but unless God is truly worshiped there in spirit and truth (John 4:24), nothing is actually holy about it at all. Many a lofty cathedral has become defiled by false teaching and unbelieving hearts, whereas the barest and darkest hut, if filled with the worship of true believers and the faithful preaching of God's Word, is as holy as any other place on earth. The same is true of people. It is the presence of God in our lives through the Holy Spirit that makes us holy, and without God in our lives even the most impressive good works or religious shows remain unholy. Years after this psalm was likely written, the prophet Zechariah wrote to encourage the Jews who had returned to Jerusalem to rebuild the temple after its destruction. Some of them were depressed by the outward appearance, which was nothing compared to Solomon's original. But God said, "I will be the glory in her midst" (Zech. 2:5). So it was for Mount Zion in Psalm 87:1: "On the holy mount" God's city rested.

The second glorious thing said about Zion is just as important. Not only did she rest "on the holy mount," but she is "the city he founded" (Ps. 87:1). Jerusalem may have been conquered by King David and its construction supervised by his son Solomon. But it was God who founded and established the holy city. It was God who provided the ark of the covenant, which rested on Mount Zion, who caused his glory cloud to fill the temple (1 Kings 8:10–11), and who accepted the offerings sacrificed there for forgiveness of sin. In short, the religious system established on Mount Zion was God's gift of grace for the salvation of his people.

What is said of ancient Jerusalem is even more evidently true of the Christian church that it symbolized: it is sovereignly established by God's grace. We might think of this in two ways. The first is that the church has a foundation laid in the eternal decree of the Lord. Charles Spurgeon writes:

> The foundation of the church, which is the mystical Jerusalem, is laid in the eternal, immutable, and invincible decrees of Jehovah. He wills that the church shall be, he settles all arrangements for her calling, salvation, maintenance and perfections, and all his attributes, like the mountains round about Jerusalem, lend their strength for her support.[7]

We should also think of the church as being founded and established by the perfect and finished work of Jesus Christ. Paul wrote that the church is "built on the foundation of the apostles and prophets, Christ Jesus himself being the cornerstone" (Eph. 2:20). This means that the church is built by the preaching of God's Word, the message of which is the saving achievement of Jesus in his virgin birth, perfect law-keeping life, sin-atoning death, glorious resurrection, and mighty ascension to the right hand of God in heaven. With perhaps both of these in mind—God's sovereign decree and Jesus' finished work—Newton's famous hymn celebrates the ultimate security and assurance of those within the church:

> On the Rock of Ages founded, what can shake thy sure repose?
> With salvation's walls surrounded, thou may'st smile at all thy foes.[8]

Psalm 87:2 adds a third glorious thing about the city of God: "the Lord loves the gates of Zion more than all the dwelling places of Jacob." Just as the city is founded by God's election and the gospel salvation accomplished there, she is beloved of God for the same reasons. Why this city and these people? Moses told Israel that it was not because of any virtue of their own that God chose and loved them, "but it is because the Lord loves you and is keeping the oath that he swore to your fathers" (Deut. 7:7–8). God loved

7. Charles Haddon Spurgeon, *The Treasury of David*, 3 vols. (Peabody, MA: Hendrickson, n.d.), 2a:477–78.

8. Newton, "Glorious Things of Thee Are Spoken."

the Israelites because he loved them, with no cause other than his own gracious choice, and he loved Mount Zion for the same reason. He further loved it because of his Word that was preached there and the worship offered that was dear to his holy heart.

Psalm 87:2 specifies not only God's love for the city but specifically that he loves "the gates of Zion more than all the dwelling places of Jacob." God loved all the places where the Israelites lived, but it was the gates of Zion that he loved the most. This probably speaks of the gates as centers of social gatherings when the people of the nation streamed into Zion for sacred assemblies. We can well imagine how many Israelites agreed to meet at one or another of Jerusalem's gates when they arrived there for Passover or some other festival. This would be analogous today to the gathered worship of the church on the Lord's Day. Private and family worship are, of course, important and are blessed by God. But it is particularly the assembly of his church inside the gates of Zion that is precious to God. We are to love the church of which we are members, and especially its public worship services. It should not be difficult to get Christians to be regular and fervent in attending Sunday worship, realizing how precious it is to God himself. Robertson writes of Zion's gates: "At this place God's people consecrated themselves to him. They brought their hearts as living sacrifices to the Lord. They sang the songs of Zion. They rejoiced in God, the mighty Saviour who delivered them at the very gates of Zion from [enemy] armies."[9]

God's special love for his gates reminds us of the vital significance of the local congregation. At the same time, Psalm 87 calls us to love the entire worldwide church of all true believers. In the age to come, when the church has come to her glorious maturity, all congregations and denominations will have been assembled at the gates of the one heavenly city of God. We ought to be looking forward to that day with keen expectation, and that awareness ought to spur us on to a love for all faithful churches and all true believers.

The Song of the Citizens

One way in which we can be sure that Psalm 87 is fulfilled by the church in the gospel age is to consider the song of the citizens in verses 4–6. Here, we find the evil nations surrounding Israel incorporated into the city as

9. Robertson, *Psalms in Congregational Celebration*, 223.

fellow believers and worshipers. This never took place in the Old Testament, although numerous individual Gentiles became believers. Psalm 87 celebrates the fulfillment of a prophecy that is directed to the age following the coming of the Messiah, which is designated "the latter days" of redemptive history. Isaiah foretold, echoing Micah: "It shall come to pass in the latter days that the mountain of the house of the LORD shall be established as the highest of the mountains . . . ; and all the nations shall flow to it" (Isa. 2:2).

Psalm 87:4–6 anticipates the ingathering of believers from all nations in the most sweeping terms. Five nations are mentioned, representing various directions of the map. To the south is "Rahab," which in the Bible represents Egypt (see Ps. 89:10), and to the east is "Babylon." To the west is "Philistia," with "Tyre" to the north. "Cush" is added, referring to modern-day Ethiopia, to represent the distant peoples outside the ancient Near East. These names provide us with the best guess as to the time when Psalm 87 was written. Since Babylon is mentioned, and the northern menace of Assyria is not cited, it is likely that the psalmist wrote in the early or mid-seventh century, after Babylon emerged and conquered the Assyrian strongholds. The point, however, is that pagan Gentiles from all the nations—south, east, west, and north, together with distant lands—will become citizens of the city of God.

These five names also suggest different characteristics out of which God's people are saved. The name *Rahab* for Egypt suggests her pride. Babylon was noted for sensuality. The Philistines were marked by long hatred of their neighbors. Tyre was a merchant city of greed. Cush was far off and largely ignorant of God's truth. All these kinds of people were hostile or indifferent to Zion and its cause. Yet it is the glory of God's city not merely that its enemies are defeated but also that so many are brought inside and made wholehearted citizens. This roster of nations, with their distinctive evil, shows that a past record of sin does not bar anyone from God's salvation. Moreover, we see the error of those who would ever define the church on a racial or socioeconomic basis. Even when the city of God was physically located on Mount Zion, the gates were open to all who could come to know and worship God on the basis of faith. Just as Psalm 87 depicts it, a healthy church today is one that is welcoming to sinners of all kinds and is used by God to make them true converts, whose allegiance is changed from the world to the lordship of Jesus Christ.

Five Characteristics of the Church

In this brief but remarkable description of God's city in "the latter days" (Isa. 2:2), that is, the New Testament church, we can observe five significant characteristics. The first is seen in Psalm 87:4, describing people from these nations as "those who know me." This indicates that the church's calling is to reveal the knowledge of God through its life and worship. This will take place primarily through the clear teaching of God's Word. The church is not called to entertain members of the surrounding culture, to market worldly goods and services, however valuable they may be, or to gain secular power in society, but to shine forth the light of the knowledge of God for the saving of the souls of men and women, boys and girls.

Jesus said, "And this is eternal life, that they know you, the only true God" (John 17:3). This means that saving faith must include essential biblical knowledge about who God is—Father, Son, and Holy Spirit—and what God has done through Jesus for our redemption. It is not a saving knowledge of God merely to say that you believe in God or believe in Jesus Christ, in the sense of a mere acknowledgment. We must trust Christ and his saving work and surrender ourselves to the God of the Bible. This faith then results in a personal relationship with Jesus, like that between a sheep and its shepherd. Jesus declared, "I am the good shepherd. I know my own and my own know me" (John 10:14). Saving faith also includes a relationship of knowledge and love with God the Father as a devoted and trusting child.

Second, the church consists of citizens who are born again into God's spiritual family. Probably the most remarkable feature of Psalm 87 is its teaching that pagan members of enemy nations are not merely subdued and incorporated into God's city, but become natural-born residents. Of the converts from Egypt, Babylon, Philistia, Tyre, and Cush, it is said, "This one was born there" (Ps. 87:4). But despite their worldly origin, once they come by faith to Zion, God records them as having been born in his city: "This one was born there" (v. 6). This does not mean that worldly people are literally born a second time in Zion, but it means that the converts are received and registered with the status of natural-born citizens. H. C. Leupold notes that the citizens of God's city are accepted as true, native members "as though they had actually seen the light of this world within her walls."[10]

10. H. C. Leupold, *Exposition of the Psalms* (Columbus, OH: Wartburg Press, 1959), 625.

It is this passage that provides the idea of the church as the mother of God's people. The early church father Cyprian of Carthage wrote, "He cannot have God for his Father who will not have the Church for his mother."[11] In the Septuagint (LXX), the third-century B.C. Greek translation of the Old Testament, Psalm 87:5 is slightly different. Instead of saying, "And of Zion it shall be said," the LXX reads, "Mother Zion shall say." It seems that the apostle Paul was referring to this translation when he wrote that "the Jerusalem above . . . is our mother" (Gal. 4:26). The Roman Catholic Church wrongly draws on this to teach that membership in the church determines one's salvation—a teaching deeply at odds with biblical teaching that God saves through faith alone in Jesus. Taken rightly, however, Psalm 87 teaches that individual salvation makes one a member of the family of God and mandates one's participation in a local visible church. Moreover, the idea of "Mother Kirk" identifies the church as the primary vehicle for God's saving work in the world.

The most important point for us is the necessity of the new birth. One may be a member of the visible church on earth by making profession of faith or by being the child of a believer. But membership in the true church and citizenship in the heavenly Zion requires true saving faith through the new birth by the Holy Spirit. When Jesus said, "You must be born again" (John 3:7), he noted that only God can save by means of the regeneration that enables a heart to believe and trust personally in Christ.

Moreover, we should note as well the wonderful privilege that the new birth gives to believers, as we all become true members of God's family and native-born members of his city. There are no second-class citizens in the city of God. Hebrews 12:23 goes so far as to call it "the assembly of the firstborn who are enrolled in heaven." Firstborn were given preference in ancient families, but God's family consists entirely of firstborn children through union with Christ. Every Christian has the full loving attention and diligent care that a firstborn child receives from faithful and devoted parents.

Additionally, the realization that all believers are native-born members ought to influence the quality of life within the church. There are regions of the country where newcomers are likely to be told that they will never fit in because they lack the proper family connections and were not native-born.

11. *Treatise on the Unity of the Church*, 6.

But this attitude ought never to be the mood of the church. To the people of God, the church is a family. While many of us are blessed to have strong ties of love and support within an extended earthly family, we ought never to forget that we have been born again into a family where many others do not have that same earthly support system. We have privileges and obligations to our fellow Christians, especially in the local church, that are just as valuable and important as those in our natural families, if not more so. In particular, as Psalm 87 suggests, our attitude toward new members and new converts ought to be one not of suspicion or indifference but of loving interest and self-sacrificing welcome.

The third characteristic of the church seen in Psalm 87 is that its members are sovereignly chosen by God. Verse 6 shows that the action takes place by God's will and choosing: "The Lord records as he registers the peoples, 'This one was born there.'" We know from the New Testament that God predestined each of his people "before the foundation of the world" (Eph. 1:4). Yet here we find that as each of his elect people is actually brought to saving faith through the spiritual new birth, his own hand registers that person as a full member of his city. This ought to give every believer a certainty of hope through faith in Christ. As you trust in Jesus, you can rest your soul on the certain knowledge that God has placed your name on the roll of his city. When Christ returns, believers will hear the words of the great beatitude of Revelation 22:14, "Blessed are those who wash their robes, so that they may have the right to the tree of life and that they may enter the city by the gates." Murdoch Campbell urges us to note

> God's act in writing down each soul who is born into His kingdom. So precious is their salvation to Him that He does not leave this to men or angels, for only He knows all those who are His. . . . We speak with all reverence when we say that He is the heavenly Registrar in whose Book of Life are to be found the names of all who belong to the Church of the first-born.[12]

Fourth, the final verse depicts the joy of the redeemed as they sing and dance before the Lord: "Singers and dancers alike say, 'All my springs are in you'" (Ps. 87:7). These are the words of men and women who are conscious that they were once strangers to God's people, "having no hope and without

12. Murdoch Campbell, *From Grace to Glory: Meditations on the Book of Psalms* (Edinburgh: Banner of Truth, 1970), 137.

God in the world" (Eph. 2:12), who realize that they have been forgiven and reconciled to God by the blood of Christ, and have received a place and a home in the eternal blessings of his city.

For all its reverence and the serious nature of its work, the church is a joyful society of redeemed sinners who delight in their Savior. Do you take joy in the wonder and the blessing of your salvation and your membership in the city of God? John Newton was a brutal slave trader, once the slave of drunkenness, but he found freedom and abounding joy in Jesus Christ. The second stanza of his hymn from this psalm not only expounds his grateful spirit, but aptly describes the joy that flows to all Christians from the grace of God:

> See, the streams of living waters, springing from eternal love,
> Well supply thy sons and daughters, and all fear of want remove:
> Who can faint, while such a river ever flows their thirst t'assuage?
> Grace which, like the Lord, the giver, never fails from age to age.[13]

The fifth characteristic of the church is a passionate desire for the glory of God. "All my springs are in you," the believer cries, with grateful praise to God (Ps. 87:7). This is a way of saying that my spiritual life, with the forgiveness of sins through Christ's blood, the new birth and its spiritual enlightenment, and God's loving provision for all my soul's needs, flows from the source of eternal life that is the sovereign grace of God. Have you learned to rejoice in God's grace for you, and do you desire that God would have glory from your life? As Newton concludes his hymn, based on Psalm 87, he urges us therefore to take a bold stand before the world in witness of the salvation we have received in Jesus Christ:

> Savior, if of Zion's city I, through grace, a member am,
> Let the world deride or pity, I will glory in thy name:
> Fading is the worldling's pleasure, all his boasted pomp and show;
> Solid joys and lasting treasure none but Zion's children know.[14]

13. Newton, "Glorious Things of Thee Are Spoken."
14. Newton, "Glorious Things of Thee Are Spoken."

17

A Soul Full of Troubles

Psalm 88

For my soul is full of troubles, and my life draws near to Sheol.
(Ps. 88:3)

One of the best advertisements for the book of Psalms is that it delves into every emotional state known to humanity. If you turn to the Psalter, you will find a chapter that connects with what you are going through. But do the Psalms connect even with the believer who has seemingly lost all hope and is barely clinging to God? The answer is yes, and the proof is Psalm 88. John Calvin writes that this psalm "contains very grievous lamentations, poured forth by its inspired penman when under very severe affliction, and almost at the point of despair."[1] Robert Godfrey describes Psalm 88 as "the bleakest psalm in the whole Psalter. Here is the crisis of faith at its deepest."[2]

Unlike most other psalms, which start in distress but work themselves up to hope and praise, this psalm has its only clear statement of faith in the first verse. All that follows is a continual lament until as his final word the

1. John Calvin, *Calvin's Commentaries*, 23 vols. (1848; repr., Grand Rapids: Baker, 2009), 5:405–6.

2. W. Robert Godfrey, *Learning to Love the Psalms* (Orlando, FL: Reformation Trust, 2017), 153.

psalmist utters the word *darkness*. While Psalm 88 is not a pleasant chapter of the Bible, we may be grateful for its inclusion, lest we believe that true faith can never wrestle in such spiritual depression. James Boice writes that Psalm 88 "reminds us that life is filled with trouble, even to the point of despair, even for mature believers."[3]

This psalm is the only known contribution from Heman the Ezrahite, who is mentioned in 1 Kings 4:31 as a wise man and poet in or before the time of King Solomon. Many commentators speculate about the kind of trouble that he was experiencing. Some consider it to be a dreadful physical illness, perhaps leprosy, since this ailment was medically hopeless and isolating. Others associate this psalm with Job, who suffered devastation in his personal and family life and was afflicted by accusing friends. The psalm is also connected with the sufferings of Christ, whose cry of lament from the cross was a quotation from Psalm 22 but embraced the doleful spirit of Psalm 88. Whenever we feel ourselves at a loss, lacking hope and seeing only darkness, we may join our Lord and many other great figures from the Bible in sharing the lament of Psalm 88.

Since Psalm 88 proceeds as a litany of complaints, there are different ways to organize its verses. I will treat it in three sections. Verses 1–5 show a suffering spirit pleading to God. In verses 6–12, we see an afflicted spirit questioning God. In the final section, verses 13–18, we observe a broken spirit clinging to God. That final statement is the key to Psalm 88, for while Heman does not find relief within the stanzas of this poem, he nonetheless holds fast to God even in his darkness, trusting in the God of his salvation.

A Suffering Spirit Pleading to God

The only positive statement in Psalm 88 occurs in the first verse: "O Lord, God of my salvation, I cry out day and night before you." The psalmist begins with the covenant name of God, *Yahweh*, and extols him as the Savior in whom he trusts. This beginning shows that the context for all that will follow is not unbelief, but a suffering soul wrestling in faith. Heman the Ezrahite knows that the covenant promises of God grant him the right to

3. James Montgomery Boice, *Psalms*, 3 vols. (Grand Rapids: Baker, 1996), 2:716.

pray for deliverance and to expect the help of God in his need. He is not turning from God, as if the Lord were the problem, but turning to God as the answer, even if the answer he seeks eludes him. J. J. Stewart Perowne writes that God's salvation "is the pledge of his deliverance, though he cannot yet taste its comfort."[4]

It is because he knows that salvation comes from God that the psalmist says, "I cry out day and night before you" (Ps. 88:1). He pleads, "Let my prayer come before you; incline your ear to my cry!" (v. 2). Heman realizes that when God chooses to leave a believer in affliction, among the Lord's purposes is to teach constancy and persistence in prayer. The psalmist takes advantage of this privilege to unburden his soul day and night.

Psalm 88:3 makes an initial statement of his condition, presenting his inward and his outward state: "For my soul is full of troubles, and my life draws near to Sheol." The psalmist is in a desperate situation, perhaps slowly dying or with deadly danger unavoidably drawing near. In today's setting, Heman might be slowly withering with cancer, sensing that each new day will bring new weakness and distress. He feels the cold claws of despair and a rising sense of panic. Rather than be smothered by grief, however, he turns to vent his anguish into God's hands.

The dominant image in these verses is that of the grave, to which "Sheol" refers. Whatever the psalmist's affliction, it is not a mild or temporary one: Heman feels that he is about to be destroyed. He says that he is considered "among those who go down to the pit" (Ps. 88:4). As such, he is "a man who has no strength." He uses the image of the bodies of those who have been slain and have not yet had a proper burial: "like the slain that lie in the grave" (v. 5). He adds the idea of being forsaken and forgotten, like one buried in an unmarked grave: "like those whom you remember no more, for they are cut off from your hand" (v. 5). In short, the most dreadful end is staring him in the face, and he feels that he is without strength to oppose it and without help to save him. He feels that he will be a nameless casualty, like one of a host of bodies strewn across a field of war.

If we doubt that such a fate is possible for a Christian, we need only consult church history. Think of the early martyrs who were burned in the gardens of Nero or slaughtered by wild animals in the Colosseum. Presbyterians

4. J. J. Stewart Perowne, *The Book of Psalms*, 2 vols. (1878; repr., Grand Rapids: Zondervan, 1976), 2:141.

remember the "Killing Time" in Scotland from 1684 to 1688. Afflicted with a state church that neither preached God's Word nor practiced biblical worship, faithful people gathered in fields to pray and hear unauthorized preachers hold forth the gospel. The royalist authorities responded by pursuing them with mounted dragoons and hunting dogs, condemning as outlaws all who practiced true Christianity outside the corruptions of the established church.

When we read Psalm 88, we think of believers such as John Brown, a lay preacher in the parish of Moorkirk, who opened the Scriptures to the faithful and led them in prayers under broad skies. In 1682, John married, and after the vows were taken, the preacher gravely addressed the bride: "Isabel, you have got a good man; but you will not enjoy him long. Prize his company, and keep linen by you to be his winding-sheet; for you will need it when ye are not looking for it, and it will be a bloody one."[5] A few short years later, the godly woman stood in the doorway of her house, clutching two small children. The royal authorities had come to execute her husband without a trial, and after John had prayed and kissed her goodbye, a firing squad cut him down. After the dragoons rode away, Isabel knelt alone in the dirt, gathering pieces and scattered organs of her husband's body so that she could bury him with her own hands behind the house. In time, other family members arrived, including Brown's mother. For all his faith and service to God, John Brown was just one of countless casualties of a ruthless world, leaving his loved ones in the bitterness of loss. A witness records: "We can see them still, these kinsfolk in grief, one with the white hair and the other with the dark, as they wept and prayed together."[6] Though they trusted in Christ, their souls were full of troubles with no relief in sight.

An Afflicted Spirit Questioning God

As the middle portion of Psalm 88 elaborates on the psalmist's woes, we notice that a shift has taken place. His griefs are not merely things happening to him but things that God is doing to him: "You have put me in the depths of the pit," he laments, "in the regions dark and deep" (Ps. 88:6).

5. Quoted in Alexander Smellie, *Men of the Covenant* (1903; repr., London: Banner of Truth, 1960), 404.

6. Smellie, *Men of the Covenant,* 405–7.

It is here that Psalm 88 reminds us of the book of Job. Job had led a "blameless and upright" life (Job 1:1), drawing Satan's disgusted attention. The devil was soon in God's presence, complaining that Job honored God only because the Lord had "blessed the work of his hands, and his possessions have increased in the land" (v. 10). Satan added that if God were to afflict Job, "he will curse you to your face" (v. 11). So God tested Job, delivering him into the most horrid suffering, the kind that would break anyone's spirit. After his children had been slain, his property destroyed, and his body afflicted with sores, Job still had no idea of the cause of his troubles, yet the reader of Job is aware that God himself had permitted these calamities.

Many a well-informed Christian endures under great afflictions by being aware of God's sovereignty over all things. Jesus emphasized the Father's control over even the smallest of events by saying that not even a sparrow "will fall to the ground apart from your Father" (Matt. 10:29). For many believers, it is precisely this knowledge of God's control that makes afflictions harder to bear. They ask, "How could my loving Father do this to me?" and wonder what they have done to deserve such suffering from God.

In addition to complaining that God has put him at the brink of destruction, the psalmist adds: "Your wrath lies heavy upon me, and you overwhelm me with all your waves" (Ps. 88:7). It is not clear that Heman feels personally punished by God, but at least he knows that God has cursed this present world because of sin. It is God's wrath that causes death, grief, suffering, and despair. Heman feels like Jonah, when he was so pursued by God's anger that he cast himself overboard, except that no great fish has yet rescued the psalmist from the depths.

To make matters worse, the psalmist is cut off from all friendship: "You have caused my companions to shun me; you have made me a horror to them. I am shut in so that I cannot escape" (Ps. 88:8). Job had his accusing friends, who wrongly blamed him for his sorrows. Heman, similarly, is rejected by horrified former companions. Perhaps it is an illness that they fear to contract or persecution that they are unwilling to share. It may also be that in his panic, the psalmist only feels this way, so that in loneliness he imagines the rejection of his friends. Many suffering souls feel isolated by their trauma and in many cases make it difficult for even willing friends to draw near. It is easy to think that no one understands our situation, that we are the only one who has ever faced a particular trial. All Heman can do is to weep uncontrollably and cry out to God: "My eye grows dim through sorrow. Every day I call upon you, O Lord; I spread out my hands to you" (v. 9).

At this point, the psalmist poses a series of questions to God that are practically accusations. The general drift is to challenge God's wisdom in allowing Heman's destruction. "Do you work wonders for the dead?" he asks, pointing out that soon it will be too late for God to intervene. "Do the departed rise up to praise you?" he queries (Ps. 88:10), arguing that those in the grave offer no worship to the Lord. "Is your steadfast love declared in the grave, or your faithfulness in Abaddon?" (v. 11). All talk of God's gracious character is lost on those who lie lifeless in the netherworld. "Are your wonders known in the darkness, or your righteousness in the land of forgetfulness?" (v. 12).

These statements reveal an extremely negative view of life in the grave, leading some scholars to argue that Old Testament believers knew nothing of life after death. It was these and similar statements that led C. S. Lewis to write that the Old Testament had "no belief in any sort of future state whatever."[7] This is untrue, since many other psalms celebrate a view of life after death that enriches even the New Testament's teaching on the resurrection and eternal life, such as Psalms 16, 23, and 116. In his despair, however, the writer of Psalm 88 cannot access this hope. He is depressed by afflictions, and his mind can see only gloom ahead. Christians may experience a similar dread of death, even with our hope for life beyond death with Jesus. The psalmist is right, so far as this world is concerned, that God is praised and his love known only by those who are rescued by God's answer to prayer. William Plumer accurately describes the psalm's challenge: "The sole object is to show that in the present conflict and trouble, if God would show himself on the side of the Psalmist, he must manifest his favor before death supervenes and leaves the point apparently settled against his servant."[8]

The point of the psalm is simply that the author feels abandoned in the face of despair. In this lament, and its expression through prayer to God, he has the companionship of Jesus Christ on the cross. Before we ever think to rebuke and correct a broken spirit crying out with broken heart about

7. C. S. Lewis, *Reflections on the Psalms* (New York: Harcourt, Brace & World, 1958), 38.
8. William S. Plumer, *Psalms* (1867; repr., Edinburgh: Banner of Truth, 1975), 821.

God's will, let us remember the cry of Jesus, "My God, my God, why have you forsaken me?" (Matt. 27:46). Jesus could utter that cry without a shred of doubt in God. With that in mind, our best ministry to depressed believers will often be simply to offer a patient heart of sympathy. We should also direct their faith to the Savior, who suffered both with and for them. The despairing believer, trusting in Christ, will find Jesus a true companion in sorrows—a friend who both understands and offers spiritual help.

Elsewhere the Bible does give answers to those who are troubled by God's sovereignty over the afflictions of his people. One answer was given at the end of Job. After listening to several chapters of complaints in which his wisdom was maligned, the Lord appeared in person. This was not what Job had been expecting! "Then the LORD answered Job out of the whirlwind" (Job 38:1). God appeared in his sovereign majesty and began asking questions back to his self-pitying servant. "Who is this that darkens counsel by words without knowledge?" he demanded (v. 2). "Where were you when I laid the foundation of the earth? Tell me, if you have understanding" (v. 4). If Job was so wise, God asked, where had he been "when the morning stars sang together and all the sons of God shouted for joy?" (Job 38:7). On it went for two long chapters, until finally "the LORD said to Job: 'Shall a faultfinder contend with the Almighty? He who argues with God, let him answer it'" (40:1–2). By this time, Job was thoroughly chagrined. He decided that rather than making his own accusations, he would do better to let God be God and admit that the divine counsel does not answer to his demands. "Behold, I am of small account," he replied; "what shall I answer you? I lay my hand on my mouth" (v. 4).

Humble silence will be the best counsel for many grieving believers, especially after they have vented themselves at God for a while. The time comes to take up the posture commanded in Psalm 46:10, "Be still, and know that I am God." To this, Job added an awareness of his own sin in the presence of God's pure holiness. After he had seen God in his glory, he concluded: "I had heard of you by the hearing of the ear, but now my eye sees you; therefore I despise myself, and repent in dust and ashes" (Job 42:5–6). When we see ourselves through God's eyes, our questions are reversed. Instead of marveling at how bad things could happen to good people like us, we stand amazed that God has done anything good at all for proud sinners like us, much less sent his own Son to die for our sins.

In addition to seeing our own puniness and sinfulness in the presence of God's greatness and holiness, there is another answer to the "problem" of God's control over our suffering. This answer is to realize that God's sovereignty is actually our best and only hope. Plumer applies this lesson personally: "To the pious mind it is a relief to know that troubles come from the hand of God. He then knows they are not sent in wantonness. . . . It says, God can do no wrong, yet he afflicts me thus."[9] Since God is holy, his purposes are all holy, including my bewildering affliction. Since "God is love" (1 John 4:8), in the end even my wounds will be seen as strokes of tender mercy necessary for the cause of my salvation and the gospel's work in the world.

A Broken Spirit Clinging to God

The final section of Psalm 88 shows that it is not necessary for us to have all the answers in order to continue to hold fast to the Lord for salvation. The psalmist has vented his troubled soul to his patient and long-suffering God, who yet has not willed to come with help. So the psalmist does the only thing he can do. Even as a broken spirit in despair, he continues to cling to God: "But I, O Lord, cry to you; in the morning my prayer comes before you" (Ps. 88:13). Some writers argue that the expression "in the morning" indicates the psalmist's optimism that the night is virtually over. Optimism, however, is not the spirit of this psalm. We should rather take it that after a sleepless night of anguish, the morning has come and he is continuing to lay hold of God in the weakness of his faith. After everything that he has suffered in his dark night of the soul, he is still praying.

This is the point and lesson of Psalm 88. There will be times when the only thing we can do is to just keep holding on to the Lord, crying to him and trusting against all apparent hope. Like Jacob when he wrestled with God in Genesis 32, we may emerge limping at the end, but if our hands simply remain clenched in faith to the Lord, we will not be lost. Marvin Tate comments: "The speaker is on the brink of death, but prayer is the lifeline which keeps him/her from the Pit."[10]

So the psalmist continues praying all the way to the end of Psalm 88. In verse 14, he complains again: "O Lord, why do you cast my soul away? Why

9. Plumer, *Psalms*, 822.

10. Marvin E. Tate, *Psalms 51–100*, Word Biblical Commentary 20 (Waco, TX: Word, 1990), 405.

do you hide your face from me?" But notice that he is still clinging to the Lord despite his bitterness. He looks back over an entire lifetime of suffering, the precise circumstances of which we do not know: "Afflicted and close to death from my youth up, I suffer your terrors; I am helpless" (v. 15). Looking forward, he sees no release from his torment: "Your wrath has swept over me; your dreadful assaults destroy me. They surround me like a flood all day long; they close in on me together" (vv. 16–17). Yet Heman is still praying, still holding to God with the lifeline of faith, and still connected to the one he first addressed as the "God of my salvation" (v. 1). We must do the same in our own valleys of despair.

If we look for a happy ending in the final verse, we will be disappointed. The psalmist rehearses his abandonment from family and friends: "You have caused my beloved and my friend to shun me" (Ps. 88:18). In exquisite self-pity and perhaps bitter self-awareness, he admits that he is not totally alone. "My companions have become darkness," he says (v. 18). If he has a friend, it is the depression that has become comfortable and familiar. Though nothing else presents itself, the darkness is there. In the Hebrew text, *darkness* is the final word of this psalm. Yet still the psalmist clings to God, and so must we even when our spirit is broken by fear and grief.

Do Christian stories really end this way, at least so far as this present life is concerned? Consider the grief that consumed one of the great theologians of the nineteenth century, James Henley Thornwell. In 1859, Thornwell returned from church meetings to Columbia, South Carolina, where he pastored the First Presbyterian Church. He had hurried home in order to officiate at the wedding of his daughter, Nannie, with whom he had a particularly special bond of faith and love. Thornwell arrived to find that she had become deathly ill. Within a few days the wedding guests began to arrive, only to find that they had come instead to a funeral. Nannie's wedding dress was delivered, and it became the shroud for her burial. Benjamin Morgan Palmer records that "just a little after the day when she should have plighted her vows before the altar, the very attendants who, in a different scene, should have 'rejoiced, hearing the bridegroom's voice,' with their white gloves lifted the bier, and bore it to the grave." There she lies still in the Elmwood Cemetery in Columbia, with a marble slab that records her name and age, together with the inscription: "Prepared as a bride adorned for her husband."[11]

11. Benjamin Morgan Palmer, *Life and Letters of James Henley Thornwell* (Richmond, VA: Whittet

It would be wrong to say that Thornwell responded to his dear daughter's death by living out the bitter experience of Psalm 88, and especially its bitter attitude toward the Lord. He had the benefit of the New Testament and its triumphant message of resurrection hope through Jesus Christ. But it would also be false to say that he recovered from the grief. He never did. His biography reads:

> It was a sorrow from which the stricken father never fully recovered. From this time his health became feebler, a tinge of sadness rested upon his countenance, the Christian graces became sweeter and softer every day, and it was evident to all that he was himself mellowing rapidly, to be gathered above with her who had gone.[12]

DARKNESS THE FINAL WORD?

The conclusion of Psalm 88 begs the question: is darkness really the final word? The New Testament, with its message of the open tomb of Jesus Christ, assures us that it is not. It was, no doubt, the New Testament message that enabled the grieving Scots during the dreadful Killing Time not to fall into the despondency of Psalm 88 and helped James Henley Thornwell continue to rejoice in the Lord even as grief stole the remaining years from his life. Indeed, darkness was evidently not even the final word for Heman the Ezrahite, since after all he lived long enough to publish this psalm. Yet we miss the point if we conclude our study of this psalm on an upbeat note.

Psalm 88 proves that great suffering is sometimes the lot of God's people; indeed, all Christians will experience deep sadness and grief if only we live long enough. The reason given by the psalmist in verse 7 is that God's wrath lies on this cursed world, which is thus the realm of death. Afflicted Christians should therefore not consider themselves abandoned by God, as if suffering were unexpected. First Peter 4:12 asserts: "Beloved, do not be surprised at the fiery trial when it comes upon you to test you, as though something strange were happening to you." It is not strange for Christians to suffer, even grievously, since we are called to fellowship with the suffering of Christ. Realizing this, we should turn to God and not pull away from him, saying with Heman the Ezrahite, "But I, O LORD, cry to you" (Ps. 88:13).

---

and Shepperson, 1875), 439.

12. Palmer, *Life and Letters of James Henley Thornwell*, 440.

Psalm 88 reminds us that while we suffer, we are not alone. This psalm may itself be a companion to grieving Christians if they have no other. Godfrey writes: "It shows us that we are not alone in our doubts, confusions and complaints. Not only have other believers felt the same things, but God has inscripturated those sentiments to assure us that it is legitimate to feel such things and to pour them out in prayer."[13]

Moreover, knowing what trials to expect in this life, Christians see this present age as a work in process, looking for our deliverance to the future when Christ returns. Just as there was for Jesus a cross and then a crown, so, too, must we suffer with him in order to reign with him in glory (see 1 Peter 4:13). This was the hope that sustained even Job in his great sorrows: "For I know that my Redeemer lives, and at the last he will stand upon the earth. And after my skin has been thus destroyed, yet in my flesh I shall see God" (Job 19:25–26). This was also Jesus' perspective on our present lives: "In the world you will have tribulation. But take heart; I have overcome the world" (John 16:33).

Finally, as we watch the broken psalmist holding fast to the Lord in his darkness, we are reminded of what true victory looks like for the followers of Christ. Some preachers insist that Christian faith must result in earthly riches, good health, and social approval. Paul saw things quite differently when he wrote in Romans 8:37 that Christians "are more than conquerors through him who loved us." In the preceding verse, the apostle made clear the circumstances in which believers triumph, situations much like that of the Scottish Covenanters, meeting secretly in the fields to hear God's Word, or like James Henley Thornwell, tearfully saying goodbye to a dying daughter in her wedding gown, or even like Heman the Ezrahite, with darkness as his only friend. Paul said, "For your sake we are being killed all the day long; we are regarded as sheep to be slaughtered" (Rom. 8:36). Where is the victory in that? Paul answers with the words of triumph that will sustain us through the darkness of this dying, sinful world, if only we cling in faith to the God of our salvation:

> For I am sure that neither death nor life, nor angels nor rulers, nor things present nor things to come, nor powers, nor height nor depth, nor anything else in all creation, will be able to separate us from the love of God in Christ Jesus our Lord. (Rom. 8:38–39)

13. Godfrey, *Learning to Love the Psalms*, 94.

18

The Steadfast Love of the Lord

Psalm 89:1–18

I will sing of the steadfast love of the Lord, *forever; with my mouth I will make known your faithfulness to all generations.*
(Ps. 89:1)

As we study the Psalms, we notice that many of them begin with complaints and conclude with praise. Psalm 89 is notable for following the opposite pattern: it begins with praise and only toward the end brings complaints and requests before the Lord.

Psalm 89 seeks the revival of Israel's fortunes in light of a great reversal. Some commentators place the psalm shortly before the fall of Jerusalem, which took place in 587 B.C. The lament's claim in verses 44–45 that God has cast the king from his throne and "cut short the days of his youth" is taken by some to refer to Nebuchadnezzar's removing King Jehoiachin after he had reigned only three months (see 2 Kings 24:8–12). This certainly was a lamentable tragedy for Israel. Other commentators note that this psalm is ascribed to Ethan the Ezrahite, who according to 1 Kings 4:31 was one of the four wise men of Solomon's reign. This would place the psalm toward the beginning of the Davidic kingdom, perhaps lamenting the rebellion against Solomon's son Rehoboam when the ten northern tribes broke away from Judah (1 Kings 12:1–19).

Whichever event is referred to, a calamity has struck the throne of David, and the psalmist is responding in the right way: he appeals to the throne of God in prayer. His example has been followed by Christians whenever the church has become conscious of a need for spiritual revival. In fact, God's motivating his people to call on him in prayer often proves to be the beginning of revival. Eric Alexander points out the failure of many Christians to realize the significance of prayer and the error of the church in not granting a higher priority to intercession: "Prayer is the essence of the work to which God calls us. We frequently speak about praying *for* the work, but essentially it is prayer which is the real work. There is no harder or more demanding ministry."[1]

As the psalmist prays for the revival of the Davidic kingdom, we may divide Psalm 89 into four sections. First, he praises God for his faithful, covenant love in verses 1–18. Second, in verses 19–37, he remembers before the Lord the terms of God's covenant with David. The third section, verses 38–45, presents his dismay that God could allow the Davidic throne to be laid so low. The final section, verses 46–52, pleads with God to manifest his power and defend his honor. We will tackle this lengthy psalm in three chapters, starting with David's praise for God's steadfast love in the opening section.

The Believer's Attitude of Prayer

The first section of the psalm gives praise to God while recalling the reasons why his faithfulness can be trusted: "I will sing of the steadfast love of the Lord, forever; with my mouth I will make known your faithfulness to all generations" (Ps. 89:1).

We are reminded by this beginning that the believer's proper attitude in praying to God is that of praise. Alexander urges that "even when we are in days of great darkness, deeply burdened for the cause of God, all our thinking and all our crying to God must be from a posture of worship."[2] The psalmist is persuaded that God always deserves the praise of his people—not

1. Eric J. Alexander, *Our Great God and Saviour* (Edinburgh: Banner of Truth, 2010), 174.
2. Alexander, *Our Great God and Saviour*, 175.

only when he is acting in ways that we approve but also when we find it hard to understand his purpose. God is to be praised at all times because of who he is—that is, because of the glory of his attributes. When things seem to be going poorly for believers, the reason is not that God has changed but that we have changed and need to repent, or else that God is working according to plans that will ultimately bring us blessing.

We see this attitude of praise in many of the great prayers of the Old Testament. In 701 B.C., the Assyrian conqueror Sennacherib overran all the surrounding area of Judea and laid siege to Jerusalem. Hezekiah went in before the Lord to pray and began by praising God: "O LORD, the God of Israel, enthroned above the cherubim, you are the God, you alone, of all the kingdoms of the earth" (2 Kings 19:15). Hezekiah did not express doubt in God simply because his situation had turned sour, but he began his plea with confidence in God and a concern for his glory. He asked God to deliver him, so "that all the kingdoms of the earth may know that you, O LORD, are God alone" (2 Kings 19:19). We see a similar attitude of trust and praise in Jehoshaphat's prayer when beset by the armies of the East (2 Chron. 20:5–12) and in Daniel's prayer for Israel's restoration (Dan. 9:4–19).

It is likewise good for us to begin our prayers with adoration for God and a concern for his glory. This is especially true of public prayers in the church, but it should be true of family and private prayers as well. When we are wavering in faith or doubting God's care, we will strengthen ourselves in prayer by carefully rehearsing the reasons for God's praise before we come to him with requests.

WHY GOD'S PEOPLE PRAISE HIM

One biblical approach to praising God is to meditate on his attributes. These are the characteristics of God that are revealed in Scripture. In Psalm 89, the writer focuses on God's faithfulness as a prime reason why his people praise him. Both verses 1 and 2 highlight God's "steadfast love" and "faithfulness," which is "to all generations." The Hebrew word for "steadfast love" is *hesed*, which speaks of God's unfailing love and covenant faithfulness, to which is added the word *amunah*, which refers to God as reliable and dutiful.

Psalm 89:2 sees God as building on a foundation of faithfulness: "For I said, 'Steadfast love will be built up forever.'" Before making his petitions, the psalmist thus notes that God's answer relies on his being always faithful. He adds that "in the heavens you will establish your faithfulness" (v. 2). The psalmist seems to note the reliability of the stars and constellations, so that observers can chart their movements. God's faithfulness to Israel is no less settled in its course, so that we may rely on God to fulfill his promises just as we can count on the stars to shine in the dark sky.

The psalmist advances in Psalm 89:3 to focus on God's faithfulness in making a covenant with David: "You have said, 'I have made a covenant with my chosen one; I have sworn to David my servant.'" This statement recounts the events recorded in 2 Samuel 7. David had just brought the ark of the covenant up to Jerusalem, and he was concerned for the honor given to God's sacred vessel, which was housed in a mere tent compared with David's magnificent palace (2 Sam. 7:2). God replied that it was not David who was building a house for God but God who would build his own house through David. The Lord then promised: "I will raise up your offspring after you, who shall come from your body, and I will establish his kingdom. He shall build a house for my name, and I will establish the throne of his kingdom forever" (vv. 12–13). We see this language reflected in Psalm 89:4: "I will establish your offspring forever, and build your throne for all generations."

On the one hand, the psalmist is introducing the theme that will form his chief concern, namely, that the Davidic throne seems in jeopardy. On the other hand, he is pointing out God's faithfulness to David and Israel in making this covenant. God had earlier anointed David to the kingship and promised to make his throne secure, but God then followed up with a covenant to make those promises sure. Notice how the terms "made a covenant" and "sworn" are prominent in Psalm 89:3: "I have made a covenant with my chosen one; I have sworn to David my servant." A covenant is a solemn promise sealed with an oath. God does not need to be bound by such a procedure, since his mere Word is always reliable. But as a kindness in helping us to know that his promises are certain to be fulfilled, God binds himself to a covenant that puts him under an oath. The writer of Hebrews used this same language to note how faithful God is in granting us the assurance we need:

> So when God desired to show more convincingly to the heirs of the promise the unchangeable character of his purpose, he guaranteed it with an oath, so that by two unchangeable things, in which it is impossible for God to lie, we who have fled for refuge might have strong encouragement to hold fast to the hope set before us. We have this as a sure and steadfast anchor of the soul. (Heb. 6:17–19)

At a time when the Davidic kingdom seemed to be tottering, the psalmist looked back to God's covenant with David to remind himself of the Lord's faithfulness. How much better a vantage point we believers have today on the same divine faithfulness! The believing Israelite may well have wondered how God was going to fulfill his promise to David, and how a mere human could ever have his throne established eternally. But Christians look back on these same verses and see that they even better describe Jesus Christ as the one who truly fulfills God's promise to David. Psalm 89:3–4 speaks of the king as God's "chosen one" and "servant," who will build his "throne for all generations"—descriptions that more fittingly refer to Jesus rather than to David himself.

The psalmist may have wondered at how God would fulfill his covenant with David. But the Christian realizes that God has secured the throne of David in the royal ministry of his divine ancestor, Jesus Christ. Believers no longer have to wonder how God will keep such an audacious covenant, realizing how his eternal Son became flesh and was exalted to sit on God's throne forever. Looking back on this fulfillment of God's covenant with David, Christians have a strong basis both to trust God for his faithfulness and to praise him as well.

Why the Heavens Praise Him

Having stated the faithfulness of God as a reason why his people may always trust and praise him, the psalmist proceeds to marshal evidence to back up this claim. In Psalm 89:5–7, he points out why the angels in the heavens praise the Lord. If we are to trust God's faithfulness, we need to be reminded of the greatness of his person. And if beings so great as the angels worship and obey God, then he is one who is great enough for us to trust.

Psalm 89:5 exclaims, "Let the heavens praise your wonders, O Lord, your faithfulness in the assembly of the holy ones!" The "assembly of the holy ones" is undoubtedly the host of the angels in heaven. The Bible records them as unceasingly adoring God in fervent worship. Moreover, even the angels praise God especially for his faithfulness. This indicates that as God has performed his wonderful works of redemption for his people, the angels have themselves marveled with astonishment. Peter wrote that the gospel involves "things into which angels long to look" (1 Peter 1:12). Jesus said that there is "joy in heaven over one sinner who repents" (Luke 15:7). So God's faithfulness is a theme that causes wonder and joy even among the holy angels of heaven!

Psalm 89:6 adds: "For who in the skies can be compared to the Lord? Who among the heavenly beings is like the Lord . . . ?" The fact that God stands alone among the heavenly beings as the sole true deity is seen throughout the Bible. For instance, after Israel had passed through the parted waters of the Red Sea, the Song of Moses extolled him: "Who is like you, O Lord, among the gods? Who is like you, majestic in holiness, awesome in glorious deeds, doing wonders?" (Ex. 15:11). God's glory is seen in the worship of the angels that attends his works. When Jesus was born, the angels appeared, singing, "Glory to God in the highest" (Luke 2:14).

The book of Revelation opens a window into the unceasing worship of heaven, and shows that God sits enthroned as Father and Son, with the angels gathered all around to offer unending adoration. John writes: "Then I looked, and I heard around the throne and the living creatures and the elders the voice of many angels, numbering myriads of myriads and thousands of thousands." The angels joyfully acknowledge God's sole right to be worshiped, crying: "To him who sits on the throne and to the Lamb be blessing and honor and glory and might forever and ever!" (Rev. 5:11–13).

Moreover, the angels themselves hold God in awe and terror: "a God greatly to be feared in the council of the holy ones, and awesome above all who are around him" (Ps. 89:7). The idea here is that the greatness of God "begets deep reverence in the hearts of all who consider who He is,"[3] including even the angels. One of the great worship scenes of the Old Testament occurred when the prophet Isaiah entered the temple. The Lord appeared on his throne, high and lifted up, and "above him stood the seraphim," each of which "had six wings: with two he covered his face, with two he covered his feet, and with two he flew" (Isa. 6:2). This is an astonishing scene. The

3. H. C. Leupold, *Exposition of the Psalms* (Columbus, OH: Wartburg Press, 1959), 635.

name *seraphim* means "burning ones," which indicates that these are angels of a particularly glorious kind. Yet how submissive they were in the presence of God. With two wings they maintained constant readiness to do his bidding. With two wings they covered their feet as an expression of creaturely modesty before the Creator. Then with two wings they covered their faces. So overwhelming is the sheer glory of God that even the "burning ones" cannot bear to gaze on him. The seraphim hold God in the deepest reverence as one who is awesome and to be feared. How much more ought we lower beings to do the same?

Psalm 89:8 also refers to the angels when it addresses God as the "LORD God of hosts." To call him by this name is to acclaim him as the commander of the armies and awesome resources of heaven, which enable him to be faithful to all that he promises. William Plumer writes: "Jehovah has all armies, all causes, all agents at his disposal. He marshals the stars. He guides the angels. He is the God of battles. He is a man of war. He is in all, through all, over all."[4] Seeing that God is held in such reverent awe in his command of legions of angels, we should never doubt the mightiness that enables the Lord to be faithful.

WHY THE EARTH PRAISES HIM

As if Ethan the Ezrahite had not already marshaled enough data to prove the faithfulness of the Lord, he turns from the heavens to the earth to prove that God is mighty to uphold his steadfast love. The earth, like the church and the angelic hosts above, gives praise to God as one who is able to maintain his steadfast love forever.

We can see that a new section of Psalm 89 begins in verse 8 because the psalmist turns to the second person. Here he begins to focus on God's mighty power. Is God able to keep to his promises? He answers: "O LORD God of hosts, who is mighty as you are, O LORD, with your faithfulness all around you?" The point of verses 8–9 is that God's rule over creation, where he maintains the boundaries of the earth and sea, proves his power to keep all his promises: "You rule the raging of the sea; when its waves rise, you still them" (Ps. 89:9). In the Old Testament, the sea was the ultimate symbol of chaos and violence, which no man could ever master. The sea was a place

4. William S. Plumer, *Psalms* (1867; repr., Edinburgh: Banner of Truth, 1975), 827.

of terror where people were in constant danger. Yet the Old Testament shows God as constantly mastering the sea, both in his establishment of its boundaries (Gen. 1:9–10) and in his ability to control its waters. We can think of many biblical examples, including God's targeting Jonah's sailing ship with a violent tempest and God's parting the waters of the Red Sea when Israel needed a passage to escape from the army of Pharaoh. A God who can rule the waves can handle the challenges that threaten our salvation.

Christians read Psalm 89:9 and remember one of Jesus' greatest miracles as he calmed the waves and stilled the winds on the Sea of Galilee by the mere word of his command. Mark 4:39 tells us that Jesus cried, "'Peace! Be still!' And the wind ceased, and there was a great calm." Believers in Christ have long seen this episode as proof that we can trust Jesus to preserve us through all the tumults of life. Katharina von Schlegel wrote:

> Be still, my soul: the waves and winds still know
> His voice who ruled them while he dwelt below.[5]

In addition to the seas, the psalmist speaks of God's creation of the mountains: "The north and the south, you have created them; Tabor and Hermon joyously praise your name" (Ps. 89:12). Different suggestions are given about the meaning of this verse. It could be that the psalmist is looking over all Israel, from the north and the south and also from the east to the west, since these two mountains stood on the east and west of the nation. Over all the land, the mountains bear testimony to God's power, since their rocky heights were created by him. The verse could also draw from the fact that Tabor is a relatively low mount, whereas Mount Hermon towered at nine thousand feet, so that God's power is seen both lengthwise from north to south and also heightwise from east to west. The overall point is clearly stated in verse 13: "You have a mighty arm; strong is your hand, high your right hand."

God showed his power not only in creating the seas and the mountains but also in his ruling over the affairs of history. This is the point of Psalm 89:10: "You crushed Rahab like a carcass; you scattered your enemies with your mighty arm." Rahab was the mythical monster of the Nile, so here God's rule of the seas is symbolized in mythic terms. It is likely that Egypt is specifically in view as the land of the Nile. We see allusions to Egypt at

5. Katharina von Schlegel, "Be Still, My Soul" (1752).

various points in this psalm, including verse 8, which is virtually a quote from Moses' song after Israel passed through the parted Red Sea. God's power is seen all through biblical history as God intervened in a mighty way to rescue and defend his threatened people. The passage of the Red Sea is one of the great instances that is often cited by God's people as a reminder that we can and should trust him. God was faithful to deliver Israel out of desperate danger in Egypt by the kinds of supernatural intervention that are so easily possible to him. When we come to God in prayer, our faith should enter into the joyous refrain of those who discovered God's covenant faithfulness because of his glorious might. Moses sang: "The Lord is my strength and my song, and he has become my salvation; this is my God, and I will praise him, my father's God, and I will exalt him" (Ex. 15:2).

Psalm 89:14 sums up the conclusions that the psalmist has drawn not only from God's rule over the created elements but also from all that has been said in this psalm about the faithfulness of God. He envisions the throne of God as being upheld by mutually supportive divine attributes, all of which make him constant in his steadfast love: "Righteousness and justice are the foundation of your throne; steadfast love and faithfulness go before you." Marvin Tate understands these attributes as a pedestal on which God sits enthroned: the Lord's throne "is founded upon and characterized by the fundamental, cosmic characteristics of right order and justice. Loyal-love and Faithfulness are personified as royal attendants who do the bidding of the Cosmic King."[6] When we think of God's throne, we naturally think of our approach to him in prayer. Especially when we are dismayed by troubles, we should approach God in a spirit of praise like that of the psalmist. God's kingdom is established in righteousness and justice, so we can count on his upholding our cause against the assaults of evil. Moreover, since his steadfast love and faithfulness never fail, he will be certain to forgive our sins through his covenant of grace in the blood of Christ and will keep all his promises to those who believe.

Blessed to Praise the Lord

Psalm 89 reminds us that we should always pray to God in a spirit of praise, and that we have abundant reasons to trust his steadfast love forever.

6. Marvin E. Tate, *Psalms 51–100*, Word Biblical Commentary 20 (Waco, TX: Word, 1990), 422.

As the psalmist concludes the opening portion, he points out blessings that come to us when we live for the praise of God through faith in his Word. "Blessed are the people who know the festal shout," he writes, speaking of the trumpets and acclamation that announced the beginning of worship at the temple in Jerusalem (Ps. 89:15). This notes a joyful attitude in praise and the blessings that come to those who rejoice in the Lord.

Four blessings are listed, which we may take as applications of this psalm's exhortation to come to God in a spirit of worship and praise. The first is that we will "walk, O LORD, in the light of your face" (Ps. 89:15). To walk in the light of God's face is to know him and be confident of his covenant favor. But how can we know that we have God's blessing, especially when we, like the Israelites, so often fall into sin and folly? The answer is discovered in the gospel of Jesus Christ. Jesus said, "I am the light of the world. Whoever follows me will not walk in darkness, but will have the light of life" (John 8:12). To walk in the light is to know Jesus as Savior and to trust him as Lord, living by faith through obedience to his Word. What a blessing this brings, enabling us to know many other blessings from God as we walk before him through a living faith in his Son.

A second blessing for those who come to God in joyful praise is that they will be lifted up in their spirits with a sense of the glory that belongs to him. The psalmist tells us that they are blessed "who exult in your name all the day and in your righteousness are exalted" (Ps. 89:16). The psalmist evidently knew this for himself. The psalm will indicate that he was in great distress and even some perplexity over what had happened. Nonetheless, he was not spiritually defeated because he contemplated the steadfast love and faithfulness of God. Often it will be enough for us simply to know that God reveals his glory through the afflictions of his people, so that our attitude changes from despair to delight in our knowledge that our great and faithful God is sure to manifest his grace at the right time.

Very much in the spirit of Psalm 89, Stuart K. Hine contemplated both the power of God revealed in creation and the blessings of his saving grace to lift his soul up in a spirit of adoration. He began his famous hymn by contemplating the way in which creation glorifies God:

> O Lord my God, when I in awesome wonder
> Consider all the worlds thy hands have made,

I see the stars, I hear the rolling thunder,
Thy pow'r throughout the universe displayed.

Hine advanced to recall the wonders of the gospel and its promised salvation:

And when I think that God, his Son not sparing,
Sent him to die, I scarce can take it in,
That on the cross, my burden gladly bearing,
He bled and died to take away my sin.

From both creation and redemption, his soul was blessed in being lifted up, so that he concluded: "Then sings my soul, my Savior God, to thee: how great thou art, how great thou art!"[7]

A third blessing is seen in Psalm 89:17: "For you are the glory of their strength; by your favor our horn is exalted." Here we add to the blessing of inward glory the accompanying grace of spiritual strength. Prayer to God in a spirit of praise, extolling his steadfast love and mercy, will leave us strengthened in our precious faith.

The final result of joyful worship in prayer is the inward peace and calm that God gives when we trust in his steadfast love. Paul had this in mind when he wrote that we should "not be anxious about anything, but in everything by prayer and supplication with thanksgiving let your requests be made known to God. And the peace of God, which surpasses all understanding, will guard your hearts and your minds in Christ Jesus" (Phil. 4:6–7). The psalmist gave the same message: "For our shield belongs to the Lord, our king to the Holy One of Israel" (Ps. 89:18). He was distressed because he was relying on the Davidic king who had been cast down by a stronger enemy. But seeing and reminding himself that God reigns above in covenant faithfulness and power, he is content simply to wait on the Lord for salvation.

Are you able to say with peace that whatever happens, God is your shield, and that the things in which you trust are all overseen and governed by the

7. *How Great Thou Art.* Words: Stuart K. Hine. Music: Swedish folk melody/adap. and arr. Stuart K. Hine. © 1949, 1953 The Stuart Hine Trust CIO. All rights in the USA, its territories and possessions, except print rights, administered by Capitol CMG Publishing. USA, North and Central American print rights and all Canadian and South American rights administered by Hope Publishing Company. All other North and Central American rights administered by The Stuart Hine Trust CIO. Rest of the world rights administered by Integrity Music Europe. All rights reserved. Used by permission.

holy God of heaven? You can know this if you gain access to God's love through the Savior he has sent. Then you will be able to approach all your own trials with the spirit of faith that is taught to us by our Lord. As Jesus exhorted: "In the world you will have tribulation. But take heart; I have overcome the world" (John 16:33).

19

God's Covenant Faithfulness

Psalm 89:19–37

My steadfast love I will keep for him forever, and my covenant will stand firm for him. (Ps. 89:28)

One of the most beloved Christian hymns celebrates one of the most glorious attributes of God:

> Great is thy faithfulness, O God my Father;
> There is no shadow of turning with thee;
> Thou changest not, thy compassions, they fail not;
> As thou hast been thou forever wilt be.[1]

Wonderful as it always is to sing such a hymn, the reminder of God's faithfulness is most needed in times of darkness and seeming despair. So it was for Ethan the Ezrahite in Psalm 89, which reveals a dismayed concern for the downcast throne of the house of David. It is little wonder, then, that the psalmist, seeking a rock on which to stand, rehearses the Bible's teaching of God's covenant faithfulness.

1. Thomas O. Chisholm, "Great Is Thy Faithfulness" (1923).

Psalm 89 is the work of a prayer warrior for God's people. How valuable are those few men and women who maintain a prayerful watch over the church and its people! The psalm also shows that true prayer is rooted in God's Word. Eric Alexander comments: "When God creates prayer warriors he begins by making them Bible students."[2]

Ethan mines the Scriptures, looking particularly for promises that he can set before the Lord. This middle portion of his prayer is seeded with "I will" statements from God. The psalmist focuses on the promises of what is known as the *Davidic covenant*, found in 2 Samuel 7:1–16. By considering God's faithfulness to David, God's faithfulness to his covenant, and then God's faithfulness in discipline, Ethan anchors himself in the solid rock of sovereign grace as he advances toward the mournful pleas that will come at the psalm's end.

God's Faithfulness to David

Since Psalm 89 is concerned with a calamity that has befallen the throne of the house of David, the author looks back to the grace by which God first established David as king over his people. As Ethan looks to David as a source of hope for Israel's kingship, Christians will see the pattern of salvation that God provides in their own experience. God revealed his faithfulness in choosing, strengthening, protecting, and exalting David. Regardless of our present difficulties, we who trust in Jesus may be confident of God's being faithful to us in the same way.

First, God was faithful in choosing David to be Israel's king: "Of old you spoke in a vision to your godly one, and said: 'I have granted help to one who is mighty; I have exalted one chosen from the people'" (Ps. 89:19). The book of 1 Samuel emphasizes David's faithfulness to God in making him suitable to serve as Israel's true king. Samuel described him as "a man after [God's] own heart" (1 Sam. 13:14). Speaking of young David, the prophet noted that "man looks on the outward appearance, but the Lord looks on the heart" (16:7). Yet whenever we find a man's or woman's faith being praised in Scripture, the ultimate reason is always to highlight the free grace of God at work in his or her life. Jesus said to his disciples, "You did not choose me, but I chose you" (John 15:16). Likewise, David was sovereignly

2. Eric J. Alexander, *Our Great God and Saviour* (Edinburgh: Banner of Truth, 2010), 177.

chosen by God, and it was the grace of God that made him all that he would become. David was not a self-made man but a God-chosen man, and God's grace gave the psalmist confidence that God would complete the good work he had begun in David's call (see Phil. 1:6).

The psalmist notes further that in choosing David, God was faithful in providing for Israel's need of a godly king. David's ministry as God's royal servant expressed not Israel's deserts but God's grace for his people. Christians who trust in Jesus but doubt their own ability to withstand the storms of doubt or temptation may look to God's sovereign election as a source of confident hope. In Isaiah, God said of Israel: "'You are my servant, I have chosen you and not cast you off; fear not, for I am with you" (Isa. 41:9–10). Christians know that God chose us when there was no good in us (see Rom. 3:9–10; Titus 3:4–5). It was by his own purpose that he gathered us for salvation, so we can be certain that his will cannot ultimately fail (see Eph. 1:4, 11).

God was faithful not only in choosing David but also, second, in strengthening him during the challenges of life: "I have found David, my servant; with my holy oil I have anointed him, so that my hand shall be established with him; my arm also shall strengthen him" (Ps. 89:20–21). James Boice writes: "God does not abandon to their own strength or devices those upon whom he has set his love."[3]

When God tells us that he "anointed" David with "holy oil" (Ps. 89:20), he is referring to the occasion when the prophet Samuel obeyed his command by anointing David to be Israel's king. More important was the equipping that this anointing symbolized: "And the Spirit of the Lord rushed upon David from that day forward" (1 Sam. 16:13). God provides the same spiritual equipping for everyone who is chosen to come to Christ in faith. The Holy Spirit regenerates our nature so as to be able to believe, implants within us a spirit of holiness, provides spiritual gifts with which we serve the Lord, and causes God's Word to be effective in bringing us to godliness. Jesus promised that God will be faithful to strengthen prayerful believers with the very provision he gave to David: "If you then, who are evil, know how to give good gifts to your children, how much more will the heavenly Father give the Holy Spirit to those who ask him!" (Luke 11:13).

The Lord adds that "my arm also shall strengthen him" (Ps. 89:21). Are you troubled that you are weak in faith and vulnerable to fear and temptation?

3. James Montgomery Boice, *Psalms*, 3 vols. (Grand Rapids: Baker, 1996), 2:727.

Keep trusting in the Lord, who is faithful to strengthen those who walk with him in faith. God will mold your character in godliness, increase your faith, and teach you how to live according to his Word so that you will become strong to face the trials and demands of life in this world. The psalmist invites you to realize that even such a spiritual giant as David was not strong in himself, but persevered only by the same grace on which you rely. God, having chosen David by his grace, did not abandon him to his weakness but strengthened him by that same grace.

Third, God was faithful to protect David from all the threats to his life and success: "The enemy shall not outwit him; the wicked shall not humble him. I will crush his foes before him and strike down those who hate him" (Ps. 89:22–23). The story of David's years as a fugitive from King Saul's mad hatred read like a page-turning novel. Time and again, young David was cornered, trapped, or abandoned. Each time, God protected him and ultimately brought down his enemy. Once David became king, God put foe after foe under David's feet. Christians will find that the same is true when it comes to their precious faith. Even Peter, when he was assailed by Satan and denied Jesus three times because of his fear, was upheld by the grace of God at work through the ministry of Christ. "I have prayed for you that your faith may not fail," Jesus reassured Peter (Luke 22:32). While it is certainly true that Christians may suffer every kind of abuse and violence from ungodly powers, Paul nonetheless insisted that "we are more than conquerors through him who loved us" (Rom. 8:37).

Fourth, the Lord was faithful to exalt David, both in his reign and in his relationship to God. Psalm 89:24 promises, "My faithfulness and my steadfast love shall be with him, and in my name shall his horn be exalted." This verse declares the prominence that God did in fact give to David among the other earthly rulers of his day. His victories over the Philistines to the west and his enemies to the east even as far as the rivers of Babylon, which are recorded in 2 Samuel 8, are promised in Psalm 89:25: "I will set his hand on the sea and his right hand on the rivers." More important still is the intimacy of David's special relationship with God: "He shall cry to me, 'You are my Father, my God, and the Rock of my salvation'" (v. 26). We need only think of the many beautiful psalms in which David's communion with the Lord is poetically expressed to see the fulfillment of Ethan's promise. The reference to David as God's son speaks of his special relationship as king over the Lord's people. Verse 27 adds, "And I will make him the firstborn, the highest of the kings of the earth." Firstborn sons had prominence, position, and possessions above those of other sons. In this way, David's singular honor above all other kings is shown. God was faithful not only to choose, strengthen, and protect him, but also to exalt him. Likewise, those who trust in Christ claim an eternal inheritance as the firstborn people of God (see Heb. 12:23). Paul writes that when Jesus returns, all Christians will be "heirs of God and fellow heirs with Christ" (Rom. 8:17).

As we read of God's faithfulness to David, the record of which is seen in the Old Testament, like Ethan the Ezrahite, we may be greatly strengthened in our assurance of salvation. Do we believe in Jesus Christ with a true and saving faith? Then this has occurred only because God was faithful to choose us and strengthen our faith by his Spirit. Possessing this grace ensures that God will protect us from every threat to our souls and will ultimately exalt us with Christ when he returns. The famous "golden chain" of Romans 8:30 outlines what Psalm 89 declares about God's faithfulness to David, and to us: "those whom he predestined he also called, and those whom he called he also justified, and those whom he justified he also glorified" (Rom. 8:30). On the basis of God's faithfulness, we, too, may pray to God with confidence amid trials, resting our hopes on the faithfulness of our sovereign and gracious God.

God's Faithfulness to His Covenant

If we look back and consider the terms of God's covenant with David, as the psalmist has done in this prayer, we will soon realize that its fulfillment can be fully seen not in David but only in David's greater son, the Lord Jesus Christ. Jesus came to fulfill God's promises to David and to become the royal Savior who brings the fullness of the kingdom of heaven. We see this in 2 Samuel 7:13, where God promised that David's offspring would "establish the throne of his kingdom forever." This promise obviously could not refer to any mere human, but looked forward to the eternal Son of God, who would become incarnate as a descendant in the line of David.

In considering God's faithfulness to David in Psalm 89, we likewise find our thoughts directed beyond David to his true heir, Jesus Christ. Verse 26 says, "He shall cry to me, 'You are my Father, my God, and the Rock of my salvation.'" It seems that David had a privileged status as God's son by virtue of his kingship over Israel. Yet there are no references of David's actually addressing God this way. It is Jesus who first addressed God as his Father, speaking this way in the Gospel of John alone no fewer than sixty times. Hebrews 1:5 tells us explicitly that the promise to be God's Son is made specifically to Jesus: "You are my Son, today I have begotten you" and "I will be to him a father, and he shall be to me a son." Thus, it is Jesus alone who ranks as the true firstborn of God (see John 3:16; Rom. 8:29; Col. 1:15).

Seeing that the covenant with David had its true reference in the person and work of Jesus Christ, we realize that the psalmist is anticipating the greater saving arrangement that God made through his divine Son. David Dickson wrote: "As David was in type, so Christ is in truth, and in all respects, more eminently than David, a strong helper, mighty to save, appointed of the Father to help us in all cases, and to whom we are directed to God, that we may find help . . . [and] that out of his fullness we may all receive grace for grace."[4] Thus, when Psalm 89:28 says that "my covenant will stand firm for him," it refers not merely to David but also to the entire covenant of grace, at the heart of which is God's unbreakable promise to reward Christ's saving work with the salvation of everyone who believes. In this way, we can see that the psalmist is celebrating not merely God's faithfulness to David personally, but also God's faithfulness to his covenant, on which every believer may completely rely amid the broken promises of this world.

God gave his covenants to establish a firm and inviolable basis on which his people could rely on his promised salvation and respond to him in faith and obedience. When Jesus taught that "whoever believes in the Son has eternal life" (John 3:36), he was making reference to this provision of the covenant of grace. God's covenant with his people is not merely a legal arrangement, although this is vital, but "also a personal commitment."[5] Since God is faithful to his covenant, those who trust in him may be sure to be saved in the end. In Psalm 89:34, God assures his people: "I will not violate my covenant or alter the word that went forth from my lips." Therefore, Christians may look to his covenant oath in Christ and find, as Hebrews 6:19 puts it, "a sure and steadfast anchor of the soul."

4. David Dickson, *A Commentary on the Psalms* (1653; repr., Edinburgh: Banner of Truth, 1995), 2:118–19.

5. Eric Lane, *Psalms 1–89: The Lord Saves* (Ross-shire, Scotland: Christian Focus, 2006), 394.

God kept his covenant by fulfilling all his promises to Jesus, just as he fulfilled all his promises to David. When Jesus was baptized by John the Baptist, God spoke from heaven: "This is my beloved Son, in whom I am well pleased" (Matt. 3:17). At that moment, the Holy Spirit descended like a dove upon Jesus. Even though Jesus was very God in his divine nature, his human nature needed to be strengthened by God's Spirit, even as David was strengthened in his anointing. As David was made strong and protected from his enemies by God, so Jesus prayed and found his pleas answered from heaven. Just as we must do, Jesus employed the Word of God in victorious warfare against the devil, saying in response to temptation, "Man shall not live by bread alone, but by every word that comes from the mouth of God" (Matt. 4:4).

One might object to the claim that Jesus was strengthened by God, since after all Jesus was allowed to be arrested, beaten, mocked, and finally crucified in agony. Where was God's faithfulness then? The answer is that God was fulfilling in Christ the demands of his covenant for the Lamb of God to take away our sins (John 1:29). After he suffered and died for our sins, then God exalted Jesus by raising him from the grave, ascending him into heaven, and seating him at his own right hand in glory (see Acts 2:24–25; Eph. 1:20–22). By means of faith, Christians behold the faithfulness of God to his Son and our Savior when we look to Jesus now enthroned in heaven, where he is interceding for us (Rom. 8:34). The entire world will see God's faithfulness to Christ, to the dismay of unbelief, when he returns on the clouds of glory and sits in judgment over the living and the dead (Matt. 25:31–32; 1 Thess. 4:16–17). God promised to set David's hand "on the sea and his right hand on the rivers" (Ps. 89:25). But his greater promise to Jesus is dominion over heaven and earth, "so that at the name of Jesus every knee should bow, in heaven and on earth and under the earth, and every tongue confess that Jesus Christ is Lord, to the glory of God the Father" (Phil. 2:10–11).

Most vital for us, God is faithful not only in exalting Jesus but also in giving him the promised reward of a people to belong to himself through saving faith. It is only of Jesus that God has promised: "My steadfast love I will keep for him forever, and my covenant will stand firm for him. I will establish his offspring forever and his throne as the days of the heavens" (Ps. 89:28–29). Dickson notes how this promise secures the eternal salvation of the church: "Whence learn, Christ hath, from age to age, a succession of children, whom he, by his word and Spirit, begetteth unto a spiritual life; and this succession shall not be cut off, but one generation shall follow another."[6] Thus, when Christians read of God's solemn oath for Jesus to reign on his eternal throne, it is our kingdom of which he speaks and the reign of the Savior we trust that is established forever.

God's Faithfulness to Discipline

It may seem surprising that as Psalm 89 celebrates one aspect of God's faithfulness followed by another, we are drawing closer to his dismay in verses 38–51 over the apparent collapse of David's throne. The final section of Psalm 89 involves bitter groaning under oppressors, yet it is preceded by an explanation in God's faithfulness to discipline those called to him in faith.

When we ask how a reminder of God's covenant faithfulness helps the psalmist to deal with calamity and failure, the first answer is given in Psalm 89:30–32: "If his children forsake my law and do not walk according to my rules, if they violate my statutes and do not keep my commandments, then I will punish their transgression with the rod and their iniquity with stripes." The point is that the very covenant by which God promised an eternal throne to David also warned about these very sanctions that would occur in the case of unfaithfulness and sin on the part of David's descendants (see 2 Sam. 7:14). The psalmist's particular point, then, is that God allowed the Davidic throne to suffer calamity precisely because he was faithful to his covenant, which had warned of this discipline in advance.

What was true for the Davidic kingdom in the Old Testament is true for believers today. When calamities strike us and our hearts are broken by trials and sorrows, it is not because God has become unfaithful to us. The reality is that we are sinners and that God disciplines and chastens us so that we will advance in holiness. Peter therefore wrote: "Beloved, do not be surprised at the fiery trial when it comes upon you to test you, as though something strange were happening to you" (1 Peter 4:12). In fact, the Bible tells us that "the Lord disciplines the one he loves, and chastises every son whom he receives" (Heb. 12:6). Fatherly punishment for sin is a mark of God's love for us, as well as of his commitment to his own holy standards.

6. Dickson, *Psalms*, 2:122.

This is not to say that all our trials occur as God's chastisement, since he has many gracious purposes at work in us. But when God does bring earthly discipline into our lives, it is because he is faithful to his Word. John Calvin explains: "God does not adopt us as his children, to encourage us to take liberty to commit sin with the greater boldness."[7] Rather, as Dickson insists, God's discipline consists of "fatherly corrections, medicinal preservatives against sinning afterward, and tokens of God's hating sin."[8]

A second way that we see God's faithfulness in discipline is that he does not allow the consequences of our sin to overthrow his covenant promises of salvation. The psalm continues: "but I will not remove from him my steadfast love or be false to my faithfulness. I will not violate my covenant or alter the word that went forth from my lips. Once for all I have sworn by my holiness; I will not lie to David" (Ps. 89:33–35). The fact that David's successors had been unfaithful to God did not mean that God would be unfaithful to David and his covenant promises to him. God had promised David an everlasting throne, and that oath would be kept. For this reason, God's chastisements would not go so far as to cut off the future for David's kingdom. In light of the calamity he faced, the psalmist may not have known how God would still raise up the throne of David so that his offspring would reign forever. But today we know that despite the sins of David's offspring, God fulfilled his promise to David in the kingdom reign of Jesus Christ.

Likewise, in our trials, God will show a merciful restraint so that we do not suffer the full punishment we deserve, including eternal condemnation, but will still be saved according to his promises of his gospel. These words are a special comfort to Christians who fear the results of continual and ongoing sin. God may discipline us in the way that a faithful father does. But will a true believer be lost because of his or her sins? God answers, "I will not remove from him my steadfast love or be false to my faithfulness. I will not violate my covenant or alter the word that went forth from my lips" (Ps. 89:33–34). We also trust the gospel promise of John 3:16, that whoever believes in Jesus "should not perish but have eternal life." We trust 1 John 1:7, which declares that "the blood of Jesus [God's] Son cleanses us from all sin." If my sin and folly require God's faithfulness to discipline me in this life, I can still know that, trusting in Jesus, my soul will enter into

7. John Calvin, *Calvin's Commentaries*, 23 vols. (1848; repr., Grand Rapids: Baker, 2009), 5:442.
8. Dickson, *Psalms*, 2:123.

heaven and I will be justified through faith on the day of final judgment. The key, of course, is faith in Jesus Christ, by which God's covenant promise is confirmed to me. If I possess the gift of saving faith, then God declares to me, "I have loved you with an everlasting love; therefore I have continued my faithfulness to you" (Jer. 31:3).

The third reason that we can see God's being faithful in his discipline is explained in the final verses of this central section of Psalm 89: "His offspring shall endure forever, his throne as long as the sun before me. Like the moon it shall be established forever, a faithful witness in the skies" (Ps. 89:36–37). The point here is not only that God is faithful to his covenant by fulfilling its warnings or that God is faithful in showing mercy even in anger, but further that God's discipline has the purpose of actually securing us for salvation. In this light, we see that when God executed such terrible judgments as the destruction of Jerusalem and the Babylonian captivity, his purpose was to save his people from the sin of idolatry that would have destroyed them forever. His ultimate purpose was seen in the planned return of his people with their idolatry chastened and removed. Calvin applies this principle to our own fatherly discipline from God: "God has nothing else in view than to correct the vices of his children, in order that, after having thoroughly purged them, he may restore them anew to his favor and friendship."[9] This agrees exactly with Jesus' promise to the church before his departure into heaven: "And behold, I am with you always, to the end of the age" (Matt. 28:20).

The evangelist Harry Ironside told of an occasion when he was preaching the gospel in a series of places, only to realize that the offerings he collected did not provide enough money for him to continue. Indeed, he was so poor that he had to check out of his hotel and spend the night under a tree with nothing to eat. There, Ironside thought of God's promise in Philippians 4:19, "My God will supply every need of yours according to his riches in glory in Christ Jesus." He complained in his spirit against God, who seemed not to have kept this promise, since Ironside was practically starving. Yet as he prayed that night, perhaps not unlike Ethan the Ezrahite, Ironside remembered reasons why he should trust and glorify God despite his hardships.

The next day, some friends found him and gave the provision that enabled him to return to his home. What is interesting is that before leaving that

9. Calvin, *Commentaries*, 5:443.

town, Ironside stopped into the post office and found that a letter from his father had come. His father had written to him some days earlier: "God spoke to me through Philippians 4:19 today. He promised to supply all our need. Some day he may see that I need a starving, and if he does, he will supply that." Ironside saw that, all along, God had been providing him with discipline that was intended to strengthen his faith and make him wiser for the sake of his ministry.[10]

Great Is Thy Faithfulness

Would God be faithful to David and to his own covenant, just as he was faithful to discipline Israel for its sins? The final verses provide a tangible assurance that he would: "His offspring shall endure forever, his throne as long as the sun before me. Like the moon it shall be established forever, a faithful witness in the skies" (Ps. 89:36–37). David was to look into the sky, see the sun and moon, and remember that God had made them witnesses of his promise. Seeing them still shining in the heavens, Ethan remembered that God must still remain faithful. We look back, and from our perspective in history we can see how God did fulfill his promise to David by sending his own Son into the line of David's house to restore that kingdom. As Christians, we look in faith to heaven and know that Jesus is reigning at the right hand of God the Father. His death and resurrection are proof of God's faithfulness for our salvation. We can therefore sing of God's faithfulness together with all others who look to him in faith:

> Pardon for sin and a peace that endureth,
> Thine own dear presence to cheer and to guide,
> Strength for today and bright hope for tomorrow,
> Blessings all mine, with ten thousand beside!
>
> Great is thy faithfulness! Great is thy faithfulness!
> Morning by morning new mercies I see:
> All I have needed thy hand hath provided—
> Great is thy faithfulness, Lord, unto me![11]

10. Taken from Boice, *Psalms*, 2:728.
11. Chisholm, "Great Is Thy Faithfulness."

20

Where Is Your Faithfulness?

Psalm 89:38–52

Lord, where is your steadfast love of old, which by your faithfulness you swore to David? (Ps. 89:49)

Psalm 89 celebrates the attribute of God's faithfulness as few other chapters of Scripture do. It does this, that is, until we get to the final sections, which suddenly ask, "Where is your steadfast love of old, which by your faithfulness you swore to David?" (Ps. 89:49). This prayer refers to some calamity that has befallen the Davidic throne in Jerusalem. The most common suggestion is that it relates to the downfall of King Jehoiachin, when his reign was cut short after three months and the eighteen-year-old ruler was deported into exile in Babylon. The statement of verse 45 especially suggests this context: "You have cut short the days of his youth; you have covered him with shame." Whatever the exact circumstances, they are so shocking that this psalmist who has been rejoicing in God's faithfulness now finds himself questioning this very attribute. More precisely, he expresses concern that the horrid circumstances will cast doubt on God's faithfulness. After all, he complains to God, "You have renounced the covenant with your servant; you have defiled his crown in the dust" (v. 39).

What You Have Done

The main complaint is listed in Psalm 89:38–45, which speaks first of the casting down of the Davidic throne, whether in calamity or in defeat: "But now you have cast off and rejected; you are full of wrath against your anointed" (Ps. 89:38). The crown was "defiled . . . in the dust" (v. 39), the king's splendor ceased and his throne cast down (v. 44), and the king's own days cut short shamefully in his youth (v. 45).

Along with the fall of the monarchy, the city itself has been abandoned by God's protection: "You have breached all his walls; you have laid his strongholds in ruins" (Ps. 89:40). As a result, God's city has "become the scorn of his neighbors," so that Israel's enemies have their right hand exalted with rejoicing (vv. 41–42). Those who would defend Jerusalem find themselves with no strength: "You have also turned back the edge of his sword, and you have not made him stand in battle" (v. 43).

At the center of this dire situation is God's apparent rejection of his royal promises: "You have renounced the covenant with your servant" (Ps. 89:39). It is clear that this refers to God's covenant with David as Israel's king: "you have defiled his crown in the dust" (v. 39). The word *renounced* is a strong statement of God's not merely changing but disavowing his covenant arrangement. This statement is remarkable when we move back a mere five verses to read, "I will not violate my covenant or alter the word that went forth from my lips" (v. 34). While it is clear that God is upset with the conduct of Israel's king, the psalmist is chiefly concerned with God's own actions, which seem to contradict the promises that he swore.

Uniformly, the actor in these verses is God: the key word is *you*. "You have renounced," "you have defiled," "you have breached" and "laid his strongholds in ruins." "You, you, you, you," the psalmist continues, regarding the strengthening of the wicked, the overthrow of the city's defenders, the shaming of the kingship, and the cutting short of the king's years. This claim of divine responsibility is in line with the Bible's teaching on the absolute sovereignty of God over all things. Jesus said that even though two sparrows are sold for a penny, "not one of them will fall to the ground apart from your Father" (Matt. 10:29). So none of these things happened without God's will. Moreover, God himself is the active agent in these judgments. Psalm 89:38 says that "you are full of wrath against your anointed," so that all these things have come about as God's chastisement against the sins of his people.

On the one hand, it is terrible when God strikes down in judgment on his people. Hebrews 10:31 declares, "It is a fearful thing to fall into the hands of the living God." This is especially true for those who die in unbelief and face an eternity of condemnation for their unforgiven sins. But it is also terrible for God's justified people, who look forward to heaven through faith in Christ, nonetheless to experience God's chastising hand in temporal judgments. Israel gave itself over to idolatry, which is such an abomination to the Lord, and in judgment God cast down its royal throne, caused strong enemies to overrun its walls, and ultimately cast the entire nation into exile. Christians should therefore learn to fear particularly grievous sins, to which God may respond with life-crushing chastisements.

It is also true, on the other hand, that God's sovereignty over our judgments and trials is the greatest source of our hope. James Boice writes: "If God is behind what happens, then although we may not understand what God is doing we can know that there is a purpose somewhere and that a solution to the problem will be found, if not in this life, then in the next."[1]

When God finds it necessary to cut us down a notch because of sinful patterns in our lives, it hurts and scars our lives. Many Christians live with the reality of significant long-term losses because of what God has done in response to their sin. Some are financially crippled because God refused to bless a gambling habit. Christian men and women deal with the long-term pain of divorce because one of them indulged in sexual infidelity, and their children also deal with the heartbreak of broken families. Men who permit themselves to indulge in pornography may lose the capacity for loving intimacy in the way that God designed sex. I know a Christian man who went to prison for embezzling funds, inflicting vast pain on his family. I also know pastors who crippled their churches through sins that they knew perfectly well not to commit. The list could go on. Not only does sin carry its own harmful consequences, but God himself actively blocks his people from profiting from sin and strikes blows to wayward believers that are designed to stop them in the tracks of rebellion.

As the psalmist sees it, the chief calamity is not the pain that our sins cause to us but the damage they do to God's reputation. When he cries out, "You, you, you did this!," his burden is not that of resentment but of holy alarm for the glory of God. This is why he asks, toward the psalm's end:

1. James Montgomery Boice, *Psalms*, 3 vols. (Grand Rapids: Baker, 1996), 2:733.

"Lord, where is your steadfast love of old, which by your faithfulness you swore to David?" (Ps. 89:49). His tone is not that of anger against God, in the way that many Christians respond to God's discipline today, but that of holy concern for God's honor. The watching world knows that the church claims great promises from God, but now look what has happened to these people who believed!

This concern for God's glory is an attitude that our generation in the church greatly needs to cultivate. When the church is disgraced in society, is our first concern for the reputation of Christ and his gospel? When Christians are chastised because of our sin, is our first reaction to weep for ourselves or for the shadow that is cast across God's honor? When the apostle Paul walked through Athens and saw idols filling that great city, the word that expressed his grief might be translated in terms to the effect that he had a heart attack (Acts 17:16; Greek, *paroxuneto*). Eric Alexander comments on Psalm 89: "It is this spirit which I find so lacking in my own soul and in the contemporary evangelical church. . . . We need to ask ourselves why we do not share the psalmist's distress over our situation." Why do not the downcast state of the church today and the widespread contempt shown for the gospel grieve us more than they do for God's sake? Alexander writes: "Is it perhaps because we do not share [the psalmist's] zeal for the honour of the name of God which is brought into reproach?"[2]

How Long, O Lord?

Indeed, if the Bible is to be believed, not merely some but all Christians will suffer temporal pains and losses because of God's discipline on our sins. Hebrews 12:6 teaches that "the Lord disciplines the one he loves, and chastises every son whom he receives." This means that there are sins that we would "get away with" in the short term if we were not Christians but that God punishes for the sake of our holy calling as believers. So how do we handle the grief over lost love, lost health, lost reputations, or lost careers that result from our own folly and sin? One answer is seen in Psalm 89, where the psalmist responds to the calamity of fallen Jerusalem by asking God to defend his own glory by manifesting his covenant faithfulness to restore Israel's condition.

2. Eric J. Alexander, *Our Great God and Saviour* (Edinburgh: Banner of Truth, 2010), 181.

First, the psalmist asks, "How long, O Lord?" (Ps. 89:46). This plea shows that he is speaking to God in faith, not in unbelief. He knows that God will ultimately be faithful, but wonders only how long it will be before this faithfulness is revealed. When God told Isaiah that the people of Israel would harden themselves against the Lord's Word, the prophet asked, "How long, O Lord?" (Isa. 6:11). The watchman Habakkuk prayed, "O Lord, how long shall I cry for help, and you will not hear?" (Hab. 1:2). In the book of Revelation, the saints in heaven ask God when Christ will come in the final judgment: "O Sovereign Lord, holy and true, how long before you will judge and avenge our blood on those who dwell on the earth?" (Rev. 6:10). Here, in Psalm 89, Ethan the Ezrahite asks the Lord how long he will withhold the solution that his people need.

In Psalm 89:46, the psalmist proceeds to ask God, "Will you hide yourself forever?" So the problem is not really God's faithfulness, but his timing in revealing his sovereign, saving presence. Ethan does not deny God's justice in casting down the throne and subjecting the city to attack and ridicule. These are deserved, even under the terms of God's covenant. But how long will God permit this to go on? Because of the promises of God's Word, he knows that the defeat cannot be final and the judgment cannot be everlasting. So the question "is not the *event* of an enemy victory but its *duration*."[3] Moreover, the psalmist realizes that God has not really turned against his people but only removed the evident signs of his protection and favor. Nonetheless, he realizes that this very situation is a fearful judgment: "How long will your wrath burn like fire?" (v. 46). By asking "How long?" to these questions, John Calvin notes, the psalmist "tacitly intimates that all will be well as soon as God is pleased to look upon his chosen people with a benignant countenance."[4] What an encouragement it is to prayer when we realize that God's gracious answer, when his wisdom chooses to provide it, is the answer to all our needs.

In Psalm 89:47–48, the psalmist marshals his plea with two supporting arguments. First, he points to the brevity of human life, so that if God waits long, it will be too late: "Remember how short my time is! For what vanity you have created all the children of man!" (Ps. 89:47). The psalmist's plea

3. Eric Lane, *Psalms 1–89: The Lord Saves* (Ross-shire, Scotland: Christian Focus, 2006), 396.

4. John Calvin, *Calvin's Commentaries*, 23 vols. (1848; repr., Grand Rapids: Baker, 2009), 5:452–53.

assumes that God created and redeemed his people not only to bless them but also to employ them in the service of his gracious reign. None of these aims can be attained while God's presence is hidden and his wrath is burning! The brevity of life argues on the one hand for a speedy repentance on the part of wayward Christians who are under God's affliction. Let us straighten our accounts in the presence of the Lord, putting right the causes of his affliction and committing ourselves anew to forms of obedience that we have neglected! An aid to this goal is consistency in reading our Bibles, so that we are reminded of our duties and of God's prohibitions. Once we have removed the cause for offense, we present a strong argument, coupled with the brevity of our lives, for God to restore us to his favor.

The second supporting argument points out that we have no remedy for the terror of death: "What man can live and never see death? Who can deliver his soul from the power of Sheol?" (Ps. 89:48). Faced with such a threat, believers need God himself to intervene. Indeed, it is only the believer who finds a true answer to this great problem that threatens us all. True comfort in the form of God's resurrection promises belongs only to the covenant people of God's household, who entered in by faith in Jesus Christ. Jesus offered the true remedy to this plea in saying, "I am the resurrection and the life. Whoever believes in me, though he die, yet shall he live" (John 11:25).

A related question is uttered in Psalm 89:49. Whereas the psalmist first asked *when*, here he requests to know *where* God's faithfulness is: "Lord, where is your steadfast love of old, which by your faithfulness you swore to David?" Here we see the psalmist encouraging his faith by remembering God's faithfulness in prior times. The Bible affords records of situations similar to ones that we face, in which God's people struggled to keep up their faith. But God proved faithful to believers in the past. Did it not seem that God had abandoned Israel and forsaken his promises as the chariots of Pharaoh bore down to destroy the nation as it was trapped by the Red Sea? But God's faithfulness appeared and the waters were parted, providing a highway for Israel and a grave for Pharaoh's army. Christians look back to the saving events of Jesus' crucifixion, when the disciples scattered in dismay, thinking that Jesus' promises had failed. But God sent his angels to roll away the stone from Jesus' tomb, and his resurrection appearance brought life and power back to the church. There are other biblical examples pertaining specifically to God's relenting from showing his wrath to his people. When Israel was in Babylon, it may have seemed that God had written the nation off, just as Christians who face crushing trials may feel that God's faithfulness has failed them. But when the prescribed seventy years were over (Jer. 25:10–11), and the prophet Daniel prayed in repentance to God, the Lord responded by causing the Persian king to order the restoration of Jerusalem (see Ezra 1; Dan. 9). These mighty events that are recorded in Scripture plead eloquently for our hold on God to be strengthened through faith.

Whereas Psalm 89:39 complains that God has "renounced the covenant" with Israel's king, the psalmist suddenly remembers that God by his faithfulness swore a promise to David. This being the case, appearances must be deceiving. There were, indeed, long centuries during which Israel had no king, David's throne having been cast down in the Babylonian conquest. But there were believers such as Ethan the Ezrahite who knew that God had promised an eternal throne to the line of David and who trusted that God's faithfulness could never fail. Among them were Anna and Simeon, venerable believers who were present when the baby Jesus was brought to be presented at the temple. Simeon responded in song: "Lord, now you are letting your servant depart in peace, according to your word; for my eyes have seen your salvation" (Luke 2:29–30). Beleaguered Christians today, who suffer either under the chastisement of God or under the cruelty of a godless world, may look to the second coming of Christ and know that however long it takes for God to return in faithfulness, our own personal history with a promise-keeping God will make us eyewitnesses when the Lord returns.

Remember, O Lord!

It is in light of God-centered historical perspective that the striking feature of the final verses in this long psalm is its concern for the glory and honor of God in the midst of the world's scoffing: "Remember, O Lord, how your servants are mocked, and how I bear in my heart the insults of all the many nations, with which your enemies mock, O Lord, with which they mock the footsteps of your anointed" (Ps. 89:50–51).

The word *remember* functions here as a covenantal term: God is to look on this situation in light of his covenant bond with his people, remembering his obligation to them. But here the specific concern deals with the link between God's honor and his covenantal bond with his people. It is "your servants" who are mocked and "your enemies" who are doing the mocking (Ps. 89:50–51). The state of Israel's throne and city seemed to be a public disgrace to the promises of God, just as the low state of the church in the world today often presents a similar shame. Calvin points out that when we pray to God out of a sincere concern that is primarily directed to his own glory in the state of the church, then we have offered the most effectual prayers: "It is a more powerful plea for obtaining favour in the sight of God, to beseech him to maintain his own cause, because all the reproaches by which the simplicity of our faith is held up to scorn recoil upon himself," since God is himself "wounded in the person of his church."[5] If we were more concerned for the glory and honor of God in our prayers, they would likely receive a swifter answer from God, who wants us to give his glory the place of priority in our hearts.

Perhaps the most striking statement in the conclusion of Psalm 89 is that "they mock the footsteps of your anointed" (Ps. 89:51). H. C. Leupold notes that ancient Jewish interpreters took this verse to mean that the Israelites' enemies mocked them over the delay of the Messiah's coming.[6] Jewish religion hoped in a Savior. Where was he? If Leupold's interpretation is correct, then the psalmist is praying for the Messiah to come, a prayer that was answered in the incarnation of Jesus Christ.

Whether or not the psalmist meant to refer to Christ explicitly—he might merely have been referring to the Davidic king with the title of "anointed"—it is doubtless true that the ultimate fulfillment of God's covenant with David is seen in the person and work of Jesus Christ.

In this respect, Christians today can answer the challenges of Psalm 89, with its concern both for God's coming to his people in their need and for the glory of God that is bound to our salvation, by reference to the gospel of Jesus Christ.

The circumstances by which Christians suffer are different from those that afflicted Ethan the Ezrahite, but the spiritual issues are the same. At the root of Israel's troubles lay the guilt of the people's sins before God. Whether or not our trials result directly from our sins, our alienation from God because of sin is the chief problem in each of our lives. The gospel

5. Calvin, *Commentaries,* 5:457–58.
6. H. C. Leupold, *Exposition of the Psalms* (Columbus, OH: Wartburg Press, 1959), 640.

answers this need by reference to the finished work of Jesus. We have not lived before God as we should, so Jesus fulfilled the law on our behalf. We deserve the penalty of death for our sins, so Jesus bore those sins, receiving the wrath of God and satisfying God's justice so that we might be forgiven through faith in him. With what triumph Paul writes in Romans 8:1: "There is therefore now no condemnation for those who are in Christ Jesus"! Through faith in the blood of God's Son, shed for our sins, sinners "are justified by his grace as a gift" (Rom. 3:24).

The gospel brings good news not only about Christ's past work but also about his present ministry as our exalted Savior in heaven. In this way, Christ is the answer to the trials that we face. While our prayers may plead with God to remove our afflictions, it is often his will to leave us in weakness while providing us with his own resources of strength from heaven. Jesus currently stands "at the right hand of God, . . . interceding for us" (Rom. 8:34), sending us the "Spirit [who] helps us in our weakness" (v. 26). In Paul's estimation, our afflictions thus become a source of boasting, "so that the power of Christ may rest" on us (2 Cor. 12:9).

What about the frustrations in life associated with our failures? Ethan looked on the calamity of the fall of Jerusalem and the disgrace of the Davidic line as the culmination of generations of Israel's idolatry. Christians today will have occasion to look on the church with drooping heads, wearily observing the many failures of the church and its earthly leaders. Here again, the apostle Paul points to the gospel as our confidence. His letters are filled with references to unending difficulties among the Christians and disputes among their leaders. For all the glory that we associate with the early church, the reality was that it was an outwardly insignificant movement in the great affairs of the day. But Paul looked to the gospel that he had the privilege of bearing, together with his fellow believers, and his head was lifted up. "I am not ashamed of the gospel," he exulted, "for it is the power of God for salvation to everyone who believes" (Rom. 1:16). For all our failures, Christians possess a mighty source of optimism and an awareness of certain success in the end, through the good news of Jesus.

The psalmist pleaded, "Lord, where is your steadfast love of old, which by your faithfulness you swore to David?" (Ps. 89:49). "How long, O Lord?" was his plea (v. 46). Beleaguered Christians will pray to God in this same spirit. When will our salvation be fully revealed? When will Jesus come again to relieve us of all our earthly troubles? The answer is found in the great day of glory that is fast approaching—what Paul called "our blessed hope, the appearing of the glory of our great God and Savior Jesus Christ" (Titus 2:13).

Remember the cry of the saints in Revelation 6:10: "O Sovereign Lord, holy and true, how long before you will judge and avenge our blood on those who dwell on the earth?" Jesus himself gives the answer to this plea, which is the final and greatest answer to Psalm 89. He says: "Behold, I am coming soon, bringing my recompense with me, to repay each one for what he has done. I am the Alpha and the Omega, the first and the last, the beginning and the end" (Rev. 22:12–13). The church gives its response in Revelation 22:20: "Amen. Come, Lord Jesus!"

Bless You, Lord!

The editor who completed this third book of the Psalter must have had a similar perspective in mind, because he concluded Psalm 89 and book 3 of the Psalms with these words, to which there can be no improvement: "Blessed be the Lord forever! Amen and Amen" (Ps. 89:52). Yes, even in circumstances like those afflicting godly Ethan the Ezrahite, our believing hearts may yet give praise to God. If believers today fix our eyes on Jesus (Heb. 12:2), remembering all that he has done, is doing now, and has promised to do in his glorious return, we will take up this same spirit of praise, giving him a most potent witness in our troubled times. Regardless of our present trials, we will join Ethan and all the other saints in declaring, "Blessed be the Lord forever! Amen and Amen."

Psalms 90–106: Book 4 of the Psalter

The Lord Reigns!

21

Lord, Our Dwelling Place

Psalm 90

Lord, you have been our dwelling place in all generations.
Before the mountains were brought forth, or ever you had
formed the earth and the world, from everlasting
to everlasting you are God. (Ps. 90:1–2)

A number of hymns are associated with specific events in the life of the church. "Blest Be the Tie That Binds" is sung when receiving new church members. When children are baptized, we often sing "Children of the Heavenly Father." Another occasional hymn is Isaac Watts's "Our God, Our Help in Ages Past," based on Psalm 90. We sing this hymn at funerals, just as the psalm was placed in the funeral service of the Church of England's *Book of Common Prayer.* It reminds us that while earthly life comes to an end, believers have an eternal resting place in God:

> Our God, our help in ages past, our hope for years to come,
> Our shelter from the stormy blast, and our eternal home.[1]

1. Isaac Watts, "Our God, Our Help in Ages Past" (1719).

It has been my practice for many years to have the congregation I serve sing Watts's hymn to start the last worship service of the ending year. The year-end is a time both to reflect on the ephemeral nature of our lives and to set before the Lord all that we have done in order that he would establish our work, two chief themes in Psalm 90.

Psalm 90 is the only psalm ascribed to Moses, the great leader of Israel through the exodus. Many scholars question his authorship, however, in part because the psalm numbers our lives at seventy or eighty years, whereas Moses lived much longer. Yet even in the time of Moses, many lives were of about this duration. Moreover, there are good reasons why Moses would have written these lines. James Boice suggests that Moses wrote Psalm 90 during the events of Numbers 20, which records the death of his sister, Miriam, and his brother, the high priest Aaron, and also Moses' sin of striking the rock twice, for which sin he would die.[2] In that case, Moses would understandably have been reflecting on the brevity of life under God's righteous judgment. More generally, we may think of Moses as reflecting on the long sojourn of Israel in the wilderness, in which the entire generation of the exodus died. Moses wanted Israel to learn its lesson: while our sin has brought death and frustration, God's people may look with hope to God, who is eternal in his life and unchanging in his saving will. It is in this light that Moses concludes by praying for God's mercy on Israel, the blessing of God's presence during trials, and God's establishment of the work of his generation.

A Home in the Eternal God

It is a good practice in our prayers to focus on an attribute of God that will bring consolation in our trials. As Moses faced mortality, God's eternal nature was a source of great solace. He therefore began with these immortal lines:

> Lord, you have been our dwelling place
> in all generations.
> Before the mountains were brought forth,
> or ever you had formed the earth and the world,
> from everlasting to everlasting you are God. (Ps. 90:1–2)

2. James Montgomery Boice, *Psalms*, 3 vols. (Grand Rapids: Baker, 1996), 2:740–41.

In contrast to man in his weakness and transitory nature, God exists beyond time, unreached by the influences of change or circumstance. Stephen Charnock pointed out the significance of this aspect of the divine being:

> Eternity is a negative attribute, and is a denying of God any measures of time.... Eternity is the duration of his essence; and when we say God is eternal, we exclude from him all possibility of beginning and ending, all flux and change. ... His duration is as endless as his essence is boundless: he always was and always will be, and will no more have an end than he had a beginning.[3]

By comparison to the apparently everlasting mountains, Moses cites God's eternity as proof of his changelessness. Here, in a frightening world of change, the believer may find a sure and stable hope. Before the mountains rose up, "or ever you had formed the earth and the world," God dwells "from everlasting to everlasting" (Ps. 90:2). Moreover, God exists without succession in his experience, thoughts, or plans, so that all history is an eternal present to him. Verse 4 extols: "a thousand years in your sight are but as yesterday when it is past, or as a watch in the night." The evening hours were divided into three or four watches, during which sentinels would stand guard. But for God, even a millennium is but a single watch in the night, during which he sleeplessly oversees his people and will. Think of all that history packs into a thousand years, mused Charles Spurgeon: "the rise and fall of empires, the glory and obliteration of dynasties, and countless events ... which elude the pens of historians. Yet this period ... is to the Lord as nothing."[4] For the psalmist, God's eternal being is tied to his utter sovereignty over all things. Who or what can interfere with God's rule, when God is before and after all, together with the almighty power by which he created the mountains and the whole world? How blessed is this thought to the failing and faltering believer who is relying on God for his eternal salvation! Charnock notes: "The eternity of God is the foundation of the stability of the covenant, the great comfort of a Christian."[5]

It is precisely the connection between God's eternal being and our salvation hope that Moses makes: "Lord, you have been our dwelling place in all

3. Stephen Charnock, *The Existence and Attributes of God*, 2 vols. (1883; repr., Grand Rapids: Baker, 1996), 1:281.

4. Charles Haddon Spurgeon, *The Treasury of David*, 3 vols. (Peabody, MA: Hendrickson, n.d.), 2b:61.

5. Charnock, *Existence and Attributes of God*, 1:279.

generations" (Ps. 90:1). To know God according to his Word and trust him in saving faith involves dwelling in him as the source of our protection and care.

It will help for us to think of dwelling in God in terms of Moses' experience with Israel in the sojourn of the exodus. Israel was a pilgrim people, having departed from the bondage of Egypt and traveling through great trials to the promised land. But God dwelt in the midst of Israel's camp at the tent of meeting. When Israel set out, the shekinah glory of God went before the people, a pillar of cloud by day to shade them from the sun's harsh rays and of fire by night to guide them. So it is for the Christian! God dwells within us by his Spirit, and we sojourn under the protecting care of his faithful love, guided by the shining light of his Word. Psalm 121 expresses this very help and care:

> He will not let your foot be moved;
> he who keeps you will not slumber. . . .
> The LORD is your keeper;
> the LORD is your shade on your right hand.
> The sun shall not strike you by day,
> nor the moon by night.
> The LORD will keep you from all evil;
> he will keep your life. (Ps. 121:3–7)

Since God is our eternal dwelling place, no Christian walks through this life without a home. Though rejected by the world and beset with many trials, at times like Jesus without a place to lay our head (Matt. 8:20), yet the believer may look to God with the faith of Abraham, who "called . . . on the name of the LORD, the Everlasting God" (Gen. 21:33). Paul rejoiced at the end of his life of trials: "The Lord will rescue me from every evil deed and bring me safely into his heavenly kingdom" (2 Tim. 4:18).

Unlike the dwellings of merely mortal man, which prove so transient and insecure, Christians find a sure repose in the eternal God of heaven. Spurgeon writes: "King's palaces have vanished beneath the crumbling hand of time—they have been burned with fire and buried beneath mountains of ruins, but the imperial race of heaven has never lost its regal habitation. . . . Where dwelt our fathers a hundred generations since, there dwell we still."[6]

6. Spurgeon, *Treasury of David*, 2b:61.

The Fleeting Nature of Mortal Life

In light of our eternal dwelling in God, Moses turns his attention to the mortal existence of mankind. Most people cannot endure a sober reflection of their mortal condition because of the anxiety that springs from their lack of hope. But the believer can see the truth about himself or herself under the protection of God's covenant love. Moses, nearing the end of his own life, sees the value of a sober realism, which will cast us more fully into the arms of our Savior.

First, man faces the troubling prospect of death at the end of his decades of life: "You return man to dust and say, 'Return, O children of man!'" (Ps. 90:3). Some of the earliest members of our race lived what seems to us an exceedingly long life, capped by Methuselah's 969 years. Yet even this long life ended in the grave, passing like an evening watch for the Lord (v. 4). For most of us, life will be much shorter: "The years of our life are seventy, or even by reason of strength eighty" (v. 10). If we look on a church congregation and fast-forward a hundred years, virtually all of us will have died by then. Men take pride in achievements, but in the end all are laid low. Wise Solomon saw this fact as humbling to our race: "For what happens to the children of man and what happens to the beasts is the same; as one dies, so dies the other. They all have the same breath, and man has no advantage over the beasts, for all is vanity" (Eccl. 3:19). However admirable may be the form of a man or a woman, by God's decree a little time will return our frame to dust. As our own days get closer to the average that Moses cites, or even beyond them, we wisely begin to turn our thoughts more frequently to eternal things.

Second, even while we live, mankind is subjected to sudden overthrow: "You sweep them away as with a flood" (Ps. 90:5). Think of how a sudden downpour results in a torrent of floods, carrying all things away. Mankind lives every moment under this possibility. Or consider the grass that springs up with life when the sun shines out after rain. So are the affairs of mortal man. "They are like a dream, like grass that is renewed in the morning: in the morning it flourishes and is renewed; in the evening it fades and withers" (vv. 5–6). A visit to the doctor, the impact of distant events on the stock market, or fleeting changes to human affections may turn our lives upside down in a moment. All of us know people who have suffered sudden anguish in these and other ways. We live in this world under constant insecurity. What folly it is to build the house of our eternal security on the shifting sands of worldly hopes!

To make matters worse, Moses notes that even the normal affairs of our lives are beset with "toil and trouble" (Ps. 90:10). The young worker looks forward to a promotion, only to crumble under responsibility when he gets it. The girl longs for marriage and children, but when they arrive they crease her brow with anxiety and strain. Solomon laments: "This also is vanity and a great evil. What has a man from all the toil and striving of heart with which he toils beneath the sun? For all his days are full of sorrow, and his work is a vexation" (Eccl. 2:21–23).

These insights are known by everyone, not merely readers of the Bible. But what unbelieving man does not know—though he struggles in thought and shakes his frustrated fist—is the true cause of this deplorable situation. Moses did know, by revelation from God's Word and as confirmed in his experience. The cause of man's earthly woe is God's wrath for our sins: "For we are brought to an end by your anger; by your wrath we are dismayed. You have set our iniquities before you, our secret sins in the light of your presence" (Ps. 90:7–8).

We remember that Moses was the human author of Genesis 3, where Adam and Eve fell under the curse of death because of sin. Not only would man die (Gen. 2:17), but as punishment for breaking God's covenant Adam and his race would suffer lives of toil and pain:

> By the sweat of your face
>   you shall eat bread,
> till you return to the ground,
>   for out of it you were taken;
> for you are dust,
>   and to dust you shall return. (Gen. 3:19)

Moreover, Moses had experienced the woeful effects of sin while leading Israel in its exodus. Having begun with such remarkable instances of God's supernatural aid, the people nonetheless fell into sin, complaining against the Lord and refusing to obey. As a result, God sentenced that generation to wander in the desert until all the offenders had died. Those Israelites, who could have long since been enjoying the blessings that God had offered in the promised land, instead wore themselves out in the hard climate of the Sinai desert. Only when all that generation had died would Israel enter Canaan. Even godly Moses would be forbidden to enter because of his sin against God in striking twice on the rock (Num. 20:12). Sin is the great problem of every life, though we tend not to think in this way. When Moses cries that "we are brought to an end by your anger" (Ps. 90:7), the problem is not some petulant defect in the divine character but rather God's perfect, glorious, and unchanging holiness in response to the sins for which we are at fault. God's judgment for sin makes sense of this troubled life. As H. C. Leupold put it: "Life could not be the futile thing that it is if God were not thoroughly displeased with men."[7]

We do not think of sin as our problem because we so easily forget our failings. But God in his perfect holiness cannot forget our sins. Moses notes: "You have set our iniquities before you, our secret sins in the light of your presence" (Ps. 90:8). The Bible is filled with people who vainly hoped their sins were unseen by God. Like David in his sin with Bathsheba, we may employ earthly power and cunning to tie up our dirty loose ends. But the whole sordid episode concluded with: "the thing that David had done displeased the Lord" (2 Sam. 11:27). David's subsequent life would be scarred by the wages of divine judgment. So, too, are our sins the cause of pain and sorrow throughout life. What folly it is for Christians to treat their sins so lightly! Although through faith in Christ we are forgiven of all our sins (1 John 1:7), sins yet make a quagmire of our relationships and endeavors. Moses thus asks, "Who considers the power of your anger, and your wrath according to the fear of you?" (Ps. 90:11). It is a mark of God's grace at work in our lives if we are able to take a sober estimate of sin. As Proverbs 9:10 states: "The fear of the Lord is the beginning of wisdom."

Given this assessment of man's mortal frailty—with our short duration, filled with danger and troubles, and ending with the grave, all because of God's just wrath on our sins—Moses calls on the Lord with his primary request in this psalm: "So teach us to number our days that we may get a heart of wisdom" (Ps. 90:12).

Most people respond to such a sober assessment of life by praying for God to grant us an exception from fallen human experience. Moses, who knew better, asks for God to enable us to reflect wisely on our situation. In

7. H. C. Leupold, *Exposition of the Psalms* (Columbus, OH: Wartburg Press, 1959), 646–47.

this sense, Psalm 90 is one of the most realistic of all the psalms, without a trace of bitterness for our wretched mortal state. The reason for this is that Moses knew God, who was in the end the safe dwelling place where his hopes were secure.

On average, twenty-seven thousand Israelites died every year during their wilderness trek. So if death is such a constant, it is vital that we profit from its lessons. This wisdom involves realizing that each day is numbered, and that one of them will be our last. As we have noted, wisdom involves a watchful opposition toward sin and its false claims. William Plumer thus suggests these resolutions: "Let us cherish rather than reject solemn reflections on the mortality of man, the vanity of his course and the shortness of his life . . . . Let us be anxious rather to live well than to live long."[8] Whenever we attend a funeral, we should carefully note the lessons to be learned from the life that has passed into eternity. Chief among these lessons must be the vital difference between the believer, who passes out of life into the eternal dwelling of God's grace, and the unbeliever, who dies in the guilt of his sin to face the dreadful prospect of eternal judgment from God. Hebrews 9:27 declares the immortal truth that "it is appointed for man to die once, and after that comes judgment." If we have prepared for that judgment by placing our sins onto the cross of Jesus Christ, where God's Son died to pay our penalty, we have embraced the very heart of wisdom in the face of life and death.

Three Prayers for Sinful Man

In 1192, England's King Richard the Lionhearted was returning home from the Third Crusade when he was captured by Leopold V, Duke of Austria. Leopold turned Richard over to Henry VI, the Holy Roman Emperor, who had grievances against Richard stemming from the war. Henry needed money to fight his wars in Italy, so he communicated to England that Richard could be released only upon the payment of a ransom of 150,000 marks. This amount was three times the annual revenue of the entire kingdom. Meanwhile, England was languishing under the corrupt rule of Richard's brother, Prince John. Feeling their misery and longing for the return of their king, the English people and church heroically raised the needed amount

8. William S. Plumer, *Psalms* (1867; repr., Edinburgh: Banner of Truth, 1975), 845–46.

at great sacrifice to themselves. In February 1194, Richard was released and finally arrived home to his people, a scene celebrated in legend and literature. With the strong and lionhearted monarch safely returned to his people, England would be safe and whole again.

The English people's fervent longing for the return of their king finds an echo in the first of three petitions with which Moses concludes Psalm 90. He has gathered up his wisdom, resting in the secure dwelling of God's eternity and facing the truth of his own mortal weakness. The petitions that conclude this psalm therefore set a model for what a heavenly-minded believer should desire from God. The first of the three requests asks God to return to Israel not with might or riches but with mercy: "Return, O Lord! How long? Have pity on your servants!" (Ps. 90:13).

To live in this fallen world is to daily confront the presence and effects of our sin. We are like the Israelites in the wilderness, bearing great promises but suffering in our present banishment from our eternal home. What we need most, then, are reminders of God's tender love and grace, together with gospel assurances of our salvation. Verses such as Micah 7:18 should be close to our hearts: "He does not retain his anger forever, because he delights in steadfast love." Christians think often of Paul's persuasion that "neither death nor life, nor angels nor rulers, . . . nor anything else in all creation, will be able to separate us from the love of God in Christ Jesus our Lord" (Rom. 8:38–39). If England would pay so much silver and gold for the return of King Richard's valor, how much more eagerly ought Christians to hasten to the church, or make time in our daily lives to search our Bibles, for the return of God's blessing with good news of his saving grace!

The second of Moses' concluding petitions involves another form of wisdom. He realizes that Israel is yet in the wilderness and that by God's will this present life is designed for the testing of our faith through various trials. Therefore, instead of wasting his prayer by asking for a change in his circumstances, Moses prays for an alteration to his attitude. Specifically, he prays that the Lord would convey a spirit of joy that arises from the mere presence of the Lord: "Satisfy us in the morning with your steadfast love, that we may rejoice and be glad all our days" (Ps. 90:14).

The Lord's "steadfast love" speaks of God's faithfulness to his covenant promises. What joy there is in reflecting on the promises of God to his people, together with our knowledge that he will fulfill them all. Leupold writes: "To know that the nation dwells under the shadow of that love is sufficient to lay the basis for an enduring gladness over against the oppressive grief that had now for some time brooded over the people. If one can only be sure of that love, then there is reason enough for exulting and being glad all the days of one's life."[9]

Moses adds his plea that the long years of striving would be answered with corresponding times of blessing: "Make us glad for as many days as you have afflicted us, and for as many years as we have seen evil" (Ps. 90:15). This prayer was answered in the entry of Israel into the land of Canaan. Plumer rightly observes: "The generation that grew up under those great displays of wrath and mercy in the wilderness was the best generation of Jews that ever lived."[10] The tribes that entered Canaan with Joshua, casting down the fortress of Jericho and seizing God's holy land, had learned well the wages of sin and unbelief through the strivings of the desert. Taught in hardship to rely on God's gracious provision, they rejoiced in the Lord when he strengthened them with might to conquer the land.

Paul makes a similar appeal in the fourth chapter of Philippians. That wonderful book contains numerous proofs of God's steadfast love. Paul writes that "he who began a good work in you will bring it to completion at the day of Jesus Christ" (Phil. 1:6). He reminds his readers that "to live is Christ, and to die is gain" (v. 21). He extols the servant love of Jesus that caused him to humble himself by setting aside his glory and obediently bearing the cross (2:8). He reminds them that through faith in Christ, we have "righteousness from God," knowing our Lord in "the power of his resurrection" (3:9–10). What, then, is Paul's exhortation? It is the same as Moses' appeal to God that a spirit of joy would arise in believers' hearts: "Rejoice in the Lord always; again I will say, rejoice" (4:4).

Moses has three concluding appeals: first for a return of God's mercy and second for joy in our afflictions because of his love. His final appeal is one that speaks to us in our various Christian callings:

> Let your work be shown to your servants,
>   and your glorious power to their children.
> Let the favor of the Lord our God be upon us,

9. Leupold, *Exposition of the Psalms*, 648.
10. Plumer, *Psalms*, 844.

> and establish the work of our hands upon us,
> yes, establish the work of our hands! (Ps. 90:16–17)

What a blessing it is in the brief years of our lives to have a meaningful calling from the Lord that will provide an enduring legacy! Notice that Moses does not ask God merely to give his blessing to our work. Rather, he appeals for the Lord to show us his work and then to allow that work to shine as a display of his power for the faith of our children. Moses realizes that he needs two things in order to play a meaningful role in the work of God's salvation: for God's work to be shown to him and for God's blessing to spread through that work. Alexander Maclaren joins these together:

> Our work will be established if it is His work. . . . And our work will stand if we quietly leave it in His hands. . . . In the great summing up of everything at the end, the tiniest deed that was done for God, though it was done far away up amongst the mountain solitudes where no eyes saw, shall live and be represented, in its effects on others and in its glad issues to the doer.[11]

Moses' prayer shows that those who are most keenly aware of God's purpose in the world are most concerned that their children would embrace the Lord in faith. This should form a regular prayer at the beginning and end of every church year: that through the Word that is preached, the prayers that are answered, and the godly works that are performed, our children would become aware of the reality of God and the priceless value of his salvation. "Let us spend our lives not on our works, but on your works," we should pray. And it is the heart of those who love the people of God that concludes with Moses' fervent appeal: "establish the works of our hands upon us; yes, establish the work of our hands!" (Ps. 90:17).

Our God in Jesus Christ

If we sum up Psalm 90, we may say that Moses' great psalm is very much like David's most famous poem, Psalm 23. Moses lifts his heart to the eternal Father in whom his hope of dwelling lies. David looks to God as the loving Shepherd, and ultimately to Jesus Christ, who guides his people into everlasting

11. Alexander Maclaren, *Expositions of Holy Scripture*, 17 vols. (Grand Rapids: Baker, 1982), 4b:182–83.

life. The final verse of Psalm 23 connects closely with the opening verse of Psalm 90. Whereas Moses celebrates his dwelling in the eternal God, David rejoices: "Surely goodness and mercy shall follow me all the days of my life, and I shall dwell in the house of the LORD forever" (Ps. 23:6).

The question we should ask of Psalm 23 pertains to Psalm 90's key to gaining this eternal dwelling in God. Does David extol the strength of the sheep? Does David write that what makes the difference is being able to navigate the journey of life on your own, forging your own way through the valley of the shadow of death? Not at all! For Psalm 23, the key to entering the house of the Lord forever is being able to say with David in its opening line, "The LORD is my shepherd." Anyone who can look to Jesus Christ, the Good Shepherd who laid down his life for the sheep, and declare, "He is my Savior! Jesus is my Lord and my Guide!," can also declare with absolute confidence, "I shall dwell in the house of the LORD forever."

The same is true for Psalm 90. Do you long for an eternal home, safe in the heavens? Do you feel in your heart the desire for a significance and meaning that lasts beyond these short years of mortal life? Do you feel frustration over the ravages of sin in society and your own experience? The key to your fulfillment lies in the final verse, where Moses pleads: "Let the favor of the Lord our God be upon us." Moses can call the Creator of all things "the Lord our God." Can you say of God, "He is my God"? Can you rejoice to know, "He is the faithful God of his people, and I am one of them"? You can know your acceptance with God through faith in his Son, Jesus. God's Word declares that "to all who did receive him, who believed in his name, he gave the right to become children of God" (John 1:12). Believing in Jesus, you, too, will be able to rejoice in your Father God as your eternal home. And when your brief life has come to its end, you will experience with Moses the fulfillment of his longing plea: "Satisfy us in the morning with your steadfast love, that we may rejoice and be glad all our days" (Ps. 90:14).

22

In the Shelter of the Most High

Psalm 91

He who dwells in the shelter of the Most High will abide in the shadow of the Almighty. (Ps. 91:1)

The opening verse of Psalm 91 contains a couplet that is as beloved and comforting as any other in Holy Scripture: "He who dwells in the shelter of the Most High will abide in the shadow of the Almighty." This verse affirms, writes Matthew Henry, "that all those who live a life of communion with God are constantly safe under his protection, and may therefore preserve a holy serenity and security of mind at all times."[1] Believers in all kinds of trouble have gained strength of heart by meditating on these inspired words. Charles Spurgeon tells of a period early in his ministry when a deadly plague coursed through London. Coming home from yet another funeral and concerned for his own safety, Spurgeon passed a shop where the merchant had hung a handwritten sign bearing the opening line of Psalm 91. "The effect upon my heart was immediate," he later wrote. "I felt secure, refreshed, girt with immortality.

1. Matthew Henry, *Commentary on the Whole Bible*, 6 vols. (Peabody, MA: Hendrickson, n.d.), 3:479.

I went on with my visitation of the dying in a calm and peaceful spirit; I felt no fear of evil, and I suffered no harm."[2]

Psalm 91 has a number of valuable features. It is intensely theological, portraying God's ability to care for his people in moving terms. It is also personal, as the unnamed psalmist applies these truths to his own condition and urges his heart to a more fervently trusting faith. It is a Christological psalm, the message of which is most pointedly fulfilled in the experience of Jesus Christ. And Psalm 91 offers promises from the mouth of God that inspire believers to find their satisfaction in him. "Because he holds fast to me in love, I will deliver him," God tells his servant. "With long life I will satisfy him and show him my salvation" (Ps. 91:14, 16).

The Believer's Shelter

The theological emphasis comes first in Psalm 91, as the names and saving mercy of God are presented as a refuge for believers. Four different names for God appear in verses 1–2, each of which provides a strong basis for our confidence: God is *Elyon*, "the Most High," *Shaddai*, "the Almighty," *Yahweh*, the covenant "Lord," and *Elohim*, the Creator "God." These four names give a sufficient hope to all who know him. As "the Most High" and "the Almighty," God is sovereign in authority and infinite in power. As "Lord," he has pledged his covenant care to his people. As God "who made heaven and earth" (Ps. 121:2), he can help when every earthly solace fails.

Because of who and what God is, believers may dwell in him as a refuge. The word for "shelter" carries the idea of a hidden compartment, which is why several versions render it as "the secret place" (e.g., KJV). Corrie ten Boom tells of how her family home in Amsterdam was modified during the Nazi occupation to create a secret compartment where Jewish refugees could hide from arrest. God's protection is like that for a believer.[3] A sense of peace that the unbeliever can scarcely imagine comes to our hearts when we trust the Lord, like a secret refuge that the world cannot reach.

Saying that believers "abide in the shadow of the Almighty" (Ps. 91:1) reminds us of a great rock beneath which desert dwellers find life-preserving shade. Dwelling under God's shadow may also be a reference to the taber-

2. Charles Haddon Spurgeon, *The Treasury of David*, 3 vols. (Peabody, MA: Hendrickson, n.d.), 2b:92.
3. Corrie ten Boom, *The Hiding Place* (Grand Rapids: Baker, 1984), 101–3.

nacle, where Israel drew near to God as the ark of the covenant rested under the shadow of angelic wings. John Calvin notes that believers "dwell under his shadow, in the sense that they experience to what a rich extent his protection reaches."[4]

Psalm 91:1 may be taken as one of the most compelling descriptions of prayer that is found in all the Bible. Taking "shelter" as a "secret place," we are reminded of Jesus' teaching that we should go to a private place "and pray to your Father who is in secret" (Matt. 6:6), an analogy that Jesus may have drawn from this verse. In this light, we see Psalm 91:1 as providing an awesome depiction of the life of devoted prayer. To dwell in the secret place of prayer with the Most High is to "abide in the shadow of the Almighty," that is, to meet with God in spirit and experience the reflection of his glory on our souls.

Psalm 91:2 adds that God is "my refuge and my fortress." The word for "fortress" is *matzudah*, referring to a mountaintop stronghold. After the Roman destruction of Jerusalem in A.D. 70, a thousand Jewish zealots occupied the Masada, a mountain fortress in southern Judea, where they held off an entire Roman legion for months. While the Masada was finally breached, the fortress that is God in his sovereign omnipotence can never be overcome.

In speaking of God's protection, the psalmist emphasizes his personal relationship and access: "My refuge and my fortress, My God, in whom I trust" (Ps. 91:2). Verse 4 depicts God as responding in kind, using a surprisingly intimate illustration of devotion and care: "He will cover you with his pinions, and under his wings you will find refuge." The image is of a mother bird who draws near to her vulnerable chicks when a deadly hawk soars above, looking for prey. Spreading her wings over their little bodies, she both shields them from evil and comforts them with her protective presence. Likewise, when believers draw close to God in faith, the sense of God's nearness drives oppression from our hearts. Spurgeon writes: "Who will not see herein a matchless love, a divine tenderness, which should both woo and win our confidence. Even as a hen covers her chickens so does the Lord protect the souls which dwell in him; let us cower down beneath him for comfort and for safety."[5]

4. John Calvin, *Calvin's Commentaries*, 23 vols. (1848; repr., Grand Rapids: Baker, 2009), 5:478.
5. Spurgeon, *Treasury of David*, 2b:90.

If God's care is soft, like a mother bird's feathers, it is also firm and strong: "his faithfulness is a shield and buckler" (Ps. 91:4). The King James Version reads that God's "truth" is a shield and buckler (the latter a small, round shield), so that the believer is covered all around. This is a valid idea, since God's Word does protect us from spiritual assault. But it is better to take verse 4 as citing God's "faithfulness" as a shield and armor for his people. God does not desert us in time of need. God stands between us and all assault. While it is certainly true that Christians can suffer harm, by God's sovereign will it is not possible for even such harm to do us evil. Joseph, looking back on bitter betrayals and cruel circumstances, could affirm God's overruling faithfulness: "you meant evil against me, but God meant it for good" (Gen. 50:20). When Abraham faced danger from the five kings of the east, the Lord made a promise that Psalm 91 extends to all believers: "Fear not, . . . I am your shield; your reward shall be very great" (Gen. 15:1).

In all these ways—his divine names, his secret place and high fortress, his motherly attention, and his firm faithfulness—God is a shelter on whom we may wholly rely. Yet we must not fail to note the essential role of faith in the psalmist's hope. It is he "who dwells" in the Most High's shelter who "will abide in the shadow of the Almighty" (Ps. 91:1). The psalmist not only celebrates God as a high fortress, but adds "my God, in whom I trust" (v. 2). God is your shelter "because you have made the Lord your dwelling place" (v. 9).

There is a tendency among commentators to say that the shelter referred to in Psalm 91 belongs not to all believers but only to those who have sought the Lord with great fervor. Spurgeon states: "The blessings here promised are not for all believers, but for those who live in close fellowship with God."[6] Under this approach, it is those who actively seek God's face in prayer, who carry God's Word constantly on their heart, and who live with a zeal for God's pleasure who can claim the privileges of Psalm 91. An example is seen in the biography of the missionary-martyr Jim Elliot, who from early years showed an unflagging zeal for the Lord. The record of his remarkable life was titled *Shadow of the Almighty*, from Psalm 91.[7] The meaning was that here was a man who dwelt constantly in the presence of God and who therefore lived with a bold assurance of God's blessing.

6. Spurgeon, *Treasury of David*, 3:88.

7. Elisabeth Elliot, *Shadow of the Almighty: The Life & Testament of Jim Elliot* (San Francisco: Harper & Row, 1958).

Does this mean that God shelters only the most consistent and zealous believers? The answer is no. This is God as he is presented to each of his people. God is present as a shelter and fortress for you. The Lord desires to cover you with his wings and protect you like a shield. God is unchanging toward all his people; as Psalm 118 repeatedly celebrates, "his steadfast love endures forever." Spurgeon is right that we still must enter into God's shelter through faith. We must dwell in the shelter of the Most High in order to abide in the shadow of the Almighty. Because Jim Elliot dwelt in God's presence, being constantly aware of God's greatness, he lived with peace and a courageous purpose in life, just as we may do in the same way. In this respect, Psalm 91 invites all of God's people—weak and strong—to set their hearts firmly on the Lord, reminding themselves of all that he is to us in time of need. He is always there for us, if only we will find our shelter in him.

Do we remember God when trouble comes? Do we lay hold of his sovereignty, power, and faithfulness? Do our hearts look to him when fearful, like chicks running under their mother's uplifted wing? Do we rely on God's faithfulness to shield us from danger? The answer is that we are far more likely to receive the comfort we need in trials if we have been habitually drawing near to God. In this respect, Psalm 91 serves as both a challenge and an invitation. If we lack a sense of God's presence in time of need, might this suggest that we have neglected to dwell in his courts? Psalm 91 invites us to join in acclaiming: "My refuge and my fortress, my God, in whom I trust" (v. 2).

The Believer's Security

Having so wonderfully portrayed God as our shelter, the psalmist vividly depicts the believer's security in the Lord. Starting in Psalm 91:3, he asserts God's protection from unforeseen dangers: "For he will deliver you from the snare of the fowler and from the deadly pestilence." The fowler's snare is a bird trap into which the unwary may stumble. Likewise, "the deadly pestilence" is sudden in its coming. The "snare" may have the idea of temptations in which believers may be entangled if we do not walk closely with the Lord. Jesus taught us to pray for God's protection: "Lead us not into temptation, but deliver us from evil" (Matt. 6:13). It is true that God's people do get tripped up and are sometimes afflicted, yet Psalm 91 reminds us how often we are protected, even if unawares. How little we think of thanking God after arriving safely from a journey or upon rising from sleep after the night. Yet it is God's protection that enables us to avoid innumerable threats to our lives.

For many people, it is not so much the trials of life as the fear of danger that paralyzes our lives. For such Christians, Psalm 91 offers a remedy through our faith in the Lord: "You will not fear the terror of the night, nor the arrow that flies by day, nor the pestilence that stalks in darkness, nor the destruction that wastes at noonday" (Ps. 91:5–6). The point is to remind us, as Calvin writes, "that those whom God has taken under his care are in a state of the most absolute safety. . . . Mention is made of *the fear of the night*, because men are naturally apprehensive in the dark, . . . and our fears are apt at such seasons to magnify any sound or disturbance."[8] A famous instance of faith overcoming fear was given by the Confederate general Stonewall Jackson amid the deadly hail of Minié balls on the battlefield of First Manassas. When asked afterward why he had showed not the least sign of fear, he answered, "My religious belief teaches me to feel as safe in battle as in my bed. God has fixed the time for my death."[9]

One reason why Christians can have confidence in God's protection is the unseen ministry of angels in our times of need: "For he will command his angels concerning you to guard you in all your ways. On their hands they will bear you up, lest you strike your foot against a stone" (Ps. 91:11–12). Hebrews 1:14 describes these unseen holy agents as "ministering spirits sent out to serve for the sake of those who are to inherit salvation." Many people are superstitious in focusing on guardian angels assigned to them, but the Bible speaks of legions of angels who are on hand at God's command to preserve his people. In reality, our guardian is God and the angels are his servants for the protection of believers.

While we catalogue the specific pledges made by Psalm 91 to preserve us from unforeseen dangers, we should not downplay its even more comprehensive claim. Verses 9–10 boldly assert: "Because you have made the Lord your dwelling place—the Most High, who is my refuge—no evil shall be allowed to befall you, no plague come near your tent." The psalmist does not

8. Calvin, *Commentaries*, 5:481.

9. Quoted in S. C. Gwynne, *Rebel Yell: The Violence, Passion, and Redemption of Stonewall Jackson* (New York: Scribner, 2014), 103.

mean that Christians will breeze through life without troubles. Though we are not told who wrote this psalm, it is unlikely that a believer who spoke of such wide-ranging trials should have had no personal experience with them. Still, he boldly claims God's protection so that the Christian is not fully touched by the plague of sin and evil on our world. As a result, verses 7 and 8 exclaim: "A thousand may fall at your side, ten thousand at your right hand, but it will not come near you. You will only look with your eyes and see the recompense of the wicked." This promise especially applies to our spiritual warfare against Satan and his evil servants. Spiritual conflict seems to be in mind in the promise of Psalm 91:13: "You will tread on the lion and the adder; the young lion and the serpent you will trample underfoot." Though we may suffer greatly under spiritual assault, the New Testament reminds us of ultimate victory through the conquest of Christ. Paul writes simply: "The God of peace will soon crush Satan under your feet" (Rom. 16:20).

An example of God's wide-ranging care and protection is seen in the testimony of Corrie ten Boom. Earlier, I noted how her family built a hiding place in their home to shelter Jews threatened by the Nazis during World War II. In February 1944, an informant betrayed the ten Booms. Corrie, together with her sister, Betsie, and her aged father, Caspar, fell into the hands of the dreaded Gestapo. Huddled together in the police station, their minds assailed by terror, they were led by Caspar in prayer, quoting Psalm 119: "You are my hiding place and my shield; I hope in your word. . . . Hold me up, that I may be safe" (vv. 114–17).

The events that ensued involved shocking suffering. Corrie and Betsie were beaten, to extract information. Caspar was offered release, if he would promise to cease aiding the Jews. In calm words, he refused, and within ten days he would die from the strain of prison life. Corrie and Betsie were sent to the dreaded Ravensbrück concentration camp in Germany, where they experienced countless horrors. Working as slave laborers while their health plummeted, they clung to God as their shelter. Their victory took the form of maintaining the grace of Christ in their hearts as they ministered to fellow prisoners and sought to show love to hardened Nazi guards. Throughout the ordeal, God fulfilled the promise of Psalm 91. He provided for their spirits by arranging for them to possess a smuggled Bible, which they used to share God's Word with many broken souls. He allowed their meeting room to be infested with fleas, with the providential result that the prison guards gave them space to study the Bible and pray.

Corrie and Betsie's desperate prayers were answered with supernatural deliverances. The most notable concerned a small vial of vitamins, which was vital for maintaining life in the midst of freezing cold, starvation, and sickness. At first, Corrie sought to hoard the small amount of precious medicine. Betsie countered with the Bible story of the woman whose jar was never empty, so they decided to share their few ounces freely. Corrie later wrote, "Every time I tilted the little bottle, a drop appeared at the top of the glass stopper. It just couldn't be! . . . Yet it happened, this day, and the next, and the next, until an awed little group of spectators stood around watching the drops fall onto the daily rations of bread." When Corrie tried to reason out how so little liquid could be administered to dozens of people every day, Betsie answered: "Don't try too hard to explain it, Corrie. Just accept it as a surprise from a Father who loves you." Shortly afterward, a nurse smuggled in several jars of vitamin pills. "We'll finish the drops first," Corrie reasoned. "But that night, no matter how long I held it upside down, or how hard I shook it, not another drop appeared." God had spread his wings over them in their time of need, perhaps employing angels to keep them safe until their work was done.

Sadly, Betsie died in the prison camp. For months she had led suffering women to faith in Jesus and had rejoiced with those lingering near death over the approaching rays of heaven. Gazing now at her sister's dead body, Corrie was struck by the evident blessing: "For there lay Betsie, her eyes closed as if in sleep, her face full and young. . . . Stronger! Freer! This was the Betsie of heaven, bursting with joy and health. Even her hair was graciously in place as if an angel had ministered to her." Corrie herself was released from prison by a clerical error, just one week before the women her age in the camp were all put to death. She understood that God had intended her to bear Betsie's witness, as found in her book *The Hiding Place*. Betsie had urged Corrie with her dying words: ". . . must tell people what we have learned here. We must tell them that there is no pit so deep that [God] is not deeper still."[10] There can be no more fitting commentary on this touching scene than the words of Psalm 91:9–10: "Because you have made the LORD your dwelling place—the Most High, who is my refuge—no evil shall be allowed to befall you, no plague come near your tent."

10. This account of Corrie and Betsie ten Boom is taken from *The Hiding Place*, 139–248.

The Believer's Savior

The pledges of Psalm 91 applied especially to the experience of Jesus Christ, who is the believer's Savior in these lines. The second of Satan's three temptations of Jesus included his quotations of Psalm 91:11–12. Taking Jesus to the pinnacle of the temple, Satan urged Jesus to test God by throwing himself down. After all, God had promised, "He will command his angels concerning you," and "On their hands they will bear you up, lest you strike your foot against a stone" (Matt. 4:5–6). This occasion is the one time recorded in Scripture when Satan quotes directly from the Bible, prompting Calvin to observe that the devil "is a sufficiently acute theologian."[11] The problem was that Satan wanted Jesus to misuse the promise by presuming on God's protection. Jesus' answer showed his superior grasp of God's Word: "Again it is written, 'You shall not put the Lord your God to the test'" (Matt. 4:7).

As usual, Satan's manipulation of Scripture involved an omission. Psalm 91:11 states that God assigns angels "to guard you in all your ways." The point is that God guards us as we are seeking to serve him in the ordinary callings of our lives. We are not, however, to live recklessly under the foolish premise that God has committed to our protection even in the course of sin or neglect. Jesus said that we are not to test God or tempt him, but should receive his promises of protection as an incentive to a courageous obedience.

It was just such a life that Jesus followed perfectly during his days of mortal weakness on the earth. God responded by fulfilling the pledge of Psalm 91. We find that after Jesus overcame Satan's temptations, "the devil left him, and behold, angels came and were ministering to him" (Matt. 4:11). Likewise, Jesus was immortal against all threats until the appointed time for his sin-atoning sacrifice. Dwelling constantly in the refuge of God's presence, his faithful life received the fulfillment of Psalm 91:10: "no evil shall be allowed to befall you, no plague come near your tent."

It is therefore in the life of our Lord that the final promises of Psalm 91 find their fullest expression. God says, "Because he holds fast to me in love, I will deliver him; I will protect him, because he knows my name" (Ps. 91:14). We then think of Jesus' prayer life and how the Father so readily provided all that was asked by his holy Son: "When he calls to me, I will answer him;

11. Calvin, *Commentaries*, 5:486.

I will be with him in trouble; I will rescue him and honor him" (v. 15). The greatest instance of this fulfillment was the resurrection of Jesus. While he suffered on the cross, the religious leaders mocked him. "He trusts in God; let God deliver him now, if he desires him," they scoffed (Matt. 27:43). God answered by raising Jesus from the grave and exalting him to the highest place of glory in heaven (Eph. 1:20–22). "With long life I will satisfy him and show him my salvation," declares Psalm 91:16 in conclusion. Jesus ascended into an eternal reign of glory above. Isaiah 53:11 spoke of the satisfaction that was the Father's reward for his cross: "Out of the anguish of his soul he shall see and be satisfied; by his knowledge shall the righteous one, my servant, make many to be accounted righteous, and he shall bear their iniquities." Christ trusted in his Father throughout his saving ministry for us. God fulfilled Psalm 91 by preserving and protecting him until the coming of his hour to fulfill his atoning purpose. In raising Jesus from the grave, God has granted Jesus his highest satisfaction in gathering his people to salvation, declaring them righteous through faith in the gospel, and forgiving all their sins.

The Believer's Satisfaction

It is in Christ that God's people receive their fullness of what God has promised in Psalm 91. The psalm began by extolling the believer's shelter in God and then the believer's security under God's care. This leads to the believer's own satisfaction as these promises are extended to us through our union with Christ in faith.

The final verses of Psalm 91 catalogue the inheritance of believers in Christ. The first is a summary of God's promise to deliver: "Because he holds fast to me in love, I will deliver him; I will protect him, because he knows my name" (Ps. 91:14). This language assumes that we will be constantly surrounded by danger, both temporal and spiritual. Our calling is to hold fast to the Lord in love, clinging to the example of verse 2: "I will say to the Lord, 'My refuge and my fortress, my God, in whom I trust.'" Calvin writes: "God does not promise [believers] a life of ease and luxury, but deliverance from their tribulations."[12] "I will be with him in trouble," God says; "I will rescue him and honor him" (Ps. 91:15).

12. Calvin, *Commentaries*, 5:491.

Moreover, God promises to hear our prayers and answer according to our needs: "When he calls to me, I will answer him" (Ps. 91:15). This promise serves as the grand theme of Psalm 91: to dwell in the "shelter of the Most High" is to "abide in the shadow of the Almighty" (v. 1). God's first answer to prayer is the peace he supplies to our hearts, as well as the marvelous provision of all that we need. Faith in this promise results in the calm repose expressed by Paul in Romans 8:28: "And we know that for those who love God all things work together for good, for those who are called according to his purpose."

The final promise of Psalm 91 is the most wonderful: "With long life I will satisfy him and show him my salvation" (v. 16). In the Old Testament, a long life symbolized the blessing of God. What matters more than the length of our days, however, is the joy that we experience in the Lord for whatever time we have on earth. Indeed, when our satisfaction rests in the presence and provision of God, our hearts long not so much for more and more days here in this world, but increasingly for enjoyment of the glories of heaven with God. Spurgeon writes: "The man described in this Psalm fills out the measure of his days, and whether he dies young or old he is quite satisfied with life, and is content to leave it."[13] The Christian therefore does not fear even to die, knowing that our longest life of greatest satisfaction awaits beyond the grave, and especially in the return of our Lord. Trusting in God, we express our confidence in the promise of Psalm 91:16, with the answer given in Psalm 23:6, "Surely goodness and mercy shall follow me all the days of my life, and I shall dwell in the house of the Lord forever."

The great condition of Psalm 91 is a living faith in God and his Word, looking to their fulfillment in Jesus Christ. Have you said the words of verse 2 to Jesus: "My refuge and my fortress, my God, in whom I trust"? If you have not come in faith to Christ, let Psalm 91 remind you of the perils around you, especially the danger of your sins to your eternal soul. What could keep you from the shelter, the security, and the satisfaction of Psalm 91, all of which are found in the Savior to which it points? The angel told Joseph, Jesus' earthly father, what to name him: "You shall call his name Jesus, for he will save his people from their sins" (Matt. 1:21). If you will open your

13. Spurgeon, *Treasury of David,* 2b:94.

heart to Jesus in love, having come to know his name by believing the message of Scripture, God promises this of you: "I will deliver him; I will protect him" (Ps. 91:14).

If you are a believer, let Psalm 91 remind you of the great wisdom of living close to God in the spirit of prayer. "He who dwells in the shelter of the Most High will abide in the shadow of the Almighty" (Ps. 91:1). Let these words serve as a motto for a life of peace in his strong arms and of loving security under the caring wings of a Savior who will be faithful to you.

23

A Sunday Go-to-Meeting Psalm

Psalm 92

For you, O Lord, have made me glad by your work; at the works of your hands I sing for joy. (Ps. 92:4)

We are living in an age that exalts the individual experience above that of the larger group. This spirit not only permeates society but also has infiltrated the church. I recently read an article, aimed at Christians who have been disappointed by church, that urged them to stay at home on Sundays. God is everywhere, it exclaimed! You can worship God on your own and in the way that fits your own needs! Against this ethos, we come to Psalm 92, which bears the title "A Psalm for the Sabbath." John Gill summarizes that Psalm 92 "was made for the Sabbath-day, and to be used upon it; and directs to the work and worship of it; praising of God and celebrating his works, attending his house and ordinances."[1] Here we encounter a mandate for the gathered church in its praise to God, together with the primary lessons we are to glean from attending the house of the Lord.

1. Quoted in William S. Plumer, *Psalms* (1867; repr., Edinburgh: Banner of Truth, 1975), 856.

A Guide to the Lord's Day

A likely reason that people feel disappointed with the church is that they come to worship seeking things other than what God has appointed. In our fractured society, many people primarily seek friendships and social bonds. These are important blessings, and the church should cultivate them. But the primary reason to come to church, and the aim for which we should prepare, is to give thanks and praise to God.

The God-centeredness of Psalm 92 is evident throughout the opening section. According to the psalmist, the verb *worship* is not an intransitive verb—one that does not require a direct object. For instance, *smile* is an intransitive verb. There is no direct object. You just smile. But worship always has an object, and the proper object of worship is God. So we worship by giving "thanks to the Lord." We "sing praises to your name, O Most High" (Ps. 92:1). We "declare your steadfast love" (v. 2).

According to the psalm, worship consists primarily of thanks and praise: "It is good to give thanks to the Lord, to sing praises to your name, O Most High" (Ps. 92:1). We have abundant reasons to thank God, since he is the author of every good thing. James 1:17 states: "Every good gift and every perfect gift is from above, coming down from the Father of lights." Moreover, it is fitting that we should worship God because of his supreme worthiness. The etymology of the English word *worship* helpfully brings out the rationale for our praise. Originally, the term was *worth-ship*. The point of our praise is to extol how sublimely worthy God is of our adoration.

If someone asks why we think so highly of the Lord, we find our answer in Psalm 92:2: "to declare your steadfast love in the morning, and your faithfulness by night." *Steadfast love* refers to God's covenant mercy to believers. God's *faithfulness* refers to the integrity of his truth. David Dickson writes: "The matter of God's praise and our rejoicing, are chiefly the Lord's mercy and truth, in pitying and pardoning, and lovingly entreating sinful men, and performing the promises of the covenant to his people, contrary to their deserving."[2] For all the many and great reasons believers have to thank and praise God, none is higher than the grace he has shown to us in Jesus Christ. In Ephesians 1, the apostle Paul unfolds a summary of God's

2. David Dickson, *A Commentary on the Psalms* (1653; repr., Edinburgh: Banner of Truth, 1995), 2:150.

saving work, as Father, Son, and Holy Spirit. The purpose of this redemptive marvel is "to the praise of his glorious grace, with which he has blessed us in the Beloved" (Eph. 1:6). The highest aim of our salvation is the glory and praise of God, and the strongest motive to thank and praise the Lord is his steadfast love and faithfulness to us.

Having set before us the two basic aims of worship in the thanks and praise of the Lord, the author of Psalm 92 adds an emphasis on the works of God that will provide a trajectory for the rest of this psalm: "For you, O Lord, have made me glad by your work; at the works of your hands I sing for joy" (Ps. 92:4). When we think of God's work in history, we consider his works of creation and providence. God is praised as the Creator and Sovereign of history. With respect to providence, we glorify God for what is termed his *common grace* in overseeing all the affairs of mankind, but especially for his *special grace* in redeeming his believing people. Verse 4 considers these achievements as a unity (he is made "glad by your work"), but also in their variety ("at the works of your hands").

God's works in creation and history are a revelation of his character and glory. Psalm 92:5 marvels: "How great are your works, O Lord! Your thoughts are very deep!" H. C. Leupold writes: "Behind the works of God lie His thoughts. They, too, are characterized by a depth which the human mind can never plumb."[3] To reflect soberly on the vast scale and staggering intricacy of the creation is to glorify a mind that is infinitely higher and greater than our own. To embrace the gospel in faith, coming to the cross on which God's Son died for sinners, is to be humbled before a mystery of love that Paul says "surpasses knowledge" (Eph. 3:19).

For ancient Israelites, God's great deliverance in the exodus headed the list of works for which they gave him praise. Throughout their history, God's work defended, blessed, and saved them. In keeping with God's promises, the Israelites looked forward to God's great work in the coming of the Messiah. What they looked forward to, Christians look back on. Above all the works of God in which we rejoice is the saving ministry of Jesus Christ, centered on his atoning death for our sins. Moreover, it is in celebration of God's mighty work in raising Jesus from the grave that Christians worship together on the first day of the week in the gospel age (Acts 20:7).

In assessing worship that is focused on God, giving thanks and praise to

3. H. C. Leupold, *Exposition of the Psalms* (Columbus, OH: Wartburg Press, 1959), 660.

him, and glorying in his mighty works, the psalmist offers a considerable understatement: "It is good" (Ps. 92:1). Indeed, there is nothing better than the worship of God. Answer 1 of the Westminster Shorter Catechism tells us that the "chief end [of man] is to glorify God," and so the best thing man can do is to worship the Lord. We are reminded of God's verdict on his own work day by day during the week of creation: "and God saw that it was good" (Gen. 1:10, etc.). Looking beyond the creation to God's works of providence and redemption, the believer can only join in affirming, "It is good to give thanks to the LORD, to sing praises to your name, O Most High" (Ps. 92:1). Charles Spurgeon amplifies this goodness:

> It is good ethically, for it is the Lord's right; it is good emotionally, for it is pleasant to the heart; it is good practically, for it leads others to render the same homage. . . . Devout praise is always good, it is never out of season, never superfluous, but it is especially suitable to the Sabbath: a Sabbath without thanksgiving is a Sabbath profaned.[4]

Informative Comments about Worship

In the midst of the worship fundamentals set forth in Psalm 92, some comments are made that should inform our own attendance at church. For instance, note in verse 2 the worship that took place both morning and evening: "to declare your steadfast love in the morning, and your faithfulness by night." Few churches today schedule worship services for both morning and evening, but the psalmist sets forth this pattern as an ideal.

Some commentators take the view that "morning and evening" is a way of talking about the entire day. They take the psalmist to say, "We should thank and praise God all the time." In response, we should note that there were two daily times for public praise at Israel's temple, when the sacrifices for sin were offered in the morning and then again in the evening (Num. 28:4, 8). It is evident that Psalm 92 is considering the formal, public worship of God's people (hence the musical accompaniment and the reference to the temple courts in verse 13). Therefore, the most natural reading is that the morning and evening praises of Psalm 92 are formal gatherings in God's house.

4. Charles Haddon Spurgeon, *The Treasury of David*, 3 vols. (Peabody, MA: Hendrickson, n.d.), 2b:116.

In former times, morning and evening worship on the Lord's Day was a staple of zealous, evangelical churches. This priority has been more recently crowded out by an emphasis on church social gatherings, where the focus is directed to one another or to a desire to enjoy worldly recreations on the Lord's Day, rather than to the Lord. This practice, in effect, truncates the Lord's Day into the Lord's Morning. The psalmist offers a countering perspective. To be sure, his summons in verse 2 pertains to the daily sacrifices and not the Sabbath day gatherings, so the connection to our Lord's Day services is not direct. Nonetheless, the ideal of Psalm 92:2 urges that churches provide opportunities for us to join in the heavenly song of praise in such a way that brackets the Lord's Day.

We may observe, second, the highlighting of musical instruments to accompany the singing of praise: "to the music of the lute and the harp, to the melody of the lyre" (Ps. 92:3). This statement indicates that the worship in view is public, gathered worship. It is also highly musical worship. We gather "to sing praises to your name, O Most High" (v. 1), accompanied by musical instruments.

A number of important Christian leaders have urged that under the gospel the church should sing without instruments. The great fifth-century preacher John Chrysostom argued: "Instrumental music was only permitted to the Jews, as sacrifice was, for the heaviness and grossness of their souls."[5] John Calvin strongly urged that Christians, being indwelt by the Spirit, have need only of their hearts and voices. Likewise, Spurgeon's congregation sang without instruments. It is hard to see, however, how this opposition to instruments can be sustained in light of the strong emphasis of the Psalms. None would deny that the Psalms serve as a guide to the spirituality of worship, as well as to the content of worship. Why, then, is the practice of worship in the Psalms considered alien to the New Testament church? It is true that believers in Christ possess a fullness of the Holy Spirit not available before Jesus' coming. Yet the Holy Spirit flows freely through the book of Psalms, in which the joyful accompaniment of instruments and the singing of choirs is often extolled.[6]

5. Quoted in Spurgeon, *Treasury of David*, 2b:123.

6. This is not to say that opponents of instrumentation were uninfluenced by the Psalms. For a thorough presentation of the case against musical instruments, see John L. Girardeau, *Instrumental Music in the Public Worship of the Church* (Columbus, IN: Puritan Reprints, 2006).

Perhaps the most important comment regarding worship is made in Psalm 92:4: "For you, O LORD, have made me glad by your work." Here we see that the proper attitude for worship is joy. It is true that the Bible often emphasizes reverence before the Lord. Hebrews 12:28 urges: "let us offer to God acceptable worship, with reverence and awe." Yet our reverence is to include a joyful exuberance for the grace of the Lord. Psalm 2:11 puts them together, saying that we are to "rejoice with trembling." While the presence of God's majesty humbles us with reverence, it is our remembrance of what God has done for us—his great saving works—that makes our hearts glad. In this way, the psalm points out that the most beneficial activity for the downcast soul—whether one is perplexed, fearful, or grieving—is to join in the public worship of God. George Horne writes of the believer: "It is his duty, as being the least return he can make to his great Benefactor: it ought to be his delight, for it is that of angels, and will be that of every grateful heart, whether in heaven or on earth."[7]

Psalm 92 challenges our attitude as we come to church on Sundays. Do you think of the worship service as something to get finished with as soon as possible, perhaps so that you can have time for more enjoyable activities? Or do you look on Sunday as, in the Puritans' term, "the market day of the soul," anticipating keenly the joy of gathering with the saints to give thanks and praise to our Lord? James Boice asks, "Is Sunday a trial or a treat? Is it a delight or a deadly duty?"[8] If we think worship is a boring demand on our time and long for the service to end, does this not suggest a heart that is out of tune with Psalm 92? Obviously, we all have limitations to our attention and endurance. But the believer who appreciates the greatness and glory of God, and who is especially impacted by the marvel of God's saving work in Jesus Christ, is likely to take up the joyful passion for worship that Psalm 92 exhibits: "For you, O LORD, have made me glad by your work; at the works of your hands I sing for joy" (Ps. 92:4).

The Withering of the Wicked

If you come to church wondering, "What do I get out of this?," Psalm 92 has already answered in terms of the joy of the Lord. But as the psalmist

7. George Horne, *Commentary on the Psalms* (1771; repr., Audubon, NJ: Old Paths Publications, 1997), 403.

8. James Montgomery Boice, *Psalms*, 3 vols. (Grand Rapids: Baker, 1996), 2:754.

continues, he points out the wisdom that is gained by those who gather in faith for public worship. To this end, the remainder of the psalm involves a great contrast between the ungodly and the righteous. According to the psalm, the chief characteristic of those who do not worship God is their folly regarding life: "The stupid man cannot know; the fool cannot understand this" (Ps. 92:6).

Here, the Bible divides the human race into two groups, depending on their response to God. On the one hand are those referred to as "the stupid" and "the fool" (Ps. 92:6), contrasted with "the righteous" (v. 12). Spurgeon writes of the fool: "He may be a philosopher, and yet be such a brutish being that he will not own the existence of a Maker for the ten thousand matchless creations around him, which wear, even upon their surface, the evidences of profound design."[9] Such a person may be a statesman, a poet, an inventor, or a philanthropist. Yet the Bible's testimony still stands: "The fool says in his heart, 'There is no God'" (14:1). William Plumer comments: "Is not he a fool, who prefers time to eternity, earth to heaven, the world to its Maker, sin to holiness, death to life?"[10]

The particular folly of the unbeliever, according to Psalm 92:7, is that a present prosperity indicates that all is well. The reality for one who is alienated by sin from God is "that though the wicked sprout like grass and all evildoers flourish, they are doomed to destruction forever." This point is one that God's people need to know. Like Asaph in Psalm 73, we are foolish to envy the ungodly. He complained: "I was envious of the arrogant when I saw the prosperity of the wicked. For they have no pangs until death; their bodies are fat and sleek" (Ps. 73:3–4). When Asaph came to his senses—which, incidentally, happened when he returned to the church and its worship—he said: "then I discerned their end. Truly you set them in slippery places; you make them fall to ruin" (vv. 17–18). The reality is, under God's rule, that the very prosperity that the ungodly take "as a pledge of their happiness" is instead "a preparation for their ruin."[11]

When Psalm 92:7 says that "the wicked sprout like grass," the psalmist refers to plants that spring up quickly but have no root. The result is an inevitably short life. Thus, while "all evildoers flourish, they are doomed to

9. Spurgeon, *Treasury of David*, 2b:118.
10. Plumer, *Psalms*, 859.
11. Matthew Henry, *Commentary on the Whole Bible*, 6 vols. (Peabody, MA: Hendrickson, n.d.), 3:483.

destruction forever" (v. 7). Their exaltation is thus God's preparation for eternal humiliation. When God's people see the phenomenal wealth of those who worship money and the lordly power of those who seek to dominate, they should remember God's higher authority that has destined even these fleeting delights to serve the purpose of their judgment.

In contrast to the insecure perch of the ungodly is the eternal reign of God in heaven: "but you, O LORD, are on high forever" (Ps. 92:8). Verse 8 occupies the middle point of Psalm 92, and on this its teaching depends. It is for this that the church gathers on the Lord's Day to exalt his name. How worthy God is of our adoration and praise! And how enduring will be his glory after the towers of earthly praise have all fallen! Matthew Henry exhorts us: "Let us not therefore fear that pride and power of evil men, nor be discouraged by their impotent menaces, for the moth shall eat them up as a garment, but *God's righteousness shall be for ever.*"[12]

God's enduring glory is the first great truth that we learn by faithful attendance in the Lord's Day worship: "For behold, your enemies, O LORD, for behold, your enemies shall perish; all evildoers shall be scattered" (Ps. 92:9). As Psalm 1:4 asserts, "The wicked . . . are like chaff that the wind drives away." The hopes of the ungodly will fail. Their achievements will be broken and forgotten. The foretaste of God's victory over the wicked is, of course, the triumph of Jesus Christ in cleansing our sins and rising from the grave. For as Satan's designs in Jesus' death turned against his own kingdom of darkness, so also all the ungodly will find that in the end their rebellion to God was the greatest of follies, resulting in an eternal separation from the only eternal glory (2 Thess. 1:9).

The Thriving of the Righteous

There is a second great truth that the faithful discover at church and are reminded of week to week. Corresponding to the withering of the wicked is the thriving of the righteous.

Here, the psalmist is able to give his own testimony: "But you have exalted my horn like that of the wild ox; you have poured over me fresh oil" (Ps. 92:10). The horn was a symbol of strength, analogous to the might associated with large and virile animals. Joined to it is the symbol of blessing in

12. Henry, *Commentary,* 3:484 (italics original).

the pouring of anointing oil. These gifts are bestowed on him from the Savior who reigns on high. Whatever weakness or trouble he may have in a worldly sense is more than compensated for in spiritual power and the joy of the Lord.

Since anointing oil was applied to an office-bearer in Israel—a prophet, priest, or king—it may be that this anointing consists of a fresh consecration to sacred calling. In this respect, the great exemplar of this verse was Jesus Christ. Though poor and humble in the world, Jesus rejoiced: "The Spirit of the Lord is upon me, because he has anointed me to proclaim good news to the poor" (Luke 4:18). This same joy belongs to all his people today who are granted the inestimable privilege of bearing his gospel to the world through Spirit-transformed lives. It is more likely that the anointing oil exemplifies an especially joyous occasion, in which Israelites would generally be anointed with abundant, luxurious oil. His testimony, then, is of how God supplies his people with spiritual vigor and blessing in order that they may exult in him. Dickson comments: "Whatever weakness or grief the godly lie under for a while, they shall have in due time festiful refreshment, comfort, and encouragement from God's Spirit and powerful providence."[13]

The psalmist also confirms that he has seen God's judgment put things right: "My eyes have seen the downfall of my enemies; my ears have heard the doom of my evil assailants" (Ps. 92:11). Far from expressing a malicious delight in the suffering of unbelievers, the psalmist expresses relief to see their evil designs fail. Joined with this is the satisfaction of witnessing God's righteous judgment on an ungodly rebellion. We think of the defeat of Sennacherib in his siege of Jerusalem, the fall of Babylon in the time of the prophet Daniel, and the rejoicing of angels in Revelation 19 for the downfall of the great harlot. They sing to God: "Hallelujah! Salvation and glory and power belong to our God, for his judgments are true and just; for he has judged the great prostitute who corrupted the earth with her immorality, and has avenged on her the blood of his servants" (Rev. 19:1–2). This reminds us that the great fulfillment of this testimony will be the triumphant Jesus Christ in his second coming, after which his people will enjoy their resurrection in glory and the wedding feast of the Lamb of God. Looking forward to the certainty of this future, Christians have the satisfaction of knowing

13. Dickson, *Psalms*, 2:153.

that evil will fall to God's judgment, even while we labor in gospel witness to deliver sinners from God's wrath through faith in Christ.

The final stanza of Psalm 92 presents a vivid image of the blessed situation of those who belong to the Lord. This is the lesson, along with the folly of the ungodly, that is pressed on the hearts of those who gather in God's house for sacred worship: "The righteous flourish like the palm tree and grow like a cedar in Lebanon" (Ps. 92:12).

The palm tree is honored in the Middle East, possessing a strong and tall trunk, a spreading bough for shade, and pleasant fruit. Like the stately cedar of Lebanon, it has the special character of being evergreen. Derek Kidner writes: "The *palm* tree is the embodiment of graceful erectness; the *cedar*, of strength and majesty."[14] While the wicked spring up like grass, they also soon wither under God's judgment. By contrast, those who are righteous through faith in Christ are able to rise upward in spiritual stature and bear a sweeter, fuller fruitfulness from their hearts year by year.

Many Christians have testified to God's ability to keep them flourishing even in the midst of the greatest troubles. Art Matthews and his family were the last missionaries to escape from China after the Communist takeover. They lived in a single room with only a stool for furniture. All contact with outside friends and financial support was cut off. With only a small stove, they often shivered in the cold, their food reduced to a daily meal of rice cooked over manure that Art had gathered in the streets. But all through this trial, they trusted God, they spoke to him in prayer, and they strengthened themselves by his Word. After they escaped, they told their story. The title of the book was drawn from Jeremiah 17:7–8, which has the same idea as our psalm. The book is titled *Green Leaf in Drought Time*, their testimony that God's people do not wither in the most barren soil but persevere in the joy of their fellowship with him. "Blessed is the man who trusts in the Lord," Jeremiah said. "He is like a tree planted by water, that sends out its roots by the stream, and does not fear when heat comes, for its leaves remain green." John Newton wrote of this same provision from God to all his people:

> See, the streams of living waters, springing from eternal love,
> Well supply thy sons and daughters, and all fear of want remove:

14. Derek Kidner, *Psalms 73–150*, Tyndale Old Testament Commentaries 16 (Downers Grove, IL: InterVarsity Press, 1975), 337.

> Who can faint, while such a river ever flows their thirst t'assuage?
> Grace which, like the Lord, the giver, never fails from age to age.[15]

Psalm 92:13–14 relates the source and the outcome of a life that flourishes through divine grace. "They are planted in the house of the Lord; they flourish in the courts of our God" (Ps. 92:13). The lives of God's people flourish because they are well planted by him in good soil, with a stream of living water flowing through the roots of their faith and into the branches of their lives. Jesus referred this idea to himself, saying: "I am the vine; you are the branches. Whoever abides in me and I in him, he it is that bears much fruit, for apart from me you can do nothing" (John 15:5). In the context of this Sabbath psalm, we may also think of the believer planted in the courts of God's church, where the means of grace provide spiritual nurture. Henry explains:

> The trees of righteousness do not grow of themselves; they are planted, not in common soil, but in paradise, in the house of the Lord. Trees are not usually planted in a house; but God's trees are said to be planted in his house because it is from his grace, by his word and Spirit, that they receive all the sap and virtue that keep them alive and make them fruitful.[16]

This is not to say that physical presence in the church brings spiritual life. Rather, it is believing participation in the worship, service, and life of the church—especially as we are taught God's Word and ministered to through prayer—that serves as soil for a strongly growing Christian palm or cedar. Palm trees, especially, require a strong nearby water source to flourish. It is through a living union with Christ through faith, nurtured in the church, that believers live evergreen lives regardless of settings or trials.

God's work to make us flourish results in Christians who bear fruit into old age: "They still bear fruit in old age; they are ever full of sap and green" (Ps. 92:14). Christians who dwell in Christ through faith and in the church for sustenance will regularly exert a lifelong influence for salvation and godliness. It is not necessary for the cares of elder years to collapse our virtues into vice. The long-gracious believer thus evidences a life in union

15. John Newton, "Glorious Things of Thee Are Spoken" (1779).
16. Henry, *Commentary*, 3:484.

with Christ and in the courts of his church. While the earthly frame recedes, God provides a spiritual compensation, making aged believers fresh, like trees full of sap and green with still-healthy growth. Experience shows that believers who thrive in godliness often maintain a perpetually youthful outlook, still bright-eyed and keenly interested in God's work even as the body fails.

Life that is rooted in the house of God—made to flourish by his Spirit, staying green even to later years—most nobly glorifies God in the course of a human life. With this emphasis, Psalm 92 concludes on the same theme of praise to God with which it began: "to declare that the LORD is upright; he is my rock, and there is no unrighteousness in him" (Ps. 92:15). Would not our lives serve the Lord well if they gave living proof to the truthfulness of his Word, the safety of his grace, and the power of his Spirit in the life of one who trusts in him? What a return we will gain on an initial investment of being regularly present in church in order to thank and praise the Lord together with his people. In this respect, the long-serving, faith-displaying Christian may look on his or her own life as a source of praise to God for his work. What a high ambition it is that when our souls arrive in heaven, we will be able to point to our own lives and cry the words of Psalm 92: "For you, O LORD, have made me glad by your work . . . . How great are your works, O LORD!" (vv. 4–5).

24

The Lord Reigns

Psalm 93

The Lord *reigns; he is robed in majesty; the* Lord *is robed;*
he has put on strength as his belt. (Ps. 93:1)

Psalm 93 begins a mini-collection within book 4 of the Psalter that is focused on the kingdom of God. The collection extends to Psalm 99, which like Psalm 93 begins, "The Lord reigns." Psalms 92 and 100 may also be included, since both focus on offering praise to the Lord for his sovereignty.[1] In Psalm 93, it is because God's reign is eternally established that the world is made stable, the wicked are subdued, and God's people are made holy. Yet in the end, it is the faithfulness of God's Word that proves his sovereign reign and establishes believers as his holy people.

The Character of God's Kingdom

Psalm 93 begins with an acclamation of divine kingship: "The Lord reigns" (v. 1). Derek Kidner argues that this opening statement deserves an exclamation point, having "the ring of a proclamation."[2] God's people need

1. O. Palmer Robertson, *The Flow of the Psalms* (Phillipsburg, NJ: P&R Publishing, 2015), 153–57.

2. Derek Kidner, *Psalms 73–150*, Tyndale Old Testament Commentaries 16 (Downers Grove, IL: InterVarsity Press, 1975), 338.

to be forcefully reminded of the Lord's enthronement. When godly King Uzziah died, the prophet Isaiah was grieved and concerned about the vacant throne in Jerusalem. Walking into the temple, he saw a vision designed to remind him that Israel's true throne never is or can be empty: "I saw the Lord sitting upon a throne, high and lifted up; and the train of his robe filled the temple" (Isa. 6:1). Likewise, the church today needs a fresh vision of God's kingship. "The LORD reigns" is just as true, relevant, and comforting today as it was in the time of the psalmist. Psalm 93 does not merely proclaim God's kingship in an abstract sense, in that he is the Maker and owner of all things, but it proclaims God's reign in action: governing and overseeing all things according to the counsel of his will.

Psalm 92 introduced this theme of God's kingship, boasting that "you, O LORD, are on high forever" (Ps. 92:8). The effect of Psalm 93 is to expound on this theme and shed further light on God's kingship. If we inquire, "What is God's kingdom like?," Psalm 93 provides an answer, identifying four characteristics of God's reign.

First, the Lord's reign is *majestic*: "The LORD reigns; he is robed in majesty" (Ps. 93:1). *Majesty* is difficult to define, but it deals with the grandeur and stateliness of a king's person and rule. One way to see the majesty of God is to observe the awe of those who behold him. I mentioned how Isaiah was comforted by God's kingship in a time of trouble. But this comfort occurred only after he had been overawed by the divine majesty. Not only did Isaiah see the Lord "high and lifted up," but also "the foundations of the thresholds shook at the voice of him who called, and the house was filled with smoke" (Isa. 6:1, 4). Isaiah responded by coming undone in terrified awe. He especially realized his sinful depravity, "for I am a man of unclean lips, and I dwell in the midst of a people of unclean lips; for my eyes have seen the King, the LORD of hosts!" (v. 5). To see God in his majesty is inevitably to see ourselves as puny and corrupt.

The psalmist speaks of the Lord as putting on or robing himself with majesty. It is common for earthly monarchs to portray themselves as majestic. To this end, gold and jewels will adorn the crown and the throne will be high and imposing. The etiquette of the court is likewise intended to give a majestic impression. Yet while earthly kings put on the veneer of majesty, the heavenly Lord puts on majesty itself. Matthew Henry comments:

> The majesty of earthly princes, compared with God's terrible majesty, is but like the glimmerings of a glow-worm compared with the brightness of the sun when he goes forth in his strength. Are the enemies of God's kingdom great and formidable? Yet let us not fear them, for God's majesty will eclipse theirs.[3]

Jesus humbled himself during his incarnation, but his divine majesty could not be entirely suppressed. Consider how the kings of the East responded upon finding the virgin-born child: "And going into the house, they saw the child with Mary his mother, and they fell down and worshiped him," showering him with kingly gifts (Matt. 2:11). When Jesus was betrayed by Judas to the temple guards, his majesty was briefly permitted to overawe: "When Jesus said to them, 'I am he,' they drew back and fell to the ground" (John 18:6). In his death, the centurion standing by declared: "Truly this was the Son of God!" (Matt. 27:54). How much more majestic Jesus is now, having risen from the grave and robed himself fully in the majesty of his divine glory. The opening scene of the book of Revelation depicts Jesus in full majesty, so that even his intimate friend the apostle John "fell at his feet as though dead" (Rev. 1:17). Jesus spoke to John in terms that fulfill Psalm 93:1's claim of his majesty: "I am the first and the last, and the living one. I died, and behold I am alive forevermore, and I have the keys of Death and Hades" (vv. 17–18).

Second, God's kingdom is *mighty*: "the Lord is robed; he has put on strength as his belt" (Ps. 93:1). God's reign is not like that of a dispossessed prince, who has nothing left but a title and some discarded palace furniture. The Lord's majesty is accompanied with royal power and might. Here, as with majesty, the psalmist speaks of God's putting on his might. His power, therefore, is not derived from others. God does not gain his power from his worshipers, much less from worldly rulers who grant him permission. God's power derives from his own divine nature, a power displayed in his creating all things out of nothing by the mere word of his mouth. All the power that his people need—whether for faith and obedience or for the success of our gospel mission—is found in God.

Third, God's kingdom is characterized by his absolute *sovereignty*: "Yes, the world is established; it shall never be moved" (Ps. 93:1). The point of this statement is not that the earth is fixed in space, with the sun orbiting around

3. Matthew Henry, *Commentary on the Whole Bible*, 6 vols. (Peabody, MA: Hendrickson, n.d.), 3:485.

it, as some early medieval scholars claimed. The emphasis is moral and decretal, not scientific or astronomical. God's order and righteousness cannot be overthrown, despite the presumptions of earthly governments that seek to replace God's law with perverse demands. God's will for the world is unshakable and fixed. When Christians pray, "Your kingdom come, your will be done, on earth as it is in heaven" (Matt. 6:10), we can be sure that it will in fact be done. Charles Spurgeon writes: "That there is any stability, either in the world or in the church, is the Lord's doings, and he is to be adored for it."[4] Hebrews 1:3 speaks of this sovereignty as being exercised specifically by the exalted Jesus Christ at the Father's right hand: "he upholds the universe by the word of his power."

God's will is immovable because God himself cannot be manipulated or changed. This is because of the fourth characteristic, that God's kingdom is *eternal*: "Your throne is established from of old; you are from everlasting" (Ps. 93:2). God's kingdom did not have a beginning. God the Creator reigns even before Genesis 1:1 declares that he "created the heavens and the earth." God's existence prior to and above the entire universe establishes his right to rule. Everything that exists has its being from God and owes to him both worship and obedience.

Given these characteristics of God's kingdom, we have every reason to trust and serve him. God in his majesty is worthy of our praise. God in his power may be appealed to for any help we need. God in his sovereignty may be relied on to fulfill all that he has promised. And God in his eternal being may be trusted to remain always the same. He will be at the end as he was in the beginning, and his Word cannot be broken. As such a God, he always demands our attention and adoration. James Boice writes: "We may try to ignore him, but ignoring him will not work. One day we will have to give an accounting to him before whom all hearts are open and all desires are known."[5]

Triumphant over Turmoil

The fact that God rules everything by right does not keep sinful men from rebelling against him. Thus, the second stanza of Psalm 93 speaks of great powers below that seek to bring turmoil to the world over which God

4. Charles Haddon Spurgeon, *The Treasury of David*, 3 vols. (Peabody, MA: Hendrickson, n.d.), 2b:135.
5. James Montgomery Boice, *Psalms*, 3 vols. (Grand Rapids: Baker, 1996), 2:763.

rules. Verse 3 depicts this rebellion in terms of the raging seas and their tumult: "The floods have lifted up, O Lord, the floods have lifted up their voice; the floods lift up their roaring." The metaphor of the raging sea is often applied in Scripture to the rebellion of sinners against God. Perhaps the most famous example is found in Isaiah 57:20: "'the wicked are like the tossing sea; for it cannot be quiet, and its waters toss up mire and dirt. There is no peace,' says my God, 'for the wicked.'"

The description of the ungodly in Psalm 93:3 emphasizes the noise made by their actions: they have "lifted up their voice" and are "roaring." The same perspective is given in the more famous opening lines of Psalm 2:

> Why do the nations rage
> and the peoples plot in vain?
> The kings of the earth set themselves,
> and the rulers take counsel together,
> against the Lord and against his Anointed, saying,
> "Let us burst their bonds apart
> and cast away their cords from us." (Ps. 2:1–3)

From our perspective, the raging and plotting of worldly powers against God's rule are quite threatening. Likewise, the imagery of floods in Psalm 93:3 conjures up thoughts that frighten us. Today, Christians around the world face propaganda from the media and government against the teachings of the Bible, sometimes accompanied with threats of violence that are quite real. Psalm 93 has stated that the world is established under God's sovereignty, but it sometimes seems that his ways are under effective assault. The repetitions of verse 3 reflect the panic that God's people sometimes feel: "The floods . . . , the floods . . . ; the floods"!

A lesson in wisdom is provided, however, in that Psalm 93:3 brings the roaring of the ungodly to the attention of the Lord. David Dickson comments: "The best way to encounter threatenings and fears is to oppose God unto them, and to lay them before the Lord, that he may answer them."[6] When Christians take their fears and concerns before the Lord, they find that he is more than able to uphold their cause: "Mightier than the thunders of many waters, mightier than the waves of the sea, the Lord on high is

6. David Dickson, *A Commentary on the Psalms* (1653; repr., Edinburgh: Banner of Truth, 1995), 2:156.

mighty!" (Ps. 93:4). Our wisdom, therefore, in responding to the threats of earthly powers should be like that of godly King Hezekiah, when he prayed against the Assyrian siege of Jerusalem: "Incline your ear, O LORD, and hear; open your eyes, O LORD, and see; and hear the words of Sennacherib, which he has sent to mock the living God" (2 Kings 19:16). Hezekiah asked God to defend his own name, and the Lord's angel slew the Assyrian host outside the holy city.

However mighty the forces of idolatry may seem, the power of God is far greater still. The psalmist therefore praises him: "Mightier than the thunders of many waters, mightier than the waves of the sea, the LORD on high is mighty!" (Ps. 93:4). Despite the surging powers of the ocean waves, it is God who sets the limits of their advance. Likewise, God is able to restrain, govern, and even employ all earthly rebellions for his own purposes and praise. The Lord is enthroned high above every worldly source of strength, unassailable in his person and decrees. Henry writes: "The unlimited sovereignty and irresistible power of the great Jehovah are very encouraging to the people of God, in reference to all the noises and hurries they meet with in this world."[7]

When Christians study the Gospels, they find that Jesus often trained his disciples not merely by permitting them to face earthly trials but by intentionally sending them into dangerous waters. His aim was to build their faith by the experience of his salvation. On one occasion, Jesus "made his disciples get into the boat and go before him to the other side" (Mark 6:45). As they crossed in the night, "the wind was against them" (v. 48) and their boat came into trouble. Where was Jesus? they wondered. The answer is that Christ was atop a nearby mountain, just as Psalm 93 describes "the LORD on high" above the flood (v. 4). Jesus had his eye on them the entire time. And what was he doing? Mark 6:46 explains that he had gone "up on the mountain to pray." Before long, Jesus came to them, "walking on the sea" in his sovereign power as Lord and God, causing the winds to cease and the waves to be still (Mark 6:48–51).

The raging tumults of this world result from the power of sin, especially as it works in the schemes of wicked earthly rulers. But Christ has ordained these trials for the good of his people, especially so that we will better learn to know and trust him. J. C. Ryle comments:

7. Henry, *Commentary*, 3:486.

> By affliction He teaches us many precious lessons, which, without it we should never learn. By affliction He shows us our emptiness and weakness, draws us to the throne of grace, purifies our affections, weans us from the world, and makes us long for heaven.[8]

Realizing that our Savior is sovereign over our trials comforts us amid the storms. Earthly difficulties therefore supply us with precious opportunities to show our faith and display the power of God's grace before a watching world. And when we cry out in panic, "Where is the Lord?," we should remember where in fact he is. Paul reminds us in Romans 8:34: "Christ Jesus is the one who died—more than that, who was raised—who is at the right hand of God, who indeed is interceding for us." Katharina von Schlegel helpfully applied these truths to our faith in her famous hymn:

> Be still, my soul: your God will undertake
> To guide the future as he has the past.
> Your hope, your confidence let nothing shake;
> All now mysterious shall be bright at last.
> Be still, my soul: the waves and winds still know
> His voice who ruled them while he dwelt below.[9]

Christians today are part of a church that has proved the words of Psalm 93:4 over many centuries and in countless trials: "Mightier than the thunders of many waters, mightier than the waves of the sea, the Lord on high is mighty!" The raging of the Roman emperors only made the martyrs the seed of the church. The mocking of Enlightenment rationalism was unable to stem the power of the gospel as it spread through early America in the revivals of the Great Awakening. The terrors of Communist rule in China were inflicted on the evangelists of the house-church movement, but proved unable to slow the spread of Christian faith to tens of millions of people in our own lifetime. "In the world you will have tribulation," Jesus assured us. "But take heart," he added; "I have overcome the world" (John 16:33).

Faithful in His Word

The kingdom of God is majestic, mighty, sovereign, and eternal, able by his power to stem and control all the raging waters of sin and unbelief. The

8. J. C. Ryle, *Expository Thoughts on Mark* (1857; repr., Edinburgh: Banner of Truth, 1985), 83.
9. Katharina von Schegel, "Be Still, My Soul" (1752).

concluding stanza, in Psalm 93:5, reminds us that God rules in this world by his Word, on which we may completely rely: "Your decrees are very trustworthy; holiness befits your house, O Lord, forevermore."

The Hebrew word translated as "decrees" (*edah*) has the primary meaning of "God's statutes and testimonies." Think of God's Word going out from a herald who proclaims the edicts and declarations of the king. H. C. Leupold writes: "The emphasis would seem to be chiefly on the promissory aspect of the divine words, . . . that whatever the Lord says can be absolutely relied on in spite of appearances to the contrary."[10] Psalm 93 thus declares the promises, prophecies, and doctrine of God's Word as trustworthy and true.

How could the majestic, almighty, sovereign, and eternal God ever fail in his Word? And who can overthrow what he has promised? Certainly not the powers of this world, over which God rules from on high with omnipotent power! In ancient times, God promised to send his people a Redeemer who would free them from their sins. Abraham spoke of this promise to his son Isaac: "God will provide for himself the lamb for a burnt offering, my son" (Gen. 22:8). In God's perfect timing, John the Baptist pointed to Jesus, walking beside the river Jordan: "Behold, the Lamb of God, who takes away the sin of the world" (John 1:29). Jesus fulfilled all that the Old Testament foretold in his perfect life, atoning death, and life-giving resurrection. Now we look ahead to what God has promised still to do. Jesus declared: "All that the Father gives me will come to me, and whoever comes to me I will never cast out. . . . For this is the will of my Father, that everyone who looks on the Son and believes in him should have eternal life, and I will raise him up on the last day" (John 6:37, 40).

The psalmist simply declares: "Your decrees are very trustworthy" (Ps. 93:5). Just as the mighty God is able to defend his people, so can he keep all his Word. Spurgeon writes: "As the rocks remain unmoved amid the tumult of the sea, so does divine truth resist all the currents of man's opinions and the storms of human controversy."[11] And of all that is sure in God's Word, surely nothing is more certain than all that God has proclaimed regarding the kingdom of salvation in his Son. Jesus said: "Heaven and earth will pass away, but my words will not pass away" (Matt. 24:35).

10. H. C. Leupold, *Exposition of the Psalms* (Columbus, OH: Wartburg Press, 1959), 667.
11. Spurgeon, *Treasury of David*, 2b:135.

Because God's Word is so trustworthy, the great need of every age is for God's people to believe the Holy Scriptures and stand immovable in faith on them. Moreover, it is our special privilege to spread abroad God's Word for the salvation of many. In his parable of the soils, Jesus described the kingdom of God, saying, "A sower went out to sow his seed" (Luke 8:5). Then he explained, "The seed is the word of God" (v. 11). God's saving rule spreads with the preaching of his Word and the witness of his people to the gospel. Jesus gave this task as the Great Commission to his church: "Go therefore and make disciples of all nations, baptizing them in the name of the Father and of the Son and of the Holy Spirit, teaching them to observe all that I have commanded you" (Matt. 28:19–20).

The word for "trustworthy" in Psalm 93:5 (*ne'emnu*) comes from the root word *amen*, the word we use to affirm our faith in God's Word. Have you given your *Amen* to the testimonies of the Bible? You can, because they are "very trustworthy." You should, because they are the very Word of God. Having given our *Amen*, we should take our stand on the Bible, if need be against all the counsels, arguments, and ragings of the world. Jesus said, "Everyone then who hears these words of mine and does them will be like a wise man who built his house on the rock. And the rain fell, and the floods came, and the winds blew and beat on that house, but it did not fall, because it had been founded on the rock" (Matt. 7:24–25).

After we have received God's Word in faith, something else remains for us to do. Verse 5 makes the obvious application to all that Psalm 93 has said about the Lord and his kingdom: "holiness befits your house." The household of God in this world is the Christian church. As the blessed subjects of God's saving kingdom, we have as our calling the taking up of the manners and habits of our King, making his ways our own. Peter stated that "as he who called you is holy, you also be holy in all your conduct, since it is written, 'You shall be holy, for I am holy'" (1 Peter 1:15–16). God's house is sacred to him, as is the life of every blood-bought believer. If God will reign in us by his Word and Spirit, the inevitable result is that we will turn from sin and walk in his ways. Jesus said: "If you love me, you will keep my commandments" (John 14:15). Holiness befits God's majestic reign and his holy house.

So it will be, "O LORD, forevermore" (Ps. 93:5). The fashions of man change, and worldly morals wax and wane with the tides. But the ways of God's kingdom never change, his own nature being eternal. The writer of

Hebrews urges us to learn the habits of holiness from those who walked in faith before us. He urges this practice: "Remember your leaders, those who spoke to you the word of God. Consider the outcome of their way of life, and imitate their faith" (Heb. 13:7). But how can the ways of former times apply to the fashions of our generation? He answered: "Jesus Christ is the same yesterday and today and forever" (v. 8).

How important is the final word of Psalm 93, which in the Hebrew is "to the end of days." The psalmist states that God's Word will be trustworthy for all time as the heritage of his people, and calls us to the privilege and duty of a faith that yields the good fruit of holiness in our lives. Dickson concludes:

> The dignity, duty, and privileges of God's people, and especially this of consecration, sanctification in affection and carriage, and vindication from sin and misery, belong not to any one time or age, but are perpetual, belonging to all such as study to be approved unto God, protected and made blessed by God, in all times and ages, in all places and company, all the days of their life: for, *holiness becometh thine house forevermore.*[12]

The Song of the Church

By extolling God in his marvelous kingdom, together with his power over earthly tumult and his rule in his holy house, Psalm 93 is the song of the church in our world. According to the Bible, at the end of history a new song will rise from the hearts of both angels and the redeemed. Revelation 19 looks forward to the time when God has judged and cast out all evil and gathered his people for the joyous wedding feast of the Lamb of God, Jesus Christ. At that feast there is singing, and how closely that new song resembles the old song of Psalm 93:

> Hallelujah!
> For the Lord our God
>   the Almighty reigns.
> Let us rejoice and exult
>   and give him the glory,
> for the marriage of the Lamb has come,
>   and his Bride has made herself ready;

12. Dickson, *Psalms*, 2:157.

> it was granted her to clothe herself
> with fine linen, bright and pure. (Rev. 19:6–8)

In our worship on earth, we practice for the worship of heaven by exalting God in his majestic, mighty, sovereign, and eternal glory, and by celebrating Christ's victory over sin and evil. We also practice for heaven by the biblical and prayerful cultivation of holy lives. Psalm 93:5 says to God that "holiness befits your house." Likewise, the voices of heaven in Revelation 19:8 conclude their song with praise for the clothing of those who attend Christ's wedding feast: "the fine linen is the righteous deeds of the saints."

25

A Cry for Justice

Psalm 94

But the Lord has become my stronghold, and
my God the rock of my refuge. (Ps. 94:22)

The fact that the church is the people of God does not preserve us from great trials in this world. To the contrary, Christians are often persecuted precisely because of our godliness, together with our witness to a message that annoys worldly powers. So it was that the early church suffered cruel persecutions from the Roman Empire, experiencing harassment, imprisonment, and violence for two centuries until God brought Rome under the power of the gospel. During the Protestant Reformation, John Calvin's efforts to spread the gospel in his native France earned his seminary the nickname "Calvin's School of Death," since so many of his graduates died the death of martyrs within a few years or even months of their ordination. The English Reformation took hold only after scores of courageous Christians had been publicly executed for their faith, in many cases by the terrible trial of being burned to death. In the late seventeenth century, the Covenanters were hunted like quail on the moors of Scotland. So it continues today in many places of the world, where allegiance to Jesus Christ results in harassment, imprisonment, and violent death.

Psalm 94 seems to have been written during a time when the godly in Israel were abused by tyrannical powers. It is possible that the situation involved outside oppression, as when Israel suffered under the lash of slavery in Pharaoh's Egypt. There are statements in the text, however, to indicate that the oppressors were corrupt rulers within the nation of Israel. An example is Manasseh, who in the time of the prophet Isaiah exercised a brutal tyranny in which God's faithful remnant suffered terrible violence (2 Kings 21:1–18).

Psalm 94 assumes that when godly people suffer, God is angered and roused on their behalf. In this respect, Psalm 94 fits into the collection of psalms that celebrate God's kingship (Pss. 93–99). One of a king's most important duties is to establish justice in his realm. When injustice reigns, the king must be roused to relieve affliction. Psalm 94 asserts that God is in fact reigning over history as Sovereign and Judge, even when heavy trials are inflicted on the church. Instead of doubting God's rule, we should, as John Calvin writes, "pray for help from God, who, though he connives at wickedness for a time, eventually comes to the deliverance of his people."[1] Christians who rely on God's sovereign rule of the world find themselves able to bear even great afflictions as they are upheld by the Lord until their faith is rewarded with the overthrow of the wicked and the restoration of righteousness.

A Call to the Lord

Psalm 94 begins with a cry to the Lord to rise and bring judgment against the wicked: "O Lord, God of vengeance, O God of vengeance, shine forth!" (Ps. 94:1). In giving this call, the psalmist appeals to God according to his proper office as Judge. As Abraham reasoned, "Shall not the Judge of all the earth do what is just?" (Gen. 18:25). The New Testament confirms God's commitment to overthrowing evil: "Vengeance is mine, I will repay, says the Lord" (Rom. 12:19). This is why the King James Version renders Psalm 94:1: "O Lord God, to whom vengeance belongeth." The Creator and Ruler of all holds jurisdiction over the entire earth, so the psalmist calls him to appear in this office.

Some interpreters raise a complaint over the psalmist's manner of speaking.

1. John Calvin, *Calvin's Commentaries*, 23 vols. (1848; repr., Grand Rapids: Baker, 2009), 6:13.

Is it right, since Jesus told us to love our enemies (Matt. 5:44), to pray for God to bring justice on the wicked? These interpreters fail to distinguish between selfish revenge and judicial retribution. It is true that Christians are not to act in vengeance, but are to leave judgment to the Lord. So here is an instance in which we are to do as God says, not as God does, precisely because God is the one who is qualified to judge in holy vengeance. When Paul says, "Beloved, never avenge yourselves," he adds "but leave it to the wrath of God" (Rom. 12:19). The psalmist therefore acts rightly in calling for God to appear in judgment of the wicked. In this prayer, he shows that while Christians are to look with grace on our enemies, we are nonetheless to oppose injustice and oppression in our hearts, deeds, and prayers. Alexander Maclaren wrote:

> They who have no profound loathing of sin, or who have never felt the crushing weight of legalized wickedness, may shrink from such aspirations as the psalmist's, and brand them as ferocious; but hearts longing for the triumph of righteousness will not take offence at them.[2]

An example of this righteous spirit was given by John Milton when he heard about the massacre of whole Protestant families in northern Italy during the seventeenth century. Drawing from Psalm 94, he wrote: "Avenge, O Lord, thy slaughtered saints whose bones lie scattered on the Alpine mountains cold."[3] Milton's response is vindicated by its parallel in Revelation 6:10, where the martyrs of heaven cry out: "O Sovereign Lord, holy and true, how long before you will judge and avenge our blood on those who dwell on the earth?"

In this same spirit, the psalmist continues his plea: "Rise up, O judge of the earth; repay to the proud what they deserve!" (Ps. 94:2). The call for God to "rise" indicates that, so far at least, the Lord has done nothing to intervene against the ungodly powers. How desperate would be the cause of believers if they lacked the ability to call on God in prayer! Yet possessing this great resource, they appeal to the Lord, making plain their frustration and the urgency of their need: "O Lord, how long shall the wicked, how long shall the wicked exult?" (v. 3).

We have all experienced pleasant days when the time seemed to fly away. But how slow and painful is the passage of time when under injustice! It

2. Alexander Maclaren, *Expositions of Holy Scripture*, 17 vols. (Grand Rapids: Baker, 1982), 4b:40–41.
3. Quoted in James Montgomery Boice, *Psalms*, 3 vols. (Grand Rapids: Baker, 1996), 2:769.

of course glorifies God that he is patient even with the wicked. Yet under duress, the godly are dismayed—even as the martyrs of heaven wonder—at the apparent delay in God's appearing. Twice the psalmist complains, "How long?" Charles Spurgeon describes the psalmist's spirit: "Truly in these evil days we need a manifest display of his power, for the ancient enemies of God and man are again struggling for the mastery, and if they gain it, woe unto the saints of God."[4]

A mere subject does not arouse an earthly king without proper justification. How much more does the psalmist seek to justify his prayer for the vengeance of God. To this end, he first appeals to the boasting of the ungodly: "They pour out their arrogant words; all the evildoers boast" (Ps. 94:4). It is characteristic of bullies to boast about their abuses, and so it is with those afflicting God's people. When Proverbs lists the seven things that God especially hates, the first is "haughty eyes" (Prov. 6:17). Here is an appeal to God that is likely to gain a holy response, since the Bible declares, "The boastful shall not stand before your eyes" (Ps. 5:5).

Even worse than boasting is the sheer violence against God's helpless people: "They crush your people, O Lord, and afflict your heritage" (Ps. 94:5). The psalmist thus reminds the Lord of his vested interest in those who are suffering violence: they are his heritage. It is therefore God's plans and people that are being struck down and afflicted. Jesus confirmed that God feels deeply when his people are hurt when he rebuked the persecutor Saul of Tarsus: "Saul, Saul, why are you persecuting me?" (Acts 9:4). To afflict the church was to persecute Christ personally. Matthew Henry comments: "This is a very good plea with God, in our intercessions for the church: 'Lord, it is thine; thou hast a property in it. It is thy heritage; thou hast a pleasure in it, and out of it the rent of thy glory in this world issues.'"[5] Surely, the psalmist reasons, God will come and defend that which is his very own, evicting those who trample his own vineyard!

It was bad enough that the wicked were targeting believers, but they especially took advantage of those who were weakest in society, whom God had placed under his special protection: "They kill the widow and the sojourner, and murder the fatherless" (Ps. 94:6). Psalm 68:5 styled the Lord as "Father of the fatherless and protector of widows." How moved God is

4. Charles Haddon Spurgeon, *The Treasury of David*, 3 vols. (Peabody, MA: Hendrickson, n.d.), 2b:143.
5. Matthew Henry, *Commentary on the Whole Bible*, 6 vols. (Peabody, MA: Hendrickson, n.d.), 3:487.

when the weakest and most vulnerable are abused. Christians today rightly pray for God to intervene against the slaughter of the unborn by a calloused society, even as many around the world pray for God to relieve the sufferings of the church under persecution.

Finally, having pointed out the boasting of the wicked and the crushing of the needy, the psalmist alerts the Lord to what the oppressors are saying: "The Lord does not see; the God of Jacob does not perceive" (Ps. 94:7). The wicked have based their entire program on the premise that God will not take notice or act to remove their sway. This statement suggests that the psalmist refers to legalized criminality by ungodly powers who have seized the government of Israel. Such authorities believe they have cloaked their injustice by passing statutes in support of their oppression. The psalmist sets this offense before God, knowing that the Lord is all the more angered when slaughter is established by supreme courts and corruption is protected by executive order. Far from bowing to such presumptuous human authorities who cloak their violations of God's law under legal pretense, the psalmist expects a more rapid appearing of God because of the affront to his rule.

A Rebuke to the Wicked

Having called on the Lord for help, the psalmist turns his voice to the evil oppressors. Appealing to them in frustration, he writes: "Understand, O dullest of the people! Fools, when will you be wise?" (Ps. 94:8). The word translated as "dullest" means "beast" in its noun form, so the idea is that the boastful fiends are brutish in their ways. However impressive they may be in their worldly status, they conduct themselves like animals. Thinking themselves wise, they are in reality fools. Derek Kidner writes: "These people are adopting a bovine view of life; they are capable of better things, and the psalmist now appeals to them to use their minds."[6]

The psalmist challenges the tyrants particularly in the third of the charges made in the first stanza: "they say, 'The Lord does not see; the God of Jacob does not perceive'" (Ps. 94:7). This belief that they sin with impunity, since God has apparently taken no notice, is at the heart of their folly. In three rhetorical questions, the psalmist discloses the error of their view, dealing

6. Derek Kidner, *Psalms 73–150*, Tyndale Old Testament Commentaries 16 (Downers Grove, IL: InterVarsity Press, 1975), 341.

in turn with how God's knowledge is proved by creation, providence, and general revelation.

First, the evidence of creation makes it obvious that the Creator is not incapable of gaining new information about the world that he made. "He who planted the ear," the psalmist asks, "does he not hear?" If God created the ear, then he must himself have the capacity to hear. Moreover, "He who formed the eye, does he not see?" (Ps. 94:9). If God has given these abilities to man, does this not argue that God possesses them himself? William Plumer writes: "Shall he who imparts powers of perception have no powers of perception himself? . . . If the creature has such faculties, must not the Creator have glorious perfections?"[7]

Second, God's works of providence also indicate that he judges the affairs of men: "He who disciplines the nations, does he not rebuke?" (Ps. 94:10). Even at this earlier stage of history, there was abundant proof that God does judge nations that are given over to evil. Virtually every culture on earth preserves a memory of Noah's flood, which occurred as God's judgment for sin. Israel's history included God's wrath on the Amorites when Israel ejected them from the land of Canaan. If God judges the nations in this way, is it reasonable that he will treat individuals differently?

This argument from God's providence is especially potent in Western nations today, when worldly powers in education, the media, and the government conspire to overthrow the moral heritage of Christianity. Their frequent claim that Christians are "on the wrong side of history" is tragically ironic. Under their evolutionary paradigm, they mean that historical forces inexorably ensure the victory of their atheistic cause. In reality, history teaches exactly the opposite. Throughout history, every civilization that has turned to moral and sexual debauchery has soon fallen to more virtuous competitors. The examples of the ancient world include Babylon, Greece, and Rome, all of which grew to vast power through civic virtue and moral commitments, but then turned to tyranny and sensual pleasure, resulting in their calamitous fall. This very process is happening today in secular humanistic Europe. Having rejected the worship and moral commitments of their Christian past, European societies today are not even able to sustain their population levels. Their citizens no longer motivated for parenthood, European countries have imported vast numbers of Muslim immigrants to

7. William S. Plumer, *Psalms* (1867; repr., Edinburgh: Banner of Truth, 1975), 866.

uphold their labor force. These unassimilated Muslims, who place a high value on children, now threaten the very fabric of European society. The lesson of history—that is, of God's providential rule over the world—sounds a loud condemnation of the ungodliness being promoted by the cultural tyrants of the West, arguing that their debauchery will not succeed.

Third, the psalmist notes that all earthly knowledge derives from God, "who teaches man knowledge" (Ps. 94:10). How could God be ignorant, when all truth is revealed by either his general revelation in nature or his special revelation in Scripture? Calvin observes that "all the knowledge which is in the world is but as a drop from his own inexhaustible fullness,"[8] so that any theory founded on divine ignorance is itself ignorant in the extreme.

In particular, God "knows the thoughts of man, that they are but a breath" (Ps. 94:11). It is because of man's unbelief and atheism toward God that the rest of his thinking goes astray. Indeed, the only way for men and women to live wisely and to leave a true legacy is to proceed from an accurate knowledge of God. Still, even the wisest men embarrass themselves before God by the vanity of their thoughts. H. C. Leupold summarizes that "there has, perhaps, never been a more devastating demonstration of the foolish thinking which men occasionally become guilty of when they imagine that the Lord is not aware of what they are doing."[9]

A Blessing on God's Discipline

In the third stanza of Psalm 94, the writer turns to afflicted believers with encouragement. For all their suffering, and despite God's apparent delay in sending aid, they should trust that God is working in and through their oppression to do them spiritual good. "Blessed is the man whom you discipline, O Lord," he writes, "and whom you teach out of your law" (Ps. 94:12).

Believers need to remember that they, too, need a continuing education from the Lord, including God's dealing with their sin. Therefore, even as the psalmist appeals to the wicked to grow in wisdom, he acknowledges that God uses affliction to discipline his beloved people. Spurgeon writes:

8. Calvin, *Commentaries*, 6:18.

9. H. C. Leupold, *Exposition of the Psalms* (Columbus, OH: Wartburg Press, 1959), 671.

"The afflicted believer is under tuition, he is in training for something higher and better, and all that he meets with is working out his highest good, therefore he is a blessed man, however much his outward circumstances may argue the reverse."[10] This was Paul's assumption in Romans 8:28: "And we know that for those who love God all things work together for good, for those who are called according to his purpose." Experience shows that believers often receive their best and most profitable instruction from God in the midst of difficult trials, which cast them onto the Lord and draw them near to God in prayer.

Christians not only may realize that God is growing their character under trials, but may also lean on the Lord's grace for solace. Thus the psalmist expresses God's purpose: "to give him rest from days of trouble, until a pit is dug for the wicked" (Ps. 94:13). In Psalm 73, Asaph improved his attitude by remembering the certain judgment of the wicked in the final judgment, if not sooner. He wrote: "I went into the sanctuary of God; then I discerned their end" (73:17). In contrast to the fate of the wicked, the believer realizes that the Lord has promised vindication for him through faith. His troubled life is leading him to eternal blessing, whereas even in prosperity the wicked oppressors are merely storing up wrath for the day of judgment. What solace an afflicted believer receives by meditating on the promises of Scripture! Romans 8:31–34 argues:

> If God is for us, who can be against us? He who did not spare his own Son but gave him up for us all, how will he not also with him graciously give us all things? Who shall bring any charge against God's elect? It is God who justifies. Who is to condemn? Christ Jesus is the one who died—more than that, who was raised—who is at the right hand of God, who indeed is interceding for us.

This ability to find rest from God while still under trials is a mark of the true believer. The merely outward professor of faith is prone to falling away when there is a price to be paid for his shallow convictions. Jesus cited this scenario as typical of false believers, whose faith is like a seed that fell on rocky ground. Though he may receive God's Word joyfully in pleasant times, "yet he has no root in himself, but endures for a while, and when tribulation

10. Spurgeon, *Treasury of David*, 2b:145.

or persecution arises on account of the word, immediately he falls away" (Matt. 13:21). With this potential calamity in mind, the believer finds his fidelity to God's Word under trial to be a great encouragement, since it testifies to the reality of his salvation. When the affliction has finally been relieved, such a Christian realizes the blessing spoken of by 1 Peter 1:6–7:

> though now for a little while, if necessary, you have been grieved by various trials, so that the tested genuineness of your faith—more precious than gold that perishes though it is tested by fire—may be found to result in praise and glory and honor at the revelation of Jesus Christ.

Of particular solace to the troubled Christian is the Bible's testimony that God will never abandon his own: "For the Lord will not forsake his people; he will not abandon his heritage" (Ps. 94:14). Plumer writes: "Sad and suffering as the saints may be, yet this is their joy and their glory, that in the darkest hour of life they are still the people and the heritage of God. They may be cast down, yea, they may be cast out, but they shall not be cast off, nor cast away."[11] Given this biblical warrant, the most troubled of saints, especially those targeted with injustice because of their faith, may look with certainty for God to set things right: "for justice will return to the righteous, and all the upright in heart will follow it" (v. 15).

A Testimony to the Savior

The final section of Psalm 94 takes up the call to which all believers should aspire when they find themselves oppressed: the psalmist glorifies God for his faithfulness and bears testimony to his saving presence.

To this end, the psalmist admits that he had gone through a time of great frustration and even doubt. Apparently, his chief complaint was that no one seemed to take a stand alongside him: "Who rises up for me against the wicked? Who stands up for me against evildoers?" (Ps. 94:16). So low were his spirits that if the Lord had not rendered him personal aid, he trembles to think of the deadly fate to which he may have fallen: "If the Lord had not been my help, my soul would soon have lived in the land of silence" (v. 17).

Both experience and Scripture show that even the strongest of saints may

11. Plumer, *Psalms*, 870–71.

be cast into depression when it seems that they are abandoned by their fellow believers. Perhaps the greatest example is that of Elijah, when he fell into sudden despair after achieving one of the most heroic victories of his ministry. In 1 Kings 18, Elijah squared off against the priests of Baal, who were in the pay of wicked Queen Jezebel. By God's power, Elijah shamed the idolaters on Mount Carmel, leading the people of Israel to rise up and put them to the sword. To our great surprise, however, when Jezebel turned her daggers in the prophet's direction, mighty Elijah turned in panicked flight, running all the way to Mount Sinai in the desert. There, the Lord inquired, "What are you doing here, Elijah?" (1 Kings 19:13). The prophet answered, "I have been very jealous for the Lord, the God of hosts. For the people of Israel have forsaken your covenant, thrown down your altars, and killed your prophets with the sword, and I, even I only, am left, and they seek my life, to take it away" (v. 14). Elijah was wrong about this, since the Lord then told him of "seven thousand in Israel, all the knees that have not bowed to Baal" (v. 18). If even so great a prophet as Elijah was panicked at the thought that he stood alone against the ungodly, how easily we may be cast down by similar thoughts!

Even when believers do stand alone against the ungodly, the Lord is faithful to take our side. This was Paul's testimony when he faced Caesar without anyone to support him. "But the Lord stood by me and strengthened me," he testified, "so that through me the message might be fully proclaimed and all the Gentiles might hear it" (2 Tim. 4:17). The psalmist had a similar experience: "When I thought, 'My foot slips,' your steadfast love, O Lord, held me up" (Ps. 94:18). He learned from this experience that God can be appealed to, if not to render outward aid, then certainly to give spiritual encouragement: "When the cares of my heart are many, your consolations cheer my soul" (v. 19). Calvin writes that "the word of God provides us with abundant ground of comfort, and . . . none who rightly avails himself of it need ever count himself unhappy, or yield himself to hopelessness and despondency."[12]

One great truth that the psalmist learned in Scripture is that God will never ally himself with the ungodly, but is certain to take cause on behalf of his afflicted people: "Can wicked rulers be allied with you, those who frame injustice by statute? They band together against the life of the righteous

12. Calvin, *Commentaries*, 6:21.

and condemn the innocent to death. But the LORD has become my stronghold, and my God the rock of my refuge" (Ps. 94:20–22). Even while the afflictions lasted, the prophet found God as a fortress to make his faith grow strong, and as a refuge in which he could rest from his fears. William O. Cushing expressed this conviction in the words of his memorable hymn:

> O safe to the Rock that is higher than I
> My soul in its conflicts and sorrows would fly;
> So sinful, so weary, thine, thine would I be;
> Thou blest Rock of Ages, I'm hiding in thee.
>
> In the calm of the noontide, in sorrow's lone hour,
> In times when temptation casts o'er me its pow'r,
> In the tempests of life, on its wide, heaving sea,
> Thou blest Rock of Ages, I'm hiding in thee.[13]

From this high perch in the refuge of God's saving presence, the psalmist looked down on his foes, no longer panicked, but secure in the certainty of God's judgment: "He will bring back on them their iniquity and wipe them out for their wickedness; the LORD our God will wipe them out" (Ps. 94:23).

Steadfast against Evil

An obvious application of this psalm comes from the complaint of the psalmist in Psalm 94:16: "Who rises up for me against the wicked? Who stands up for me against evildoers?" With God as our fortress, and with our awareness of God's certain judgment against all evil, Christians are emboldened not to go into hiding. There is no reason to deny our faith or give in to evil, as the psalmist was tempted to do. Perhaps we will be like Obadiah, a contemporary of Elijah's who had the misfortune to serve as an official in the court of wicked King Ahab. At great risk to his own life, Obadiah did what he could to protect the weak and vulnerable from oppression, hiding the prophets of the Lord in caves and providing food and water for them while they escaped Ahab's persecution (1 Kings 18:13). Or perhaps we will be called to be like Elisha, who trained under Elijah to take up his calling

13. William O. Cushing, "O Safe to the Rock That Is Higher Than I" (1876).

as a prophet to the Lord. Maybe God will call you to be bold like they were. Perhaps you serve as a government or business leader. How can you take a stand against corruption and abuse? Perhaps you teach in a secular college. Do you pray for God's wisdom in countering denials of his Word? Or maybe you are a mother in a home, or a member in a church. Can you be bold for truth and godliness in answering the call of Psalm 94:16: "Who rises up for me against the wicked? Who stands up for me against evildoers?"

Whatever our calling, we can all take refuge in God's protection in order to give a bold and compassionate witness to the grace that God gives to every sinner who believes. For this calling, we have great encouragement in God's Word. Paul writes that "everyone who calls on the name of the Lord will be saved" (Rom. 10:13). That "everyone" includes great persecutors just as Paul himself had once been. It is our privilege to give this witness, even to the wicked in the midst of oppression, as Paul went on to reason:

> How then will they call on him in whom they have not believed? And how are they to believe in him of whom they have never heard? And how are they to hear without someone preaching? And how are they to preach unless they are sent? As it is written, "How beautiful are the feet of those who preach the good news!" (Rom. 10:14–15)

26

O Worship the King

Psalm 95

Oh come, let us sing to the Lord*; let us make a joyful noise to the rock of our salvation!* (Ps. 95:1)

One of my seminary professors summarized what he described as "the typical psalm." He said: "Most psalms have about twelve verses. The first ten verses cry out to the Lord about how terrible life is and what danger is about to strike. Then the last two verses say, "Oh, but you are in charge, Lord, so I know everything will be all right." By that standard, Psalm 95 is practically the opposite of the typical psalm. Instead of beginning with a lament for troubles and dangers, it celebrates how great the Lord is as King of his people. The last three verses, however, provide a warning to the spiritually complacent. Instead of saying, "All will be well," the psalmist warns that if the people hear but do not obey God's Word, they will fall into danger of rejection by a wrathful Lord. The only way we can be sure that "everything will be all right," he insists, is by hearing God's Word in such a way that we receive it in faith.

Psalm 95 is an act of worship. It outlines the manner in which God's people should worship, together with our motive in giving praise. In doing so, the psalmist highlights the necessity of knowing who and what God is in order to worship him as he deserves to be worshiped. The way to know God, and thus to worship him, is to carefully heed the Word of God as it is proclaimed. Eric Lane writes: "Worship is prompted by a right view of God, which in turn prompts a response to his Word."[1] In this way, Psalm 95 sets a high view on the gathered and corporate worship of God's people. At the same time, it notes that the true test of our worship takes place after we leave the sanctuary. Jesus once complained against what he considered hypocritical worship, which did not include trusting obedience to God: "This people honors me with their lips, but their heart is far from me" (Mark 7:6). Along these same lines, Psalm 95 completes its call to worship with a warning: "Today, if you hear his voice, do not harden your hearts" (Ps. 95:7–8).

COME, LET US SING!

When it comes to how the people of God are to worship, Psalm 95 calls for exuberant hearts that cry out in song: "Oh come, let us sing to the LORD" (Ps. 95:1)!

Of two attitudes that Psalm 95 commends in worship, the first is joy: "let us make a joyful noise to the rock of our salvation!" (Ps. 95:1). Israelites likely would have thought of the rock in the desert that followed Israel in order to sustain the people with life. With what joy their parched lips opened to receive water from the rock! Believers likewise bring their thirsty hearts before the Lord, opening them in gladness to be spiritually nourished. Our worship is to involve not only the giving of ourselves in praise but also finding satisfaction in the God to whom we have come. Charles Spurgeon writes:

> God is our abiding, immutable, and mighty rock, and in him we find deliverance and safety, therefore it becomes us to praise him with heart and with voice from day to day; and especially should we delight to do this when we assemble as his people for public worship.[2]

This call to joyful worship does not enshrine any particular style for worshipers. In many churches today, worshipers raise their hands aloft,

1. Eric Lane, *Psalms 90–150: The Lord Reigns* (Ross-shire, Scotland: Christian Focus, 2006), 27.
2. Charles Haddon Spurgeon, *The Treasury of David*, 3 vols. (Peabody, MA: Hendrickson, n.d.), 2b:164–65.

sigh, and cry. In other churches, the concern for reverence creates a less active physical response. What matters more than these styles is the true joy in the Lord that should characterize our attitude. To be sure, the call to "make a joyful noise" makes a hearty *Amen* more than permissible! But more than the outward form, the psalmist is concerned for the inward response of joy to the Lord, especially in our congregational singing. It is important to the writer of Psalm 95 that visitors to our worship service come away with the idea that the people rejoiced to worship the Lord.

A second characteristic of true worship is thankfulness: "Let us come into his presence with thanksgiving" (Ps. 95:2). In his book *The Religious Affections*, Jonathan Edwards pointed out, "The love and joy of the saints on earth is the beginning and dawning of the light, life, and blessedness of heaven, and is . . . the same in nature."[3] When we turn to the Bible's depictions of worship in heaven, what we see there should begin to permeate our worship here below. There, we discover an overwhelming thanksgiving to God for all that he has done in our salvation: "We give thanks to you, Lord God Almighty, who is and who was, for you have taken your great power and begun to reign" (Rev. 11:17). This thankful spirit permeates the praise songs throughout the Psalter: "Oh give thanks to the Lord, for he is good; for his steadfast love endures forever!" (Ps. 118:1). Since Christ is the rock of our salvation—the source and the strength of our eternal life—our joy and thanks should mingle together in a spirit of heart-opening praise.

Psalm 95 sees this joyful thanksgiving as taking place in the gathering of God's people in his sanctuary: "Let us come into his presence with thanksgiving; let us make a joyful noise to him with songs of praise!" (Ps. 95:2). Notice the call for the gathering of the church: "Oh come, let us sing . . . . Let us come into his presence" (vv. 1–2). Our times have seen a de-emphasis on public, congregational worship, with many opting instead to watch a video church service at home or to replace public worship with socially oriented fellowship gatherings. The proliferation of live computer broadcasts of church services has been a great blessing for the homebound and infirm, and home fellowship groups can provide important spiritual support to believers. But they should never be seen as substitutes for being physically present in the gathering of the saints whenever possible. When the hymn is being sung and the Word is being preached, there is nothing to compare

3. Jonathan Edwards, *The Religious Affections* (1746; repr., Edinburgh: Banner of Truth, 1986), 42.

with being "in the room." For this reason, when the writer of Hebrews warned his disciples about "not neglecting to meet together" (Heb. 10:25), the emphasis lay on the public gatherings of God's people for joyful, thank-filled worship.

When it comes to our meeting together, we should also note the prominence given to singing together: "Oh come, let us sing to the Lord" (Ps. 95:1). Here we see an important constant in the worship of God's people of all times and places, extending into heaven. Both Old and New Testaments emphasize congregational singing as an important element of praise. Singing incorporates nearly all the aspects of Christian worship. We worship God with our minds, so it is important that our songs inscribe sound doctrine. Worship is also a matter of our hearts, and singing expresses thoughts in an emotionally uplifting manner. Psalm 95 commands us to "make a joyful noise" to the Lord, and what could be more joyful than a song of praise? Finally, singing is an element of worship in which all the people of God participate together. O. Palmer Robertson writes:

> There is no such thing as a person without music in his soul. God has made all human beings so that they respond to rhythm and song. Knowing this basic aspect of man, the Lord has ordained that his worship will include the offering of a sacrifice of praise through singing.[4]

One of the saddest features of much contemporary worship is that so many people in the congregation no longer sing. Instead, with the lights focused on the stage, a professional "worship team" puts on a show of lively music to which the "audience" responds by adoringly watching. But biblical singing is congregational, with the audible voices of all of God's people joined in thanks to the Rock of our salvation. In this choir of the congregation, none need worry that their voices are out of tune. All are called to "make a joyful noise."

Let Us Kneel before the King!

If the opening stanza of Psalm 95 outlines the manner of our worship, the middle section supplies abundant motives for worshiping the Lord with

4. O. Palmer Robertson, *Psalms in Congregational Celebration* (Darlington, UK: Evangelical Press, 1995), 255.

joyful thanksgiving: "For the Lord is a great God, and a great King above all gods" (Ps. 95:3). These descriptions of God tell us why he is worthy of our praise. They show us the necessity of an accurate knowledge of God for biblical worship and, correspondingly, the great motivation that arises when we consider his greatness. William Plumer comments: "If we would be strong and happy servants of Christ, let us meditate much on God's *greatness*. He is the infinite God, unmeasurable in all his glorious attributes. There is no limit to any of his perfections, and there is no perfection of God, in which his people may not find matter of exultation."[5]

God is extolled, first, as a great and sovereign King: "a great King above all gods. In his hand are the depths of the earth; the heights of the mountains are his also" (Ps. 95:3–4). In saying that he is "above all gods," the psalmist is not acknowledging the deity of other gods but noting lesser powers that are falsely treated as divine. The idols were man-made gods, with no life. They were local to a particular territory and dependent on man for their being. The idols, in short, are no gods at all! But "the Lord is a great God, and a great King" (v. 3). He reigns sovereignly over the entirety of the earth, the dimensions of which are traced out in verses 4–5. Whether we go to "the depths of the earth" or "the heights of the mountains," or even span the seas, everything is "in his hand" and under his royal control. Only by placing all things under his feet, therefore, and by extolling the God of the Bible as the true and heavenly Sovereign, do we worship him as he deserves.

Associated with God's sovereignty is his almighty power as the Creator of heaven and earth. Psalm 95:5 says, "The sea is his, for he made it, and his hands formed the dry land." Here God's sovereign rule is established in his creation of all things. Therefore, the entire world owes allegiance only to him. Even inaccessible places of the world where man seldom if ever goes—"the depths of the earth" and "the heights of the mountains"—exist under his sovereign command and for the praise of his glory.

God's sovereign kingship and almighty power as Creator supply more than sufficient grounds to motivate our worship. But Psalm 95 provides a final motivation that appeals to believers directly: "For he is our God, and we are the people of his pasture, and the sheep of his hand" (Ps. 95:7). While all people ought to praise God as their Maker, the church should be moti-

5. William S. Plumer, *Psalms* (1867; repr., Edinburgh: Banner of Truth, 1975), 875.

vated to worship in light of God's saving relationship with us. The great God, the sovereign Creator of heaven and earth, is our God, and has made us his dearly beloved people! Spurgeon writes:

> Here is the master reason for worship. Jehovah has entered into covenant with *us*, and from all the world beside has chosen us to be his own elect. If others refuse him homage, we at least will render it cheerfully. He is ours, and our God; ours, therefore we will love him; our God, therefore will we worship him.[6]

Psalm 95:7 emphasizes not only our saving relationship to the Lord, but also his tender, loving care in meeting all our needs. We are "the people of his pasture," "the sheep of his hand." The Lord watches over our souls, supplying all our spiritual needs out of his storehouse in heaven, to ensure that each of his sheep will enter his house without a single one being lost. How blessed is anyone who knows that God is his Savior through faith in Christ! What a motive for worship these saving blessings provide!

Christians cannot read Psalm 95:7 without thinking of Jesus' teaching, "I am the good shepherd. The good shepherd lays down his life for the sheep" (John 10:11). Jesus provided for our salvation by dying in our place, paying the penalty for our sins in the blood of his cross. A shepherd not only feeds his sheep but also defends them. Jesus therefore added: "I give them eternal life, and they will never perish, and no one will snatch them out of my hand" (v. 28).

Perhaps with similar thoughts of thanksgiving, the psalmist responds to this pastoral imagery with an even higher pitch of zeal for worship: "Oh come, let us worship and bow down; let us kneel before the Lord, our Maker!" (Ps. 95:6). This verse identifies God both by his covenant name, *Yahweh* (English, Lord), and as the Creator (*Elohim*). Perceiving his infinite majesty as Creator, we bow before him as mere creatures. Rejoicing in his intimate grace as our Redeemer, we kneel before the Lord with the fervent offering of our lives.

With this statement, Psalm 95 rounds out a godly attitude in worship. We come to the Lord joyfully and with great thanksgiving, singing excitedly in his presence. But we also come humbly and reverently before the awesome

6. Spurgeon, *Treasury of David*, 2b:166.

Creator and loving Redeemer. Whether we kneel physically or spiritually in the attitude of our adoration, true Christian worship is aptly described by the words of Psalm 2:11: "rejoice with trembling." Robert Grant reproduced this logic in a familiar hymn:

O worship the King all-glorious above,
O gratefully sing his pow'r and his love;
Our shield and Defender, the Ancient of Days,
Pavilioned in splendor and girded with praise.[7]

Today, Hear His Voice!

When Jesus described himself as the Good Shepherd and his people as the flock under his care, he made an important statement that connects with Psalm 95:7–8: "My sheep hear my voice, and I know them, and they follow me" (John 10:27). This teaching points in the same direction that the psalmist is taking our study of worship. Having described the main actions of worship in terms of the words *sing* and *kneel*, he now adds another priority for the people of God to *hear*. Jesus said that his true sheep are known by the way in which they respond to his voice (v. 27). "Today, if you hear his voice," the psalmist therefore writes, "do not harden your hearts" (Ps. 95:7–8).

We previously noted that it is impossible to worship rightly unless we know the Lord. This knowledge comes from the Word of God, which is why true worship is centered on the proclamation of the Holy Scriptures. We come before God singing and bow down before him in our prayers. But then the psalmist instructs us to open our ears to hear God's Word. How important it is to our lives that we attend to the Bible with a prepared and open heart! Robertson observes: "It is not the daily newspaper that is being read at worship. It is not the latest opinions of men that are being rehearsed. It is the unchanging word of the Almighty God that is being declared before the congregation. His Word must be given all the respect it deserves."[8]

At its heart, the worship service is a meeting with God in which we learn of him through the faithful teaching of his Word. When we select a church

7. Robert Grant, "O Worship the King" (1833).
8. Robertson, *Psalms in Congregational Celebration*, 257.

to attend, faithful preaching is not the *only* important factor, but it is the *most* important criterion. For the great need of our souls is to be shaped and transformed by the work of God's Word. As Paul urged: "Do not be conformed to this world, but be transformed by the renewal of your mind" (Rom. 12:2).

This principle of true worship transforming our lives forms the conclusion of Psalm 95. The psalmist makes this point with a warning that is so sudden and severe that liberal scholars have argued that it seems out of place. In fact, the psalmist is making a point that needs to be heard by our generation especially. James Boice writes that "the warning to hear the voice of God and obey it is actually a critical part of what needs to be said about the worship God accepts. Worship without obedience is a mere sham. It calls down the judgment of God the Father and Jesus."[9]

To see that this claim is not an overstatement, we need only consider the example to which the psalmist refers. "Do not harden your hearts," he writes, "as at Meribah, as on the day at Massah in the wilderness, when your fathers put me to the test and put me to the proof, though they had seen my work" (Ps. 95:8–9). This statement refers to historical incidents during Israel's exodus through the wilderness from Egypt to the promised land.

A mere three days after the people of Israel had escaped from slavery in Egypt and passed through the Red Sea, they arrived in the desert, where there was no water to drink. When the people assailed Moses, he answered: "Why do you quarrel with me? Why do you test the LORD?" (Ex. 17:3). The psalmist has this episode in mind when he describes God as saying that the Israelites' ancestors "put me to the test and put me to the proof, though they had seen my work" (Ps. 95:9). When Israel rebelled, Moses turned to the Lord, saying that the people were threatening his life. God answered by providing the rock from which water flowed after Moses struck it. Exodus 17:7 concludes: "And he called the name of the place Massah and Meribah, because of the quarreling of the people of Israel, and because they tested the LORD by saying, 'Is the LORD among us or not?'"

Another episode took place forty years later, after the Israelites had been forced to wander in the desert as punishment for their testing the Lord. Once again, the people quarreled over physical hardship, accusing Moses of leading them to their deaths and wishing that they were back in slavery.

9. James Montgomery Boice, *Psalms*, 3 vols. (Grand Rapids: Baker, 1996), 2:778.

Moses was so vexed by their hardness of heart that when God told him once more to strike the rock, Moses angrily struck it twice, committing the sin for which he was barred from entering the promised land. The Lord named that place Meribah, signifying the quarreling of Israel with the Lord (Num. 20:1–13).

It is this forty-year period—between the rebellions of Massah and Meribah—that Psalm 95 mentions in warning its readers against a similar wickedness. When facing difficulties, the children of Israel hardened their hearts to the Word of God, making demands of the Lord and assailing his goodness: "your fathers put me to the test and put me to the proof, though they had seen my work" (Ps. 95:9). God had previously shown staggering wonders, breaking the power of Pharaoh by slaying all of Egypt's firstborn sons, and then parting the waters of the Red Sea to make a way of escape for his people. Yet these miracles were not enough to quiet their anxieties and earn the Lord their trust.

This episode reminds Christians that our experience of God's saving power increases our responsibility to believe and obey God's Word. If we reflect honestly on our own hearts, we will see the relevance of the psalmist's warning. Do we not also grumble and complain when the Lord does not meet our immediate needs, despite the greater proofs of his love that we have received in the ministry and death of Jesus Christ? How vital it is for all believers—especially those facing trials—to keep their hearts soft and malleable before the teaching of God's Word! In the context of Psalm 95, this warning especially pertains to our response to God's Word as it is preached in the worship service. The psalmist asks: "Will you hear his voice *today*? Here you are, singing and bowing, but are you *listening*?"[10]

The psalmist's warning is made all the more pressing when we consider God's intense response to the unbelief of his people at Massah and Meribah: "For forty years I loathed that generation and said, 'They are a people who go astray in their heart, and they have not known my ways.' Therefore I swore in my wrath, 'They shall not enter my rest'" (Ps. 95:10–11). God was angry with the hard-hearted Israelites of the exodus, and in his wrath he caused the nation to wander in the desert until all of that generation perished (apart from faithful Joshua and Caleb). The Israelites did not enter into the

10. Michael Wilcock, *The Message of Psalms 73–150* (Downers Grove, IL: InterVarsity Press, 2001), 94.

rest of the promised land in Canaan because of the hardness of their hearts to the Word of God.

According to the Lord, our willingness to hear, believe, and obey God's Word—especially in times of trial—is a test of our faith and salvation. Notice that God looked on the Israelites not only as those "who go astray in their heart," but also as those who "have not known my ways" (Ps. 95:10). This is said of the exodus generation, the multitude that saw some of the greatest miracles of the entire Bible and received the greatest deliverance in history before the coming of Christ! The nation was delivered. God's people were saved from bondage. But at least a considerable portion of the people were not saved eternally because their hardened hearts would not believe. Could there be a more urgent warning to outwardly professing Christians today? It is not our church membership—much less our family connections or our baptism—that saves us. We are saved only through a true and living faith in God, trusting in Jesus Christ and receiving God's Word. Not surprisingly, Jesus made our perseverance under trial an essential test of true and saving faith. In his parable of the soils, Jesus spoke of "one who hears the word and immediately receives it with joy, yet he has no root in himself, . . . and when tribulation or persecution arises on account of the word, immediately he falls away" (Matt. 13:20–21). We must receive God's Word with a living faith in hearts prepared by the Spirit of God in order to be saved.

Entering God's Rest

The writer of Hebrews picked up on the warning of Psalm 95:8–11 in reminding his own generation to hold fast to the Word of God. Psalm 95 calls us to sing to the Lord with joy for our salvation, to bow before the Lord for his greatness, and to hear God's Word as it is preached in the church. According to Hebrews, two vital applications emerge from this exhortation.

First, Hebrews 3:12–13 quotes the final section of Psalm 95 and makes the following comment:

> Take care, brothers, lest there be in any of you an evil, unbelieving heart, leading you to fall away from the living God. But exhort one another every day, as long as it is called "today," that none of you may be hardened by the deceitfulness of sin.

This warning tells us that when Christians gather for their weekly worship services, they should see themselves as a source of spiritual support for fellow Christians. We have a tendency to unbelief when going through hard times. Moreover, it is because sin is so deceitful that it succeeds in hardening our hearts. We therefore need one another's encouragement—and sometimes our rebukes—as we pray for one another, bear one another's burdens, provide spiritual encouragement, and give a godly example of faith. Hebrews 3–4 sees the Christian contest as a team sport, in which our gatherings for worship are intended to provide mutual support and exhortation.

Second, Psalm 95 presents our response in worship to the Word of God as a matter of eternal life and death. God said of unbelieving Israel, "They shall not enter my rest" (Ps. 95:11). Hebrews 4:2 explains why they did not enter the promised land: "the message they heard did not benefit them, because they were not united by faith with those who listened." According to Psalm 95 and Hebrews 3–4, believers in Christ must persevere in faith if we will enter into the rest of God's eternal life in heaven. The key to persevering is our humble receiving of God's Word as it is preached.

"Today," said the psalmist, "if you hear his voice, do not harden your hearts" (Ps. 95:7–8). Now is our "today," whether we have already believed the gospel or have never previously believed. God's voice is still speaking through his Word, setting forth Jesus as the Savior of sinners. If you harden your heart, you are in danger of falling under God's wrath, never to enter his salvation rest. But if you believe today, you will have reason to rejoice together with the faithful church forever. Through faith, your heart will sing to the Lord, making "a joyful noise to the rock of our salvation!" (v. 1).

27

Declare among the Nations

Psalm 96

Worship the Lord *in the splendor of holiness;*
tremble before him, all the earth! (Ps. 96:9)

First Chronicles 16 details the crowning moment of King David's career as he brought the ark of the covenant up to Jerusalem. Having been enthroned as Israel's king, David called for the ark to be rescued from the house of Abinadab in order to install God's throne on Mount Zion. After the ark was brought up, David directed temple singers to intone verses that include a nearly verbatim recitation of Psalm 96. "Sing to the Lord, all the earth!" sang Asaph and his band of singers. "Tell of his salvation from day to day" (1 Chron. 16:23). The occasion commemorated God's open reign through David's throne: "let them say among the nations, 'The Lord reigns!'" (v. 31).

Scholars are divided on how to take the quotation of Psalm 96 in 1 Chronicles 16:23–33. It is possible that the psalm was written by David on that most significant occasion. It is also possible that Chronicles, written during the Babylonian exile many years later, used Psalm 96 as a model summary of David's song. In any case, the setting of David's bringing up the ark of the covenant fits the kingship theme of Psalm 96. Here the psalmist, perhaps

David himself, summons the people to praise God in light of his present reign and especially because of the universal reign that will arrive in the day of the Lord's coming.

Calling All People to Worship

Like most of the other lyrics dedicated to the Lord's kingship in Psalms 93–99, Psalm 96 begins with a call for the people to gather in praise: "Oh sing to the Lord a new song; sing to the Lord, all the earth!" (Ps. 96:1). A distinctive feature is the summons to sing "a new song" (recurring in Psalm 98). Here we find that worship calls for creativity in response to the fresh mercies of the Lord.

When the Bible speaks of a new song, however, its emphasis is not on man's new compositions but on God's fresh advances in redemption, which warrant a response in praise. A noted example was the Song of Moses after the Lord's parting of the Red Sea for Israel's escape. "I will sing to the Lord, for he has triumphed gloriously," Moses rejoiced; "the horse and his rider he has thrown into the sea" (Ex. 15:1).

In the case of Psalm 96, it may be that the new thing God had done involved bringing his ark up to Jerusalem, marking the beginning of his reign on Mount Zion. In David's eye, this glorious advancement warranted new praise. In Revelation 5, we encounter another "new song," which also concerns the kingship of the Lord. The chapter shows Jesus as "the Lion of the tribe of Judah" (Rev. 5:5), taking the scroll of God's sovereign will. As Jesus stepped forward and took hold of history after his ascension into heaven, the assembled host of heaven "sang a new song": "Worthy are you to take the scroll and to open its seals, for you were slain, and by your blood you ransomed people for God" (v. 9). Revelation 14 likewise tells of the scene at the end of history, when the vast assembly of God's redeemed people come to stand beside the Lamb on Mount Zion, and "they were singing a new song before the throne" (14:3). Since the "new song" celebrates the victory of God's grace in the exaltation of his reigning Son, we look back on the bringing up of the ark as anticipating the triumph of our Savior.

In the "new song" for which Psalm 96 calls, we see a facet of what makes Christianity so thrilling to believers. We look back on marvelous achievements by our God for our salvation. God saved Israel of old and he has sent his Son to earth, where Jesus conquered sin and death and ascended to heaven's throne. Yet there still remain new events for us to anticipate with joy. Each stage of redemptive history has brought and will bring out new wonders of God's grace. Yet at the same time, each new song carries forward the grand theme of saving grace that we believed at first in our salvation and that the Bible taught in its opening chapters. Katherine Hankey captured the spirit that the unfolding of redemptive history inspires in God's people:

> I love to tell the story; for those who know it best
> Seem hungering and thirsting to hear it, like the rest.
> And when, in scenes of glory, I sing the new, new song,
> 'Twill be the old, old story, that I have loved so long.[1]

In addition to calling believers to sing a new song, the psalmist summons praise to God for his person and work: "Sing to the Lord, bless his name; tell of his salvation from day to day" (Ps. 96:2). By calling us to "bless his name," the psalmist is referring to the nature and person of God. Worship should always be theological, exploring and extolling the perfections of God's marvelous attributes. God is holy, eternal, just, unchanging, faithful, and gracious. These glories—encapsulated in "his name"—deserve to be adored whenever God's people meet. Yet the emphasis of Psalm 96 falls on God's great works in history: "tell of his salvation from day to day" (v. 2). The great things that God has done for us in the past, is doing now, and has pledged to do in the future deserve to be known and praised.

Almost surprisingly, the psalmist not only calls for this praise from God's covenant people, Israel, but also summons all creation to glorify God. "Sing to the Lord, all the earth!" he begins (Ps. 96:1). "Declare his glory among the nations, his marvelous works among all the peoples!" (v. 3). This universal call to worship may seem out of sync with the historical context of God's coming to reign over Israel. Yet here we find that David's idea included God's reign through his people for the entirety of the world.

One way to see the psalm's emphasis is to note that the Jewish scholars who translated the Old Testament into Greek used the word for "evangelize" in Psalm 96:3: "Spread the good news of his glory among the nations." This

1. Katherine Hankey, "I Love to Tell the Story" (1866).

reminds us that while worship is foremost an offering of praise and glory to the Lord, so that doxology remains the primary aim of worship, it is also true that God-centered worship will always present a missionary and evangelistic appeal. Those who meet God in the church service are drawn to know him, and those who know the Lord in worship experience a great desire for everyone else to know him, too. William Plumer thus writes: "This is a missionary hymn for all ages of the church."[2]

It is always perplexing when Christians are reluctant to tell others about the glory of God's person and especially his saving works in Jesus Christ. We are usually eager to spread good personal news in the form of announcements sent out to celebrate a marriage, childbirth, or job promotion. When we discover an excellent doctor, we are eager to let our friends know, especially those who are sick. If we learn of an outstanding financial investor, car mechanic, or degree program, we are virtually certain to spread the news throughout our circles of influence. How curious it is, then, that Christians do not make it our first business, after worship, to tell everyone we know about the glory of God and the greatness of the salvation he has provided in his Son. The psalmist wants to counter this tendency: "tell of his salvation from day to day. Declare his glory among the nations, his marvelous works among all the peoples!" (Ps. 96:2–3). O. Palmer Robertson comments: "This great missionary psalm anticipates the gospel age of today. As the early Christians first experienced persecution, the book of Acts says that except for the apostles who stayed in Jerusalem, they all went out 'declaring the good news' (Acts 8:4)."[3] In following their example and in spreading God's glory to and throughout the world, Christians should seek every day—"from day to day"—to tell at least one person about the grace of our God and the cleansing blood of Jesus Christ.

Praising the Only True God

Psalm 96 presents the greatness of God as the primary reason for both worship and evangelism: "For great is the Lord, and greatly to be praised; he is to be feared above all gods" (Ps. 96:4).

2. William S. Plumer, *Psalms* (1867; repr., Edinburgh: Banner of Truth, 1975), 880.

3. O. Palmer Robertson, *Psalms in Congregational Celebration* (Darlington, UK: Evangelical Press, 1995), 269.

Why is the Lord to be praised? The psalmist's answer is that he alone is the true and living God, whereas all other gods are but "worthless idols" (Ps. 96:5). Here, the psalmist employs a parody, based on the similarity of sounds between the Hebrew words for "God" (*Elohim*) and "idols" (*elilim*). The idols seem like gods to the foolish, but they fall critically short of the reality. They are made by the hands of men and possess no power to speak or act. Today, the parallels to idols are the twisted ideas that are worshiped by secular humanists. Evolution is an idol, and a corrupt view of "tolerance" is exalted by sophisticated elites. Derek Kidner points out that Psalm 96 urges Christians to be "unimpressed by currently revered nonsense, whatever its pedigree or patronage."[4] In the light of the true God and his revealed truth, all idols will be cast to the ground in the end.

The Christian faith joins with the testimony of the psalmist: "great is the Lord, and greatly to be praised; he is to be feared above all gods" (Ps. 96:4). Only the God of the Bible displays true attributes of deity: "Splendor and majesty are before him; strength and beauty are in his sanctuary" (v. 6). Especially in the worship of the church, the truths of God's Word are to be held up and his glory alone is to be praised. Whereas the idols are "worthless," "the Lord made the heavens" (v. 5).

In this way, Psalm 96 grounds the Christian conviction of the absolute exclusivity of our faith in the greatness of God. Others may blather about all things being divine, and idolaters may be comfortable in worshiping a multitude of deities. But the believer of Psalm 96 knows that there is but one true God, the sovereign Creator, the God whose ark was established on Mount Zion, and the one to whom we offer unyielding, and even exclusive, devotion. J. Gresham Machen identified this conviction as the essential difference between Christianity and liberal religion:

> The early Christian missionaries demanded an absolutely exclusive devotion to Christ. Such exclusiveness ran directly counter to the prevailing syncretism of the Hellenistic age. In that day, many saviours were offered by many religions to the attention of men, but the various pagan religions could live together in perfect harmony; when a man became a devotee of one god, he did not have to give up the others. But Christianity would have nothing to do with these "courtly polygamies of the soul"; it demanded an absolutely

4. Derek Kidner, *Psalms 73–150*, Tyndale Old Testament Commentaries 16 (Downers Grove, IL: InterVarsity Press, 1975), 347.

> exclusive devotion; all other Saviours, it insisted, must be deserted for the one Lord. Salvation, in other words, was not merely through Christ, but it was only through Christ. In that little word "only" lay all the offense.[5]

In our postmodern, relativistic world, the Christian refusal to acknowledge any gods but the God of the Bible is considered hateful. Yet Christians cannot remain true to our Lord while acknowledging other lords. "Splendor and majesty are before him," insists the psalmist. True "strength and beauty are in his sanctuary" (Ps. 96:6). This being the case, it is not possible for a Christian to acknowledge other religions and competing worldviews as equally valid. James Boice notes: "If you are not worshiping the God of the Bible exclusively, as God says you must do, you are not worshiping God. You are not a Christian."[6]

The Lord's Coming to Reign

The first stanza of Psalm 96 calls all people to worship the Lord, and the second stanza insists that this worship belongs to him alone. The psalmist's final argument rests on the claim that God is the true Sovereign of history, and for this reason our worship should be given only to him. "Say among the nations," he cries, "The LORD reigns!" (Ps. 96:10).

The final stanza of Psalm 96 makes three claims regarding the kingship of God. First, it insists that the Lord is reigning even now: "The LORD reigns! Yes, the world is established; it shall never be moved" (Ps. 96:10). The point is that despite the turbulent affairs of men, many of which arrogantly flout God's rule, God nonetheless reigns sovereignly over all affairs.

One reason the world remains ignorant of Christ's reign is that it fails to perceive his objective. In Matthew 16, Jesus responded to Peter's faith by giving him the name *Cephas*, meaning "rock." He then declared that the bedrock of faith that Peter had shown would form the basis of his rule in this world: "on this rock I will build my church, and the gates of hell shall not prevail against it" (Matt. 16:18). With these words, Jesus declared himself sovereign in spreading his gospel throughout this age and overcoming unbelief, so as to gather believers into his church. As the early church bore

5. J. Gresham Machen, *Christianity and Liberalism* (Grand Rapids: Eerdmans, 1923), 123.
6. James Montgomery Boice, *Psalms*, 3 vols. (Grand Rapids: Baker, 1996), 2:785.

testimony, the secular powers could rage against the Christians. They could persecute believers and seek to suppress the gospel. But in the end, worldly might proves utterly impotent against the spread of salvation in Jesus' name and the building up of his holy church.

A stirring testimony to the truth of Christ's present reign has been supplied in our times by the spread of the gospel in Communist China. When Mao Zedong conquered China in 1949, some Western Christians came to the conclusion that their determined attempts to establish a Chinese church had been thwarted. Under official pressure, all the Western missionaries departed from China, leaving the remnant of the church weak before the looming threat of deadly persecution. The Communists persecuted believers, making Christian worship a legal offense and sending faithful preachers into work camps, where their health was broken by slave labor. Yet the record shows that this intense display of worldly might only fanned the flame of gospel expansion. The imprisoned evangelists devoted themselves to prayer. Christians refused to cease meeting for worship and could not be kept from speaking to many people about Jesus and his salvation. Today, under continued persecution and injustice, the movement of Christian house churches in China is estimated to contain as many as one hundred million believers.

Christ reigns as well in the lives of individual believers. An example is seen in Wang Mingdao, one of the early leaders of the Chinese house-church movement. In the 1920s and '30s, Wang had been one of Beijing's leading preachers. After the war, he was arrested by the Communists, along with his wife. In prison, Wang's strength became compromised. Plants among the prisoners terrified the minister with tales of torture. Isolated, weakened, and concerned for his wife, he broke down, promising to sign any statement and preach any message he was given by the Communists.

Released from prison, Wang was a spiritually broken man, and his support of the Communist regime and its puppet church was widely publicized. Despising himself, he wandered the streets of Beijing, muttering, "I am Peter, I am Peter," referring to the apostle's denial of Christ on the night of his arrest. But then suddenly and without warning, Wang Mingdao recovered his courage and began preaching true faith in Jesus with great boldness. The authorities were astonished and dismayed. What had restored Wang to heroic Christian faithfulness? The answer was that Wang had been reading his

Bible, and through God's Word the sovereign Lord of heaven overthrew the bondage into which he had been cast. He later pointed to a single verse in the prophet Micah as having restored his confidence: "He will bring me out to the light; I shall look upon his vindication" (Mic. 7:9). Wang remembered that through faith he would be forgiven even for the sin of betrayal and would be ultimately justified before God. He trusted the reigning Christ to give him the power to resume a faithful ministry. Over the next two decades, Wang Mingdao preached the gospel boldly and openly despite repeated arrests, bearing testimony to the reigning power of the Son of God.[7]

A second claim regarding God's kingship insists that the Lord alone must be worshiped not only because he reigns now, but also in light of the fullness of his coming reign: "for he comes, for he comes to judge the earth. He will judge the world in righteousness, and the peoples in his faithfulness" (Ps. 96:13). In the present, Christ reigns for the spread of his gospel and the building up of his church. But when he returns to the earth in the fullness of glory, he will effect the final judgment for which the godly have been yearning. "He will judge the peoples with equity," the psalmist declares (v. 10). "He will judge the world in righteousness, and the peoples in his faithfulness" (v. 13).

As a third claim regarding God's kingship, the psalmist looks forward to a time of perfect righteousness, involving both the judgment of the wicked and the vindication of the persecuted, godly church. A foretaste of this righteous rule was seen in the reign of God through King David after the ark of the covenant was enthroned in God's city. The chapters that followed this event (2 Sam. 6) saw the victory of Israel's army over all their surrounding foes (2 Sam. 8, 10) and a benevolent mercy enthroned in the rule of God's people (2 Sam. 9). The reason that this golden era did not endure was David's own sinfulness, as it exploded onto Israel through his adultery with Bathsheba and callous murder of her husband, Uriah (2 Sam. 11). David, it turned out, was not the one to bring in the eternal reign of God's righteousness. David's kingship instead served as a type and foreshadowing of Christ in his second coming, when, according to Psalm 96:13, "he will judge the world in righteousness, and the peoples in his faithfulness."

From time to time, foretastes of Christ's rule appear not only over his church but also over worldly powers. A glorious example of Christ's reign

7. Taken from David Aikman, *Jesus in Beijing* (Washington, DC: Regnery, 2003), 47–57.

in world affairs took place in eastern Europe in 1989, when the Communist power was broken. History records the fall of the Berlin Wall in response to voices crying for freedom. What the journalists largely overlooked was the decisive role of Christians and the spiritual power worked through them by the sovereign Christ. In one example, a prayer meeting at the St. Kikolai Church in Leipzig grew from a small group in 1980 to a mass movement of thousands of believers by 1989. News of this surprising expression of religious freedom spread to East Berlin, and by November 9, 1989, the Communist authorities could no longer hold back the demand of the people to be free. Although the hated Berlin Wall was not completely demolished until 1992, its repression was already broken by spiritual power spreading out from praying Christians.[8]

At the time, the Western media largely ignored the role of faith and spiritual power in the liberation of East Germany. Bud Bultman, a CNN producer, later wrote:

> We in the media watched in astonishment as the walls of totalitarianism came crashing down. But in the rush to cover the cataclysmic events, the story behind the story was overlooked. We trained our cameras on hundreds of thousands of people praying for freedom, votive candles in hand, and yet we missed the transcendent dimension, the explicitly spiritual and religious character of the story.[9]

When Christ returns at the end of the age, every injustice will be cast to the ground at the cry of the archangel, the sounding of the last trumpet, and the appearing of the Son of God in glory (1 Thess. 4:16). The result, in the final resurrection and the following age of glory, will be the renewal of the entire creation. With this event in mind, the psalmist writes: "Let the heavens be glad, and let the earth rejoice; let the sea roar, and all that fills it; let the field exult, and everything in it! Then shall all the trees of the forest sing for joy before the Lord, for he comes" (Ps. 96:11–13). The creation in all its parts rises up in rejoicing for the restoration of righteousness and life in all the earth! J. J. Stewart Perowne writes: "The world's largest hopes are to be fulfilled. A new era is to begin, a reign of righteousness and peace, a

8. Boice, *Psalms*, 2:787.

9. Quoted in Ann Clark, "The Fall of the Wall: The Untold Story," *reNews: A Journal of Presbyterians for Renewal*, December 1994, 17.

time so blessed that even the inanimate creation must be partakers of the joy."[10] When Christ returns, the creation's "eager longing" for the Lord's glory (Rom. 8:19) will result in nature itself breaking out in song when the Savior has come to reign fully and eternally. Of that time to come, for which believers join in longing, the prophet Isaiah foretold: "They shall not hurt or destroy in all my holy mountain; for the earth shall be full of the knowledge of the LORD as the waters cover the sea" (Isa. 11:9).

THE KING'S DUE

The application to the kingly declaration of Psalm 96 is given in the pointed exclamations of verses 7–10. If the Lord reigns and is coming soon to reign fully and forever, what is due to so great a King from his people? The first application, in verse 7, calls for God's people to worship the Lord with a sense of the glory that he is due: "Ascribe to the LORD, O families of the peoples, ascribe to the LORD glory and strength!"

The Hebrew word for "glory" is *kabod*, which has the meaning of "weightiness" or "value." According to the Bible, God is not a lightweight but is heavy in significance, and in the worship and lives of his people God is to be reverenced as such. Here we encounter what David Wells has described as one of the chief failings of popular Christianity in our view of "the weightlessness of God." Wells explains that to professing Christians in America, "God has become unimportant. He rests upon the world so inconsequentially as not to be noticeable."[11] Wells does not mean that something has happened to God, but rather means that something has happened to our attitude toward him. In the place of God, man sees himself on the throne. Even Christians today are preoccupied not with knowing God and his will but with matching our own preferences and suiting our own needs.

The psalmist calls for believers to renew their awareness of God's greatness and glory, and in response to offer ourselves wholly to his service: "Ascribe to the LORD the glory due his name; bring an offering, and come into his courts!" (Ps. 96:8). When he speaks of offerings, the psalmist would include the financial tithes and gifts that Christians bring to the church in

10. J. J. Stewart Perowne, *The Book of Psalms*, 2 vols. (1878; repr., Grand Rapids: Zondervan, 1976), 2:197.

11. David F. Wells, *God in the Wasteland: The Reality of Truth in a World of Fading Dreams* (Grand Rapids: Eerdmans, 1994), 88–90.

their worship. Christians who think little of spending a thousand dollars on a vacation find it difficult to leave a hundred dollars in the offering plate. Robertson exhorts us: "Whether you have a little or a lot, your money is a major manifestation of your glory. Bring a generous offering and give glory to him."[12] The psalmist urges: Consider the glory and greatness of God! Treat God and his church as weighty matters, worthy of your total commitment! Remembering the significance of God's kingdom, Christians should come to worship yearning more for what they can bring to God than for what they can take away from the service.

Second, in light of God's greatness in reigning over all things, Christians are to pursue sanctification for the holiness of their lives: "Worship the Lord in the splendor of holiness; tremble before him, all the earth!" (Ps. 96:9). In Old Testament Israel, priests donned sacred garments so as to be holy in their service to the Lord. The New Testament points out that God's true intention is not holy clothing but holy characters that we bring before him. Paul writes: "I appeal to you therefore, brothers, by the mercies of God, to present your bodies as a living sacrifice, holy and acceptable to God, which is your spiritual worship" (Rom. 12:1). If we realize God's glory and seek to be holy as his people, we will give priority to the ministry of his Word, as Paul continued: "Do not be conformed to this world, but be transformed by the renewal of your mind" (v. 2).

Finally, Christians manifest their awareness of God's greatness through a life that is committed to bearing testimony before the world: "Say among the nations, 'The Lord reigns! Yes, the world is established; it shall never be moved; he will judge the peoples with equity'" (Ps. 96:10). If we believe the declaration of this message—"The Lord reigns!"—and remember that Christ is now building his church against all earthly opposition, and if we trust that someday soon Jesus will return to establish righteousness on the earth, then we will serve as heralds of his gospel message of salvation. Are we telling others about the salvation they can find through Jesus Christ? If not, do we believe that the Lord is reigning now for salvation? Psalm 96 urges us to renew our commitment to Christ and his kingdom, not only by our worship and giving to the church, and by the sanctification of our lives, but also by the boldness of the testimony we give to the salvation that only Jesus offers.

12. Robertson, *Psalms in Congregational Celebration*, 272.

When Jesus was departing from the world, he combined the truth of his kingdom reign with the Great Commission he left to the church. "All authority in heaven and on earth has been given to me," he began (Matt. 28:18). Then he commanded: "Go therefore and make disciples of all nations, baptizing them in the name of the Father and of the Son and of the Holy Spirit, teaching them to observe all that I have commanded you" (vv. 19–20). With this command, Jesus began with a declaration and concluded with a promise that is precious to those who rely on his royal rule: "All authority in heaven and on earth has been given to me. . . . And behold, I am with you always, to the end of the age" (vv. 18, 20).

28

Exalted above All Gods

Psalm 97

The Lord *reigns, let the earth rejoice; let the many coastlands be glad!* (Ps. 97:1)

Psalms 96 and 98 are joyful songs celebrating the Lord's kingship. Lodged between them is a more sober psalm that highlights the necessity of submitting to God's rule. Psalm 97 begins by drawing on lines taken from the middle of the preceding psalm. Psalm 96:10 contains the exhortation, "Say among the nations, 'The Lord reigns,'" followed by the charge, "Let the heavens be glad, and let the earth rejoice" (Ps. 96:11). Following this up in Psalm 97, the psalmist opens with these lines: "The Lord reigns, let the earth rejoice," adding an appeal to universal praise: "let the many coastlands be glad!" (97:1). In this way, the psalmist is saying, "Let me pick up that central theme of Psalm 96 and take it deeper in Psalm 97." In particular, the psalmist here brings the urgent requirement associated with the coming of the Lord. For when God comes to bring gladness to his people, he will also cast down all that is opposed to his glory. The kingdom of Christ is a cause for great joy. Yet as James Boice writes, "we are to be under no illusions as to what is involved. God's rule will mean the confounding of all evil and the rule of perfect righteousness."[1]

1. James Montgomery Boice, *Psalms*, 3 vols. (Grand Rapids: Baker, 1996), 2:789.

The Coming of the Great King

The opening stanza celebrates the glory of the Lord in his coming to earth. Some scholars believe the psalmist was responding to some great divine intervention, such as the destruction of Babylon or the restoration of the Jewish people from their exile. While the psalmist may have had a contemporary event in mind, his perspective contains a strong dose of future hope. Psalm 97:7 is quoted in Hebrews 1:6 with respect to the coming of Jesus Christ. With this in mind, we should treat Psalm 97 as displaying God's glory whenever he acts on earth with special power, but especially in the appearing of his Son at his first and second comings.

In describing the Lord's appearing, the psalmist employs visual images that speak of God's transcendent, royal majesty. "Clouds and thick darkness are all around him," he begins (Ps. 97:2), adding: "His lightnings light up the world; the earth sees and trembles" (v. 4). This language harks back to the great theophany of the exodus, when Israel trembled before "thunders and lightnings and a thick cloud on the mountain . . . . Mount Sinai was wrapped in smoke because the Lord had descended on it in fire" (Ex. 19:16, 18). By this revelation, the psalmist stokes our reverent fear in encountering the divine King. John Calvin writes: "Thus he gives us a representation of the formidable majesty attaching to God, that he may dash and humble vain confidence and carnal pride."[2] Psalm 97 calls us to joyful thanksgiving, but never to presumption. The God who is draped in clouds and lightning is not a "buddy" to be treated lightly, but the Great King of heaven and earth!

The clouds and darkness further represent the incomprehensibility of God. He comes as the Great King, yet with a wisdom that exceeds our understanding. Paul exclaimed: "How unsearchable are his judgments and how inscrutable his ways!" (Rom. 11:33). How often in his coming the Lord conceals his aims! The wicked will be permitted to rise up in prideful might, yet God's purpose is to cast them down. The church will be assailed with persecutions, yet the Lord's plan is to purify her before an outpouring of his Spirit. How impenetrable was the wisdom of Christ in taking up the cross to die for our sins! Pontius Pilate marveled that he should be considered a king. In mockery, Pilate affixed a sign to the cross: "Jesus of Nazareth, the King of the Jews" (John 19:19). There, in his sin-atoning death, Jesus displayed

2. John Calvin, *Calvin's Commentaries*, 23 vols. (1848; repr., Grand Rapids: Baker, 2009), 6:60.

the foolishness of God that confounds the wisdom of men: the divine logic and redemptive mathematics of the forgiveness of sin and salvation by grace.

Not only is God majestic and inscrutable, but his coming is also irresistible: "The mountains melt like wax before the LORD, before the Lord of all the earth" (Ps. 97:5). Mountains serve as formidable barriers to mere human kings. The great Carthaginian Hannibal astonished Rome by his crossing of the Alps, but lost half his army in the process. The Lord encounters no such trouble in his coming despite all the pretensions of earthly opposition. The point is that when God decides to intervene in history, there is nothing to bar his way. Calvin comments that the image of mountains melting like wax before God's fire "symbolize[s] how defenseless we are, how totally unable to resist God. For if God should suddenly appear, who could withstand his furor?"[3]

Applying this truth to the kingdom of Christ, we most naturally think of his second coming, when Jesus will overthrow all evil and the world will be purged in fire (2 Peter 3:7). But we would be mistaken not to apply the same truth to the first coming of Jesus and the subsequent mission of his gospel in the world. The miracles performed by Jesus show his sovereign power in overthrowing misery and bondage, casting out the realm of Satan. Charles Spurgeon adds: "Even now where the gospel is preached in faith, and in the power of the Spirit, it burns its own way, irresistibly destroying falsehood, superstition, unbelief, sin, indifference and hardness of heart."[4] When we calculate the total depravity of fallen mankind and the strength of power through sin by which Satan reigns in this evil world, we realize that salvation can occur only through the divine power of God. It is because the Lord is so pleased to come as King that Christians can be bold and intrepid in our reliance on his sovereign Word. It is because of the truth enshrined in Psalm 97:5, in which "mountains melt like wax before the LORD," that Paul could speak of Christian ministry as conquering evil without relying on worldly manipulation:

> For the weapons of our warfare are not of the flesh but have divine power to destroy strongholds. We destroy arguments and every lofty opinion raised against the knowledge of God, and take every thought captive to obey Christ. (2 Cor. 10:4–5)

3. John Calvin, *Sermons on the Book of Micah* (Phillipsburg, NJ: P&R Publishing, 2003), 25.
4. Charles Haddon Spurgeon, *The Treasury of David*, 3 vols. (Peabody, MA: Hendrickson, n.d.), 2b:195.

In the midst of Psalm 97's statements of God's kingly power, verse 2 reminds us of the character of God's kingdom: "righteousness and justice are the foundation of his throne." It is because of God's righteousness that his coming is cause for gladness throughout the whole world. "Let the many coastlands be glad!" writes the psalmist (Ps. 97:1), referring to distant regions far beyond the knowledge of the ancient Israelites. Normally, we would be alarmed to see all power gathered into the hands of a single king. But here absolute power is gathered into absolutely righteous hands! "The LORD reigns, let the earth rejoice" (v. 1)! And so godly people celebrate!

The Conquest of the Great King

The emphasis of Psalm 97—among the nearby psalms that also celebrate the Lord's kingship—is placed on the conquest of God over all opposition in the world. "The heavens proclaim his righteousness," the psalmist writes, "and all the peoples see his glory" (Ps. 97:6). If this psalm was written to rejoice in some divine intervention such as the fall of Babylon or the restoration of Jerusalem, the idea is that God has revealed his faithfulness in keeping his promises. J. J. Stewart Perowne writes: "He comes to judge, and the act of judgement is one which the whole world shall witness."[5] While this has occurred in various ways throughout history, Christians anticipate the full and final fulfillment of God's vindication when Jesus returns in glory and power. John writes in Revelation 1:7: "Behold, he is coming with the clouds, and every eye will see him, even those who pierced him, and all tribes of the earth will wail on account of him."

When God appears in saving power, one result is the humiliation of all false gods: "All worshipers of images are put to shame, who make their boast in worthless idols" (Ps. 97:7). It is not that Christ's victory empties the idols of their glory, but rather that it exposes the vanity that has always been true of them. Isaiah made this point in memorable language when he mocked the idols of his day. "All who fashion idols are nothing," the prophet argued, "and the things they delight in do not profit" (Isa. 44:9). After all, the woodsmith "plants a cedar and the rain nourishes it. Then it becomes fuel for a man. He takes a part of it and warms himself; he kindles a fire and

5. J. J. Stewart Perowne, *The Book of Psalms*, 2 vols. (1878; repr., Grand Rapids: Zondervan, 1976), 2:201.

bakes bread. Also he makes a god and worships it; he makes it an idol and falls down before it. Half of it he burns in the fire. . . . And the rest of it he makes into a god, his idol, and falls down to it and worships it. He prays to it and says, 'Deliver me, for you are my god!'" (Isa. 44:14–17)

While Isaiah points out the perennial folly of those who worship idols, Psalm 97 points to a day when the shame of idol worship will be laid bare before all. This claim makes it possible that the psalm was written to celebrate Israel's return to Jerusalem after the Babylonian exile, since it was there that the Jews renounced the great sin of idolatry that had led to their judgment. Having seen the evil and vanity of the false gods of Babylon, Israel was ashamed of its former sin, never to take it up again.

In declaring the idols shamed by the coming of God's kingdom, Psalm 97 indicates that the renouncing of idols and false religion is inseparable from the embracing of the true God by believing his Word. Therefore, in heralding the coming of God as King, the psalmist meant that "the time was come when those who were given to idolatry should repent, and return to the worship of the true God."[6] With this in mind, verse 7 exhorts: "worship him, all you gods!"

Debate rages concerning what is meant by "all you gods." Some argue that the psalmist personally addresses the idols themselves. The idea is not that the blocks of wood and stone are capable of submitting to Christ, but that the idols are tools in the hands of demons who serve Satan by holding sinners in bondage. The problem with this view is that the demons neither can nor will repent and believe, but are destined for eternal torment in God's final judgment (Rev. 20:10). Instead, the psalmist may be appealing to the nations that worship idols, urging them to observe the power of God in redeeming his people so that they, too, will turn and be saved. To be sure, idol worship thrives in every society today. Boice writes: "What are these idols? Self, power, fame, sex, and money. The people of the world sell their souls to these idols constantly."[7] Yet through the preaching of the gospel, the people of the nations have an opportunity to, in the language of Psalm 2:12, "kiss the Son" and be blessed.

According to the New Testament, however, Psalm 97 is addressing angels, calling them to adore and worship Jesus Christ. We learn this in Hebrews

6. Calvin, *Commentaries*, 6:64.

7. Boice, *Psalms*, 2:792.

1:6, which quotes Psalm 97:7, saying: "when [God] brings the firstborn into the world, he says, 'Let all God's angels worship him.'" The writer of Hebrews thus tied Psalm 97 to the greatest event of history up to this day, the coming of God's Son, Jesus Christ, into the world as our Savior. The coming of Jesus declared God's kingdom victory, and an angel choir glorified God in the night sky of Bethlehem on the night when Jesus was born. The greatest event in our individual lives has been the preaching of Christ as Savior and Lord, by which God's kingdom came to us in power. Our highest response is to embrace him, bowing our hearts in humble adoration and lifting up our voices in faith and praise.

In the logic of Psalm 97, only the display of true religion through faith in the gospel of Jesus Christ dispels the delusion of idolatry. From one continent to the next, and one distant island to another, the missionary preaching of the gospel has broken the enslaving power of idols over the hearts of men. Whether it was John Paton declaring the grace of Christ to the cannibals of Aniwa, Hudson Taylor teaching the gospel amid the Buddhist temples of China, or D. L. Moody preaching the grace of Christ to money-worshiping stock traders in New York City, the one way of casting out the darkness of false gods is the shining of "the light of the knowledge of the glory of God in the face of Jesus Christ" (2 Cor. 4:6).

Do you realize that you have the privilege of playing your part in the liberation of enthralled idolaters? Psalm 97 reminds Christians that our witness of the gospel is for the sake of those who are enslaved in the vanity of false gods. Some people enjoy a prosperous enslavement that provides wealth, pleasure, and power—yet their idolatry nonetheless enchains their souls through unbelief. Many more people experience misery because they seek meaning through sin, worldly glory, and earthly possessions. To such a world, we preach the truth of Jesus Christ, so that sinners will turn, as Paul put it, "from idols to serve the living and true God" (1 Thess. 1:9) and receive eternal life in his name.

The Communion of the Great King

When Jesus entered Jerusalem on Palm Sunday, crowds of Jewish people greeted him with ecstatic joy. It was the fulfillment of Zechariah's prophecy: "Say to the daughter of Zion, 'Behold, your king is coming to you'" (Matt.

21:5). Jesus' first action, however, was not to raise armies for the overthrow of the Roman occupiers, as the crowd may have wanted, but rather was to cleanse the temple from corruption (vv. 12–13). His first coming was aimed to conquer sin and redeem his people from God's wrath, a message for which the proud Jewish people rejected him. They wanted God to justify them for their works, whereas God convicted them for their sins.

The psalmist could have helped Jerusalem, had she paid attention. For he knew that when God comes as King, the first priority is the vindication of his law: "Zion hears and is glad, and the daughters of Judah rejoice, because of your judgments, O Lord" (Ps. 97:8). In the context of the psalm, the church is especially happy when the spread of the gospel leads sinners away from their idols. For in the grace of God, the Lord is pleased to judge our sin by placing it onto Jesus and his cross. Nothing gives greater joy to the church, therefore, than the justification of new believers and the judging of sin through the atoning work of Jesus Christ. Spurgeon exults: "As the women of Judah went forth to meet David in the dance, singing his victory over the Philistine, so shall they chant the triumphs of David's son and Lord."[8]

In fact, Christians may rejoice in God's reign over history even when the darkest times seem to have fallen. Bulstrode Whitelock was an emissary of Oliver Cromwell to Sweden in 1653. The night before he sailed from England he could not sleep, so distressed was he by the situation facing his country. Discovering this anxiety, his Christian servant came to his room and asked a question: "Pray, sir, do you think God governed the world very well before you came into it?" The official answered, "Certainly." "And do you think he will govern it quite as well when you are gone out of it?" he continued. "Undoubtedly." "Then pray, sir, excuse me, but do you not think that you may trust him to govern it quite as well while you are living?" Whitelock gave no answer, but he did return to his bed and soon fell peacefully asleep.[9]

Likewise, Christians in troubled times may rest their hearts in God's sovereign rule over world affairs, as well as over their personal lives. Jesus taught: "Are not two sparrows sold for a penny? And not one of them will fall to the ground apart from your Father" (Matt. 10:29). The psalmist thus rejoices: "For you, O Lord, are most high over all the earth; you are exalted far above all gods" (Ps. 97:9). We, too, may lift up our faces to heaven and

8. Spurgeon, *Treasury of David*, 2b:197.
9. Quoted in Boice, *Psalms*, 2:790.

trust that God's will is being done, so that his righteous judgments—casting down the wicked and vindicating his people—are certain to be accomplished.

This awareness of God's sovereignty yields three applications. The first is that since God's people may trust in his sovereign rule, we are delivered from the temptation to serve ourselves through compromises with evil: "O you who love the LORD, hate evil! He preserves the lives of his saints; he delivers them from the hand of the wicked" (Ps. 97:10). Notice the logic: since our Lord is righteous and since we are called to love the Lord, this love is expressed by our hating the things that he hates. The Lord hates evil; therefore, "you who love the LORD, hate evil!"

For Christians to have fellowship with evil makes no sense, given our belief that Jesus will soon return to put all evil away. Our calling, then, is to shun all sin, investing in things of righteousness, truth, and beauty. We are to cultivate holy habits rather than ways that we know are under God's judgment. As the psalmist sees it, our relationship with God is the prime motivator for our sanctification. Jesus said, "If you love me, you will keep my commandments" (John 14:15). The apostle John concluded his first letter on this theme: "Little children, keep yourselves from idols" (1 John 5:21). Do we love the Lord? Then let us hate whatever is evil. If there is one thought that should keep believers in Jesus from tolerating their sins, it is the awareness of our Savior's having suffered the penalty of our sins on the cross. How, then, can we give ourselves over to that which cost the Lord Jesus so much?

Psalm 97:10 offers a valuable guide to Christian conduct in troubling political times. Christians in America face the potential of government opposition to a degree never previously known. Given intolerance of government, education, and media powers toward the Bible's teachings, significant societal conflict seems to be drawing near. For some Christian leaders, the dire needs of this situation seem to warrant a compromise with those who might provide worldly aid, even to the point of tolerating gross ungodliness. Different Christians will always cast their votes according to what they think is best for the country. But it should never be the case that God's people compromise biblical standards or ally their cause with ungodly powers, simply out of fear of worldly threat. It is God who "preserves the lives of his saints; he delivers them from the hand of the wicked." Knowing this, those who love the Lord are to hate evil, since the Lord will never compromise with it and since the Lord himself will deliver and preserve us from all evil. Michael Wilcock writes: "If we are called by his holy name (v. 12) we are expected to live a correspondingly holy life, and to take seriously the pursuit of righteousness and the hatred of sin."[10]

A second application calls for God's people to be zealous in the saving work of the Lord. Psalm 97:11 reminds us that in the midst of an evil world, God is at work spreading his salvation: "Light is sown for the righteous, and joy for the upright in heart." The key word here is *sown*, which refers to the planting of seeds. God is at work behind the scenes and beneath the surface. God is hatching sovereign plans for the display of his glory through the triumph of righteousness.

Suffering believers gain patience by knowing that whatever the appearances, God is sovereignly sowing light and joy. Trusting his providence helps us to endure the long struggle of our own sanctification as we fight besetting sins, and also to endure seasons of outward hardship and persecution. David Dickson comments:

> The Lord's children, who love him and hate evil, must not think to have the fruit of their righteousness presently in possession, but must give a time unto it, as is given to corn that is cast into the ground; and as after a time the corn springeth, and cometh to a ripe harvest; so shall the troubles of the godly have a comfortable issue: *light is sown for the righteous.*[11]

What a privilege it is for God's people to be the instruments by which God is sowing seeds for salvation. Jesus taught about God's kingdom: "A sower went out to sow his seed. . . . The seed is the word of God" (Luke 8:5, 11). Knowing that saving light and joy come through faith in the gospel of Jesus, Christians are to labor in this world with a great hope, desiring above all things for God's Word to be spread, heard, and believed. And we ourselves are like seeds planted by God in a vineyard of salvation that is certain to prosper, whatever the outward circumstances. Calvin writes that "though the righteous may be almost banished out of the world, and unable to venture

10. Michael Wilcock, *The Message of Psalms 73–150* (Downers Grove, IL: InterVarsity Press, 2001), 102.

11. David Dickson, *A Commentary on the Psalms* (1653; repr., Edinburgh: Banner of Truth, 1995), 2:184.

themselves forth in public, and hidden from view, God will spread abroad their joy like seed, or bring forth to notice the light of their joy which had been shut up."[12]

Realizing this truth supplies our third application, in the final verse of the psalm: "Rejoice in the LORD, O you righteous, and give thanks to his holy name!" (Ps. 97:12). This call to joy and thanks applies both to our personal demeanor and then especially to our constant delight in giving worship to our Lord. To the world, the kingdom of God is hidden; to us, the saving reign of God is revealed with great joy. Is there anything that should keep the followers of Christ from gathering together in public doxology, and from private worship in our homes? Sadly, for most of us, the great threat to Christian joy in worship is the business that comes from our preoccupation with the world rather than any external threat. If our eyes are open to the greatness of our King and the glory of his victory in our world, we will devote our whole lives to the praise of his glory, treasuring above all things our worship with the church.

COME, O KING!

Christians rejoice because our greatest possessions can never be taken from us. Our greatest hope can never fail. Our beloved Savior and King can never die, and his will cannot be effectively opposed. However hard and painful our passage through this life may be, every Christian can know that it will end in glory. David reminds us: "Weeping may tarry for the night, but joy comes with the morning" (Ps. 30:5).

From the perspective of Psalm 97, perhaps the best way for Christians to live with confidence and joy, while we keep ourselves from evil, is to keep constantly in view our great hope of Jesus' second coming. Confused and perhaps embarrassed by bizarre and false teachings concerning the end times, many believers today give little thought to the promised end to world history. But to the psalmist, however great his joy for what God had recently done in the world, his even greater delight centered on the promise of God's future coming to judge and to reign. Christians today look back on the wonderful first coming of our Lord—Jesus' virgin birth, his enlightening words, his staggering miracles, and his gospel message of salvation through

12. Calvin, *Commentaries*, 6:68.

faith, sealed in blood through the cross. But if we fail to look forward, knowing that even greater things are in store for us, we will cripple the passionate joy that ought to be ours. The Bible's teaching on Christ's return is clear and simple, echoing the opening lines of Psalm 97: Jesus will come in glory before all the world to put evil away and judge all sin, saving his people and bringing them into glory forever with him. It was on this basis that Paul urged us to live wholeheartedly for God in renouncing sin, and "waiting for our blessed hope, the appearing of the glory of our great God and Savior Jesus Christ" (Titus 2:13).

The return of our Lord offers special comfort to Christians undergoing severe trials in the world. Concerning the second coming, Boice observes:

> Only then will perfect justice come to this earth. There is no such thing as perfect justice now. Now those who are strong oppress the weak. The unscrupulous cheat the innocent. . . . But when Jesus returns there will be perfect righteousness. The helpless will be defended, liars confounded, and the guilty judged.[13]

Here we find grounds in this troubled world to hate evil, devote ourselves to God's Word, and rejoice in the joy of the glory of our Lord. Jesus concluded the Bible with this promise: "Surely I am coming soon," to which the saints reply, "Amen. Come, Lord Jesus!" (Rev. 22:20). Anticipating the fulfillment of this our greatest hope, Psalm 97:8 declares: "Zion hears and is glad, and the daughters of Judah rejoice, because of your judgments, O Lord."

13. Boice, *Psalms*, 2:793.

29

Joy to the World!

Psalm 98

Oh sing to the Lord *a new song, for he has done marvelous things! His right hand and his holy arm have worked salvation for him.* (Ps. 98:1)

Psalm 98 continues the series of psalms dedicated to the kingship of the Lord. At first glance, it appears as virtually a repetition of Psalm 96, beginning and ending with nearly identical words. At closer examination, however, Psalm 98 makes a distinct contribution to the praise of our Lord as King. The occasion for this royal psalm is apparently a great national victory that revealed God's supernatural intervention. Israel's history was full of such events, including the parting of the Red Sea, the slaying of Sennacherib's mighty army by the angel of death, and the deliverance of the Jews from their Babylonian captivity. As a result of some such triumph, the psalmist calls for fresh praise: "Oh sing to the Lord a new song, for he has done marvelous things!" (Ps. 98:1).

One point made by Psalm 98 is that God is praised not merely for the great things he has done, but also for the way in which these mighty deeds reveal him as reigning over the world on our behalf. Many times when ministering to discouraged believers, I have prayed for the Lord to intervene in even a small way, so long as it can be clearly seen as an answer to prayer. The benefit of such an answer is not only what God does but also the way in which he encourages our weak and faltering faith, reminding us that he really does care and that he is involved in our lives. In just this same way, Psalm 98 calls for Israel to respond to what God has done by acknowledging that he reigns as King over all. More than that, God has promised to judge the entire world on the day of Christ's return, so that even nature will be set free from bondage to praise the Lord. Realizing this now, the psalmist urges: "Make a joyful noise to the Lord, all the earth" (Ps. 98:4).

An Appeal to Israel

A distinctive feature of Psalm 98 is that each of its three stanzas is addressed to a different audience. The first section, verses 1–3, consists of an appeal to Israel to rejoice in song for God's great, saving works: "Oh sing to the Lord a new song, for he has done marvelous things! His right hand and his holy arm have worked salvation for him" (Ps. 98:1). Here God is exalted as Savior of his people. The deliverance he achieved was by his own power, in such a way that his sovereign action was made plain. "His right hand and his holy arm" alone overcame all opposition, without any human cooperation. God's strength was made clear in accomplishing what had been thought to be impossible. Derek Kidner writes: "This salvation/victory is wholly supernatural, a single-handed exploit of the Lord."[1] As such, the deliverance warrants special praise to God.

The event most commonly associated with Psalm 98 is the deliverance of the Jews from their Babylonian captivity and subsequent restoration to Jerusalem. This event certainly fits the description of "marvelous things" performed by God's supernatural intervention. In a situation in which God's people were completely vulnerable, with no political or military power at all, held as captives in a distant and ungodly land, the Lord secured their deliverance. The opening section of the book of Ezra tells how this happened. After the Medo-Persian conqueror Cyrus the Great overthrew the Babylonians, "the Lord stirred up [his] spirit" (Ezra 1:1) to make an astonishing proclamation. It seems that God had somehow communicated directly to

1. Derek Kidner, *Psalms 73–150*, Tyndale Old Testament Commentaries 16 (Downers Grove, IL: InterVarsity Press, 1975), 352.

the king that the Jews were to be restored to their homeland: "The LORD, the God of heaven, . . . has charged me to build him a house at Jerusalem, which is in Judah" (v. 2). Accordingly, Cyrus summoned the very Jews who so desperately sought to return to their home and ordered them to do that very thing, providing them with protection and provision along the way. It truly was a marvelous thing the Lord had done, working salvation by his own right hand and holy arm, through the agency of a Gentile potentate.

We should note, however, that Psalm 98 does not refer to a particular event by name. The effect is that we are not limited to thinking about only a certain instance of salvation. Rather, we are empowered to think of this language in terms of the greatest things that God has done for us, the most marvelous, sovereign, and gracious deeds for our salvation, all of which took place through the ministry of his Son, Jesus Christ. James Boice points out that the most marvelous work of the Lord is our deliverance from sin:

> The single greatest problem you and I have is our sin, not a lack of self-esteem or accomplishment or anything else. Sin both separates and destroys. It separates us from God, who is the source of all good, and it destroys relationships. In the end it will bring us to that final place of all separation, hell.[2]

It is essential for us to realize not only that our deliverance from sin is a marvelous work of the Lord, but also that it is one that God has done for us by his sovereign grace alone. The world did nothing to help us to turn from sin. We ourselves could do nothing to escape the stain of the guilt that was already upon us. But what we cannot do, God has done by his own working, according to his own plan, and by his own might. He delivered us from the penalty of sin through the atoning death of his Son, whereby Jesus took our guilt and paid its penalty on the cross. He is delivering us now from sin's power by the presence of the Holy Spirit, whom he sends in Christ's name. In the end, God will have delivered us from every vestige of sin's presence, after Christ returns and we have been glorified together with him. With this in mind, the chorus of heaven sang a new song to Jesus' glory in Revelation 5:12: "Worthy is the Lamb who was slain, to receive power and wealth and wisdom and might and honor and glory and blessing!"

2. James Montgomery Boice, *Psalms*, 3 vols. (Grand Rapids: Baker, 1996), 2:796.

The psalmist adds that God is glorified not only for the marvelous thing he has done but also for the way in which he has caused it to be known across the world: "The Lord has made known his salvation; he has revealed his righteousness in the sight of the nations" (Ps. 98:2). It was true for all of the Israelites' great deliverances that their salvation revealed God's righteousness before the eyes of the whole world. Wicked powers had oppressed God's humble people, but God intervened and they were delivered out of Egypt, from the violence of Assyria, and out of bondage in Babylon. Likewise, the changes effected in the lives of believers are obvious to people who know them. The peace that Christians receive, the power they gain for living in a new and godly way, and the love that they are motivated to show makes plain how God has worked righteously in their lives. Moreover, through his apostles, the Lord caused the gospel to spread throughout the world, a dispensation of good news that continues today. George Horne appeals to us to take up that work with great zeal: "Still let that salvation be made known, still let that righteousness be openly showed, by ministers of the gospel, until the fullness of the Gentiles be come in, and the remnant of the Jews converted; until antichrist be overthrown, and death himself fall before the all-conquering Christ."[3]

Israel should sing with joy to the Lord not only because of his marvelous deeds that are displayed before the world, but also because the nation represented God's faithfulness to his promises to them: "He has remembered his steadfast love and faithfulness to the house of Israel" (Ps. 98:3). For God to remember does not mean that he ever forgot what he had pledged to his people. Rather, this language speaks of his faithfulness, even though a long delay may have tempted his people into doubt. John Calvin explains that the language of God's remembering "implies that he was influenced by no other motive than that of faithfully performing what he had himself promised."[4] How wonderful it is that God is faithful! We may rely on him to fulfill all the remarkable claims he has made about the salvation of those who trust in his Word. "Oh sing to the Lord a new song," the psalmist writes, for "He has remembered his steadfast love and faithfulness to the house of Israel" (Ps. 98:1, 3).

3. George Horne, *Commentary on the Psalms* (1771; repr., Audubon, NJ: Old Paths Publications, 1997), 424.

4. John Calvin, *Calvin's Commentaries*, 23 vols. (1848; repr., Grand Rapids: Baker, 2009), 5:71.

We think of God's remembering long-distant promises when we think of the birth of Jesus through the virgin Mary. Mary herself seems to have understood the birth of our Savior in terms of Psalm 98, because her song of praise, known as the *Magnificat*, follows essentially the same outline. The psalmist begins, "Sing to the Lord a new song" (Ps. 98:1), and Mary began, "My soul magnifies the Lord" (Luke 1:46). "For he has done marvelous things!" extols the psalmist (Ps. 98:1), and Mary continues, "He who is mighty has done great things for me" (Luke 1:49). Mary went on in the spirit of Psalm 98: "He has shown strength with his arm . . . . He has helped his servant Israel, in remembrance of his mercy" (Luke 1:51, 54).

Sensing this same connection between the glory of salvation in Psalm 98 and the birth of Jesus, we sing a version of this psalm as one of our most beloved Christmas carols, Isaac Watts's hymn "Joy to the World!" Psalm 98:3 states not only that Israel celebrates God's faithfulness, but also adds: "All the ends of the earth have seen the salvation of our God." In similar terms, Watts wrote: "Joy to the earth! The Savior reigns: let men their songs employ."[5]

An Appeal to the World

Watts's hymn, together with the final statement of Psalm 98:3, transitions us to the second appeal of the psalm. Starting in verse 4, the psalmist urges the world as a whole to rejoice in the Lord: "Make a joyful noise to the Lord, all the earth; break forth into joyous song and sing praises!" Why should the world celebrate that Israel's Savior has been faithful to deliver? The reason lies in how this good news reveals a Savior who is sufficient to save the entire world. God was able to save Israel because of his sovereignty. Jesus, having fulfilled his saving mission, has been enthroned over all things in heaven (Eph. 1:20–22). This saving kingship over all things, by which the gospel message of salvation is spread far and wide, warrants an appeal to the world to worship Christ: "make a joyful noise before the King, the Lord!" (Ps. 98:6).

The exuberance for which the psalmist calls is appropriate to the greatness of its recipient: "break forth into joyous song and sing praises! Sing praises to the Lord with the lyre, with the lyre and the sound of melody!

5. Isaac Watts, "Joy to the World! The Lord Is Come" (1719).

With trumpets and the sound of the horn make a joyful noise before the King, the Lord!" (Ps. 98:4–6).

Many commentators urge from these statements that Christian worship must be lively, loud, and filled with excitement. So writes Boice: "Should the worship of God's people be any less exuberant today? Should we be quiet when we have come to know him who is the great King above all kings and the great Lord above all lords? Shame on us for all lackluster worship and all halfhearted praise."[6]

Two comments should be made about this call for loud and lively worship in the church. First, the scene here fits an ancient coronation service as much as or even more than the worship of Israel at the temple. For example, we are told that when Zadok anointed Solomon as king, "they blew the trumpet, and all the people said, 'Long live King Solomon!' And all the people went up after him, playing on pipes, and rejoicing with great joy, so that the earth was split by their noise" (1 Kings 1:39–40). This event was not directly analogous to weekly worship in the church today. Second, in contrast to an audience clapping with wild enthusiasm at a civic event, the worship of the church involves elements that require good order and thoughtful concentration, such as prayer, the preaching of God's Word, and the administration of the sacraments. With this being said, it should be noted that the worship at Israel's temple was so loud, with massed voices singing, that it could be heard at a great distance. Particularly our singing as a congregation should be with full hearts and open mouths. John Wesley exhorted the early Methodists: "Sing lustily, and with good courage. Beware of singing as if you were half dead or asleep; but lift up your voice with strength."[7]

Earlier, I mentioned Watts's hymn from this psalm, "Joy to the World!" It is noteworthy that Watts did not write this lyric with Christmas in mind at all. What he actually had in mind was the second coming of Christ. For it is then that the whole earth will receive Jesus as its King. We see this in the third verse, which reads:

> No more let sins and sorrows grow, nor thorns infest the ground;
> He comes to make his blessings flow far as the curse is found.[8]

6. Boice, *Psalms*, 2:800.
7. Quoted in Boice, *Psalms*, 2:800.
8. Watts, "Joy to the World!"

This does not, of course, describe our current experience, even as Christians. Alyssa Poblete, commenting on Watts's hymn, wrote: "The world is not sin-free. The world is not void of sorrow. Not yet, at least." The joy of all the earth awaits the coming of Christ to reign with sovereign power at the end of history. Yet Poblete reminds us of how Psalm 98 remains a source of joy to the world: "Although the fulfillment of all Christ's work is not fully expressed this side of eternity, we know there will be a day when it is. Christ sits at the Father's right hand, waiting until the perfect moment—a time when all good things will come to fruition. So we have hope."[9]

An Appeal to Creation

The final stanza of Psalm 98, verses 7–9, makes its appeal to the creation itself, calling on the sea, the rivers, and the hills to express their joyful praise to the Lord in his coming. Whereas Israel praised the Lord as its Savior and the world celebrated his reign as King, nature's praise is summoned forth to Christ as Judge of the earth: "Let the sea roar, and all that fills it; the world and those who dwell in it! Let the rivers clap their hands; let the hills sing for joy together before the LORD, for he comes to judge the earth" (Ps. 98:7–9).

The rising up of the creation itself in praise to its Lord is closely tied in Scripture to the return of Christ and the conclusion of world history in his final judgment. We hear similar language in Isaiah 55:12: "the mountains and the hills before you shall break forth into singing, and all the trees of the field shall clap their hands." This imagery is followed by the renewal of all creation and the final glory of the Lord: "Instead of the thorn shall come up the cypress; instead of the brier shall come up the myrtle; and it shall make a name for the LORD, an everlasting sign that shall not be cut off" (Isa. 55:13).

Two points call for our attention. The rejoicing of inanimate creation points out that the creation itself experiences deliverance through the saving work of Christ. According to the Bible, the earth came under the curse of Adam when the human race fell into sin. To Adam, God said, "Cursed is

9. Alyssa Poblete, "Joy to the World: A Christmas Hymn Reconsidered," The Gospel Coalition, December 22, 2014, https://www.thegospelcoalition.org/article/joy-to-the-world-a-classic-christmas-hymn-reconsidered/.

the ground because of you; . . . thorns and thistles it shall bring forth for you" (Gen. 3:17–18). This ancient curse explains why Psalm 98 progresses through Israel to the world to the entirety of creation. The Lord comes as a Savior in whom believers rejoice. He reigns as a King, offering the only true hope for the world. His final return will involve the judgment of all evil, so that all those who refused to believe his gospel are separated into hell, leaving the creation to be regenerated along with the glorification of Christ's faithful people. Paul thus writes in Romans 8:19–21:

> For the creation waits with eager longing for the revealing of the sons of God. For the creation was subjected to futility, not willingly, but because of him who subjected it, in hope that the creation itself will be set free from its bondage to corruption and obtain the freedom of the glory of the children of God.

The entirety of creation was made by God for the praise of his glory. Sin has corrupted not only mankind but the creation with him. In the end, when Christ has returned, not only will all his enemies be finally and eternally defeated and his people brought with him into eternal glory, but every square inch of the vast universe will resound in such manifest doxology to God that it will be as though the rivers rose up in animate praise and the hills reached out their hands to applaud the salvation of their Lord. Considering this great coming day, we should even now burst with joyful wonder at our blessing in Christ, in the words of the apostle John in his contemplation of it: "See what kind of love the Father has given to us, that we should be called children of God" (1 John 3:1). Together with ancient Job, we should be heartened even amid our present suffering, crying out: "My heart faints within me!" (Job 19:27).

A second point concerns the nature of God's judgment. Psalm 98 calls for creation to praise the Lord specifically as the coming Judge: "let the hills sing for joy together before the Lord, for he comes to judge the earth. He will judge the world with righteousness, and the peoples with equity" (Ps. 98:8–9). The final judgment, in which every wrong will be addressed and all unrepentant sinners cast off into eternal condemnation, is the joyful hope of the creation itself. It was because of the guilty deeds committed on it that the earth was cursed with futility. And just as the blood of slain Abel cried out to God from the ground (Gen. 4:10), so also will the creation rise up in grateful praise when Christ returns in judgment. With his blood having already cried out a better word than the blood of Abel (Heb. 12:24), his coming will remove every vestige of sin so that the creation may be restored to the freedom of its intended glory to the praise of God. The final judgment of God not only brings him praise in the perfect manner that it displays the purity of his justice, but also, as H. C. Leupold writes, "accomplishes so much of lasting good that men should rejoice exceedingly that the Lord does judge."[10]

How tragic it is that unbelieving man does not look on nature as his partner in giving praise to God, but either deifies it in idolatry or defiles it in self-absorption. Carl Sagan spoke for a wayward generation in the worshipful tones of the opening sequence of his television show, *Cosmos*. In an adoring mantra he intoned: "The cosmos is all that is or that ever was or that ever will be."[11] In contrast, the Christian looks on nature as a stewardship granted by God so that man may glorify his Maker together with the cosmos. The world was made by God and for God. And while nature currently languishes under the curse of sin, so that the world is neither safe nor sound, the desire of the seas, rivers, and hills is to render praise to its Lord. According to Psalm 98, the day will soon come when nature will sing its praise, together with the redeemed people who have been delivered from sin by our Savior and brought through history into glory by our eternally praiseworthy King.

The Savior Reigns

No wonder Watts wrote his famous hymn with an eye to the coming of the Lord with glory, as the Savior, King, and Judge who will cleanse the earth of sin. It is then that the final verse of "Joy to the World!" will have come true:

> He rules the world with truth and grace, and makes the nations prove
> The glories of his righteousness and wonders of his love.

Anticipating that coming day, Watts summoned every voice to praise the Lord with a glad noise even now:

10. H. C. Leupold, *Exposition of the Psalms* (Columbus, OH: Wartburg Press, 1959), 692.
11. Quoted in Boice, *Psalms*, 2:891.

> Joy to the earth! The Savior reigns: let men their songs employ;
> While fields and floods, rocks, hills, and plains repeat the sounding joy,
> Repeat the sounding joy, repeat, repeat the sounding joy.[12]

With this praise in mind, Alyssa Poblete asks why we sing this song at Christmas. Undoubtedly, Watts wrote "Joy to the World!" about the second coming, not Christ's first coming as a baby laid in the manger of Bethlehem. "It doesn't really have anything to do with the Christmas story," she wrote. "Or does it? After all, there is no second coming without a first coming."[13]

In her final assessment, Poblete rightly concludes that "Joy to the World!" should be sung by believers at all times, and especially during this present age of the world after the Savior has been born, while he reigns above on heaven's throne, and while we await his second advent to judge the world once and for all. Poblete's final comments remind us why we should indeed make a joyful noise to the Lord, anticipating the day when all creation will join in, and why Christmas is an excellent time to have these great truths in mind:

> This song is all about the fulfillment of what Christ came to do in the first place. Christmas is not only a time to look back at the grace accomplished in the past. Christmas is also a time to look forward to the grace that was accomplished for our future. When we sing these words we are proclaiming the ultimate joy to be revealed. This is why we can sing "Joy to the World" at Christmas.[14]

12. Watts, "Joy to the World!"
13. Poblete, "Joy to the World: A Christmas Hymn Reconsidered."
14. Poblete, "Joy to the World: A Christmas Hymn Reconsidered."

30

Holy, Holy, Holy!

Psalm 99

Let them praise your great and awesome name!
Holy is he! (Ps. 99:3)

It is not difficult to tell when political campaigns are taking place, because the television and Internet are jammed with political advertisements. As we study Psalm 99, we can imagine a political appeal following much the same pattern. The advertisement might begin by saying, "Joe Smith is our Senator! Vote for him!" It then appeals, "Joe Smith has passed excellent laws! Vote for him!" In conclusion it states, "These outstanding leaders endorse Joe Smith for Senator. Vote for him!"

Psalm 99 is not, of course, an advertisement for the eternal God to be elected as King. It begins with a declaration that appeared earlier in Psalms 93 and 97: "The Lord reigns" (Ps. 99:1). Instead of choosing a leader, the psalmist urges us simply to worship the Lord as he deserves: "Exalt the Lord our God; worship at his footstool!" (v. 5). Still, Psalm 99 does follow the pattern that one might suggest for a political ad. Verse 1 declares his kingship. Verse 4 points out the justice of his reign. Verse 6 adds the excellence of the Lord's servants, Moses, Aaron, and Samuel. The logical response to this appeal is for the Israelites to prioritize their praise to him: "Exalt the Lord our God, and worship at his holy mountain" (v. 9).

Scholars differ in their organization of Psalm 99. Some argue that it falls into two stanzas, each of which concludes with the exhortation, "Exalt the LORD our God" (Ps. 99:5, 9). Another approach, which I am following, notes three occurrences of the cry, "Holy is he!" (Ps. 99:3, 5, 9). While political candidates today are celebrated as being competent, charismatic, or well connected, the Lord as King is exalted for his chief attribute of holiness. In Isaiah 6:3, the angels cry before God's throne: "Holy, holy, holy is the LORD of hosts" (see also Rev. 4:8). Since the Old Testament in its original language does not employ exclamation points, this tripling of God's holiness marks the singular emphasis given to this quality. This very repetition is discovered in Psalm 99, each section concluding with an exclamation: holy, holy, holy (Ps. 99:3, 5, 9)! J. J. Stewart Perowne comments: "In this Psalm, not only the righteous sway of the King, but His awful holiness, forms the subject of praise; and the true character of His worshipers as consecrated priests, holy, set apart for His service, is illustrated."[1]

HOLY IN HIS TRANSCENDENCE

The psalm opens with the theme that has occupied each psalm going back to Psalm 93: "The LORD reigns." This statement does not entertain doubt as to the certainty of God's kingship. Whatever is happening in the earth and whatever powers are acting for good or evil, above them all is the active, sovereign rule of Israel's covenant Lord.

The transcendence of God's kingdom is indicated by the fact that he sits on no ordinary throne. There are great and famous thrones in the world. Japan's emperor occupied the Chrysanthemum Throne, while his Chinese counterpart sat on the Dragon Throne. The Marble Throne served rulers of Persia, and the Swedish monarch sat on the Silver Throne for his or her coronation. India had its Peacock Throne and Russia its Ivory Throne. But the throne of the heavenly King surpasses any earthly splendor: "He sits enthroned upon the cherubim" (Ps. 99:1).

The cherubim are mighty angelic beings who attend the Creator and support his throne. They are the "four living creatures" of Revelation 4:6, one with a face like a lion, another like an ox, the third of a man, and the

1. J. J. Stewart Perowne, *The Book of Psalms*, 2 vols. (1878; repr., Grand Rapids: Zondervan, 1976), 2:206.

fourth like an eagle. In this way, they represent the various orders of land creatures: wild beasts, domestic animals, mankind, and flying beasts. Similarly, the cherubim-throne represents God reigning as Lord over all creation. "Holy, holy, holy, is the Lord God Almighty," they cry continually (Rev. 4:8). Before the glory and the awful majesty of this thrice-holy God, there is awestruck fear: "let the peoples tremble!" "let the earth quake!" (Ps. 99:1). God's enthronement unsettles all the vain ambitions of men, even as the birth of royal Jesus disturbed the thoughts of Herod in Jerusalem.

While the Lord is enthroned over all creation, his reign is closely connected with his people on earth: "The Lord is great in Zion; he is exalted over all the peoples" (Ps. 99:2). Derek Kidner explains that God reigns "in the midst of His covenanted people, from whom His kingdom reaches out to the world."[2] It was in Jerusalem, through the ordinances of the temple and by the teaching of his Word, that God specially revealed himself in the world. It was for Israel that he reigned, restraining her sins and destroying her enemies. As the psalmist sees it, all the great affairs of the world in its mighty empires and armies find relevance through their relation to God's people and under God's overlordship.

What Zion was in the Old Testament, the Christian church now is in the New Testament era. The writer of Hebrews tells Christians that they "have come to Mount Zion and to the city of the living God, the heavenly Jerusalem" (Heb. 12:22). Believers in Christ are citizens of the heavenly Zion and the church of all ages, in which God reigns as a great Sovereign. Charles Spurgeon writes that "his church is now his favoured place, where his greatness is displayed, acknowledged, and adored."[3] Christ, having purchased the church with his blood, has been exalted by the Father to his throne above, where he is "head over all things to the church" (Eph. 1:22). Westminster Shorter Catechism question 26 asks, "How doth Christ execute the office of a king?" It answers: "Christ executeth the office of a king, in subduing us to himself, in ruling and defending us, and in restraining and conquering all his and our enemies." How great is our King in Zion! What confidence he inspires for those who trust him! And with what boldness believers should serve and worship him in the world over which he reigns! David Dickson summarizes:

2. Derek Kidner, *Psalms 73–150*, Tyndale Old Testament Commentaries 16 (Downers Grove, IL: InterVarsity Press, 1975), 354.

3. Charles Haddon Spurgeon, *The Treasury of David*, 3 vols. (Peabody, MA: Hendrickson, n.d.), 2b:222.

> Albeit the church be compassed about with enemies, as the lily among the thorns, yet, because her Lord reigneth in the midst of her, she hath reason not only to comfort herself in him, but also hath ground of defying her enemies and boasting against them.[4]

For all the impressive things said about the Lord as King, the emphasis of this first stanza remains on his transcendent holiness: "Holy is he!" (Ps. 99:3). Usually when we think of holiness, we are referring to God's moral perfection. But *holiness* has a more general meaning of the absolute separation between God and his creation. In his very being, God is holy and exalted, his infinite and eternal nature entirely separate from the finite creation.

It is fitting that since holiness is God's supreme attribute, the collection of royal psalms from Psalms 93 to 99 concludes on this theme. Previous psalms have celebrated the glory of the Lord's reign and the joy that attends his kingship. This final royal psalm brings the series to a climax with its focus on the transcendent holiness of the King, before which "the peoples tremble" and the earth quakes (Ps. 99:1), and before which his church should fall prostrate in adoration: "Let them praise your great and awesome name!" (v. 3).

The Creator-creature distinction should always be in the minds of God's people as we live before him and especially as we gather for public worship. When Psalm 99:2 declares, "The Lord is great in Zion," we remember that the God who draws near to us in our worship is also infinitely exalted above us. When Christians come together for worship, we are not a democratic assembly, but rather joyful subjects of a great and awesome King! The writer of Hebrews thus said to worshiping Christians that "you have come to Mount Zion and to the city of the living God" (Heb. 12:22). And while we rejoice in God's presence, we must still remember the cherubim and their cries of "holy, holy, holy" (Isa. 6:3). When Isaiah saw this vision, he responded, "Woe is me! For I am lost" (v. 5). When the Lord appeared in glory to Job, he answered, "I had heard of you by the hearing of the ear, but now my eye sees you; therefore I despise myself, and repent in dust and ashes" (Job 42:5–6). And when John the apostle stood before the glorified Christ in Revelation 1, he "fell at his feet as though dead," prompting Jesus to comfort him with

4. David Dickson, *A Commentary on the Psalms* (1653; repr., Edinburgh: Banner of Truth, 1995), 2:189.

"Fear not" (Rev. 1:17). Jesus speaks words of comfort and love to his blood-bought people still today. Yet spiritually aware Christians will never forget the transcendent holiness of the God before whom we come, and thus will praise his name as "great and awesome" (Ps. 99:3).

O. Palmer Robertson relates a story in which Robert McNamara, who served as U.S. Secretary of Defense during the Vietnam War, was making comments about the Persian Gulf War in 1991. Describing the chaos of managing a war, McNamara praised the then current U.S. administration: "Bush and Powell and Cheney are doing a superb job, but I tell you Jesus Christ himself can't keep one of these things under control."[5] How offensive is such flippant speech in light of the exalted holiness of Christ as described in Psalm 99! Robertson comments: "Let us pray for the day when the nations will once more tremble at the holiness of the one true and living God. Let us testify fearlessly to his role as holy Lord of the nations, that men may come to understand why things happen the way they do."[6]

Holy in His Justice

The first stanza of Psalm 99 emphasizes the Lord's holiness in the sense of his transcendent being. The second stanza sets forth the justice of God's holy rule as an occasion for praise: "The King in his might loves justice. You have established equity; you have executed justice and righteousness in Jacob. Exalt the Lord our God; worship at his footstool! Holy is he!" (Ps. 99:4–5).

It is a commonplace truth that great power has a corrupting influence on human rulers. Not so when it comes to the heavenly King! Psalm 99:4 states: "The King in his might loves justice." This connects the character of God's mighty rule to its moral holiness. Whereas other lords boast of empire, military conquest, or wealth, Israel's God extols justice as his royal insignia. A literal reading of this verse makes the point even clearer: "The might of the King loves justice." Strength and justice are commingled so that God's power effects justice and God's justice exhibits strength. Joseph Alexander summarizes: "God's power is controlled in its exercise by his love of justice."[7]

5. Quoted in O. Palmer Robertson, *Psalms in Congregational Celebration* (Darlington, UK: Evangelical Press, 1995), 281.

6. Robertson, *Psalms in Congregational Celebration,* 281.

7. Joseph A. Alexander, *The Psalms Translated and Explained* (1873; repr., Grand Rapids: Baker, 1977), 403.

Not only does the Lord aim for justice, but he has actually "established equity" and "executed justice" (Ps. 99:4). The effect of God's moral perfection is that no evil can go unchecked under his rule. Robertson writes: "The perfect holiness of God is displayed in his punishment of all wickedness and in his rewarding of all righteousness. Because of his holiness, God cannot do otherwise. He cannot be like a man and allow evil to go unpunished. . . . The holy God will see to it that in the end all the scales of justice balance out perfectly."[8]

The prime example of God's righteousness in action is seen in the life and ministry of Jesus Christ. Not only did Jesus keep every detail of God's law in its true spirit, but he was also its most penetrating teacher in the Sermon on the Mount. Throughout his ministry, Jesus opposed corruption among Israel's leaders and overturned the effects of sin in his mighty miracles. The best way for Christian leaders to follow his example is to observe carefully the commands of Scripture and imbibe the spirit of Christ's mercy. Paul advised us: "Brothers, if anyone is caught in any transgression, you who are spiritual should restore him in a spirit of gentleness" (Gal. 6:1).

Because of the holiness of God's justice, his people should be all the more eager to give him glory: "Exalt the Lord our God; worship at his footstool! Holy is he!" (Ps. 99:5). Rebellious unbelievers resent God's righteous rule because it holds them to account for their sin. But the believer worships at God's footstool, where everything comes into proper perspective. According to 1 Chronicles 28:2, "the footstool of our God" was the ark of the covenant, before which Israel presented itself at the temple. Inside this gold-covered box were kept the two tablets of the Ten Commandments, given by God to Moses on Mount Sinai. Atop the ark was a gold tray known as the *mercy seat*, affixed to which were two golden images of cherubim. Here, the high priest would come once a year on the Day of Atonement and sprinkle the blood of the sacrifice that had died to make propitiation for the people's sins. It was here that God's people saw the holiness of God's justice in terms of both its uncompromising perfection and its gracious provision of mercy. This symbolism was fulfilled by Jesus when he atoned for our sins in his sacrificial death (Rom. 3:25). Calvary is the place where God's people, though they are themselves guilty sinners, may exalt the Lord for his moral holiness! At the cross of Christ—symbolized by God's footstool, the holy ark—we

8. Robertson, *Psalms in Congregational Celebration*, 283–84.

see that God has upheld the absolute purity of his holiness while at the same time showing mercy on those who believe in his Son. John Calvin thus writes: "God cannot otherwise be properly worshipped, than when we come to him directly through Christ."[9]

Having been forgiven of our sins and regenerated by the Holy Spirit, Christians alone can love and rejoice for the perfection of holiness that characterizes the kingdom of God. How holy—how uniquely singular—is God among all the powers of this world! Spurgeon thus exhorts us to revel in God's holiness:

> The gods of the heathen were, according to their own votaries, lustful, cruel, and brutish; their only claim to reverence lay in their supposed potency over human destinies: who would not far rather adore Jehovah, whose character is unsullied purity, unswerving justice, unbending truth, unbounded love, in a word, perfect holiness?[10]

Holy in His Grace

The final stanza of Psalm 99 sees an abrupt transition from the previous two sections, citing the names of some of God's choice servants: "Moses and Aaron were among his priests, Samuel also was among those who called upon his name" (Ps. 99:6). The point is that these prominent servants were all interceding priests on God's behalf. Moses and Aaron were of priestly descent, and Samuel was known for the effectiveness of his prayers (see 1 Sam. 12:23). The ministry of these famous servants points out that God as King is holy not only in his transcendence and in his justice, but also in his grace.

God showed his grace to Israel in that his priests "called to the Lord, and he answered them" (Ps. 99:6). These particular men are noted for the mediation they performed when Israel had fallen under God's wrath for sin. In Exodus 32, after the Israelites had stained themselves by making and worshiping a golden calf, the Lord proposed to consume them in his wrath and then start again with Moses, who had not sinned with them. But Moses interceded with God, asserting that the destruction of Israel would disgrace

9. John Calvin, *Calvin's Commentaries*, 23 vols. (1848; repr., Grand Rapids: Baker, 2009), 6:79.
10. Spurgeon, *Treasury of David*, 2b:224.

God's name among the nations. "Turn from your burning anger and relent from this disaster against your people" (Ex. 32:13), Moses pleaded, reminding the Lord of his covenant promises to Abraham. As a result, "the Lord relented from the disaster that he had spoken of bringing on his people" (v. 14). Aaron performed his intercession annually on the Day of Atonement through the shed blood of sacrifices, as we noted earlier. In 1 Samuel 7:8–11, Samuel offered a sacrifice to the Lord during the oppression of the Philistines so that God routed Israel's enemies. The point of these examples is not that God so lacks mercy that he required mediators to cause his wrath to relent, but rather that God himself provided these priests for the very purpose of making effectual intercession to his grace.

These Old Testament examples, like the symbolism of the ark of the covenant, anticipated the coming of Jesus Christ, who is the one Mediator between the holy God and his sinful people (1 Tim. 2:5). Indeed, it was in light of Jesus and his appointed mediation that the intercessions of Moses, Aaron, and Samuel were successful. None of these men were qualified to turn aside God's wrath by their own pleas. They were all sinners in their own right, worthy of condemnation. Yet God appointed them to stand in Christ's stead until his true and effectual intercession could be offered. George Horne explains: "These men were heard through the intercession of the great Mediator, whom they represented."[11] Jesus' atoning death made the true and ultimate plea, which God answered in the forgiveness of sin. Now, in heaven, Jesus continues in that intercessory priesthood, mediating for his people from the holy throne of God. Paul writes in Romans 8:34: "Who is to condemn? Christ Jesus is the one who died—more than that, who was raised—who is at the right hand of God, who indeed is interceding for us." How holy is God—utterly above the thoughts and ways of men—in his marvelous grace! The prophet Micah asks: "Who is a God like you, pardoning iniquity and passing over transgression for the remnant of his inheritance? He does not retain his anger forever, because he delights in steadfast love" (Mic. 7:18).

In addition to displaying his grace in the mediation of Jesus Christ, God shows his holiness by answering our prayers: "They called to the Lord, and he answered them" (Ps. 99:6). What makes our prayers effective? The answer

11. George Horne, *Commentary on the Psalms* (1771; repr., Audubon, NJ: Old Paths Publications, 1997), 427.

is not found in some virtue in us or in a formula of words that will unlock the door of God's willingness. Instead, God answers our prayers because of his holiness in keeping his promises. "Call to me and I will answer you," he promised (Jer. 33:3). It is true that God does not always answer our prayers in the manner that we would like, for he remains sovereign, but when we come to him in the name of Christ, we can be sure that he receives our prayer in his grace. Spurgeon writes of Moses, Aaron, and Samuel: "Not in vain were their prayers; but being a holy God he was true to his promises, and hearkened to them from the mercy seat."[12]

The same was true of God's faithfulness in revealing his Word to these Old Testament saints: "In the pillar of the cloud he spoke to them; they kept his testimonies and the statute that he gave them" (Ps. 99:7). In the wilderness, the tabernacle was not only the place where the ark of the covenant rested and where the sacrifices were offered. It was also the tent of meeting where God spoke to Moses out of the glory cloud. The cloud showed the solemnity of the giving of God's Word, which is therefore referred to as *Holy Scripture*.

We usually think of God's holiness and his grace as opposites, since it is by God's grace that we are delivered from holy judgment. Yet here the psalmist celebrates God's grace and concludes, "For the Lord our God is holy!" (Ps. 99:9). How do holiness and grace stand together? The answer is that God's grace is a holy grace, achieving righteousness in the lives of his people. Verse 8 states: "O Lord our God, you answered them; you were a forgiving God to them, but an avenger of their wrongdoings." Some might see this verse as displaying opposite sides of God's dealing with men: he is on the one hand forgiving, but on the other hand, he chastens his wayward people. In fact, both sides of this equation exalt God's grace. God is gracious in forgiving sinners who come to him through faith in Christ. God is further gracious in driving sin's presence out of our lives. To be sure, God's opposition to the sins of believers is an administration of his justice. But it is God's grace that applies the justice of God to the lives of those who are forgiven, yet still in need of purging from their sins. God's grace is holy so as to forbid his people to presume in the indulgence of sin; God's discipline is gracious in accepting those who still require the removal of sin from their lives.

12. Spurgeon, *Treasury of David*, 2b:224.

Holy! Exalt Him!

We have seen that God is praised for the transcendence of his holy being and for his holy justice. In the end, we are to praise God for the holiness of his grace: "Exalt the Lord our God, and worship at his holy mountain; for the Lord our God is holy!" (Ps. 99:9). When we think of "his holy mountain," Christians may think of the worship of the saints in heaven, the Zion above. There in heaven, all the glorified believers are worshiping with praise to his holy grace in the presence of the cherubim. But remembering that the temple rested on God's holy mountain, we may also take this as an exhortation to living worship today. "I appeal to you therefore, brothers, by the mercies of God," Paul wrote, "to present your bodies as a living sacrifice, holy and acceptable to God, which is your spiritual worship" (Rom. 12:1).

The question is how we should exalt so holy a God as our God. The best answer will be seen in the example of the holy servants of the Lord listed in Psalm 99. We should be like Moses and Aaron in the faithfulness of our worship and in the intercession of our prayers for both believers and the unbelieving world. We are, Peter writes, "a royal priesthood" (1 Peter 2:9), so as Moses mediated for Israel, we, too, should labor in prayer, interceding for the salvation of the lost. Moreover, Psalm 99:7 says not only that the Lord spoke to his servants in the pillar of the cloud, but also that "they kept his testimonies and the statute that he gave them." Here was the priestly pattern set by the eminent servants who dwelt in the midst of God's visible holiness: a life of worship, prayer, and the faithful ministry of God's Word. To this we add the holiness of our own lives, pursued by God's grace at work in us. "Be holy, for I am holy," says the Lord (1 Peter 1:16). As Samuel urged: "to obey is better than sacrifice, and to listen than the fat of rams" (1 Sam. 15:22).

In pursuit of holiness, we must at the same time appeal constantly to forgiving grace in the blood of Christ for our sins. This appeal follows the pattern of Aaron in his priestly service: first he was cleansed by water and by the sacrifice of a lamb, and then he went into the tabernacle to serve the Lord. James Boice writes what therefore amounts to a watchword for those who wish to know and exalt the Lord in the beauty of his holiness: "It is only the forgiven who can worship at God's holy mountain."[13] It is always and only in the spirit of his grace that we sing to God:

13. James Montgomery Boice, *Psalms*, 3 vols. (Grand Rapids: Baker, 1996), 2:808.

Holy, Holy, Holy!

Holy, holy, holy! All the saints adore thee,
Casting down their golden crowns around the glassy sea;
Cherubim and seraphim falling down before thee,
Who wert, and art, and evermore shalt be.[14]

14. Reginald Heber, "Holy, Holy, Holy!" (1783–1826).

31

The Old Hundredth

Psalm 100

Know that the Lord, he is God! It is he who made us, and we are his; we are his people, and the sheep of his pasture.
(Ps. 100:3)

One of the most familiar and beloved hymn tunes among Protestants goes by the name *Old Hundredth*. The tune was composed in Geneva by Louis Bourgeois for the 1551 *Geneva Psalter*. William Kethe, a friend of the Scottish Reformer John Knox, arranged the words of Psalm 100 to this tune, giving it its current name. This same melody is best known to Christians today as it is sung to the words of the Doxology:

Praise God from whom all blessings flow;
Praise him, all creatures here below;
Praise him above, ye heav'nly host;
Praise Father, Son, and Holy Ghost.[1]

The poet Longfellow labeled the Old Hundredth the "grand old Puritan anthem,"[2] reflecting the close association of the Psalms in general, and Psalm 100 in particular, to the public worship of the seventeenth-century

1. Thomas Ken, "Doxology" (1709).
2. Quoted in Rowland E. Prothero, *The Psalms in Human Life* (New York: Dutton, 1904), 149.

Puritans. In the early 1600s, King James I sought to oppose the Puritans by imposing his own psalter, but the Scottish people rejected it, clinging to the *Geneva Psalter* compiled for them by Knox and especially to Kethe's Old Hundredth Psalm. Charles Spurgeon captured the experience of many when he wrote, "Nothing can be more sublime this side of heaven than the singing of this noble Psalm by a vast congregation."[3]

Psalm 100 is the only psalm that is explicitly intended for thanksgiving, as seen in its superscription, "A Psalm for giving thanks." This does not deny that many other psalms are centered on thanksgiving to God. Psalm 118 repeats the famous line, "Oh give thanks to the Lord, for he is good; for his steadfast love endures forever!" Yet we can see in the structure of Psalm 100 the classic paradigm for a thanksgiving psalm. The first stanza, in verses 1–2, summons the people with exhortations. The second stanza, verse 3, provides the basis for our thanks to God, as our Creator and Redeemer. The third stanza, verse 4, renews the call to assemble with thanks, and the fourth stanza, verse 5, extols three adorable characteristics of God: his goodness, love, and faithfulness. How fitting that this psalm follows the collection of psalms that proclaim the Lord as King, starting with Psalm 93, summing up on a note of thanksgiving and praise.

The Imperatives of Worship

The first stanza of Psalm 100 summons God's people into his presence: "Make a joyful noise to the Lord, all the earth! Serve the Lord with gladness! Come into his presence with singing!" (Ps. 100:1–2).

The first imperative calls believers to exuberance in worship: "Make a joyful noise." Christians should be excited about coming to church, as the Israelites were in appearing before the Lord's temple. It is a privilege to gain admittance to the presence of God, to have liberty of access before him, and to receive the ordinances of prayer, preaching, and the sacraments. The idea of shouting suggests a coronation service for a new king or, in contemporary terms, the acclamation of crowds for a new president who is inaugurated. With that same spirit of excitement and anticipation, believers should come before the Lord with applause for him in our hearts. Particularly as the gospel is set forth, there should be a joyful reception by God's people. David

3. Charles Haddon Spurgeon, *The Treasury of David*, 3 vols. (Peabody, MA: Hendrickson, n.d.), 2b:233.

Dickson reminds us that "according to the gospel, our persons and services are accepted, imperfections pitied, our sins pardoned, and our holy endeavours are graciously rewarded."[4] How can we not come joyfully before the Lord in thanksgiving? John Stott comments that "if God is king, what can our worship be but joyful? Away with funereal faces and doleful dirges! Joy, gladness, and singing are to be the accompaniment of worship."[5]

In addition to coming before God with a joyful noise, Psalm 100:2 calls us to "serve the LORD with gladness!" This second imperative, "serve," has the meaning of participating in public worship, and gives us the terminology *worship service*. Here, it parallels the further command to "come into his presence." This summons reminds us that while attending church is far from the entirety of the Christian life, it is nonetheless an important element of our service to the Lord. Too many Christians consider weekly worship in the church a mere option based on convenience—something to be worked into our calendar with other competing activities. The Israelites saw worship much differently. It matters that you attend church weekly: this service matters to God, matters to the church, and matters to you. It is difficult to find a Christian who is growing in faith if the person is not regularly joined together with fellow believers for the worship service on the Lord's Day.

With this said, it is also true that our service to God extends beyond going to church on Sunday. The apostle Paul takes up the psalmist's language and applies it to a holy life lived for God's pleasure. His transition from doctrine to application in the book of Romans begins with an exhortation "to present your bodies as a living sacrifice, holy and acceptable to God, which is your spiritual worship" (Rom. 12:1).

The third command summons us to come singing before the Lord: "Come into his presence with singing!" (Ps. 100:2). Those who grew up in evangelical churches may not realize that joyful singing is the special province of Christian worship. Other religions employ repetitive chants. Some offer music performed only by rarefied choirs or specially appointed clergy. But while Christless religions present a grim form of worship, Christians sing together loudly and with full hearts. Donald Grey Barnhouse writes: "Where modernism and liberalism have taken hold, the hymns become a part of

4. David Dickson, *A Commentary on the Psalms* (1653; repr., Edinburgh: Banner of Truth, 1995), 2:195.

5. John Stott, *Favorite Psalms: Growing Closer to God* (Grand Rapids: Baker, 2003), 81–82.

the service where the organ plays loudly, a paid choir sings without heart, and faint murmurs come from parts of the building where spiritual life struggles to express itself in spite of the circumstances. But wherever there is the warm knowledge of sins forgiven, wherever Christ is exalted in His grace and saving power, then the singing takes on a note of triumph."[6]

Psalm 100:2 not only tells us to sing before the Lord with gladness, but also tells us to sing *together.* All the verbs in these opening verses are plural imperatives. We applaud the Lord and worship him corporately, and our singing is likewise to consist of the joined voices of the congregation. This is why, in general, the music most suited for the worship of the church was composed with that worship explicitly in mind. D. G. Hart writes: "Music that is performed at rock concerts or sung in lounges and bars, and even music performed in symphony halls[,] . . . is the world's music. It is designed for appreciation or consumption in worldly settings."[7] Worship music should be primarily written for unison singing, instead of the soaring notes appropriate for trained soloists, and should fit the setting of reverential joy that is exhorted in Psalm 100. Hart concludes that "the church needs to give more attention to her music, and a way to do this may be commissioning musicians to write melodies that are appropriate for public worship and that fit the texts congregations use to praise God."[8]

If we were to seek words to describe the worship to which we are called in Psalm 100, we would use *joyful*, *glad*, and *musical*. But one description that we must not omit is *evangelistic*. Notice that verse 1 summons "all the earth" to praise the Lord. Worship was not the exclusive monopoly of ancient Israel, but was always intended for the people of all lands. Stott writes: "Jehovah is not the tribal deity of Israel, but the sovereign Ruler over all the earth. When we assemble for worship, therefore, we should desire not only to make a joyful noise ourselves, but that all nations should unite with us in our joyful task."[9] This evangelistic motive should not cause us to secularize the worship service so as to impress the spiritually unmotivated. But it does mean that everyone not only should be welcome to join us in worship

6. Donald Grey Barnhouse, *Exposition of Bible Doctrines, Taking the Epistle to the Romans as a Point of Departure*, vol. 3, *God's Remedy* (Wheaton, IL: Van Kampen, 1954), 245.

7. D. G. Hart and John Muether, *With Reverence and Awe* (Phillipsburg, NJ: P&R Publishing, 2002), 164.

8. Hart and Muether, *With Reverence and Awe,* 146.

9. Stott, *Favorite Psalms*, 82.

but should be specially invited and desired in the congregation where the gospel is preached and its music is sung. Even as we rejoice before our God in worship, Christians must never forget the burden of the Great Commission. Spurgeon reminds us, "Never will the world be in its proper condition till with one unanimous shout it adores the only God."[10]

The Motivations of Worship

What is it about the Lord that makes such a positive approach to worship so urgent for his people? The answers are given in Psalm 100's second stanza, which unfolds the motivations of God's people in their worship of him. Primarily, we worship with reverent joy because of our knowledge that the Lord is the true and only God: "Know that the Lord, he is God!" (Ps. 100:3).

The word *know* makes an important point about the believer's approach to worship. We do worship God not according to our feelings, needs, or desires, but based on what we know about him. Primarily, this knowledge comes from God himself in his Word. When the apostle Paul brought the gospel to Athens, he grieved that the Athenians did not know God but worshiped idols in ignorance. Passing by, he found an altar dedicated to "the unknown god." Speaking before the philosophers, Paul stated: "What therefore you worship as unknown, this I proclaim to you" (Acts 17:23). This emphasis reminds us that true "thanksgiving to God must be intelligent; we must know whom we are thanking."[11] We are motivated to worship God with an excited gladness because of what we know about him.

The first thing we know is that the Lord, the God of the Bible, is the true and only God. Other claimants to deity are false. God is not within ourselves. The earth is not God, and neither are the trees and rocks. Science is not God; neither is sensual pleasure. God is the Lord of the Bible; the Lord of the Bible is God, and it is our privilege to know him and then to render the joyful service of our worship.

There are two primary things that we also know about God, including that he is the Creator: "It is he who made us, and we are his" (Ps. 100:3). To consider the intricacies of human nature with its depths of soul and the capacity of the mind, or the wonders of the human body with the dexterity of the hand or

10. Spurgeon, *Treasury of David*, 2b:233.
11. James Montgomery Boice, *Psalms*, 3 vols. (Grand Rapids: Baker, 1996), 2:812.

the marvel of the eye, is to glorify the far greater Being who made us. To expand our vision to the skies and the starry host, we can only bow down before the Creator and exclaim that "we are his." The Lord has the right to our service, including our obedience and worship. We are made for his glory, and it is our privilege to have a relationship with the great Creator God.

In a textual variant, the expression "and we are his" appears as "and not we ourselves" (KJV), meaning that we did not make ourselves. This is also true, although most scholars prefer to read the verse "and we are his." Modern man has tried to posit himself as self-made. James Boice quotes a humanist who was described as "a self-made man who worships his creator."[12] More widespread today is the denial of God as Creator through the theory of evolution. The appeal of this theory is not simply the evidence from which it draws, but its convenience in removing the place of God from our lives. Why should we worship if God did not make us? Why should we be thankful to anyone if we are the product of chance events? We are left in our pride to thank only ourselves, having removed God all along for the sake of self-deification.

In addition to knowing God as Creator, believers delight to know him as our Redeemer. Recalling the biblical imagery of the Savior-Shepherd, Psalm 100:3 concludes: "we are his people, and the sheep of his pasture." God redeemed us specifically by sending his Son to lay down his life on our behalf. Jesus said: "I am the good shepherd. The good shepherd lays down his life for the sheep" (John 10:11). Taking up the shepherd staff, he then leads his chosen flock into heaven: "I give them eternal life, and they will never perish, and no one will snatch them out of my hand" (v. 28). Having redeemed us from the guilt of sin, Jesus our Good Shepherd now leads us out from the power of sin: "My sheep hear my voice, and I know them, and they follow me" (v. 27). Every believer can therefore rejoice to sing, "The LORD is my shepherd; I shall not want" (Ps. 23:1). Knowing God as our Redeemer through his Son, Jesus Christ, is the greatest of all motivations for fervent, joyful, and devoted worship to him. Boice summarizes: "No one should be more thankful to God than the sheep who are cared for by the Good Shepherd."[13]

Whatever trials may come to us in life, every Christian finds here ample

12. Boice, *Psalms,* 2:813.
13. Boice, *Psalms,* 2:813.

reason to give thanksgiving to God with a joyful heart. He is God! It is he, the Creator, who made us! And he has made us his own people, creating not only the human race but Israel and the church to be the pasture for his sheep. To say that we are the sheep of his pasture is to acknowledge his tender love for us, which overcomes every deterrent to thanksgiving. Do we enjoy prosperity? Then let us be sure to praise the Lord with thanks. Do we struggle in trials or suffer in sorrow? Then let us lift tear-streamed faces to the Lord and worship him who is worthy and who has loved us unto salvation. God's Word declares that "we are his." Regardless of anything else, being his own precious, beloved people—individually and together as the flock of his church—let us be zealously motivated, knowing that the Lord is God, to make a joyful noise to him, serving him with gladness, and coming into his presence with singing. Whatever else is true, "the Lord, he is God! It is he who made us, and we are his" (Ps. 100:3).

Three Admirable Characteristics

Psalm 100:4 returns to the summons of God's people into his presence: "Enter his gates with thanksgiving, and his courts with praise!" Here we have the overarching theme of thanksgiving. When the Israelites entered the temple courts, blood sacrifices were offered from lambs and goats. Because Christ has come, those sacrifices have ended. But the thank offering continues in the gratitude that should characterize our worship. Spurgeon urges: "So long as we are receivers of mercy we must be givers of thanks."[14] The call to thanks is repeated: "Give thanks to him; bless his name!" This is our desire in worship, by means of thanksgiving, to give a blessing directly to God, pleasing his loving heart, and glorifying his wonderful name.

The final stanza, in Psalm 100:5, highlights three characteristics of God that are so worthy of our adoration. Why are we thankful to the Lord? Why do we come desiring a blessing not merely for ourselves but also for him? First, because "the Lord is good" (Ps. 100:5). You could not say this about the pagan gods of the idol-worshiping people. They were not good, but rather capricious. One never knew how they would react or in what mood they would be found. But the Lord, the God of the Bible, is always good. When

14. Spurgeon, *Treasury of David*, 2b:234.

he created the earth, he made it all good (Gen. 1:4–31). The rules of his law are benevolent. Boice writes:

> When he reveals his will to us, his will is "good, pleasing and perfect" (Rom. 12:2). The word *gospel* means "the good news." The very word *God* is a shortened form of "good." No wonder the psalmist cried out: "Taste and see that the LORD is good; Blessed is the man who takes refuge in him" (Ps. 34:8).[15]

Moreover, God is good to everyone. Jesus exhorted his followers to love their enemies so as to be sons of their heavenly Father: "For he makes his sun rise on the evil and on the good, and sends rain on the just and on the unjust" (Matt. 5:45). A. W. Tozer wrote:

> The goodness of God is that which disposes Him to be kind, cordial, benevolent, and full of good will toward men. He is tenderhearted and of quick sympathy, and His unfailing attitude toward all moral beings is open, frank, and friendly. By His nature He is inclined to bestow blessedness and He takes holy pleasure in the happiness of His people.[16]

Finally, we should be thankful to God because his plans are good. No greater proof exists than the cross of Jesus Christ. Here was the most evil deed ever committed, as God's perfect Son was put to death by wicked men. But so wonderful are God's plans that he made the worst thing ever to happen into the best thing that ever occurred for those who believe. Philip Ryken concludes: "The cross has brought salvation to the world. If God brought the greatest good out of the greatest evil, he can bring good out of what seems to be evil in your own life. It is all part of God's good plan."[17]

We adore God because he is good, and also because "his steadfast love endures forever" (Ps. 100:5). The word for "steadfast love" is sometimes translated as "mercy." Of course, the two ideas go together: God's love has a merciful orientation to needy sinners. It is this merciful love that especially draws our hearts to adore the Lord. The apostle John went so far as to say

15. Boice, *Psalms*, 2:815.

16. A. W. Tozer, *The Knowledge of the Holy* (1961; repr., San Francisco: HarperSanFrancisco, 1992), 127–28.

17. James Montgomery Boice and Philip Graham Ryken, *The Heart of the Cross* (Wheaton, IL: Crossway, 1999), 131.

not only that God is loving but that "God is love" (1 John 4:8). This means that "his love finds expression in everything that He says and does."[18]

God's love is not abstract, but is directed to the believer personally. The apostle Paul looked to the cross where Jesus died for sin and found assurance of his own place in God's love. In what may be regarded as his personal credo, Paul wrote: "I live by faith in the Son of God, who loved me and gave himself for me" (Gal. 2:20). Knowing God's love in Christ was the key to Paul's assurance that "all things work together for good" (Rom. 8:28). "Not just *some* things, note, but *all* things! Every single thing that happens to him expresses God's love to him—holy, omnipotent love—at every moment and in every event of every day's life. Even when he cannot see the why and the wherefore of God's dealings, he knows that there is love in and behind them."[19] Since the Lord's steadfast love endures forever, Christians have every reason to enter his courts with thanksgiving—indeed, to enter every day with prayers of blessing to God's name.

Finally, the Lord is extolled for his admirable attribute of faithfulness. God keeps covenant with his people and fulfills every promise that he has ever made. His Word is utterly dependable. He is unchanging in his will, affections, and judgments. How wonderful it is to have solid rock on which to stand, the faithfulness of God and his trustworthy Word. Spurgeon writes: "As our fathers found him faithful, so will our sons, and their seed for ever. . . . Our heart leaps for joy as we bow before One who has never broken his word or changed his purpose."[20]

When the patriarch Jacob was young, he was forced to flee his home. That night, he slept alone on the ground with his head on a stone. The Lord came to him in a dream with promises of blessing: "I am the LORD, the God of Abraham your father and the God of Isaac. . . . Behold, I am with you and will keep you wherever you go, and will bring you back to this land" (Gen. 28:13–15). Jacob responded by committing himself to be a follower of the Lord, and he named the place "Bethel" (v. 19), meaning "house of God."

Many years later, toward the end of his long life, God summoned Jacob back to Bethel to tell how God had fulfilled the promises given there. Jacob answered the summons, saying: "let us arise and go up to Bethel, so that I

18. J. I. Packer, *Knowing God* (Downers Grove, IL: InterVarsity Press, 1979), 111.
19. Packer, *Knowing God*, 111.
20. Spurgeon, *Treasury of David*, 2b:234–35.

may make there an altar to the God who answers me in the day of my distress and has been with me wherever I have gone" (Gen. 35:3). Jacob was saying at the end of his life that God had been faithful to him, keeping all his wonderful promises. God had promised that he would be with Jacob, and now Jacob confessed that God was with him. The Lord had pledged to bring him back to the promised land, and Jacob praised the Lord that he had returned. There, at Bethel, the Lord appeared before Jacob once more, confirming his covenant anew. Jacob responded in the way that we should respond to the Lord, and the way that we will spend eternity in praise when God's faithfulness has brought us all home. Genesis 35:14 relates, "And Jacob set up a pillar in the place where he had spoken with him, a pillar of stone. He poured out a drink offering on it and poured oil on it." Jacob was saying, "Thank you, Lord, for being faithful." Since the Lord is faithful "to all generations" (Ps. 100:5), we can adore him now with thanksgiving as the faithful God we know, love, and serve.

A Prophecy of Christ

There is little wonder that the Old Hundredth has stirred the hearts of so many of God's people. We will be stirred, as well, if we can claim its heritage personally. "We are his people," says the psalmist, "and the sheep of his pasture" (Ps. 100:3). Martin Luther wrote: "This Psalm is a prophecy concerning Christ. It calls upon all to rejoice, to triumph, and to give thanks; to enter his gates with thanksgiving, and his courts and sanctuary with praise; because by the gospel and the preaching of the remission of sins, that kingdom of Christ is established and strengthened, which shall remain and stand forever."[21]

How do we enter the gates of God's blessing? We enter through the door opened for us by Christ and his atoning death. The God of Psalm 100 becomes our God, and we rejoice to be his people, through the Good Shepherd, Jesus Christ. In Psalm 100, Christ calls us to himself. "I am the door of the sheep," Jesus asserts. "If anyone enters by me, he will be saved" (John 10:7–9). Finally, he declares: "I give them eternal life, and they will never perish, and no one will snatch them out of my hand" (v. 28). What can we say to that? We can say, "Thank you!," entering his gates with a praise of blessing and rejoicing that the Lord is good, his steadfast love enduring forever and his faithfulness to all generations.

21. Quoted in William S. Plumer, *Psalms* (1867; repr., Edinburgh: Banner of Truth, 1975), 895.

32

With Integrity of Heart

Psalm 101

I will ponder the way that is blameless. Oh when will you come to me? I will walk with integrity of heart within my house. (Ps. 101:2)

When George Villiers was identified as the favorite of England's King James I (1566–1625), he received a letter of advice from the philosopher Francis Bacon. Knowing that Villiers would greatly influence selection to the royal court, Bacon urged him:

> In those the choice had need be of honest and faithful servants, as well as of comely outsides who can bow the knee and kiss the hand. King David (Psalm ci. 6, 7) propounded a rule to himself for the choice of his courtiers. He was a wise and a good king; and a wise and a good king shall do well to follow such a good example; and if he find any to be faulty, which perhaps cannot suddenly be discovered, let him take on him this resolution as King David did, "there shall no deceitful person dwell in my house."[1]

Villiers's failure to heed Bacon's advice produced a number of calamities in his public life and eventually led to his assassination. By contrast, to the

1. Quoted in E. Calvin Beisner, *Psalms of Promise* (Phillipsburg, NJ: Presbyterian and Reformed, 1988), 229.

extent that David himself followed the resolutions set down in Psalm 101, his own reign was blessed. David's psalm was called by Martin Luther "a mirror for magistrates,"[2] and through the centuries its godly declarations have provided sage advice to Christian rulers and other leaders.

Questions are raised about the occasion that prompted David to pen Psalm 101. Its content suggests that David wrote it before taking up his reign as king over all Israel. One possible clue is found in verse 2, where David pines for the Lord: "Oh when will you come to me?" This plea connects with similar language in 2 Samuel 6, at the beginning of David's kingship over the unified nation. Wanting to honor the Lord, David brought the ark of the covenant up to Jerusalem. But because David had failed to carefully study the biblical requirements for moving the ark, his attempt failed, and the Lord slew one of the servants. In frustration over his failure, David prayed to God, "How can the ark of the LORD come to me?" (2 Sam. 6:9). It may well be that in his anxiety over this matter, David desired to please the Lord by recommitting himself to the godly standards of leadership in this psalm. J. J. Stewart Perowne writes: "One who begins his reign with thoughts and resolutions such as these may well look for a happy termination of it, and nothing shows us more clearly the true nobleness of David's soul than this short Psalm."[3]

Steadfast Love and Justice

When one is considering the ideal approach to leadership, the best example to consider is that of the Lord. David therefore begins by celebrating the twin virtues that characterize God's kingdom: "I will sing of steadfast love and justice; to you, O LORD, I will make music" (Ps. 101:1). God's rule is marked by its combination of justice, so that sin is overthrown and righteousness is established, together with kindhearted mercy for those who are weak and burdened. According to Micah 6:8, God gives these same priorities to his people: "He has told you, O man, what is good; and what does the LORD require of you but to do justice, and to love kindness, and to walk humbly with your God?" Jesus once described the "weightier matters of the law" as "justice and mercy and faithfulness" (Matt. 23:23). Similarly, Psalm

2. Quoted in H. C. Leupold, *Exposition of the Psalms* (Columbus, OH: Wartburg Press, 1959), 701.
3. J. J. Stewart Perowne, *The Book of Psalms*, 2 vols. (1878; repr., Grand Rapids: Zondervan, 1976), 2:213.

85:10 extols God's kingdom, saying: "Steadfast love and faithfulness meet; righteousness and peace kiss each other." The supreme example of God's justice joining together with mercy is the cross of Christ, where God's law was fulfilled as Jesus bore our sins and as God's mercy made a way for our forgiveness in Jesus' blood.

Seeing these priorities in God's own administration, David approaches his kingship by highlighting "steadfast love and justice." It is more natural to mankind to see either mercy or justice emphasized. Some leaders are strict and unyielding, while others are more easygoing and understanding. It is the mark of God's kingdom, and of the indwelling of his Spirit, to see these apparently contrary values combined in harmony. James Boice writes: "Mercy and justice operate as checks on one another. Justice checks love that might otherwise be wrongly indulgent and therefore harmful. Love checks judgment that might otherwise be unduly harsh and therefore also harmful. David wanted his rule to be marked by both of these."[4] When David writes, "I will sing of steadfast love and justice; to you, O Lord, I will make music" (Ps. 101:1), he is dedicating his leadership to the Lord in imitation of his harmonious blending of attributes into a true and spiritual righteousness. Perowne comments: "It is as a king who would frame his own rule and his kingdom after the Divine pattern that David makes these attributes the burden of his song."[5]

A Commitment to Personal Godliness

Some years ago, a presidential election saw charges made against the moral character of one of the candidates, to which his supporters responded with the slogan, "Competence, Not Character." It is hard to deny the role of competence in public office, but if David had to choose between the two, he would highlight character first. To this end, he commits himself to a kingship of mercy and justice and also realizes that his own godliness will be necessary. Therefore, David resolves, "I will ponder the way that is blameless. . . . I will walk with integrity of heart" (Ps. 101:2).

By a "blameless" life, David does not mean that he can merit God's approval through perfectly sinless works. What he does aspire to, though,

4. James Montgomery Boice, *Psalms*, 3 vols. (Grand Rapids: Baker, 1996), 2:819.
5. Perowne, *Psalms*, 2:214.

is personal conduct that is morally upright to a high degree. The ideal guide for this resolution is the law of God that is summarized in the Ten Commandments. God's law serves multiple functions, beginning with its role in showing us our sin so that we will appeal to God for forgiveness through Jesus Christ. Here, in what is called its *first use*, the law functions as a mirror to show us the guilt of our sin. But another use of the law lies in its serving as a guide to our conduct. If David wanted to walk in a blameless manner, then he should love the Lord his God with all his heart, he should refuse to plot violence against others, he should not steal, lust, or lie. God's law should shape not only the behavior but also the desires and motives of the heart: "I will walk with integrity of heart," David resolves (Ps. 101:2). How important such a commitment is to rulers in both the civil and spiritual realms. Not only kings but also pastors and elders in the church should set God's law before them as a guide, as should fathers and mothers in the home.

Indeed, David identifies godliness in the home as especially important for anyone in a leadership position: "I will walk with integrity of heart within my house" (Ps. 101:2). Many leaders erect a facade of public righteousness that masks personal depravities or the neglect of duties in the home. Sadly, King David failed most significantly in this regard, passing on to his sons more of his vices than his virtues. The rebellion that festered in David's household, where he neglected his parental duties (1 Kings 1:6), ultimately cast his kingdom into violent disarray. Most of us tend to permit sin more readily in private than in public, yet true godliness requires a correspondence between piety in the home and in the workplace. Calvin Beisner writes: "Far from a man's private life being irrelevant to his public service, it is the most relevant thing of all. In private he is himself. There he reveals his real character, and that character will count under the pressures of public service."[6]

When we consider David's resolution to godliness, we observe not only how important this is for a ruler but also how rare such a commitment is from one who possessed great worldly power. Absolute monarchs such as David are typically free from all restraint on their personal conduct. John Calvin writes:

> We know, and it is a truth taught us by experience, that almost all kings are intoxicated with the splendours of royalty; and . . . they are so blinded by

6. Beisner, *Psalms of Promise*, 234.

> their dignity, that they . . . become arrogant and haughty in their carriage, recklessly plunge into their pleasures, and at length utterly forget themselves.[7]

An example of a monarch who indulged himself in corruption was England's James I, the king who made George Villiers his leading counselor. When James set eyes on the twenty-one-year-old Villiers at a hunt, the feature that attracted him was not intelligence or integrity but physical beauty. Noticing this, Villiers's supporters purchased him stylish clothes and arranged for him to be often in the king's presence. Before long, the king and Villiers pursued relations that were widely considered homosexual in nature, the king being said to "tumble and kiss [Villiers] as a mistress."[8] The resulting elevation of an incompetent leader to a position of high office and the resentment directed toward the king and his favorite went a long way to stirring conflict in seventeenth-century England.

How important it is for public figures who make a Christian profession of faith to think and act far differently! David not only desired to provide a more responsible and godly pattern of kingship, but committed himself to its pursuit. Notice that he states, "I will ponder the way that is blameless" (Ps. 101:2). The king made a study of his own character. No doubt he prayed about his sins and asked God to stir up godly virtues. Like the blessed man of Psalm 1, David would have testified that "his delight is in the law of the Lord, and on his law he meditates day and night" (1:2). So also for us, a godly character will not simply appear without effort and diligence on our part. David pondered a blameless life and studied integrity of heart.

Moreover, this pursuit of holiness involved shunning unworthy desires and habits. David adds: "I will not set before my eyes anything that is worthless" (Ps. 101:3). The king thus realizes that godly character requires both a yes and a no. Saying yes to God's law also means saying no to things that are perverse or sinful. Desiring to overcome temptations to sin, David starts by shunning the temptations themselves! When tempted—and here we should note his priority on control of the eyes—he was resolved to turn away without delay.

7. John Calvin, *Calvin's Commentaries*, 23 vols. (1848; repr., Grand Rapids: Baker, 2009), 6:88.

8. Robert Ruigh, *The Parliament of 1624: Politics and Foreign Policy* (Cambridge, MA: Harvard University Press, 1971), 77.

Concerted Opposition to Evil

Having set before himself the divine example of mercy joined with justice, and then having committed himself to personal godliness, David devotes most of the rest of the psalm to a concerted opposition of evil within his realm and especially his court. David knows that faithful leadership is concerned with the environment in which people live and especially in which government is exercised. Determined as he is to godly rule, he realizes how vigilant he must be against competing forces. God had commanded that "you shall be to me a kingdom of priests and a holy nation" (Ex. 19:6), and it was David's job to pursue the needed righteousness within his realm. As Francis Bacon sought to advise George Villiers, it is especially in the selection of officials and advisers—as today in the hiring of managers at work and the calling of officers in the church—that David's resolutions should be applied.

David highlights five vices against which he will oppose his rule, starting with *faithless* men: "I hate the work of those who fall away; it shall not cling to me" (Ps. 101:3). A literal rendering speaks of "the works of those who swerve," that is, who act without integrity and break agreements. Most significantly, this would refer to apostates: men who have turned from the Lord. Deeds of rebellion struck at the heart of Israel's covenant faithfulness, so David vows to "hate" such works and to forbid them to "cling to me." One cannot sing of "steadfast love" (v. 1), an idea that includes covenant faithfulness, without vigorously opposing infidelity.

Second, David commits himself to oppose the *morally depraved*: "A perverse heart shall be far from me; I will know nothing of evil" (Ps. 101:4). *Perverse* means "wicked," and it includes the idea of actively subverting that which is true and right. David plans to keep such people "far from me" and to "know nothing" of their ways. Here we see the importance of Christians' not associating with the morally depraved. How vital this is for young people who are forming habits that will influence their entire lives! Few barometers will more accurately forecast a young person's direction than the moral quality of the company that he or she keeps. The same gauge should apply to leaders with respect to the advisers that they permit into their counsel. Jesus himself expressed his determination to bar evil persons from his presence. To such depraved persons he will bar the door of heaven, even if they professed to serve him, saying: "Depart from me, all you workers of evil!" (Luke 13:27).

American society today is plagued by thought leaders who are determined to upend sound moral standards. We encounter this especially in the media, where songs promote adultery and sexual violence and where television shows depict moral perversity as wholesome. The result is a society in which relational pain and broken lives are increasingly the norm. David resolves to "know nothing" of such evil, urging believers—and especially leaders—to refuse to imbibe moral filth or grant it entry into their hearts and minds.

Third, David writes with great vehemence against the damage of *slanderers*: "Whoever slanders his neighbor secretly I will destroy" (Ps. 101:5). It may be said that "sticks and stones may break my bones, but words will never harm me," but David did not believe this. Calvin points out how deadly slander can be: "To detract from the reputation of another privily, and by stealth, is a plague exceedingly destructive. It is as if a man killed a fellow-creature from a place of ambush; or . . . like one who administers poison to his unsuspecting victim, destroys men unawares."[9] Perhaps it is the cowardliness of slander that increases David's resolve against it: "I will destroy," he says of the slanderer. A royal court, or a government office today, is typically rife with those who commit character assassination with poisoned words and pens. Only when a leader actively purges slanderers will he enjoy an environment of honest debate and wholesome collaboration within his court.

How vital it is for the Christian church that its ministries remain free from this slanderous spirit. Even when we have serious differences of doctrine or practice, godly Christian leaders must be careful to speak charitably and honorably of one another, avoiding the temptation to malign motives or misrepresent words. Beisner writes: "In our day, when gossip earns millions on newsstands and passes for 'sharing' in many church congregations, we find it hard to take the offense so seriously. Why would David think slander so wicked that those who practice it should be 'exterminated'?" He answers: "David took the covenant seriously, and slander threatened the peace and unity of the covenant people."[10] In this attitude, David followed the example of the Lord God, who commanded, "You shall not go around as a slanderer among your people" (Lev. 19:16).

9. Calvin, *Commentaries*, 6:91.
10. Beisner, *Psalms of Promise*, 237.

Fourth, David will set his regime against the *proud* of heart: "Whoever has a haughty look and an arrogant heart I will not endure" (Ps. 101:5). Those with proud hearts will pursue personal ambition over the general good, and are never satisfied with the honors they receive. Charles Spurgeon writes that "proud men are generally hard, and therefore very unfit for office; persons of high looks provoke enmity and discontent, and the fewer of such people about a court the better for the stability of a throne."[11]

Fifth and finally, David resolves to shun the *deceitful* and *dishonest*: "No one who practices deceit shall dwell in my house; no one who utters lies shall continue before my eyes" (Ps. 101:7). Whatever short-term value a cunning deceiver may provide to a ruler, such a person can never be trusted. An adviser who counsels dishonesty does not serve his leader well. Especially in the church, our aim should be both to do the right thing and also to do it in the right way, prayerfully following God's Word in both respects. Church advisers who urge deceit or other unbiblical practices inject a poison into the life of God's people. Godly leaders, in the church and in the civil realm, should guard against subordinates who treat truth and integrity as malleable substances. David resolves not to permit them in his house and tolerate them before his eyes.

David would receive an education on this last priority in the later years of his realm. His most trusted adviser was Ahithophel, a man noted for his cunning (2 Sam. 16:23). But during the rebellion of his son Absalom, David discovered that this deceitful servant had practiced his cunning on the king himself. Jesus compared Ahithophel to Judas Iscariot in lamenting that false disciple's betrayal (John 13:18; Ps. 41:9). It was the proud and deceitful Ahithophel who had manipulated Absalom's coup that drove David out of Jerusalem. Absalom, too, learned the mistake of placing this deceiver at his right hand, for the overthrow of Ahithophel's counsel spelled the end of Absalom's rebellion and his life.

If David will disassociate from and even prosecute the faithless, depraved, slanderous, proud, and deceitful, whom will he seek to serve alongside him? The answer is given in Psalm 101:6, where he counters the strong negatives with a resounding positive for the faithful and godly: "I will look with favor on the faithful in the land, that they may dwell with me; he who walks in the way that is blameless shall minister to me." A ruler has to trust some

11. Charles Haddon Spurgeon, *The Treasury of David*, 3 vols. (Peabody, MA: Hendrickson, n.d.), 2b:241.

people, bringing them close in his association, and David resolves that the faithful and godly will be advanced under his rule. Here is a verse to read prayerfully before every job interview: what was true for David as king is equally true for an executive hiring a manager or for church elders seeking pastoral leadership. The most desirable qualities in a leader are not qualifications, charisma, or connections, but personal godliness coupled with demonstrated faithfulness in one's calling.

David pledges to seek out the faithful, indicating that this pursuit would be an active priority under his rule. We can imagine him briefing job recruiters, instructing them to commit this psalm to memory. Calvin summarizes: "he will exercise discretion and care, that, instead of taking persons into his service indiscriminately, he may wisely determine each man's character, so as to have those who live a life of strict integrity as his most intimate friends, and that he may intrust them with the offices of state."[12]

In this way, David gives invaluable advice to those who desire career opportunities among those who are faithful and godly. How wise for a young person, just launching a career, to desire not merely advancement but the opportunity of service alongside truly noble leaders. Do you desire such a commendable position? Then, according to David, you should demand strict integrity in your speech and conduct, not permitting the kinds of vices he has proscribed. Make yourself a faithful servant of men and women whose leadership can be respected and whose aims are in accordance with God's Word. Few habits are more worthy of cultivation than that of servant-heartedness, coupled with a commitment to be faithful in one's duty. Jesus challenged his disciples along just these lines:

> You know that the rulers of the Gentiles lord it over them, and their great ones exercise authority over them. It shall not be so among you. But whoever would be great among you must be your servant, and whoever would be first among you must be your slave, even as the Son of Man came not to be served but to serve, and to give his life as a ransom for many. (Matt. 20:25–28)

Entering into the Joy of Our Master

As David saw it, a wide variety of ungodly people must be excluded from a wise ruler's association. So resolute is he that he concludes: "Morning by

12. Calvin, *Commentaries*, 6:93.

morning I will destroy all the wicked in the land, cutting off all the evildoers from the city of the Lord" (Ps. 101:8). The problem is that David did not follow through with this commitment. We think of an unsavory figure such as Joab, David's chief general, who spun deceit at David's side for decades, bringing division and upheaval on the realm. We have already mentioned Ahithophel, the cunning counselor who betrayed his king. To this list we should add several of David's own sons, especially Absalom, who almost overthrew David's throne, and Adonijah, who staged a nearly successful coup in David's old age. David had failed to follow Psalm 101 even among his own sons; it is no wonder, then, that his reign that began so well ended so badly.

Ultimately, it was David who betrayed himself by failing to follow through on his chief personal commitment: "I will ponder the way that is blameless. . . . I will walk with integrity of heart within my house" (Ps. 101:2). Yet the day came when David, perhaps worn down by his burdens, and having grown neglectful of his spiritual state, committed the grossest sins within his own house. He used his power to violate Bathsheba, and seeking to cover up his adultery he conspired in the murder of her husband, the very kind of man that he had earlier resolved to promote and preserve. It was out of David's personal fall that his resolutions in Psalm 101 fell to the ground shattered and broken, and with them his realm.

Fortunately, there is another David who speaks in this psalm, and whose commitment to righteousness will never fail. In the timing of God, a son of David would be born of whom it would justly be said of his entire life, "He has done all things well" (Mark 7:37). Isaiah 9:6 foretold him: "the government shall be upon his shoulder, and his name shall be called Wonderful Counselor, Mighty God, Everlasting Father, Prince of Peace."

In this life, every merely human ruler or leader, however committed at first to being godly and just, is bound to disappoint and fail us to a greater or lesser degree. But there is a King who will never fail in the resolutions of Psalm 101. Jesus will uphold both mercy and justice forever, having established them both in the blood of his cross. In his return, Christ has pledged to rid his creation of all those who are false, deceitful, and wicked. Wielding a sword of omnipotent justice, he will cleanse the world as he once drove the hypocrites out from the temple. Revelation 22:15 says of his city: "Outside are the dogs and sorcerers and the sexually immoral and murderers and idolaters, and everyone who loves and practices falsehood." Who, then, can be saved under this perfectly righteous justice? The Bible answers by appeal to the mercy of Christ for sinners who repent and believe. Revelation 22:14 declares, "Blessed are those who wash their robes, so that they may have the right to the tree of life and that they may enter the city by the gates."

Christ's rule upholds justice, as he paid the full penalty for our sins on the cross and as his final judgment will condemn all those who have refused his gospel. But it is in his mercy that sinners especially rejoice. When Monica, the mother of St. Augustine, died, her famous son was overwhelmed with grief and sorrow. But a friend snatched up a Psalter and began singing the opening lines of Psalm 101: "I will sing of steadfast love and justice; to you, O LORD, I will make music." Augustine then rose and joined in the song, rejoicing in the faith of his dear mother and the faithfulness of the Savior to whose mercy she had entrusted her soul.[13]

We, too, may rejoice in the steadfast mercy and justice of Jesus Christ. Then, having been saved by his grace, our wise ambition should simply be that of devoted and godly servanthood, longing above all other praises to receive the highest accolade on the day when Jesus returns: "Well done, good and faithful servant. . . . Enter into the joy of your master" (Matt. 25:21).

13. Rowland E. Prothero, *The Psalms in Human Life* (New York: Dutton, 1904), 17–18.

33

A Psalm from the Sickbed

Psalm 102

But you, O Lord, are enthroned forever; you are remembered throughout all generations. (Ps. 102:12)

When scholars identify messianic psalms, Psalm 102 is frequently overlooked. The famous examples include Psalm 22, which Jesus quoted on the cross: "My God, my God, why have you forsaken me?" (Ps. 22:1). Psalm 118:22 says of Jesus, "The stone that the builders rejected has become the cornerstone." Peter explained Jesus' resurrection as fulfilling Psalm 16: "For you will not abandon my soul to Hades, or let your Holy One see corruption" (Acts 2:27). Psalm 102 belongs in company with these psalms that explicitly point to Christ. We know this because its final stanza is quoted of Jesus in Hebrews 1:10–12: "You, Lord, laid the foundation of the earth in the beginning, and the heavens are the work of your hands; they will perish, but you remain."

In Hebrews 1, the message of Psalm 102 has a theological emphasis in the writer's proving the supremacy of Christ over the angels. In the original setting, the psalmist grasped these truths as a source of hope in the midst of a desperate plight. His confidence in God enabled him to overcome his terrible distress and turn his prayer into a model of intercession.

An Impassioned Lament

Psalm 102 begins with a lament for sorrow that is so intense, it can be compared with the desperate prayers of Job. Satan demanded permission to afflict faithful Job in every area of his life, striking his family, wealth, and health. In chapter 3, Job breaks down in a most pathetic lament to the Lord: "For my sighing comes instead of my bread, and my groanings are poured out like water" (Job 3:24). The author of Psalm 102 is almost as distressed: "Hear my prayer, O Lord; let my cry come to you! Do not hide your face from me in the day of my distress! Incline your ear to me; answer me speedily in the day when I call!" (Ps. 102:1–2).

Hebrew poetry relies on parallelism, usually with the second line elaborating or heightening the first. Here, the parallelism takes the form of sheer repetition to express urgency. The same appeal is made over and over again with a variety of expressions: "Hear my prayer . . . ; let my cry come to you! . . . Incline your ear . . . ; answer me speedily" (Ps. 102:1–2). This is not a mere rote reading of formal prayers, but an impassioned lament arising from desperation. Its frankness reminds us that Christians may suffer dreadful afflictions and that God invites us to open our hearts to him with boldness and candor.

The superscription of Psalm 102 describes it as follows: "A Prayer of one afflicted, when he is faint and pours out his complaint before the Lord." The details are set forth in verses 3–11, as the psalmist vividly depicts his sickness of body and soul.

First, his affliction sets his *mortality* before him, so that he dreads the approaching end of his life: "For my days pass away like smoke, and my bones burn like a furnace" (Ps. 102:3). In the heat of his suffering, his life is withering away and he feels that his bones will soon turn to ashes. Christians will likewise weaken from age and find solace in meditation on this psalm. The psalmist adds, "My heart is struck down like grass and has withered" (v. 4). So grieved is he by his deterioration that he has lost his appetite: "I forget to eat my bread."

Second, the man of affliction feels this mortality because of the intense *sickness* from which he suffers: "Because of my loud groaning my bones cling to my flesh" (Ps. 102:5). He is skin and bones; with his muscles deteriorated, he can only lie and moan. We might think today of a believer who has suffered a stroke or cancer. Laid up in a hospital bed, he feels like a mere shadow of his former self.

Third, he grieves that his sickness has forced him into *isolation*: "I am like a desert owl of the wilderness, like an owl of the waste places; I lie awake; I am like a lonely sparrow on the housetop" (Ps. 102:6–7). One of the great needs of the sick is companionship, which is why family members often take turns keeping vigil with those who are infirm. In ancient times, however, great sickness often required a quarantine, as is sometimes the case today. The psalmist sees himself as a solitary owl out in the wild, hooting in distress, or a sparrow perched alone and frightened. It was out of concern for such isolation that Jesus so praised the ministry of visiting the infirm: "I was sick and you visited me" (Matt. 25:36).

In the Old Testament world, intense sickness was sometimes seen as a divine punishment for sin. One of the worst frustrations that Job experienced was the suggestion from his friends that he must have done something to deserve his awful plight. Such words are little comfort to afflicted believers, which is why Job called his friends "miserable comforters" (Job 16:2). We should be careful to avoid such legalistic statements unless a clear relationship can be traced between the affliction and sin, and even then such words will usually just add to the suffering.

Fourth, in the case of the psalmist, it is his enemies who afflict him with *mocking*: "All the day my enemies taunt me; those who deride me use my name for a curse" (Ps. 102:8). We can think of a Christian who has sought to honor the Lord in an unbelieving family or borne testimony to the gospel in a godless workplace. When affliction comes, how eagerly scoffers taunt her for her misplaced confidence in God. "See what all your sanctity has gotten you!" some will mock. "All this time you have thought that some deity was watching over you," others will say. In stronger days, she had ready answers from Scripture and experience to counter such scoffing. But laid low with sickness, weakened and depressed, she can only suffer their barbs.

Fifth, the psalmist suffers under the suspicion that his mockers may be right. His suffering, isolation, and torment leave him *bewildered* about his relationship with God. Leslie Allen writes that the "cruelest cut is the spiritual implication of his suffering."[1] "For I eat ashes like bread and mingle tears with my drink, because of your indignation and anger," the psalmist

1. Leslie Allen, *Psalms 101–150*, Word Biblical Commentary 21 (Waco, TX: Word, 1983), 14.

prays (Ps. 102:9–10). He feels that God must have rejected him and cast him off: "for you have taken me up and thrown me down" (v. 10). It is as though his former blessings were God's simply lifting him up so as to throw him down all the more violently. In abject misery, his feels his life slipping into darkness and death: "My days are like an evening shadow; I wither away like grass" (v. 11). David Dickson writes: "The sharpest ingredient in the trouble of the godly, is the sense of God's indignation."[2] The psalmist knows that he is a sinner and that God is holy, and concludes his lament by envisioning himself sitting in an ash heap as a man accursed.

A SPIRITUAL UPTURN

So far, the psalmist provides a most pitiful example of a believer who has been overwhelmed by hard circumstances. Starting in verse 12, however, Psalm 102 becomes a crowning example of prayerful optimism. What accounts for this remarkable upturn? The answer is that the psalmist takes his mind off his afflictions and begins pondering what he knows about God: "But you, O LORD, are enthroned forever; you are remembered throughout all generations" (Ps. 102:12).

Psalm 102 reminds us that in the midst of darkness, our hearts will experience light by meditating on God and his glorious attributes. For this reason, the best advice to a downcast believer is a reminder to turn to God's Word. One of the best ministries we can offer to suffering saints is to read Scripture and encourage them with God's promises. Often, a depressed Christian should stop reading books and articles about depression or other ailments and instead read devotional material that highlights the attributes of God. This was the example given by Jonathan, when David was wearied to despair by the malice of evil King Saul. First Samuel 23:16 relates that Jonathan "went to David . . . and strengthened his hand in God." Jonathan lifted David by reminding him of God's promises. We, too, need reminders of who God is and the testimony he has given in his Word as the solace of a downcast soul.

Three great truths about God turned the psalmist around, most prominently the *eternity* of God: "But you, O LORD, are enthroned forever; you are remembered throughout all generations" (Ps. 102:12). James Boice writes:

2. David Dickson, *A Commentary on the Psalms* (1653; repr., Edinburgh: Banner of Truth, 1995), 2:205.

"In the previous verses the psalmist has described his frail and wasting condition. He is like smoke that vanishes. Ah, but he has a God who is not at all like that! He is the eternal, immutable God, and it is God whom he is trusting."[3] The point is not merely that God is immortal but that the promises of his Word cannot fail in light of his eternity. The statement "you are remembered" can be rendered, as John Calvin puts it, "the memorial of thee from generation to generation."[4] The idea is that God has borne testimony to us of his covenant purpose for our salvation. Since he is eternal, that testimony and covenant cannot fail. Calvin consoles us:

> We are like withered grass, we are decaying every moment, we are not far from death, yea rather, we are, as it were, already dwelling in the grave; but since thou, O God! hast made a covenant with us, by which thou hast promised to protect and defend thine own people, and hast brought thyself into a gracious relation to us, giving us the fullest assurance that thou wilt always dwell in the midst of us, instead of desponding, we must be of good courage; and although we may see only ground for despair if we depend on ourselves, we ought nevertheless to lift up our minds to the heavenly throne, from which thou wilt at length stretch forth thy hand to help us.[5]

Joined to the eternity of God is the Lord's *sovereignty*: "But you, O Lord, are enthroned forever" (Ps. 102:12). God is still in control. Since he has decreed all things and has sovereign authority to implement his will, our afflictions are not random or without purpose. It seems that the psalmist was living during the dark times of Israel's Babylonian exile, so that his personal ailment was joined to the nation's tragedy. But God had given assurances of his sovereign purpose even in so great a judgment. He instructed the prophet Jeremiah to send a letter to the exiles with words that lift up suffering believers even today: "For I know the plans I have for you, declares the Lord, plans for welfare and not for evil, to give you a future and a hope" (Jer. 29:11). In our afflictions today, Christians place our hope in the same sovereign and eternal God, so that trials stimulate our prayer lives and strengthen our faith.

A third attribute of God is his *mercy*: "You will arise and have pity on

3. James Montgomery Boice, *Psalms*, 3 vols. (Grand Rapids: Baker, 1996), 2:827.

4. John Calvin, *Calvin's Commentaries*, 23 vols. (1848; repr., Grand Rapids: Baker, 2009), 5:108.

5. Calvin, *Commentaries*, 6:109.

Zion" (Ps. 102:13). The Lord has proved his mercy to believers by sending his Son to bear our sins on the cross. Romans 8:32 reasons: "He who did not spare his own Son but gave him up for us all, how will he not also with him graciously give us all things?" The Father will not permit the atoning work of his Son to have been in vain, and so he will be faithful in his mercy to ensure our eternal salvation.

Psalm 102:13 concludes: "it is the time to favor her; the appointed time has come." Since the psalmist refers to God's pity on Zion, some commentators see this claim as referring to God's revelation that Israel's exile would end after seventy years (Jer. 25:10–11). We usually do not know how long God intends for us to languish, yet we know that in his mercy our affliction has an appointed end, even if in a death that ushers us into eternal blessing.

What a consolation the psalmist received by his reflection on God's character: he is eternal, sovereign, and merciful. How wonderful it is that when we cannot see a purpose for our suffering, we know that God has a purpose not only for his own glory but also guided by mercy for our ultimate good. And since he is eternal and sovereign—"enthroned forever"—his gracious purposes for us are certain to be fulfilled.

A Model Intercessory Prayer

I mentioned that one of the best ministries to the sick is to read Scripture and direct them to sound theology. Another one of the best encouragements we can give the infirm is an exhortation to intercessory prayer. Christians with long illnesses often feel useless, as well as isolated from church life. But while they may not be able to attend worship or participate in church activities, they have an ideal opportunity to engage in the vitally important ministry of prayer.

In Psalm 102:14–22, the psalmist engages in a model prayer of supplication while he waits for his own recovery. His heart has been lifted from the ash heap by the knowledge of God, and now he is freed to devote his solitude to prayer for causes that are dear to his heart.

His first concern is for the church. He has already shown confidence in God's mercy for Zion, and now he appeals for her restoration: "For your servants hold her stones dear and have pity on her dust. . . . For the Lord builds up Zion; he appears in his glory; he regards the prayer of the destitute and does not despise their prayer" (Ps. 102:14–17).

The psalmist sees a parallel between his lowly state and the downcast condition of Jerusalem. Today, there is a great need for Christians to pray for the church, especially since it is so marginalized in Western societies. All Christians should be praying for the faithfulness of the preaching, for the godliness of church leaders, for the people's zeal for holiness, for the conversion of covenant children, and for the church to be strengthened in spirit and in numbers. Christians laid up with illness have a particular opportunity to pray for the church, and their ministry of supplication is of great value. The psalmist assumed the devotion of believers even for the brick and mortar of the temple building: "For your servants hold her stones dear and have pity on her dust" (Ps. 102:14). How well this prayer aligns with Christ's purpose: "I will build my church, and the gates of hell shall not prevail against it" (Matt. 16:18). How valuable, then, are prayers of the infirm for Christ's church!

Second, the psalmist prays for evangelism: "Nations will fear the name of the LORD, and all the kings of the earth will fear your glory" (Ps. 102:15). Remembering God has turned the writer's self-pity into gospel compassion. Indeed, the psalmist treats evangelism as the fruit of God's restoration of the church. It was in the church that most of us heard the good news that brought us salvation. Moreover, as we pray for evangelism, we are led to participate in sharing the gospel. Infirm Christians in hospitals have been granted a golden opportunity to share the gospel with fellow patients and medical workers.

Third, the psalmist prays for future generations: "Let this be recorded for a generation to come, so that a people yet to be created may praise the LORD: that he looked down from his holy height; from heaven the LORD looked at the earth" (Ps. 102:18–19). Far from seeing his sufferings as pointless, he notes the link between his experience and future generations, and he asks God to leave a testimony for later believers. Few motives will so inspire us to prayer and a bold witness than a love for Christian children and grandchildren, with generations that will follow, and a fervent desire for them to be saved.

Fourth, the psalmist prays for the persecuted church: "to hear the groans of the prisoners, to set free those who were doomed to die" (Ps. 102:20). We do not know specifically whom he had in mind, though it may have been Jews languishing in Babylon. Christians should never forget the suffering of our fellow believers around the world, many of them afflicted because of their valor in standing for Christ. In our trials, let us remember those whose suffering is longer and more intense, praying for God to deliver them.

If we were to cite one unifying theme of the psalmist's intercessions, it would be the glory of God in the salvation of his people: "that they may declare in Zion the name of the Lord, and in Jerusalem his praise, when peoples gather together, and kingdoms, to worship the Lord" (Ps. 102:21–22). The psalmist knows that history is going to conclude with saints gathered from every tribe and tongue into the eternal city of God. He is thrilled to realize that among the great praises that will resound from the lips of angels, together with the redeemed, will be a commemoration of the deliverance that he received and the restoration of the church for which he prayed.

An example of the spirit of the psalmist in prayer was given by John Piper during his treatment for prostate cancer in 2006. On the eve of his surgery, Piper wrote a booklet titled *Don't Waste Your Cancer.* In it, he urged fellow sufferers to accept the disease as a gift from God, not a curse, and an opportunity to glorify the Lord through faith. Some of his meditations include these headings: "We waste our cancer if we do not believe it is designed for us by God"; "We waste our cancer if we refuse to think about death"; "We waste our cancer if we spend too much time reading about cancer and not enough time reading about God"; and "We waste our cancer if we refuse to use it as a means of witness to the truth and glory of Christ." Piper concluded: "This will be an opportunity to bear witness. Christ is infinitely worthy. Here is a golden opportunity to show that he is worth more than life. Don't waste it."[6] We can extend Piper's principle to every form of affliction and suffering. Let us not waste the opportunity granted to us by God, but let us use our suffering, even amid fear and anxiety, to bear testimony to our gracious God so that he may be praised in the church and the world.

A Messianic Reprise

In the final stanza, the psalmist makes a reprise of his initial lament. He grieves that his health has been broken in midlife and he will not reach a

6. John Piper, *Don't Waste Your Cancer* (Wheaton, IL: Crossway, 2011), 1–15.

normal lifespan: "He has broken my strength in midcourse; he has shortened my days" (Ps. 102:23). His response is like that of King Hezekiah, who learned from the prophet Isaiah that his life would soon end and began begging for the Lord to grant him an extension (Isa. 38:1–3). Likewise, the psalmist cries: "'O my God,' I say, 'take me not away in the midst of my days'" (Ps. 102:24).

Again, he responds to his anxiety by recalling the eternal nature of God: "you whose years endure throughout all generations!" (Ps. 102:24). In some of the most inspirational poetic lines of the Bible, the psalmist explains his logic. We imagine him rising from his bed of affliction to walk outside and gaze upward at the night sky. As he realizes that God is greater and more enduring than the brightest star, the thought of God's eternity revives his hope. God existed before creation, using his own hands to form the vast universe: "Of old you laid the foundation of the earth, and the heavens are the work of your hands" (v. 25). The universe, enduring as it is, has nonetheless a finite lifespan, so the day will come when the stars burn out and when God rolls up the cosmos like cast-off clothing: "They will perish, but you will remain; they will all wear out like a garment. You will change them like a robe, and they will pass away, but you are the same, and your years have no end" (vv. 26–27). The offshoot of God's eternal nature is his attribute of immutability, so that God's purpose and promises neither can nor will ever fail: "but you are the same, and your years have no end" (v. 27).

The conclusion on which the psalm ends is that God's people enjoy security and peace in the eternal and unchanging Lord: "The children of your servants shall dwell secure; their offspring shall be established before you" (Ps. 102:28). In times of distress, believers worry about what will happen to their children. But the church of all ages dwells securely in the eternal God. Long after the distant galaxies have expired, all of God's promises will still be standing firm. H. C. Leupold writes that "the race of the godly goes on and on. It is not exterminated nor overcome but is rather endlessly established before the Lord."[7] Since God is unchangeable in his nature and purpose, so that even the collapse of the universe cannot alter his person or his plans, the psalmist may rest his heart in peace and with praise to the Lord.

The Christian turns to the New Testament and finds these truths applied not merely to God the Father but particularly to his Son, Jesus Christ. This reminds us that the gospel is neither an afterthought in the plan of God nor

7. H. C. Leupold, *Exposition of the Psalms* (Columbus, OH: Wartburg Press, 1959), 714.

a temporary provision that may someday fail. Hebrews 13:8 declares: "Jesus Christ is the same yesterday and today and forever." Hebrews 7:25 reminds us that because Jesus lives and reigns forever, "he is able to save to the uttermost those who draw near to God through him, since he always lives to make intercession for them."

What is the need of your soul in time or eternity that cannot be met in Christ? Do you need pardon for your sins? See him exalted, bearing the glorified wounds of his dying sacrifice on your behalf. Do you need reconciliation to God? There he is at God's right hand, interceding with mercy for you. Do you need newness of life, with strength to follow him? From the heavenly throne Jesus sends mighty resources, even angels, to your aid. Better yet, he sends the Holy Spirit to work in you with his own power. Do you, like the psalmist, lie on a sickbed, fearing death? Look upward to heaven, where Jesus is reigning, having already conquered the grave in his glorious resurrection. Because his years will have no end, death will have no hold on you. There will never be a moment in all eternity when your all-sufficient Savior will not be reigning to secure for you both life and glory.

The writer of Hebrews applied this truth by urging us never, at any cost, to let go of the gospel: "how shall we escape if we neglect such a great salvation?" (Heb. 2:3). Jesus gave a similar application, reminding us that through faith in his Word we will, like the psalmist, prevail over the worst that life can bring: "Everyone then who hears these words of mine and does them will be like a wise man who built his house on the rock. And the rain fell, and the floods came, and the winds blew and beat on that house, but it did not fall, because it had been founded on the rock" (Matt. 7:24–25).

34

O Bless the Lord!

Psalm 103:1–5

Bless the Lord, O my soul, and all that is within me, bless his holy name! Bless the Lord, O my soul, and forget not all his benefits. (Ps. 103:1–2)

In his book *Disappointment with God*, best-selling author Philip Yancey recalls many letters he had received from Christians who expressed the sentiment of his title. They had believed in God and trusted him, but things didn't work out as they had thought they would. They were disappointed with God. One had suffered his parents' divorce despite praying a thousand times. Another had lost a child. Yet another just wasn't able to be happy, and God didn't seem to care. Instead of praising God, these correspondents doubted him, rejected him, even hated him. Yancey points out that many of these people were disappointed because they had been trusting God for things that he never promised—namely, to preserve them from pain and sorrow in this life. Furthermore, he notes, even when people get what they want, they usually fail to praise and thank God. In plenty and in want, in joy and in sorrow, our souls need help remembering to praise the Lord.

Bless the Lord, O My Soul

David recognized the signs of ingratitude in his own soul. Psalm 103 begins and ends with David exhorting his inner self to praise the Lord: "Bless the Lord, O my soul." In between, he gives reasons why his heart should offer this praise. It is often said today that what we need is heart religion, and surely David would agree. He wants praise to come from his soul, from his inner person. It is not enough for him to praise the Lord with only his feet by coming to church, or with only his mouth by speaking and singing. He knows that God rejects worship that is only outward and when our hearts are far from him (Isa. 29:13).

Yet many people say that what gets in the way of heart religion is head religion, and to this David would have strenuously objected. Certainly, there are people whose faith is a lifeless intellectualism, and that is not true faith at all. But this psalm shows how greatly the heart depends on the mind; the light shining through his believing and instructed mind warms David's otherwise cold and reluctant heart. In this psalm, David *reasons* with his heart. He preaches a sermon to his soul, just as we should frequently do. He presents truths that he expects will cause his heart to rise in fervent praise of God.

It is hard to overestimate the importance of having a heart that praises the Lord. David knew that his own spiritual life grew strong through an attitude of praise to God. He knew that hardness of heart is what caused Israel to betray the Lord. With this in mind, David implores, as should we: "Bless the Lord, O my soul, and all that is within me, bless his holy name" (Ps. 103:1).

Forget Not His Benefits

Psalm 103 breaks into three sections, in each of which David seeks to gain praise to God from his heart. Verses 1–5 speak of gratitude to God for his blessings; verses 6–14 speak of love to God in response to his love for us; and verses 15–22 conclude with awe for God's greatness and glory.

David stirs his heart to gratitude by making it remember all that God has done for him: "Bless the Lord, O my soul, and forget not all his benefits" (Ps. 103:2). If the question is how to praise the Lord, David's first answer is that praise happens when the heart gratefully remembers God's blessings in our salvation. True gratitude is one of the most powerful of all motivations; it is thanksgiving that causes us to live in praise of God. Therefore, the words of verse 2 ought to be frequently placed before every Christian's heart. Our problem is that we do forget; yet only the believer who has a fresh appreciation of what God has done in Jesus Christ is glad and longs to glorify the Lord. To this end, David calls to mind a catalogue of the benefits for which he is thankful, counting his blessings in a chain of God's grace.

It is significant that the first benefit to remember is forgiveness of sin: "Bless the LORD, . . . who forgives all your iniquity" (Ps. 103:2–3). There are so many things for which we ought to praise the Lord—our homes, jobs, wealth, and health. But none of these compare to the forgiveness of our sins! What is all the world if we should lose our souls (Luke 9:35)? If the psalm came to an end in verse 3, we would have ample reason to praise the Lord for eternity, for we can be forgiven only because he gave his Son to be punished on the cross in our place.

The primacy of forgiveness means that only those who remember their sins will really praise the Lord with thanksgiving. It is only when we realize the magnitude of our guilt and the high offense we have caused against God's holy justice by our sin that God's grace seems so wonderful to our hearts and causes us to praise him. This is one reason we should regularly confess our sins: to lead us to gratitude for God's forgiving mercy. If we are disappointed with God, it is certain that we have forgotten what we really deserve from him, namely, condemnation and wrath. But when we remember that God has forgiven us at so great a cost to himself—the sacrifice of his own beloved Son—it is implausible for us to speak of disappointment with God.

As great as forgiveness is, it is just the beginning of the benefits that Christians enjoy. If you are a recent convert, flush with the release of sins forgiven, David goes on to describe more benefits that you can anticipate with joy. If you have been a Christian for some time, then these are blessings with which you should be increasingly familiar.

With forgiveness, David pairs healing: "who forgives all your iniquity, and heals all your diseases" (Ps. 103:3). Since David is addressing his soul, we should think of this mainly as spiritual healing. Sin causes not only guilt that needs to be forgiven but also an inner corruption that needs to be sanctified. This is what Augustus Toplady expressed in the great line from his hymn "Rock of Ages": "Be of sin the double cure, cleanse me from its guilt and pow'r."[1]

So many of Jesus' miracles involved cleansing and healing. We think especially of our Savior's healing lepers from their uncleanness. This is a picture of what Christians experience in salvation: a progressive and powerful cleansing of our thoughts, attitudes, and desires. What a cause for grateful praise! We are being made whole! Light is casting out darkness! In the end, *all* our diseases, body and soul, will be healed. What else can we say but "Bless the LORD, O my soul!"

To this David adds a third benefit, namely, his deliverance from the power of sin: "Who redeems your life from the pit" (Ps. 103:4). We see such deliverance in the life of John Newton, who was for many years given over to sin as a brutal slave trader. During a voyage home to England, his ship was caught in a savage storm. Terrified, Newton worked a pump in the darkness of his ship's hold for hours on end over several days. In that pit, his mind laid hold of Bible verses that his godly mother had taught him as a boy. He cried to God to save him, and the Lord delivered him not only from the peril of that storm but also from the dark pit of his vile life. Newton's gratitude to God came through in his best-known hymn:

> Amazing grace—how sweet the sound—that saved a wretch like me!
> I once was lost, but now am found, was blind, but now I see.[2]

Forgiveness speaks of pardon from sin's guilt; healing speaks of cleansing from sin's corrupting power; redemption tells of deliverance from the misery into which sin has cast us. For some, the deliverance is from the bondage of an addiction or from a lifestyle of gross sin. For others, it is from abuse, persecution, or illness that God delivered us to safety. Or we have known the more subtle slaveries of anger, greed, lust, or pride, and God redeemed us from these pits. Ultimately, David's reference is to the pit of death. Here is an enemy that we all will face, but God will redeem our lives from the grave and join us to Christ's resurrection. Bless the Lord, O my soul!

Redemption, too, is coupled with a corresponding blessing: "who crowns you with steadfast love and mercy" (Ps. 103:4). We don't often think of being

1. Augustus M. Toplady, "Rock of Ages, Cleft for Me" (1776).
2. John Newton, "Amazing Grace!" (1779).

crowned. The idea is the bestowing of dignity and honor. Far better than the gold that crowns earthly kings are the love and mercy that God gives to us; these are jewels that shine more brightly than diamonds or emeralds. David puts these blessings together to show that while sin has dragged us to the pit, salvation elevates us to the highest honors as children and heirs of God.

Jesus depicted an amazing coronation in his parable of the prodigal son. Having scorned his father and wasted his money, the prodigal found himself in the greatest misery. So low had he sunk that he had to share the food of the pigs that he had been hired to tend. What a vivid picture of the life of sin and how it ends! Finally, the wayward son came to his senses and decided to go home. Having cast away his sonship, he longed simply to return to his father's house as a servant. But in the prodigal son's return Jesus presents a matchless description of our heavenly Father's redeeming and crowning grace: "the father said to his servants, 'Bring quickly the best robe, and put it on him, and put a ring on his hand, and shoes on his feet. . . . For this my son was dead, and is alive again; he was lost, and is found'" (Luke 15:22–24). In the father's house, the best robe signifies our imputed righteousness in Christ; the ring is a symbol of honor and authority, such as Joseph received as Pharaoh's deputy; and the shoes speak of sonship in a world where slaves walked barefoot. Like the prodigal, we, too, have suffered misery because of sin and have merited rejection, but when we return to God, he crowns us with steadfast love and mercy. Bless the Lord, O my soul!

Psalm 103:5 completes David's catalogue of saving benefits: "who satisfies you with good so that your youth is renewed like the eagle's." *Satisfaction* is a word that we seldom hear today. The Rolling Stones spoke for our age when they sang, "I can't get no satisfaction." We are a people so satiated with pleasure, much of it sinful, yet we are so dissatisfied. We have all that we want and very little of what we need.

God offers not satiation but satisfaction: He "satisfies your desires," David exults (NIV). We remember that David is addressing his soul; it is the soul that God satisfies, as only he can. Psalm 37:4 declares, "Delight yourself in the LORD, and he will give you the desires of your heart." What good news to a generation like ours! If you walk with God in faith, he will satisfy your soul! Jesus said to the Samaritan woman: "whoever drinks of the water that I will give him will never be thirsty again. The water that I will give him will become in him a spring of water welling up to eternal life" (John 4:14). "Sir," the woman replied, "give me this water" (v. 15). God will give eternal life that satisfies the soul to all who repent of their sins and come to him in faith.

This blessing does not mean that Christians will never experience hardship, sickness, poverty, or pain, or that all our worldly wants will be instantly fulfilled. Jesus said, "If anyone would come after me, let him deny himself and take up his cross daily and follow me" (Luke 9:23). But he also promised, "Truly, I say to you, there is no one who has left house or wife or brothers or parents or children, for the sake of the kingdom of God, who will not receive many times more in this time, and in the age to come eternal life" (18:29–30). Bless the Lord, O my soul!

Finally, David says that our youth will be "renewed like the eagle's" (Ps. 103:5). This is similar to what Paul states about the Christian's inward rejuvenation: "Though our outer self is wasting away, our inner nature is being renewed day by day" (2 Cor. 4:16). The eagle is a symbol of strength and vigor, and God gives these sustaining virtues to the trusting soul.

This promise is especially fulfilled in the life beyond death. The nineteenth-century preacher Dr. Edward Payson, dying in the midst of great pain, gave a testimony to which every Christian has a right: "I know that my happiness is but begun. It will last forever. . . . It seems as if my soul had found a pair of new wings and is so eager to try them."[3] Isaiah likewise said that "they who wait for the Lord shall renew their strength; they shall mount up with wings like eagles; they shall run and not be weary; they shall walk and not faint" (Isa. 40:31). With this hope, David completes his chain of benefits for which his soul should praise the Lord.

Remembering God's benefits is the first way in which we learn to praise the Lord. This principle is illustrated by something that happened shortly after the end of the American Civil War. A man in farm clothes was seen kneeling at a gravestone in the soldiers' cemetery in Nashville. An observer came up and asked, "Is that the grave of your son?" The farmer replied, "No, I have seven children, all of them young, and a wife on my poor farm in Illinois. I was drafted and, despite the great hardship it would cause, I was required to join the Army. But on the morning I was to depart this man,

3. Quoted in Murdoch Campbell, *From Grace to Glory: Meditations on the Book of Psalms* (Edinburgh: Banner of Truth, 1970), 154.

my neighbor's older son, came over and offered to take my place in the war." The observer solemnly asked, "What is that you are writing on his grave?" The farmer replied, "I am writing, 'He died for me.'"

If this is how a man naturally feels for the son of his fellow man who died in his place, holding his name precious all the days of his life, how much more ought our gratitude to prompt our hearts to praise the Lord? God's own Son came down from heaven and took up our flesh. He lived and toiled for us. He entered the battle of sin on our behalf, though he himself was exempt from it. He died in our place, suffering the wrath of God that we might be forgiven. Not only that, Jesus rose from the grave to crown us with all the blessings of heaven, to give us a future in glory and a place in the renewal of all things. Do you believe this? If you do, you surely ought to plead, "Bless the Lord, O my soul, and forget not all his benefits" (Ps. 103:2).

The Grateful Life That Pleases God

In responding to David's plea, "Bless the Lord, O my soul" (Ps. 103:1), I have been translating *bless* as "praise," and this is its main meaning in context. But another idea is involved with the word *bless*: to *please* or *minister to* the one we want to bless. Of course, this idea is linked with praise. David wants his soul to praise the Lord, and he also wants his soul to please the Lord. The two necessarily go together. Indeed, if we really want to praise the Lord, it is not going to happen merely by coming to church and singing and sitting for an hour or so, but by living in a way that is inspired by God's grace and is offered up for his pleasure. Gratitude for God's blessings not only causes our hearts to *praise* the Lord, but also motivates us to *please* the Lord in the manner of our living.

Most Christians want to live in a godly way so as to please the Lord. But the question is how to gain the necessary influence over our hearts—over our desires, passions, and affections. One important answer is given here in the opening section of Psalm 103: by facing the reality of our *guilt* before God, by perceiving in faith the great gift of God's *grace*, and then by responding to him with a *gratitude* that wants to bless the Lord. Guilt, grace, and gratitude mark the progress of the heart that wants to bless and please the Lord.

In the prayer that he taught to his disciples, Jesus emphasized that having been forgiven of our sins, we best please the Lord by forgiving others of their sins against us: "and forgive us our debts, as we also have forgiven our debtors" (Matt. 6:12). One of the most important responses, then, to God's grace in our lives is to extend that same grace toward others by forgiving their sins.

In an earlier chapter, I mentioned the experience of Corrie ten Boom, who experienced the amazing protection and care of God during her years in a Nazi concentration camp. Through terrible suffering, her soul learned to bless the Lord, just as David's did in this psalm. In a remarkable intervention that Corrie ascribed to God, she was delivered through an administrative error that released her from prison shortly before her certain execution. But after the war, Corrie admitted to struggling with anger and bitterness. She wrote a vilifying letter to the man who had informed on her family to the Nazis, causing so much torment and leading to the death of her immediate family members, and denounced him for his betrayal. But she also found grace to tell him how God had helped her and that he could be saved through repentance and faith in Christ. She concluded the letter by writing that God was helping her to forgive him and that she would pray for his salvation. Days later, the man was executed for his crimes by the Dutch authorities.

In the years after the war, Corrie began traveling to tell her story of God's faithfulness. In her public addresses, she stressed God's love and his grace in saving those without hope. She founded a home for people who had suffered during the war, a dream of her dying sister, Betsie, as well as a camp for former prisoners and refugees. Because of her remarkable experiences and powerful message, she began to write books and as a result came into demand as a speaker. All these actions were a fitting way of blessing the Lord.

Yet a defining moment awaited Corrie after one occasion when she had shared the gospel. Here is how she tells the story:

> It was at a church service in Munich that I saw him, the former S.S. man who had stood guard at the shower room door in the processing center at Ravensbruck. He was the first of our actual jailers that I had seen since that time. And suddenly it was all there—the roomful of mocking men, the heaps of clothing, Betsie's pain-blanched face.
>
> He came up to me as the church was emptying, beaming and bowing, "How grateful I am for your message, *Fraulein*." He said, "To think that, as you say, He has washed my sins away!"
>
> His hand was thrust out to shake mine. And I, who had preached so often . . . the need to forgive, kept my hand at my side.

> Even as the angry, vengeful thoughts boiled through me, I saw the sin of them. Jesus Christ had died for this man; was I going to ask for more? Lord Jesus, I prayed, forgive me and help me to forgive him.
>
> I tried to smile, I struggled to raise my hand. I could not. I felt nothing, not the slightest spark of warmth or charity. And so again I breathed a silent prayer. Jesus, I cannot forgive him. Give me Your forgiveness.
>
> As I took his hand the most incredible thing happened. From my shoulder along my arm and through my hand a current seemed to pass from me to him, while into my heart sprang a love for this stranger that almost overwhelmed me.[4]

For a long moment they grasped each other's hands, the former guard and the former prisoner, the former tormentor and the former victim. How can you explain this? Corrie later did, quoting her sister's dying words: "There is no pit so deep that He is not deeper still."[5]

"Bless the Lord, O my soul," David writes, as a man who had been in the deepest pit, "and forget not all his benefits" (Ps. 103:2). This appeal is not just for famous or special Christians. It is for all of us. It is for you. Corrie ten Boom remembered all that God had done for her, and it changed her heart. Like her, we can look at this catalogue of blessings that David writes about in Psalm 103, and we can be grateful for what God has done and is doing for us. He heals our souls; he redeems us from the pits into which our sin and the sins of others have cast us. He crowns us with mercy and love, he satisfies our souls with spiritual delights, and he promises an eternity in glory, our youth renewed like the eagle's. But most of all—and surely it was remembering this that most enabled Corrie ten Boom to forgive a man who had tormented her so—God has forgiven our sins at so great a cost to himself.

We need to remember these things. We need to meditate on these verses and pray for God to fill our hearts with gratitude and praise. And if we do that, surely there will be a difference in our lives. Surely we will long to bless the Lord, who has blessed us so in Christ, and it will change the way that we think, speak, and act. "Bless the Lord, O my soul, and all that is within me, bless his holy name!" (Ps. 103:1).

4. Corrie ten Boom, *The Hiding Place* (Grand Rapids: Baker, 1984), 247–48.
5. Ten Boom, *Hiding Place*, 227.

35

How to Worship the Lord

Psalm 103:6–22

The Lord *is merciful and gracious, slow to anger and abounding in steadfast love.* (Ps. 103:8)

In the previous chapter, we looked at the first portion of Psalm 103, in which King David seeks to motivate his heart to praise: "Bless the Lord, O my soul" (Ps. 103:1–2). In verses 2–5, we saw the powerful role of gratitude in spurring praise to God. "Forget not all his benefits," David argues, and he follows up with an impressive recounting of the blessings for which every Christian should gratefully praise the Lord: forgiveness, healing, redemption, crowning, satisfaction, and renewal. If we really want to live for the glory of God, then we will exercise our hearts with this kind of remembering; we will read and meditate and pray with the goal of becoming increasingly grateful for all that God has done for us.

The remainder of Psalm 103 focuses on two other motivations to live in praise of God: love for him and awe for his greatness and majesty. To be balanced in our spiritual life, we need both of these: to love him and to fear him. Jerry Bridges writes: "To seek to grow in the fear of God . . . without also growing in our comprehension of His love can cause us to begin to view God as far-off and austere. Or to seek to grow in our awareness of the love of God without also growing in our reverence and awe of Him can cause us to view God as a permissive and indulgent heavenly Father who does not deal with our sin."[1] By this standard, David strikes a perfect balance in Psalm 103:6–22, presenting his soul with ample reasons both to love God and to hold him in fearful awe.

Love for the Love of God

First, let's consider David's marvelous depiction of God's love for us in salvation (Ps. 103:6–14), a picture that is calculated to cause his heart and our hearts to respond with love for God.

Psalm 103:8 is the key to this section: "The Lord is merciful and gracious, slow to anger and abounding in steadfast love." As Paul would later be prone to do, David draws together various words to lift our hearts in praise. These are the glories of God's love from which our whole salvation flows: from mercy we gain pardon; from grace we gain favor; from long-suffering we gain his patience; and from steadfast love we receive God's bountiful kindness. If only David's heart can realize the great, compassionate love of God, to see how beautiful and precious is his loving-kindness, his heart will surely respond with love for God in return. In verses 6–14, David develops his case for God's love: first, he *proves* God's love; then he *displays* God's love; third, he *measures* God's love; and finally, he *illustrates* God's love.

We remember that David was writing ten centuries before Christ, and in his day the great episode of salvation was the exodus of Israel. David therefore turns to this event as a sure *proof* of God's love: "The Lord works righteousness and justice for all who are oppressed. He made known his ways to Moses, his acts to the people of Israel" (Ps. 103:6–7). In the exodus, God provided justice for his people by breaking the bonds of their captivity and leading them in freedom to the promised land. More importantly, God provided a way of righteousness for his people, through the blood sacrifices that pointed forward to the cross of Jesus Christ. Through the exodus deliverance, God proved to David and his people how much he loved them. This is what Moses himself stressed in Deuteronomy 7:7–8:

> It was not because you were more in number than any other people that the Lord set his love on you and chose you, for you were the fewest of all peoples, but it is because the Lord loves you and is keeping the oath that

1. Jerry Bridges, *The Practice of Godliness* (Colorado Springs: NavPress, 1996), 47.

> he swore to your fathers, that the Lord has brought you out with a mighty hand and redeemed you from the house of slavery, from the hand of Pharaoh king of Egypt.

The exodus proved God's love for his people, and it called for their love to him in return. Deuteronomy 6:5 says—and Jesus referred to this as the chief command of the whole Old Testament—"You shall love the Lord your God with all your heart and with all your soul and with all your might."

If David looked back in his time to the exodus and saw there a great proof of God's love, what must Christians say about the cross of Christ? Surely this is the greatest of all proofs of God's love for a wayward world. The Puritan Jeremiah Burroughs wrote:

> Behold the infinite love of God to mankind and the love of Jesus Christ that, rather than God see the children of men to perish eternally, would send His Son to take our nature upon Him and thus suffer such dreadful things. Herein God shows His love; . . . it pleased the Father to break His Son and to pour out His blood. Here is the love of God and of Jesus Christ. Oh, what a powerful, mighty, drawing, efficacious meditation this should be to us![2]

Burroughs's enthusiasm for the cross extends David's own line of reasoning, and if we will realize what Paul asserts in Romans 5:8, we will never doubt God's love for us, even in the midst of the greatest trials of life. There, Paul likewise points to the cross, proclaiming that God proved his love for us "in that while we were still sinners, Christ died for us." How can you doubt the love of someone who dies in your place? This is what God has done for you in the person of his Son, Jesus Christ, so that, among other reasons, you might love him in return.

Psalm 103:9–10 goes on to tell us that God's love is put on its greatest *display* in how he reacts to our sin: "He will not always chide, nor will he keep his anger forever. He does not deal with us according to our sins, nor repay us according to our iniquities." The very fact that God placed us on this green earth, causing the sun to shine and the rain to fall, proves his love for us. But the greatest display of his love is seen in his response to our sin. On the one hand, God is angry when we sin, and he seeks to bring our hearts to conviction. But God does not berate us constantly, nor does he

2. Jeremiah Burroughs, *Gospel Worship* (1648; repr., Morgan, PA: Soli Deo Gloria, 1990), 353.

harbor grudges. If he responded only in holy justice, then God would eradicate us upon commission of our first sin. But "he does not deal with us according to our sins." This points to another principle acting in God: his love for us. Isn't it wonderful to know that God will not harbor resentment toward you for your sins? Awareness of their sins overly depresses many Christians because they assume that God will turn against them permanently. But without making light of our sins themselves, they should cause us to praise God because of his love, which is not overcome even by our transgressions. What a display of love this is: "He does not . . . repay us according to our iniquities." Bless the Lord, O my soul!

Verses 11 and 12 of Psalm 103 are among the most beloved in all the Psalms, presenting the measureless *measure* of God's love. Verse 11 declares, "For as high as the heavens are above the earth, so great is his steadfast love toward those who fear him." God's love is infinite—beyond measure or calculation. There was a famous incident many years ago when the first Russian cosmonaut broke through into space. Being an atheist, he mocked to all the world, "I have entered heaven, but I don't see any God here." In light of this verse, he should have cried, "Having entered into space, I see that there is an infinite distance to the heavens. As high as this measure is, the infinite span of heaven, God's love is even greater for those who trust him! Bless the Lord, O my soul!"

Psalm 103:12 applies this measure directly to the crucial matter of forgiveness: "as far as the east is from the west, so far does he remove our transgressions from us." This is a question that comes to our minds—to what extent can I really be forgiven? We realize how difficult it is for us to forgive the things that others have done to us, and we suspect that the same is true for God. But here is God's answer. The east is the farthest thing from the west, infinitely and absolutely and categorically distant. So far has God removed our sins in Christ. This is the measure of God's love for his people.

This utter removal of guilt was dramatized in Old Testament Israel by one of the rites on the Day of Atonement, the one day of the year when the whole nation came to God to be forgiven, as explained in Leviticus 16. The high priest took two goats, one of which was sacrificed, symbolizing the blood of Christ to atone for our sins. The other was called the *scapegoat*. On this goat the priest laid his hands, symbolically placing on it the sins of all the people.

The scapegoat was then led out to a distant place where it was released and disappeared from the people's sight forever. Whereas the goat that was killed symbolized Christ's atoning blood, the scapegoat symbolized what then happened to our sins: "as far as the east is from the west, so far does he remove our transgressions from us" (Ps. 103:12).

When you confess your sins and come to God for cleansing through Jesus Christ, you will never hear about those sins from him again. God will not bring them up years from now, for they are gone. They will not hang over your head and embitter your relationship with him, in the way that so many human relationships are sadly embittered by unforgiven sins. As soon as our sins are confessed and forgiven, they no longer stand in the way of God's love. As he promises in Hebrews 8:12: "I will be merciful toward their iniquities, and I will remember their sins no more."

When we think of the measure of God's love, we naturally think of the distance measured by the spread of Jesus' arms on the cross. J. I. Packer comments:

> The measure of love is how much it gives, and the measure of the love of God is the gift of His only Son to be made man, and to die for sins, and so to become the one mediator who can bring us to God. No wonder Paul speaks of God's love as "great", and passing knowledge! (Eph. 2:4; 3:19). Was there ever such costly munificence?[3]

BLESS THE LORD, O MY SOUL

Verses 13–14 of Psalm 103 complete David's presentation with an *illustration* of God's love: "As a father shows compassion to his children, so the LORD shows compassion to those who fear him. For he knows our frame; he remembers that we are dust." Fathers feel for their children by an inner drive of love, as Jesus immortalized in the parable of the prodigal son. Henry Lyte's great hymn on our text says:

> Fatherlike, he tends and spares us; well our feeble frame he knows;
> In his hands he gently bears us, rescues us from all our foes.[4]

3. J. I. Packer, *Knowing God* (Downers Grove, IL: InterVarsity Press, 1979), 114.
4. Henry F. Lyte, "Praise, My Soul, the King of Heaven" (1834).

Because of this love that David has proved, displayed, measured, and illustrated, our hearts should cry out to bless the Lord with love for him in return. In the previous chapter, I mentioned Philip Yancey's book *Disappointment with God.* There, Yancey reveals that when he was just a baby, his father died of polio. He grew up without a dad and never really felt a father's love. Years later, Yancey found at his mother's house a crumpled photo of himself as a baby. He asked her why she had held on to such a mangled picture when she had other good ones. She explained that this was the photo that she had wedged inside the iron lung that encased his father during his dying weeks. She told him of how his father had spent his last months gazing on him, praying for his upbringing, delighting in just a picture of the infant boy. Yancey writes, "Someone I have no memory of . . . spent all day every day thinking of me, devoting himself to me, loving me as well as he could."[5] This is how a father loves, and it is but an illustration of the great love for us that fills our heavenly Father's heart. Bless the Lord, O my soul!

Let me apply this message to anyone who has never come to God for salvation. If you have refused to believe and trust in God, this is the love you are rejecting. It is the love of a father, for which all of us yearn. In this life we know only an imperfect love from our human fathers, but God is the perfect Father for whom we all have longed.

These verses on God's love speak not only to those who have rejected God, but especially to so many of us who feel rejected by him. The apostle John, in his first epistle, makes some powerful statements on this theme. He states, in 1 John 3:20, that "whenever our heart condemns us, God is greater than our heart." His point is that we need to silence our inward sense of guilt and unworthiness with God's overwhelming testimony of love, which is greater than the testimony of our burdened conscience.

We are all trained to seek love by trying to make ourselves lovely or lovable. If we want to be loved—and we do—then in our world we have to earn it. The result is a performance mentality that offers no real peace or lasting joy, for the simple reason that we are always aware of how unlovable we really are. "How can God really love me?" we secretly wonder. But the Bible teaches that God loves us because of a vast love within himself. "God is love," John says (1 John 4:8). "In this the love of God was made manifest

5. Philip Yancey, *Disappointment with God* (Grand Rapids: Zondervan, 1988), 255.

among us, that God sent his only Son into the world, so that we might live through him. In this is love, not that we have loved God but that he loved us and sent his Son to be the propitiation for our sins" (vv. 9–10). Therefore, he adds that "we know and rely on the love God has for us" (v. 16 NIV). "There is no fear in love, but perfect love casts out fear" (v. 18). And finally, "We love because he first loved us" (v. 19). Our hope for love does not have to rest on something lovable in us, but instead may rest securely on the great, conquering love that is in God. The only thing for us to do is to love God in return. Bless the Lord, O my soul!

If you want to love God, to really learn to love him as you should, then you must start by learning and believing how great is his love for you in Jesus Christ. When this happens, you will show your love for God by thinking about him, by reading and obeying his love letter that is the Bible, by serving him, and by holding a special love for all believers, knowing that they are also beloved of the Lord.

Awe for God's Greatness and Glory

How should we praise the Lord? First, there is gratitude for blessings received (Ps. 103:1–5). Second, there is adoring love in response to God's perfect love for us (vv. 6–14). Third, David worships God in awe for his greatness and glory (vv. 15–19).

In Psalm 103:15–16, David shows that praise for men is misplaced, for in all that man lacks, God abounds in greatness: "As for man, his days are like grass; he flourishes like a flower of the field; for the wind passes over it, and it is gone, and its place knows it no more." We are finite, but God is infinite; his love has no beginning and no end. God loved his people before we were created, and his faithful love, unchanging and unchangeable, endures forever. David declares, "The steadfast love of the LORD is from everlasting to everlasting on those who fear him, and his righteousness to children's children, to those who keep his covenant and remember to do his commandments" (vv. 17–18). This eternal love is cause to praise the Lord, as the hymnist says:

> Frail as summer's flow'r we flourish, blows the wind and it is gone;
> But while mortals rise and perish, God endures unchanging on.

> Praise him, praise him, praise him, praise him, praise the High
> Eternal One.[6]

Finally, David exclaims, "The LORD has established his throne in the heavens, and his kingdom rules over all" (Ps. 103:19). The very throne of heaven is established by his hand. Stephen Charnock writes, "It is fixed, not tottering; it is an unmovable dominion; all the strugglings of men and devils cannot overturn it, not so much as shake it. . . . His dominion, as himself, abides forever. And as his counsel, so his authority, shall stand; and 'he will do all his pleasure' (Isa. 46:10)."[7]

This awe before God in his greatness may be the one thing above all else that we most greatly need to recover today. Yes, we need gratitude to God for the benefits of salvation—it is hard to place anything ahead of that. And we need to lovingly adore God in response to his fatherly love for us. But isn't this what we have most lost today—a sense of the grandeur, glory, and greatness of God? Isn't this why so many Christians are bored with God? We have forgotten his benefits, so he disappoints us. We have trivialized his love, so our hearts are untouched. But surely our greatest need today, both as individual Christians and as a church, is to recover a sense of wonder and awe, to see God as he is, as David does in this psalm, enthroned on high and reigning over all in his awesome majesty. Bridges writes:

> In our day we must begin to recover a sense of awe and profound reverence for God. We must begin to view him once again in the infinite majesty that alone belongs to Him who is the Creator and Supreme Ruler of the entire universe. There is an infinite gap in worth and dignity between God the Creator and man the creature, even though man has been created in the image of God. The fear of God is a heartfelt recognition of this gap—not a putdown of man, but an exaltation of God.[8]

What a difference this reverent attitude would make for us! Think of how it would transform our devotional lives—instead of looking to get "a little something" to help us through the day, we would come to the awesome God simply for worship and to learn of him for his own sake. Think how it would

6. Lyte, "Praise, My Soul, the King of Heaven."

7. Stephen Charnock, quoted in Charles Haddon Spurgeon, *The Treasury of David*, 3 vols. (Peabody, MA: Hendrickson, n.d.), 2:295.

8. Bridges, *Practice of Godliness*, 21.

transform our attitude in gathered worship—instead of looking to leave church feeling good about ourselves, we would make it our chief end to please God according to his Word and to give glory to his name. Think of how it would transform our attitude to the whole of our lives, in both the simplest and the greatest tasks we perform. To see God as holy and great will make us holy in all that we do, and we will make his pleasure the chief yardstick by which we measure everything.

Let Everybody Praise the Lord

Psalm 103 concludes with an observation. David shows us that the heart that praises God seeks companions for worship. Those who praise the Lord want others to praise him, too. David searches high and low, calling out for all to praise the Lord:

> Bless the Lord, O you his angels,
> you mighty ones who do his word,
> obeying the voice of his word!
> Bless the Lord, all his hosts,
> his ministers, who do his will!
> Bless the Lord, all his works,
> in all places of his dominion. (Ps. 103:20–22)

This shows the link between worship and witness. If our hearts are gripped by the gospel, are inspired by gratitude, love, and awe, then we will tell others about it. We will speak of salvation's blessings, of God's great forgiving love, of his majesty that is high above all earthly glory. And we will desire above all else to be present where God is truly praised, saying, as David does in conclusion, "Bless the Lord, O my soul" (Ps. 103:22).

Let me add a question to David's exclamation: Do you go to God's house with a heart desire to praise the Lord? Or is it with just your hands, feet, and lips that you praise him? Do you go through the motions while your mind and especially your heart are far from God? It is so easy to slip into a spiritual slumber; we all know what this is like. But Psalm 103:17 says that "the steadfast love of the Lord is . . . on those who fear him." David is talking about those who glorify God in awe for thought of his majesty, who place him first in the order of all things. Does this describe you?

A lukewarm spirituality is as dangerous today as it was in biblical times. Jesus gave a stern warning to the Laodiceans in Revelation 3:16: "because you are lukewarm, and neither hot nor cold, I will spit you out of my mouth." With this warning in mind, we, like David, need to lay hold of God's Word and apply it to our hearts so that we really praise the Lord. We need to count our blessings in Christ with thanksgiving, we need to look in love to God for his boundless love for us, and we need to kneel before him in awe as the great God and Lord of all. If you do these things, then by God's grace your heart will surely respond in the way that David's did, exclaiming, "Bless the Lord, O my soul, and all that is within me, bless his holy name!" (Ps. 103:1).

36

God's Glorious Works

Psalm 104

O Lord, how manifold are your works! In wisdom have you made them all. (Ps. 104:24)

The great American Puritan Jonathan Edwards was converted to saving faith in Christ at the age of seventeen. He later described a "new sense of things" that filled his heart, a "sense of divine things," so that he wanted to glorify and enjoy God fully. This conversion centered on a personal apprehension, in Edwards's words, "of Christ, and the work of redemption, and the glorious way of salvation by him." For Edwards, his personal faith in Christ made all things new, especially the works of God's creation that surrounded him. He later recalled that

> there seemed to be, as it were, a calm, sweet cast, or appearance of divine glory, in almost every thing. God's excellency, his wisdom, his purity and love, seemed to appear in every thing; in the sun, moon, and stars; in the clouds, and blue sky; in the grass, flowers, trees; in the water, and all nature which used greatly to fix my mind. I often used to sit and view the moon for continuance; and in the day, spent much time in viewing the clouds and sky, to behold the sweet glory of God in these things; in the mean time, singing forth, with a low voice my contemplations of the Creator and Redeemer.[1]

1. Quoted in Iain H. Murray, *Jonathan Edwards: A New Biography* (Edinburgh: Banner of Truth, 1987), 35–36.

Edwards's experience, with his desire to glorify God for his works of creation, illustrates the motivation of Psalm 104. This is a companion to Psalm 103, which praises the Lord for his works of redemption. Both psalms begin with the plea: "Bless the LORD, O my soul." Taken together, the twin psalms teach us, in the words of David Dickson, that:

> The Lord is to be praised by his children, not only for benefits bestowed upon them, but also for his own glorious majesty and greatness; not only is he to be praised for the works of redemption and grace to his elect children, but also for the works of creation and what he hath bestowed upon his creatures.[2]

Psalm 104 praises God for the marvel and wisdom of his works (Ps. 104:24). Answer 8 of the Westminster Shorter Catechism categorizes God's works into "the works of creation and providence." Along these lines, the psalmist praises the Lord in Psalm 104 for creating and governing the world with remarkable wisdom.

This praise psalm loosely follows the progression of events in the first week of creation, describing how each realm of creation brings glory to the Lord. The result is considered a rare masterpiece of sacred poetry. Yet the psalmist's study has not only the creation itself exclusively in view, but especially the glorious wisdom of the Creator. J. J. Stewart Perowne thus describes the psalm as "a bright and living picture of God's creative power, pouring life and gladness throughout the universe."[3]

God's Glorious Creation

The first two days of creation show God saying, "Let there be light" (Gen. 1:3), and then separating the skies above the earth (vv. 6–8). Looking on this realm of the air, the psalmist praises the Lord for his glory: "Bless the LORD, O my soul! O LORD my God, you are very great! You are clothed with splendor and majesty, covering yourself with light as with a garment" (Ps. 104:1–2). The idea of God's clothing himself with light makes the point that though

2. David Dickson, *A Commentary on the Psalms* (1653; repr., Edinburgh: Banner of Truth, 1995), 2:224.

3. J. J. Stewart Perowne, *The Book of Psalms*, 2 vols. (1878; repr., Grand Rapids: Zondervan, 1976), 2:232.

God is invisible in his nature, he makes himself known by his creation. God reveals himself by his works, which he puts on like a robe. John Calvin writes that "as he irradiates the whole world by his splendor, this is the garment in which He, who is hidden in himself, appears in a manner visible to us."[4]

Moreover, the Lord "stretch[es] out the heavens like a tent" (Ps. 104:2). Here, we see the idea that God takes up his dwelling with his creation, stretching out the heavens like a tent over his head. The world is therefore alive with the presence and power of its Maker. "He lays the beams of his chambers on the waters" (v. 3), by which the psalmist envisions the tabernacle of the skies resting securely on the pillars of the horizon.

The heavenly King also possesses royal transport, making "the clouds his chariot; he rides on the wings of the wind" (Ps. 104:3). On Mount Sinai and in the dedication of Solomon's temple, the Lord appeared in his radiant glory cloud. Gazing on the cotton-ball clouds rolling through the skies, the psalmist thus thinks of God's sovereign effects on the earth: "he drives about the winds and clouds at his pleasure, . . . sending them hither and thither as swiftly as he pleases."[5]

Psalm 104:4 seems to make a similar point, saying that the Lord "makes his messengers winds," except that the quotation of this verse in Hebrews 1:7 shows that it refers to angels. The angels belong with the heavenly objects of this opening section. "His ministers a flaming fire" (Ps. 104:4) likely means the *seraphim*, a title that refers to the holiness of these angels as "burning ones." The angels in their glory reveal the higher glory of the Lord, together with his goodness in making these "ministering spirits sent out to serve for the sake of those who are to inherit salvation" (Heb. 1:14).

Starting in verse 5, the second stanza of Psalm 104 expounds on the land masses that emerged out of the seas on the second day of creation (Gen. 1:9). Psalm 104:5–8 shows that God set "the earth on its foundations," and then "covered it with the deep as with a garment," so that "the waters stood above the mountains." Then at God's "rebuke they fled; at the sound of your thunder they took to flight. The mountains rose, the valleys sank down to the place that you appointed for them." This description shows God as covering the earth with water until the continents rose out from

4. John Calvin, *Calvin's Commentaries*, 23 vols. (1848; repr., Grand Rapids: Baker, 2009), 6:145.
5. Calvin, *Commentaries*, 6:146.

the deep through great convulsions. The picture approximates the findings of geological science, except that it shows God as the active moving force. It was his rebuke that parted the waters and his thunder that drove up the undersea mountains. The area of these continents has remained remarkably unchanged over long ages. The psalmist asserts God's decreed limits as the cause for the earth's stability: "You set a boundary that they [the seas] may not pass, so that they might not again cover the earth" (Ps. 104:9).

If it seems that the waters are viewed as enemies of God that need to be subdued, the third stanza sees them as subservient to the Lord's life-giving purpose: "You make springs gush forth in the valleys; they flow between the hills; they give drink to every beast of the field; the wild donkeys quench their thirst" (Ps. 104:10–11). These verses correspond to God's work on the third day of creation, in which the earth sprouted with vegetation, seed-bearing plants, and fruit trees. Emphasis is given to the way in which waterways are directed by the Lord to reach all his creatures. These creatures include "the wild donkeys," which inhabit remote regions, and "the birds of the heavens," which perch high in trees and yet have streams from which to drink. The psalmist completes the first three days of creation with a sense of the joy of new-made earth: "they sing among the branches. From your lofty abode you water the mountains; the earth is satisfied with the fruit of your work" (vv. 12–13).

The six days of God's creation may be divided into two halves, with the first three days spent preparing the earth as a habitation and the final three days spent filling it with inhabitants. As the fourth stanza relates to day 4 of creation, the psalmist turns to the way in which the world was designed to foster life and blessing: "You cause the grass to grow for the livestock and plants for man to cultivate" (Ps. 104:14). The marvels of plant life and horticulture are truly apt to give praise to God. The most abundant resource, green grass, makes livestock fat and healthy. Meanwhile, man is challenged to use his God-given ingenuity in cultivating the wide variety of plant life. It is man who "bring[s] forth food from the earth" (v. 14) by his labor and scientific genius. As man's understanding progressed, we harvested wheat, tended olive vineyards, and reaped tall stalks of corn, along with rich livestock. It is not mere subsistence that God designed, but delightful foods and drinks: "wine to gladden the heart of man, oil to make his face shine and bread to strengthen man's heart" (v. 15). Here, we find that all things made by God are good when properly used (1 Tim. 4:4). The psalmist thus describes an entire ecosystem of bounteous goodness, all bearing testimony to the wisdom of God.

Psalm 104:16 sees God himself tending the creation as a gardener: "The trees of the LORD are watered abundantly, the cedars of Lebanon that he planted. In them the birds build their nests; the stork has her home in the fir trees. The high mountains are for the wild goats; the rocks are a refuge for the rock badgers" (Ps. 104:16–18). Even in remote places, where man seldom casts his eye, the Creator still works wonders. Drawing moisture from the ground, sap climbs up to the tops of tall trees where birds nest, even the massive constructions of the stork. On lofty heights the mountain goats frolic, and God's bountiful creation accommodates their needs, even as the crevices provide refuge for the shy and vulnerable rock badger, also known as the hyrax.

Not only did God create the earth as a teeming garden of life-giving delights, but he also placed heavenly bodies in the sky to mark the passage of time: "He made the moon to mark the seasons; the sun knows its time for setting" (Ps. 104:19). We take the consistency of time and seasons, with the predictably stable movements of heavenly objects, as an assumption of nature. But the orderly passage of the earth on its axis and its orbit around the sun are upheld by God in his faithfulness. Hebrews 1:3 tells us that it is Christ who "upholds the universe by the word of his power," so it is God who deserves the praise for the reliability of our measures of time.

Starting with Psalm 104:20, the theme of time and the introduction of the creatures on the fifth day of creation overlap. First, the psalmist considers how God designed the animals to do their hunting at night so as not to pose a danger to mankind: "You make darkness, and it is night, when all the beasts of the forest creep about. . . . When the sun rises, they steal away and lie down in their dens. Man goes out to his work and to his labor until the evening" (Ps. 104:20–23). God in his wisdom designed a time for man to work and a time for rest. Those who live by God's timing, rising with the sun and going early to bed, are helped to live a wholesome life.

Having surveyed God's creation of the heavens and the earth—not as a static painting but as a living panorama—the psalmist finally arrives at his intended exclamation: "O LORD, how manifold are your works! In wisdom have you made them all; the earth is full of your creatures" (Ps. 104:24). The word for "manifold" elsewhere means "myriad" or "ten thousands," so that the idea is that of staggering abundance and variety. The Lord's works in creation are beyond counting, so that after millennia of study, man is still scratching the surface in terms of our knowledge of God's incredible design. Derek Kidner writes: "What the sceptic sees as a meaningless swarm of life, the psalmist teaches us to view as giving some inkling of the Creator's wealth, and of the range and precision of His thought."[6] We can see why his meditations on Scripture amid the beauty of nature so powerfully summoned young Jonathan Edwards's spirit to worship. The more that we see all the wonders of the world around us as the works of God's hands, the more fervently we will open our hearts to him in praise.

Meanwhile, the psalmist's elegant poetry preserves us from the grievous errors of the unbelieving world, which looks on the creation and fails to see its Creator. For instance, Psalm 104 rules out pantheism, the view that all is God so that nature itself is deified. For all his marveling over nature, it is not the heavens, the oceans, the mountains, or the stars before which the psalmist bows, but God the Creator only. In his *Reflections on the Psalms*, C. S. Lewis agreed:

> To say that God created nature, while it brings God and Nature into relation, also separates them. What makes and what is made must be two, not one. Thus the doctrine of creation in one sense empties Nature of divinity. . . . But in another sense the same doctrine which empties Nature of her divinity makes her an index, a symbol, a manifestation of the Divine. . . . By emptying nature of divinity, . . . you may fill her with Deity, for she is now a bearer of messages.[7]

Just as Psalm 104 opposes those who make a god out of nature, so it also rebukes those who would remove God from creation altogether. Seemingly anticipating the challenge of the theory of evolution, Calvin said that the psalmist "reproves the madness of those who dream, that the world has been brought into its present form by chance."[8] It is no wonder that one of the gravest threats to the cultural hegemony of evolutionary theory comes from

6. Derek Kidner, *Psalms 73–150*, Tyndale Old Testament Commentaries 16 (Downers Grove, IL: InterVarsity Press, 1975), 371.

7. C. S. Lewis, *The Inspirational Writings of C. S. Lewis* (1958; repr., New York: Inspirational, 1987), 172–73.

8. Calvin, *Commentaries*, 5:164.

those who stress the intelligent design inherent to nature. The earth and its ecosystems have such an irreducible complexity that they cannot conceivably have emerged from chance progressions of random forces. Eighteenth-century writer William Paley argued that if a watch was found, its complexity would show that it did not occur by random chance but that it must have been designed.[9] Yet the world described in Psalm 104 is infinitely more complex than a mere watch, something that scientists have to admit about the subatomic world as well as observable nature. Creation reveals God's wisdom, together with his goodness and power, so that man's only reasonable response is that of the psalmist, who prays, "Bless the Lord, O my soul!" (Ps. 104:1).

God's Glorious Providence

Having waxed so eloquently on God's glorious work of creation, the psalmist more briefly turns to the second realm of God's work: his providence. Answer 11 of the Westminster Shorter Catechism defines God's providence as "his most holy, wise, and powerful preserving and governing all his creatures, and all their actions." God's providence has been intimated throughout Psalm 104, given that the verbs are mostly in the present. John Stott notes that "the nineteenth-century deists believed that God had wound up the universe and set it in motion like a gigantic clockwork toy. The Bible teaches, however, that God is a living God, ceaselessly active in the control and the care of what he had made."[10]

The psalmist is fascinated by God's wonderful activity in and for his creation, and in Psalm 104:25–30 he highlights the Lord's governance of movements, provision of needs, and control over life and death.

Psalm 104:25–26 looks on the sea and views the various sea creatures, together with ships, as a cause for praise to God: "Here is the sea, great and wide, which teems with creatures innumerable, living things both small and great. There go the ships, and Leviathan, which you formed to play in it." What activity there is just in the oceans, with fish and whales and ships moving to and fro! In his sermon to the philosophers of Athens, Paul pointed out that God has not only made all mankind but also "determined

9. William Paley, *Natural Theology*, ed. Frederick Ferre (New York: Bobbs-Merrill, n.d.), 3.

10. John R. W. Stott, *Favorite Psalms: Growing Closer to God* (Grand Rapids: Baker, 2003), 90–91.

allotted periods and the boundaries of their dwelling place, that they should seek God, and perhaps feel their way toward him and find him" (Acts 17:26–27). Thus, while the activity of earth may appear random, it is in fact controlled by God for his purposes, especially his plan for salvation.

Verses 27–28 of Psalm 104 progress to God's personal involvement in providing for the needs of his creatures: "These all look to you, to give them their food in due season. When you give it to them, they gather it up; when you open your hand, they are filled with good things." For all the vast number of creatures on earth, every one of them requires daily food. Not only does the Lord provide a store of bounty to meet these needs, but he also provided marvelous instincts that make each creature able to gain its needed store. As the psalmist sees it, each time a mother bird drops a worm into the throat of its chick, a lion tracks its prey, or a hummingbird drinks its nectar, God's own loving hand has opened to meet its daily need, just as a child at the zoo opens its hand full of pellets to welcome the eager mouth of a hungry lamb. Each living being dwells in constant dependence on God, so that when every need is met, we ought to pause and offer a benediction to the faithfulness of our Keeper.

Divine providence is further displayed in God's sovereign gift of life: "When you hide your face, they are dismayed; when you take away their breath, they die and return to their dust. When you send forth your Spirit, they are created, and you renew the face of the ground" (Ps. 104:29–30). Calvin notes: "We continue to live, so long as he sustains us by his power; but no sooner does he withdraw his life-giving spirit than we die."[11] In the mysterious natural process of life and death, the earth is daily renewed according to our Sovereign's purpose. Life itself is the gift of God, so that his creatures should offer the days he has provided for glorifying his name.

There are people, including Christians, who deny God an active and total sovereignty over the affairs of earth, large and small. Instead, they argue, even if God is the Maker, he has stepped down from his throne to give sway to the free will of man. To the psalmist, such an idea is absurd. Reflecting simply on the data of creation, as Paul reasons in Romans 1:19–21, what is known about God as clearly revealed in nature demands its only reasonable response in that we "honor him as God" and "give thanks to him."

11. Calvin, *Commentaries*, 6:167.

Three God-Glorifying Desires

The psalmist concludes with three applications that are very much in line with Paul's thinking. First, he expresses a desire above all else that God should be glorified for his creation: "May the glory of the Lord endure forever; may the Lord rejoice in his works, who looks on the earth and it trembles, who touches the mountains and they smoke!" (Ps. 104:31–32).

God rejoices in his creation because it displays his glory. Jonathan Edwards wrote that the end for which God created the world is the display of the perfections of his attributes.[12] We self-centeredly assume that the earth exists for our pleasure, whereas the psalmist insists that its first priority is to serve the glory and pleasure of God. With this in mind, having shown how God's work of creation glorifies his wisdom, goodness, and power, the psalmist expresses his most fervent desire for this glory to endure forever. James Boice writes: "This is not a wish for something that possibly might not happen, but rather a confident assertion that this is precisely what will happen. . . . Because the glory of the Lord will endure forever, so will God's rejoicing in creation."[13]

The psalmist notes that the creation itself responds to God's presence: "who looks on the earth and it trembles, who touches the mountains and they smoke!" (Ps. 104:32). The holiness of God prompts the awed response of nature itself; how much more should God's glory inspire us to "offer to God acceptable worship, with reverence and awe" (Heb. 12:28).

As a second application, the psalmist resolves to devote all his days to praising God: "I will sing to the Lord as long as I live; I will sing praise to my God while I have being" (Ps. 104:33). Then, feeling immediately how unworthy he is even to give praise to God, he adds, "May my meditation be pleasing to him, for I rejoice in the Lord" (v. 34). Here, we discover the true essence of worship, as the psalmist concerns himself not with what he will get out of worship but rather with what God will think of his praise. What good news it is for the believer to learn that our praises are acceptable to God when offered through the mediation of his Son! Especially when we worship according to the Word of God, redeemed believers may have the confident joy of knowing that our worship is pleasing to God. Hebrews 13:15

12. Jonathan Edwards, *The Works of Jonathan Edwards*, 2 vols. (1834; repr., Peabody, MA: Hendrickson, 1998), 1:94–121.

13. James Montgomery Boice, *Psalms*, 3 vols. (Grand Rapids: Baker, 1996), 2:841.

says of Jesus, "Through him then let us continually offer up a sacrifice of praise to God."

The psalm concludes with a plea for the wicked to be judged: "Let sinners be consumed from the earth, and let the wicked be no more! Bless the LORD, O my soul! Praise the LORD!" (Ps. 104:35). The psalmist's reasoning is that the rebellion of sinners on the earth mars the Lord's delight in what he has made. With this God-centered passion, he prays for this offense to the Lord to be removed. As a third application, Christians should be grieved that unbelieving mankind denies to the Lord the glory due to his works. Our privilege in Christ is to pray and labor for their conversion to faith through our witness of the gospel. Meanwhile, the Christian knows that rebellious sinners who persist in unbelief will nonetheless end up glorifying God. Through our salvation in Christ, we glorify the grace of God. But should "sinners be consumed from the earth," God will still have the praise he deserves, in this case for the glory of his perfect justice and wrath.

How Great Thou Art

When Jesus was encouraging the faith of the Emmaus road disciples, he "interpreted to them in all the Scriptures the things concerning himself" (Luke 24:27). Where, we might then ask, is Jesus found in Psalm 104, a psalm of praise to the Creator? We can see Jesus all through Psalm 103, with its thanks to God for his works of redemption. But can we find things concerning Jesus in this psalm?

One valid answer would be to point out that Christ, as the Word, was present with the Father in his work of creation. John 1:2–3 says that Jesus "was in the beginning with God. All things were made through him, and without him was not any thing made that was made." An equally valid approach was given by Stuart Hine, in his hymn "How Great Thou Art," in which he sees the wonder of God's creation as a foretaste of his thanks for the greater work of redemption in Christ. He invites us to take up this theme of praise to the glory of our Creator and Redeemer God:

> When thro' the woods and forest glades I wander
> And hear the birds sing sweetly in the trees,
> When I look down from lofty mountain grandeur,
> And hear the brook and feel the gentle breeze;

Then sings my soul, my Savior God, to thee:
How great thou art, how great thou art!

And when I think that God, his Son not sparing,
Sent him to die, I scarce can take it in,
That on the cross, my burden gladly bearing,
He bled and died to take away my sin.
Then sings my soul, my Savior God, to thee:
How great thou art, how great thou art![14]

14. Stuart K. Hine, "How Great Thou Art" (1949).

37

Remembering God's Faithfulness

Psalm 105

He remembers his covenant forever, the word that he commanded, for a thousand generations, the covenant that he made with Abraham. (Ps. 105:8–9)

The fourth book of the Psalter (Pss. 90–106) concludes with four psalms that are arranged in couplets. Psalms 103 and 104 each begin with the plea, "Bless the Lord, O my soul," providing reasons why the psalmist's heart should offer praise. Psalm 103 praises God for his works of redemption, and Psalm 104 praises him for his mighty works of creation. The final two psalms, Psalms 105 and 106, also form a pair. For this reason, the ancient Greek translation of the Old Testament, the Septuagint, places the concluding line of Psalm 104 at the beginning of Psalm 105. This seems to be right, since with this change, both Psalms 105 and 106 begin and end with *Hallelujah*, "Praise the Lord." These final psalms contrast God's faithfulness with the infidelity of his people. Psalm 105 calls for praise in remembrance of God's faithfulness, while Psalm 106 concludes the fourth book of the Psalms with a remembrance of man's need to be saved because of his sin.

Many scholars argue that these psalms were written either during Israel's Babylonian exile or after the nation's return to Jerusalem. The chief problem with this view is that the last fifteen verses of Psalm 105, together with the last two verses of Psalm 106, along with the majority of Psalm 96, are also found in 1 Chronicles 16:8–36—the song that David gave to Asaph and his brothers during the ceremony of bringing the ark of the covenant up to Jerusalem. Since Chronicles was compiled after the exile, scholars argue that the Chronicler inserted these later psalms into David's mouth in an attempt to reproduce the kind of thing that David might have written. There is no compelling reason to take this view, but if the Chronicler did read back a later psalm into David's worship, we can be sure that under the inspiration of the Holy Spirit it provided an accurate sense of the original event. Undoubtedly, Psalm 105 offers suitable thanks to God at any time, including during and after the exile, and also for us today.

Psalm 105 is a long psalm, which breaks down into three main sections. The first stanza, verses 1–6, summons the readers to wholehearted praise for the Lord. The second stanza, verses 7–11, provides the main theme, and the cause for thanking God, in his covenant faithfulness: "He remembers his covenant forever" (Ps. 105:8). The rest of the psalm (vv. 12–45) recounts the details of God's covenant faithfulness, starting with Abraham and continuing through Israel's exodus from Israel. Throughout this historical praise, the context of suffering and hardship for God's people presents the backdrop for the display of his wonderful faithfulness.

Praise from God's Chosen People

Assuming that the *Hallelujah* of Psalm 104 really does belong at the start of Psalm 105, the psalm begins with a call to worship that is worked out in a series of appeals. The motive joined to this praise is given in verse 1: "Oh give thanks to the Lord." In other words, we are constrained to worship God not only because of the glory of his person but also because of the faithfulness of his works in our salvation. If one asks, "Why should we give praise to God?," Psalm 105 answers, "Because we are thankful for his faithfulness to us."

This call to worship is followed by a series of exhortations regarding the content of worship. Verse 1 of Psalm 105 continues: "call upon his name;

make known his deeds among the peoples!" Here is a summons to both prayer and preaching. We are to praise the Lord by invoking his blessing and appealing to his care. But then our great desire is that his great deeds be publicized as widely as possible. We find a notable example of this principle in the ministry of the Puritan Richard Baxter, which resulted in a spiritual transformation of the town of Kidderminster, where he served. Inscribed on Baxter's pulpit were the words of this verse: "Give thanks unto the LORD; call upon his name; make known his deeds among the people" (KJV).[1] This statement should form the goal of every Christian minister: that his pulpit ministry should result in thanks based on the knowledge of what God has done for us in Christ. God-glorifying thanks should provide the ambition of every Christian. When families gather around their meal with a prayer and a reading from God's Word, their aim is to stir up thanks for God by making known his deeds.

Verse 2 of Psalm 105 adds praise to the prayer and preaching of verse 1: "Sing to him, sing praises to him; tell of all his wondrous works!" Notice that the ministry of music is an adjunct to the teaching ministry of God's Word. To accomplish this goal, suitable music for Christian worship must contain sound doctrine instead of repetitive emotional appeals. The Psalms provide ideal examples, because they lift our hearts musically to poetry that exalts God's faithful deeds. The Psalms touch every human emotion, yet do not begin with the emotional experience of the worshiper. Rather, psalm after psalm tells about the Lord and his works for our salvation and his deliverance in trials. This, in turn, prompts the worshipers' heartfelt response. In this way, verse 3 urges: "Glory in his holy name; let the hearts of those who seek the LORD rejoice!" Our glory is in the Lord: all that he is, has done, and will do. Worship singing is not merely a musical exercise but is filled with a spiritual purpose in seeking God's praise. George Horne comments:

> In whom should the redeemed "glory," exult, and triumph, but in their Redeemer . . . ? They who "seek" the Lord Jesus by prayer . . . will soon exchange the galling cares and tormenting desires of the world, for the light yoke and easy burden of [their] Savior, in whom [they] will find rest, and peace, and comfort.[2]

1. James Montgomery Boice, *Psalms*, 3 vols. (Grand Rapids: Baker, 1996), 2:846.

2. George Horne, *Commentary on the Psalms* (1771; repr., Audubon, NJ: Old Paths Publications, 1997), 455.

Psalm 105:4 states that we should seek from the Lord "his strength" and "his presence continually." The idea is that our worship should include a deep sense of our dependence on God. David Dickson writes: "It is a part of God's praise and of our thankfulness, to profess our need of God, and in the consciousness of our emptiness and his unsearchable riches, to seek our supply in him."[3] It is the mark of genuine believers that they know the indwelling power of God's Holy Spirit and make it their desire in worship to be strengthened in faith through prayer.

To this end, the psalm's theme will be remembering God's great and faithful works: "Remember the wondrous works that he has done, his miracles, and the judgments he uttered" (Ps. 105:5). In the psalmist's mind, his readers are bound up in the salvation revealed to Abraham and continued through his descendants. The wondrous works of salvation done for their ancestors were also done for their salvation. Moreover, those ancient miracles reveal a faithful God on whom they, too, can rely. The psalmist addresses them as "offspring of Abraham, his servant, children of Jacob, his chosen ones!" (v. 6). Believers who read the psalm today have the same identity. The New Testament states that Abraham's true offspring are spiritual descendants through faith in Christ and his gospel. Galatians 3:29 teaches: "If you are Christ's, then you are Abraham's offspring, heirs according to promise." This means that the story that will unfold in Psalm 105 is part of the family history of every believer, and thus its record should prompt us to thank God for his faithfulness to us.

Since the Bible's history is the story in which every Christian belongs, Calvin Beisner once set out to praise God by recounting all that God had done for him, starting with the fall of Adam and concluding with the events of Beisner's conversion to faith in Jesus. It was for him that God promised Eve an offspring who would crush the serpent's head. God summoned Noah to preserve Beisner's ancestors through the great flood. God called Abraham and established a covenant with him, together with Isaac and Jacob, preserving their line through Joseph in Egypt. When Pharaoh threatened and oppressed Beisner's spiritual forebears, the Lord brought them out with a mighty hand and placed them in the promised land. There, God answered Hannah's prayer for a son and used Samuel to lead Israel to reformation.

3. David Dickson, *A Commentary on the Psalms* (1653; repr., Edinburgh: Banner of Truth, 1995), 2:237.

Samuel anointed David as king over the nation, and through David God would also bring the promised Messiah. Jesus was born in fulfillment of the prophecies and in order to die on the cross for Beisner's sins. Jesus called the disciples, who became the gospel-spreading apostles. The early church was strengthened in faith to withstand the great Roman persecutions and then to sift through the doctrinal confusions of the third and fourth centuries so that Christian faith would pass forward to our time. For Beisner's sake, God tormented the conscience of a German monk so that Martin Luther reclaimed the gospel and published it in the Reformation, together with Calvin, Bucer, Zwingli, Knox, and Rutherford. When faith languished in England and the American Colonies, God enflamed the great evangelists Wesley, Whitefield, and Edwards. In 1836, God moved the heart of Charlotte Elliott to write the hymn "Just As I Am, without One Plea." Then, when Beisner was in the seventh grade, the Lord prompted his father to take the family to a Billy Graham crusade, where God used Elliott's song to persuade Beisner of his need to embrace the gospel for forgiveness of sin. Beisner comments that the Israelites sang Psalm 105 "because they were members of the same covenant, descendants of Abraham."[4] If we are believers, then we, too, are part of the great story of Scripture, and we are called to remember what God has done and make known his deeds to the world.

God's Covenant Faithfulness

If we are asked, "What exactly has God done to prompt our praise?," the answer of Psalm 105 is that God has been faithful to his covenant with Abraham: "He remembers his covenant forever, the word that he commanded, for a thousand generations, the covenant that he made with Abraham" (Ps. 105:8–9). God's covenant with Abraham was an oath-bound promise to supply Abraham with both a vast number of offspring and a home in the land of promise. Genesis 15:17 tells how God made the covenant a unilateral commitment by passing through the divided pieces of severed animals in the form of a torch and a smoking firepot. Normally, both parties making the covenant would pass through the bloody pieces, signifying death for breaking the covenant. In this case, God signified his sovereign commit-

4. E. Calvin Beisner, *Psalms of Promise* (Phillipsburg, NJ: Presbyterian and Reformed, 1988), 215–17.

ment to supply everything needed for Abraham's blessing by putting his servant into a trance while "a smoking fire pot and a flaming torch passed between these pieces" (Gen. 15:17). God's holy nature was thus symbolized, along with his unilateral commitment to fulfill his covenant with Abraham.

The bulk of this psalm will recount how Israel persevered through the most severe trials only to emerge victorious. But why did God preserve the people and bless them? The answer is not that they were deserving in some way but that the Lord was faithful to his covenant. Likewise, "the Christian's confidence in the ultimate outcome of his faith rests not on himself but on God's faithfulness to His promise."[5] John the Baptist's father, Zechariah, saw this same faithfulness as the cause for which the Lord fulfilled his promise of a Messiah through the coming of Jesus: "to remember his holy covenant, the oath that he swore to our father Abraham," in order that God's people "might serve him without fear, in holiness and righteousness before him all our days" (Luke 1:72–75).

God's covenant with Abraham was renewed and reconfirmed to each successive generation. The Abrahamic covenant became God's "sworn promise to Isaac, which he confirmed to Jacob as a statute, to Israel as an everlasting covenant, saying, 'To you I will give the land of Canaan as your portion for an inheritance'" (Ps. 105:9–11). The blessings of these generations came, therefore, from their birthright in God's grace rather than by their own achievements. The Christian likewise learns in God's Word that, as John Calvin explains, his salvation "has not been induced from anything out of himself to prefer us to others, but that [God] was pleased to do so purely from his own free grace."[6] This was eminently the case for ancient Israel: "the ancient covenant was the cause of the deliverance granted to the chosen tribes; for in order that God might faithfully keep his promises, it behooved him first to be merciful."[7]

The promise of the land serves as a symbol for the entirety of the great salvation that God had promised through Abraham. Psalm 105 recounts the various stages by which Israel entered into this inheritance. The Christian, looking on from a more advanced position in redemptive history, sees

5. Beisner, *Psalms of Promise*, 218.

6. John Calvin, *Calvin's Commentaries*, 23 vols. (1848; repr., Grand Rapids: Baker, 2009), 6:177.

7. Calvin, *Commentaries*, 6:177.

the promise of Abraham as symbolic of the eternal life promised in Christ for those who believe. What took place because of the Lord's covenant faithfulness from Abraham all the way to Israel's entry into the promised land is a type of the same salvation we experience through our faith in Jesus. The psalmist anticipates these achievements in verse 7 by calling out: "He is the LORD our God." The Christian finds the same desire to own our relationship to God the Father through our confidence in Jesus Christ. Just as the psalmist declares that "his judgments are in all the earth" (Ps. 105:7), speaking of God's actions to deliver his people, so also the Christian looks with confidence on God's overthrow of evil through Christ.

God's Wonderful Faithfulness to Israel

Starting in Psalm 105:12, the psalmist begins to recount the great story of God's covenant faithfulness from Abraham until the entry of Israel into the promised land. We may track this journey in four movements: God's selection of Abraham; the Lord's sovereignty in sending Israel into Egypt; God's power in delivering Israel out from Egypt; and God's faithfulness in seeing the nation safely into the land of promise. In each of these phases, God proved his faithfulness to his covenant not by preserving his people from the experience of trials but by his mighty deliverance of them out of and through afflictions.

Verses 12–15 of Psalm 105 tell of God's call of Abraham and his immediate offspring to be strangers and pilgrims in the land under the Lord's sovereign protection. Emphasis is given to the grace by which God chose Abraham apart from any consideration on his part to deserve it: "When they were few in number, of little account, and sojourners in it," the Lord made Abraham's household his own (Ps. 105:12). Later Israelites were not in a position, therefore, to claim merit for their boasting as God's covenant people. As Moses recounted: "It was not because you were more in number than any other people that the LORD set his love on you and chose you, for you were the fewest of all peoples, but it is because the LORD loves you and is keeping the oath that he swore to your fathers" (Deut. 7:7–8). Christians have no place for boasting in our salvation, since we were likewise chosen by God's sovereign grace apart from any merit of our own (Titus 3:3–7). In their proud desires, the Israelites would like to look back and say, "We were the princes of ancient history, those who stood out above all others." The reality was exactly the opposite, since Abraham was a marginal figure and a sojourner on the earth.

Here we see God's grace especially in protecting Abraham and his sons from the dangers around them: "he allowed no one to oppress them; he rebuked kings on their account, saying, 'Touch not my anointed ones, do my prophets no harm!'" (Ps. 105:14–15). When Abraham and Sarah went into Egypt, the Lord intervened to protect them, despite Abraham's sin and deceit (Gen. 12:10–20). When the kings of the East came raiding, the Lord granted Abraham victory with a relatively small force (Gen. 14:1–16). The saying "Touch not my anointed ones, do my prophets no harm!" applied to Abraham as the Lord's covenant head and also as a prophet. The point is that God's servants have been seen to receive his protection until their work is done.

Revelation 11 typifies the testimony of the church in the form of two witnesses, one in the guise of Elijah and the other of Moses. Sadly, their worldly enemies rise up and slay them, leaving their bodies in the streets. This represents the deadly opposition poised against the gospel. But this oppression is permitted only "when they have finished their testimony" (Rev. 11:7). Moreover, though Moses and Elijah are slain and left on the ground, with their enemies gloating over them, after three and a half days (a reference to their union with Christ in his resurrection) they are brought back to life by God, to the astonishment of the world (vv. 7–11). At that moment, the faithful servants are gathered into heaven to God's glory just before an earthquake destroys the city (vv. 12–13). This imagery describes the experience of the patriarchs, who could not be slain by any opposition and died only when their work with God was finished. Throughout church history, God's servants—especially his preachers and evangelists—will be immortal until their task is finished and they are delivered out of death and into glory.

A second phase of redemption began in the time of Jacob and his twelve sons. Israel's entry into Egypt occurred by the sovereign moving of God: "When he summoned a famine on the land and broke all supply of bread" (Ps. 105:16). God had prepared for this event, recorded in Genesis 46, by arranging in advance for Joseph to go ahead of his family (Ps. 105:17). Through wicked cruelty, Joseph "was sold as a slave" by his faithless brothers. Verse 18 provides information about his sufferings not found in Genesis: "His feet were hurt with fetters; his neck was put in a collar of iron." Joseph's sufferings were intense, all the more so because of their injustice. His brothers had wrongly assailed him, and when he was a servant in the house of the Egyptian Potiphar, a false accusation landed him in jail. Yet even these events resulted from the Lord's faithfulness to his covenant. Joseph suffered "until what he had said came to pass, the word of the LORD tested him" (Ps. 105:19). Genesis 40 tells how Joseph was given the extraordinary ability to interpret divinely sent dreams, with the result that he was eventually brought before Pharaoh to provide this service. When Joseph interpreted Pharaoh's dreams and informed him of God's intention to follow seven years of plenty with seven years of overwhelming famine, Pharaoh "made him lord of his house and ruler of all his possessions" (Ps. 105:21). Even the other lords of Egypt were placed under Joseph's lordship: "to bind his princes at his pleasure and to teach his elders wisdom" (v. 22).

What a remarkable outworking of God's sovereignty is seen in the life and sufferings of Joseph! God had indeed sent him into Egypt ahead of the covenant family in order to provide for them in the famine. Joseph recognized God's faithfulness in all that had taken place, saying to his wicked brothers: "As for you, you meant evil against me, but God meant it for good, to bring it about that many people should be kept alive, as they are today" (Gen. 50:20). Moreover, we see in Joseph's experience a common theme in the Lord's covenant faithfulness. It is through the humbling experience of trials that God's people are prepared for blessing and high position. Dickson writes: "It is not strange to see the man whom the Lord mindeth to exalt most humbled before he be exalted, and cast into prison before he be lifted up to liberty."[8] So it would be in the experience of Jesus that the cross would come before the crown. The same is true of our trials and hardships, some of which will seem most unfair and hard to bear: Peter explains that these have come "so that the tested genuineness of your faith—more precious than gold that perishes though it is tested by fire—may be found to result in praise and glory and honor at the revelation of Jesus Christ" (1 Peter 1:6–7).

The third phase of God's faithfulness was the deliverance of Israel out of Egypt. Psalm 105:23–25 tells how Israel came to the Nile, where God "made his people very fruitful and made them stronger than their foes" (v. 24), so that the Egyptians first distrusted and then hated them. Indeed, this was

8. Dickson, *Psalms*, 243.

God's plan for Israel's return to the land of Abraham: "He turned their hearts to hate his people, to deal craftily with his servants" (v. 25).

If the experience of Joseph in Egypt showed how God uses trials to prepare his people for his blessings, we see in Moses and Aaron the necessity of our obedience in receiving God's aid: "He sent Moses, his servant, and Aaron, whom he had chosen" (Ps. 105:26). Notice again that there was nothing special about these two men, apart from God's sovereign grace and their subsequent obedience to his commands. Calvin comments: "Moses is called the servant of the Lord, to teach us that he was not self-elected to his office, and that he attempted nothing by his own authority, but, being the minister of God, executed the office with which he was intrusted."[9]

What follows, in Psalm 105:27–36, is a lengthy recitation of the ten plagues by which God displayed his power to Egypt, broke the power of Pharaoh and his false gods, and set his people free from bondage. Notice the prominence of the pronoun *he* to describe God's sovereign actions: "He sent darkness . . . . He turned their waters into blood . . . . He spoke, and there came swarms of flies" (Ps. 105:28–31). In the plagues that struck Israel, the sovereignty of God that operates continually in our lives was made plain to see.

One curiosity of this psalm is that it presents only eight of the ten plagues and changes the order in which they appeared. The first plague cited was actually the ninth (the great darkness over the land, Ps. 105:28). After this, we return to the historical sequence, with the first plague of the Nile's being turned into blood so that all the fish died (v. 29). The third and fourth plagues, however, are inverted (flies and then gnats, instead of the opposite, v. 31).

In order to understand the psalmist's purpose, we should recognize that the plagues against Egypt were intended to humiliate the false deities of the Egyptian pantheon. James Boice comments that "they were directed against the gods and goddesses of Egypt and were intended to show the superiority of the God of Israel to the Egyptian gods."[10] It seems that the psalmist desired to see this warfare in a certain order, which accounts for his reorganization of the historical data: first, against the Egyptian gods of the sky and heavens (the plague of darkness, Ps. 105:28); then against the gods of the waters (the

9. Calvin, *Commentaries*, 6:195.
10. Boice, *Psalms*, 2:849.

turning of the Nile into blood, together with the death of fish and the swarming of frogs, vv. 29–30); and finally, the Lord's victory over the false Egyptian gods of the earth (flies, gnats, vines and fig trees, locusts, and the devouring of the vegetation, vv. 31–35). The last plague was the most severe, the Lord's *coup d'état*. It was a terrible judgment, but one that justly fitted Pharaoh's evil against Israel in slaying the sons of God's people. Yet even this plague did not cause Pharaoh to repent, just as our witness will not always result in salvation. The point is that God was faithful to deliver his people, even to the point of such awesome and public displays of his sovereign power.

The final phase of Israel's deliverance involved the journey of Israel out of Egypt and into the promised land. So eager were the Egyptians to be rid of the people of so savage a God that they loaded them down "with silver and gold" (Ps. 105:37). "Egypt was glad when they departed, for dread of them had fallen upon it" (v. 38). The final verses highlight episodes from the journey through the wilderness that speak of God's supernatural provision: "He spread a cloud for a covering, and fire to give light by night" (v. 39). God provided manna from heaven, and when they asked for meat, "he brought quail" (v. 40). To supply so vast a nation with water in the desert, the Lord "opened the rock, and water gushed out" (v. 41). The point is that God is able to preserve and provide for his people in any situation and will do so, all because "he remembered his holy promise, and Abraham, his servant" (v. 42). The result was that his people came into the land of promise, in fulfillment of all that God had foretold, with joy and singing, taking possession of a rich land by the grace of God alone (vv. 43–44).

So it will be for every believer when history has run its course. God will have been faithful to his covenant promises in Jesus Christ. We will be strengthened through every trial, be delivered from every foe, be released from every bondage, and receive provision for every need, until God has the glory of the salvation he promised to us by grace alone in his covenant with Abraham and the gospel promises of Jesus Christ. John Newton used the scenes from these final verses of Psalm 105 in his hymn "Glorious Things of Thee Are Spoken":

> Round each habitation hov'ring, see the cloud and fire appear
> For a glory and a cov'ring, showing that the Lord is near;

Thus deriving from their banner light by night and shade by day,
Safe they feed upon the manna which he gives them when they pray.[11]

A Holy People

The only question left is how to praise a God who is so faithful to his covenant in the manner he deserves. One answer is by telling the story as Psalm 105 has done for the years between Abraham and Joshua. Another answer is seen in the words that occur at the beginning and end of the psalm: "Praise the Lord!" We are to worship the Lord with exuberant singing and joy in our hearts. But the emphasis given in the final verse is on our lives of obedience to his Word: "that they might keep his statutes and observe his laws" (Ps. 105:45). Derek Kidner explains: "the final verse shows why grace abounded: not that sin might also abound, but (to quote a New Testament equivalent of verse 45) 'that the righteousness of the law might be fulfilled in us, who walk not after the flesh but after the Spirit' (Rom. 8:4)."[12]

In short, the best praise that we can give to God, given his wonderful faithfulness to the promises of his covenant—all the more so in light of the ultimate fulfillment in the death and resurrection of Jesus Christ—is our giving our lives in his service through obedience to his will. Peter understood this, making the application so briefly stated by the psalmist: "as he who called you is holy, you also be holy in all your conduct, since it is written, 'You shall be holy, for I am holy'" (1 Peter 1:15–16). Do we think of our obedience as an act of worship? Jesus did. He said to his disciples, precisely in the spirit of Psalm 105: "If you love me, you will keep my commandments" (John 14:15).

11. John Newton, "Glorious Things of Thee Are Spoken" (1779).

12. Derek Kidner, *Psalms 73–150*, Tyndale Old Testament Commentaries 16 (Downers Grove, IL: InterVarsity Press, 1975), 377.

38

Steadfast Love Forever

Psalm 106

Praise the Lord*! Oh give thanks to the* Lord*, for he is good, for his steadfast love endures forever!* (Ps. 106:1)

A good movie or book comes to its end with a dramatic and usually uplifting scene. A good preacher, likewise, aims to conclude his sermon with a stirring application. But as we come to the close of the fourth book in the Psalms, it seems that Psalm 106 concludes on a sour note. We learned in our previous study that Psalms 105 and 106 fit together, both of them beginning and ending with a *Hallelujah*: "Praise the Lord." But while Psalm 105 celebrates the Lord's covenant faithfulness, Psalm 106 tells a miserable tale of his people's faithlessness. It may seem, therefore, that while Psalm 105's *Hallelujah* is warranted, the final psalm of book 4 gives less reason. Yet the two psalms actually give the same message from two different perspectives. While Psalm 105 tells of God's faithfulness in terms of "the wondrous works that he has done" (v. 5), Psalm 106 also tells the story of God's faithfulness through his remarkable patience for his most wayward followers. Derek Kidner writes: "This psalm is the dark counterpart of its predecessor, a shadow cast by human self-will in its long struggle against the light."[1] Yet though it exposes man's

1. Derek Kidner, *Psalms 73–150*, Tyndale Old Testament Commentaries 16 (Downers Grove, IL: InterVarsity Press, 1975), 377.

ingratitude, "this is a psalm of praise, for it is God's extraordinary longsuffering that emerges as the real theme."[2]

Not only does Psalm 106 sound a suitable reason for God's praise to end this portion of the Psalms, but it also excels in being realistic and accurate about our situation. When we recount God's goodness to us, there is a tendency to think that we have somehow merited our favorable position. Psalm 106 reminds us that this way of thinking is off base. The psalm cites a litany of Israel's many and varied sins, from the exodus until the captivity in Babylon. Yet amid such gross failures on Israel's part and the calamities that resulted, the Lord retains his compassion and remembers his covenant. It is on this same basis—God's faithfulness to us and to his promises—that we may join in the prayer that concludes not only this psalm but the fourth book of the Psalter, adding our *Amen* and *Hallelujah* to that of the psalmist.

God's Extraordinary Long-Suffering

The psalm begins with a call to worship: "Praise the Lord!" Then, characteristically of the Psalms, the Lord is given thanks first for his wonderful person and then for his mighty works. "Oh give thanks to the Lord, for he is good." This goodness finds expression in his faithfulness to a wayward people, "for his steadfast love endures forever!" (Ps. 106:1). Israel had turned away and sinned time and again, yet the Lord remained faithful to his covenant. While all of God's attributes deserve to be praised, the Lord's abounding grace especially prompts us to adore him. Not only the church as a whole, but every individual Christian should feel this motivation to praise God's steadfast love. James Boice writes: "We do not praise God because he is wonderful and we are wonderful too. We praise him because he is kind to us even when we sin and merciful to us when we don't deserve his mercy."[3]

The psalmist not only urges praise for God's mercy, but also points out that we will never be able to say enough about the works that the Lord has done: "Who can utter the mighty deeds of the Lord, or declare all his praise?" (Ps. 106:2). John Calvin notes that "there is no man who has ever endeavoured to concentrate all his energies, both physical and mental, in the praising of God, but will find himself inadequate for so lofty a subject,

2. Kidner, *Psalms 73–150*, 378.

3. James Montgomery Boice, *Psalms*, 3 vols. (Grand Rapids: Baker, 1996), 2:854.

the transcendent grandeur of which overpowers all our senses."[4] The entire enterprise of science consists, knowingly or not, in the exploration of praise to the vastness and intricacy of God's creation. The subject of God's redemption in sending his incarnate Son supplies an even vaster store of praise. Paul writes that in us God has revealed "the unsearchable riches of Christ . . . , so that through the church the manifold wisdom of God might now be made known to the rulers and authorities in the heavenly places" (Eph. 3:8–10).

Psalm 106:3 adds a comment that may seem out of place, until we remember the content of this psalm: "Blessed are they who observe justice, who do righteousness at all times!" Anticipating the miseries that befell the Israelites, the psalmist notes in advance that the reason for their distress is not found in God's unfaithfulness. Had God's people responded in faith, honoring the Lord in justice and righteousness, none of the recorded calamities would have occurred. The point is that "all the glory of Israel's history is confessed to be due, not to her heroes, her priests, her prophets, but to God; all the failures which are written upon that history, all discomfitures, losses, reverses, the sword, famine, exile, are recognized as the righteous chastisement which the sin of the nation has provoked."[5]

Before entering into the litany of Israel's sins, the opening stanza concludes with a personal plea from the psalmist: "Remember me, O Lord, when you show favor to your people; help me when you save them" (Ps. 106:4). The evidence suggests that Psalm 106 was completed sometime after Israel's exile into Babylon, where the psalmist may be languishing together with the remnant of God's people. But he knows that this misery will not continue forever, because of the steadfast love of the Lord. The day will come when the Lord will "show favor" to his people, and the psalmist asks God to include him in that salvation. We are reminded of the thief who was crucified next to Jesus. Though he was guilty, he recognized Jesus as the Savior and pleaded, "Jesus, remember me when you come into your kingdom" (Luke 23:42). The thief was thinking far ahead when Christ would return in glory. But Jesus surprised him by stating, "Truly, I say to you, today you will be with me in paradise" (v. 43). The thief would not have to wait for a future deliverance

4. John Calvin, *Calvin's Commentaries*, 23 vols. (1848; repr., Grand Rapids: Baker, 2009), 5:207.

5. J. J. Stewart Perowne, *The Book of Psalms*, 2 vols. (1878; repr., Grand Rapids: Zondervan, 1976), 2:257.

but would pass with Jesus immediately into heaven. Likewise, the psalmist desires to "look upon the prosperity of your chosen ones," to "rejoice in the gladness of your nation," and to "glory with your inheritance" (Ps. 106:5). Calling on the Lord in faith, the psalmist can therefore look forward to his own participation in Israel's salvation, and may even enjoy its spiritual benefit immediately.

We should study the Bible in this same spirit. When we read of what God has done for Israel, we should pray, "Lord, I am trusting you to be the same kind of Savior to me!" When we see tender mercies and long-suffering from his grace, we should plead for the same steadfast love. And when we look in Scripture on the great glory of God's kingdom, we should echo the psalmist in asking to partake of the prosperity of the elect, rejoicing in the joy of God's church, and glorying with Christ in the riches of his inheritance. Do you wish to participate in the salvation of which the psalmist speaks? Then follow the example that he goes on to set: confessing his sin, recalling God's past goodness, and looking to him in faith for every blessing.

Israel's Sin in Leaving Egypt

Starting in Psalm 106:6, the psalmist begins confessing the sins of Israel, drawing from history. Charles Spurgeon writes, "Confession of sin is the readiest way to secure an answer to the prayer of verse 4."[6] The psalmist does not merely confess the past sins of his fathers but admits that the same sins persist in God's present people: "Both we and our fathers have sinned; we have committed iniquity; we have done wickedness" (Ps. 106:6). Notice the humble candor of this confession: there is no equivocation, there are no excuses. While many today dismiss sin as a triviality, the psalmist admits that his people have offended God with sin, iniquity, and wickedness.

The psalmist follows with eight specific instances in which Israel sinned, during three periods. The first was the sin of rebellion during the time when Israel was departing from Egypt in the exodus: "Our fathers, when they were in Egypt, did not consider your wondrous works; they did not remember the abundance of your steadfast love, but rebelled by the sea, at the Red Sea" (Ps. 106:7). The people were backed up against the great waterway, with Pharaoh's chariots bearing down on them, and they forgot all about the ten

6. Charles Haddon Spurgeon, *The Treasury of David*, 3 vols. (Peabody, MA: Hendrickson, n.d.), 2b:365.

plagues that were celebrated in Psalm 105 for winning their release from slavery. This problem is repeated by us today, whenever we find ourselves in trouble and forget all that the Lord has done for us. When we are in danger, do we remember how Jesus spoke and caused the winds and the waves to be still? When we are in want, do we recall how Jesus fed ten thousand people with a few loaves and fishes? Forgetting such things was the sin of our fathers, and we need to confess our forgetfulness as well.

Having forgotten the Lord's steadfast love, some of God's people complained to Moses: "Is it because there are no graves in Egypt that you have taken us away to die in the wilderness? What have you done to us in bringing us out of Egypt?" (Ex. 14:11). They urged Moses that it would be better to go back to Egypt than to die by the sea. Yet the Lord "saved them for his name's sake, that he might make known his mighty power" (Ps. 106:8). The Lord had his own reasons for saving Israel, including his faithfulness to the covenant with Abraham. And how easy it was for the Lord to do! Moses had only to lift up his staff and the waters of the Red Sea parted, allowing Israel to pass through before they came crashing down to drown the pursuing army of Egypt. Verses 9–10 call God's deliverance to mind: "He rebuked the Red Sea, and it became dry, and he led them through the deep as through a desert. So he saved them from the hand of the foe and redeemed them from the power of the enemy." It was by his Word that God performed yet another mighty deed to save his people. Our great need today is to trust the power of God's Word to save and defend his church.

Psalm 106:12 concludes this period in Israel's history with another episode of spiritual significance: "Then they believed his words; they sang his praise." Israel's sin is shown in that the people believed only *after* God had stretched forth his power. Spurgeon comments: "This is mentioned, not to their credit but to their shame. Those who do not believe the Lord's word till they see it performed are not believers at all. . . . Their song was very excellent, . . . but sweet as it was, it was quite as short, and when it was ended they fell to murmuring."[7] Is not this behavior characteristic of us as well? Do you forget all that the Lord has done when times become hard, and then rebel against the Bible's teaching? Our growth in faith will be seen when the Word of God is enough to stir our faith, so that we believe God before he acts and honor him by trusting obedience.

7. Spurgeon, *Treasury of David*, 2b:366–67.

Sins in the Desert

Starting in Psalm 106:13, the psalmist proceeds to the sins of Israel during the exodus passage through the desert. Here, he lists six separate sin events, in each of which the Lord showed his faithfulness by bearing with his people and saving them from trouble.

The second sin of Psalm 106 was the Israelites' discontentment with their worry over food: "But they soon forgot his works; they did not wait for his counsel. But they had a wanton craving in the wilderness, and put God to the test in the desert" (Ps. 106:13–14). The record of Exodus 16 is almost comical, as the Israelites spoke longingly of the good old days when they were still slaves in Egypt: they "grumbled against Moses and Aaron in the wilderness, and the people of Israel said to them, 'Would that we had died by the hand of the Lord in the land of Egypt, when we sat by the meat pots and ate bread to the full'" (Ex. 16:2–3). Christian singer Keith Green satirized this longing to return to Egypt in a song with the humorous chorus:

> Eating leeks and onions by the Nile:
> Oh, what breath for dining out in style.[8]

The psalmist records how the Lord provided the people with manna that fell from heaven, but notes that with it he gave them a sourness in their bodies and souls: "he gave them what they asked, but sent a wasting disease among them" (Ps. 106:15). How often, when we, too, complain about the provision that God has arranged, we would have been happier with contentment beforehand rather than the bitter answer that God grants to our unappreciative prayers!

The next sin in the desert is recorded in Numbers 16, when Korah and his 250 allies spoke out in jealousy against Moses and Aaron: "When men in the camp were jealous of Moses and Aaron, the holy one of the Lord, the earth opened and swallowed up Dathan, and covered the company of Abiram. Fire also broke out in their company; the flame burned up the wicked" (Ps. 106:16–18). Instead of envying and harassing those whom God has placed in leadership over his church, we should be grateful for them and supportive of the burdens they bear. But so great was this hostility toward

8. Keith Green, "So You Wanna Go Back to Egypt" (1980).

the very leaders who had led Israel out of bondage that even after the conspirators were swallowed by the earth, the Lord sent a plague that slew over fourteen thousand people before Aaron offered a sacrifice that quelled God's anger.

The fourth sin of Israel consisted of idolatry, when Moses ascended Mount Sinai to be with God, and Aaron capitulated to the people's desire for more accessible worship: "They made a calf in Horeb and worshiped a metal image. They exchanged the glory of God for the image of an ox that eats grass" (Ps. 106:19–20). The apostle Paul quoted from this verse when in Romans 1:23 he said that idolaters "exchanged the glory of the immortal God for images." Their sin involved not only making a golden calf to worship the Lord, but also an orgiastic sexual romp, in keeping with the Egyptian worship of the bull god Apis (Ex. 32:25). The psalmist mocks their folly, noting that they "exchanged the glory of God for the image of an ox that eats grass. They forgot God, their Savior, who had done great things in Egypt, wondrous works in the land of Ham, and awesome deeds by the Red Sea" (Ps. 106:20–22). Spurgeon remarks: "It is clear that they must altogether have forgotten the nature and character of Jehovah, or they could never have likened him to a grass-eating animal."[9] The best way to remember who God is and therefore our best defense against idolatry is a continual study of the Bible's teaching about God in his person and works.

The Lord was so angered by the golden calf, and the orgy that broke loose at the very foot of Mount Sinai, that at this time the people "were in greater peril of destruction than at any other time during the course of their wanderings in the wilderness."[10] The psalmist comments: "Therefore he said he would destroy them—had not Moses, his chosen one, stood in the breach before him, to turn away his wrath from destroying them" (Ps. 106:23). These words record the greatest moment in Moses' life, when he offered himself to be condemned in place of the people (Ex. 32:32). To say that Moses "stood in the breach" means that he sought to bridge the gap between God and the nation by offering himself as a sacrifice. The prophet sets an example for Christians today, who should stand in the breach through prayer and our witness of the gospel, interceding for wayward children, lost friends, and, indeed, the entire world under judgment for sin.

9. Spurgeon, *Treasury of David*, 2b:369.
10. H. C. Leupold, *Exposition of the Psalms* (Columbus, OH: Wartburg Press, 1959), 748.

At this point, we might not see how God is to be praised in these events for his mercy, since he was intending to wipe out the nation until first Aaron, and then Moses, intervened. Aaron offered an atoning sacrifice, and Moses offered himself to assuage God's wrath. But these are human actions. Where is the divine mercy? The answer is found in realizing that it was God himself who had established these two men as mediators for the sake of the people. God had arranged the intercession of his priests, so that his justice might be satisfied in a way that offered grace for the people. Robert Godfrey explains: "God used them in the salvation of His people to begin to teach us how His righteous anger and His mercy could meet."[11]

In light of the Bible's further revelation, we realize that Aaron's and Moses' mediation succeeded only because of the true Mediator whom God would send later. Why was the Lord pacified when Aaron offered the blood of animals, except that this offering looked forward to and relied on the true atonement that would be made by Jesus, the true Lamb of God (John 1:29)? Moses' mediation is especially striking. He pleaded, "If you will forgive their sin—but if not, please blot me out of your book that you have written" (Ex. 32:32). Moses was offering to bear the punishment of his people in their place. The problem was that Moses was not a suitable sacrifice, since his own sins made him guilty before God. God accepted Moses' mediation, therefore, on Christ's behalf alone. O. Palmer Robertson comments that Moses' "willing proposal finds its fulfillment in the self-offering of Isaiah's Suffering Servant, who alone was capable of standing in the breach. That which Moses could only offer to do, Jesus Christ has done."[12] Robertson refers to Jesus' offering of himself on the cross to redeem us from sin. As Isaiah 53:6 foretold: "All we like sheep have gone astray; we have turned—every one—to his own way; and the Lord has laid on him the iniquity of us all."

Even this remarkable instance of God's grace, for so great a sin, did not make a lasting impression on Israel. With all that the psalmist has revealed, we still have three great sins in the wilderness to consider—three more episodes of sin from a third period in Israel's history. The fifth sin involved unbelief, when God arranged for spies to go ahead into the promised land

11. W. Robert Godfrey, *Learning to Love the Psalms* (Orlando, FL: Reformation Trust, 2017), 191.

12. O. Palmer Robertson, *Psalms in Congregational Celebration* (Darlington, UK: Evangelical Press, 1995), 307.

and the people responded by rejecting their report: "Then they despised the pleasant land, having no faith in his promise. They murmured in their tents, and did not obey the voice of the LORD" (Ps. 106:24–25). For this great sin, the Lord consigned the generation of the exodus to wander in the wilderness until they had all perished: "Therefore he raised his hand and swore to them that he would make them fall in the wilderness, and would make their offspring fall among the nations, scattering them among the lands" (vv. 26–27).

Sixth was the terrible sin of apostasy, when the Israelite men indulged in sexual immorality with the women of Moab and were led into worship of their false gods: "Then they yoked themselves to the Baal of Peor, and ate sacrifices offered to the dead" (Ps. 106:28). The last statement indicates that they participated in necromantic rituals. Once again, the Lord was "provoked . . . to anger with their deeds, and a plague broke out among them" (v. 29). This time it was Phinehas, Aaron's son, who intervened. Numbers 25:8 records how Phinehas drove a spear through an Israelite man and a Midianite woman as they were committing adultery, prompting the Lord to stay his anger after twenty-four thousand people had died of plague. The psalmist writes: "Then Phinehas stood up and intervened, and the plague was stayed. And that was counted to him as righteousness from generation to generation forever" (vv. 30–31). The last statement refers to a perpetual priesthood that God granted to Phinehas' descendants in memory of his faith (Num. 25:13).

Israel's seventh sin was the insurrection at Kadesh when the people lacked water. This event is chiefly remembered as the instance when Moses so lost his patience that he sinfully struck the rock at Meribah twice, so that God punished him by not permitting him to enter the promised land. "They angered him at the waters of Meribah, and it went ill with Moses on their account, for they made his spirit bitter, and he spoke rashly with his lips" (Ps. 106:32–33). Of this episode, Spurgeon comments: "We ought also to be very careful how we treat the ministers of the gospel, lest by provoking their spirit we should drive them into any unseemly behavior which should bring upon them the chastisement of the Lord. Little do a murmuring, quarrelsome people dream of the perils in which they involve their pastors by their untoward behavior."[13]

13. Spurgeon, *Treasury of David*, 2b:372.

Sins in the Promised Land

The final account of Psalm 106 concerns the period after the Israelites had entered into Canaan and occupied the promised land. Here, an eighth sin is noted: their assimilation into the ways of the evil world. Their initial error here was in failing to "destroy the peoples, as the Lord commanded them" (Ps. 106:34). God had promised to provide the strength to drive out the Canaanites, warning Israel not to make an accommodation with the ungodly, "lest it become a snare in your midst" (Ex. 34:12). This is precisely what happened: "they mixed with the nations and learned to do as they did. They served their idols, which became a snare to them" (Ps. 106:35–36).

Psalm 106:37–39 covers a period of many generations, from the entry into Canaan until the Babylonian captivity, recording a deplorable record of sin that resulted from Israel's assimilation into pagan ways: "They sacrificed their sons and their daughters to the demons; they poured out innocent blood, the blood of their sons and daughters, whom they sacrificed to the idols of Canaan, and the land was polluted with blood. Thus they became unclean by their acts, and played the whore in their deeds." Notice that idol worship is exposed as service to the demons who are operating behind the idols. And how satanic was the practice of offering children on idol altars! What a terrible end can result from the seemingly small beginning of accommodating to worldly ways of thinking and acting. Spurgeon writes:

> Who knows how far evil will go? . . . Had they thought for a moment they must have seen that a deity who could be pleased with the blood of babes spilt by their own sires could not be a deity at all, but must be a demon, worthy to be detested and not adored. How could they prefer such service to that of Jehovah?[14]

These most detestable sins of Israel's history are mirrored in our culture by the mass, industrial slaughter of preborn children on the altar of sexual pleasure and self-centered lifestyles. By this sin alone, the once-Christian West has become unclean before God and in urgent peril of his judgment.

14. Spurgeon, *Treasury of David*, 2b:373.

God's Long-Suffering Faithfulness

In the final section of Psalm 106, the psalmist sums up this historical review by noting two primary actions of the Lord in response to such wanton sin, both of which glorify his faithfulness. Verses 40–43 note the Lord's response of placing his people under judgment: "Then the anger of the Lord was kindled against his people, and he abhorred his heritage; he gave them into the hand of the nations, so that those who hated them ruled over them. Their enemies oppressed them, and they were brought into subjection under their power" (Ps. 106:40–42). Many times in Israel's history, the Lord responded to gross sin by subjecting his people to harsh oppression, until finally the Babylonians were brought to destroy Jerusalem and carry the nation into exile. How was this an expression of God's faithfulness? The answer is that this judgment was the very punishment envisioned by God's covenant through Moses (Deut. 28:15–68). The Lord was faithful to inflict the judgments about which he had warned, remembering promises that the people had forgotten.

Particularly marvelous, however, is the record of God's ongoing compassion for even this faithless people: "Nevertheless, he looked upon their distress, when he heard their cry. For their sake he remembered his covenant, and relented according to the abundance of his steadfast love. He caused them to be pitied by all those who held them captive" (Ps. 106:44–46). These verses give reference to the Lord's earlier covenant with Abraham, which promised a multitude of offspring who would enter into eternal blessing through faith (Gen. 17:7–8). They also reference the people's prayers of distress, asking the Lord for deliverance on the basis of his faithful, covenant love.

It is on the basis of this covenant faithfulness that the psalm concludes with both prayer and praise to the Lord. We can easily imagine the psalmist offering his prayer from Babylon, where he anxiously awaited deliverance with other faithful Jews: "Save us, O Lord our God, and gather us from among the nations, that we may give thanks to your holy name and glory in your praise" (Ps. 106:47). This is a prayer that we may offer with even greater boldness in the name of Jesus Christ, though we, too, petition God as a pilgrim people afflicted in the world.

With confidence in the Lord's answer, the psalmist concludes the entire fourth book of the Psalter with words of praise: "Blessed be the Lord, the

God of Israel, from everlasting to everlasting! And let all the people say, 'Amen!' Praise the Lord!" (Ps. 106:48). We are gathered as God's people today because that praise is true: God delivers his people from everlasting to everlasting, and all who trust in Jesus Christ are certain to be delivered into glory. Now is the time, therefore, to give our *Amen* to God, inviting others to join us, in all things offering the *Hallelujah* of praise to our long-suffering and faithful Savior.

Bibliography

Aikman, David. *Jesus in Beijing.* Washington, DC: Regnery, 2003.

Alexander, Eric. *Our Great God and Saviour.* Edinburgh: Banner of Truth, 2010.

Alexander, Joseph A. *The Psalms Translated and Explained.* 1873. Reprint, Grand Rapids: Baker, 1977.

Allen, Leslie. *Psalms 101–150.* Word Biblical Commentary 21. Waco, TX: Word, 1983.

Augustine. *The City of God.* Translated by Gerald G. Walsh, Demetrius B. Zemu, Grace Monahan, and Daniel J. Honan. New York: Doubleday, 1950.

———. *Confessions.* Translated by William Watts. Cambridge, MA: Harvard University Press, 1919.

Barnhouse, Donald Grey. *Exposition of Bible Doctrines, Taking the Epistle to the Romans as a Point of Departure.* Vol. 3, *God's Remedy.* Wheaton, IL: Van Kampen, 1954.

Beisner, E. Calvin. *Psalms of Promise.* Phillipsburg, NJ: Presbyterian and Reformed, 1988; 2nd ed. P&R Publishing, 1994.

Boice, James Montgomery. *Psalms.* 3 vols. Grand Rapids: Baker, 1996.

Boice, James Montgomery, and Philip Graham Ryken. *The Heart of the Cross.* Wheaton, IL: Crossway, 1999.

Bridges, Jerry. *The Practice of Godliness.* Colorado Springs: NavPress, 1996.

Brueggemann, Walter. *The Psalms and the Life of Faith.* Minneapolis: Fortress, 1995.

Burroughs, Jeremiah. *Gospel Worship.* 1648. Reprint, Morgan, PA: Soli Deo Gloria, 1990.

———. *The Rare Jewel of Christian Contentment.* Edinburgh: Banner of Truth, 1964.

Calvin, John. *Calvin's Commentaries*. 23 vols. 1848. Reprint, Grand Rapids: Baker, 2009.

———. *Sermons on the Book of Micah*. Phillipsburg, NJ: P&R Publishing, 2003.

Campbell, Murdoch. *From Grace to Glory: Meditations on the Book of Psalms*. Edinburgh: Banner of Truth, 1970.

Charnock, Stephen. *The Existence and Attributes of God*. 2 vols. 1883. Reprint, Grand Rapids: Baker, 1996.

Delitzsch, Franz. *Biblical Commentary on the Psalms*. Translated by Francis Bolton. Vol. 2. Grand Rapids: Eerdmans, n.d.

Dickson, David. *A Commentary on the Psalms*. 1653. Reprint, Edinburgh: Banner of Truth, 1995.

Edwards, Jonathan. *The Religious Affections*. 1746. Reprint, Edinburgh: Banner of Truth, 1986.

———. *The Works of Jonathan Edwards*. 2 vols. 1834. Reprint, Peabody, MA: Hendrickson, 1998.

Elliot, Elisabeth. *Shadow of the Almighty: The Life and Testament of Jim Elliot*. San Francisco: Harper & Row, 1958.

Ferguson, Sinclair B. *The Grace of Repentance*. Wheaton, IL: Crossway, 2000.

Godfrey, W. Robert. *Learning to Love the Psalms*. Orlando, FL: Reformation Trust, 2017.

Hart, Benjamin. *Faith and Freedom: The Christian Roots of American Liberty*. San Bernardino, CA: Here's Life Publishers, 1988.

Hart, D. G., and John Muether. *With Reverence and Awe*. Phillipsburg, NJ: P&R Publishing, 2002.

Henry, Matthew. *Commentary on the Whole Bible*. 6 vols. Peabody, MA: Hendrickson, n.d.

Horne, George. *Commentary on the Psalms*. 1771. Reprint, Audubon, NJ: Old Paths Publications, 1997.

Jones, Douglas, and Douglas Wilson. *Angels in the Architecture: A Protestant Vision for Middle Earth*. Moscow, ID: Canon Press, 1998.

Kidner, Derek. *Psalms 73–150*. Tyndale Old Testament Commentaries 16. Downers Grove, IL: InterVarsity Press, 1975.

Lane, Eric. *Psalms 90–150: The Lord Reigns*. Ross-shire, Scotland: Christian Focus, 2006.

Leupold, H. C. *Exposition of the Psalms*. Columbus, OH: Wartburg Press, 1959.

Lewis, C. S. *The Inspirational Writings of C. S. Lewis*. 1958. Reprint, New York: Inspirational, 1987.
———. *The Magician's Nephew*. New York: Harper Collins, 1955.
———. *Mere Christianity*. New York: Macmillan, 1958.
———. *Reflections on the Psalms*. New York: Harcourt, Brace & World, 1958.
Lloyd-Jones, D. Martyn. *The Cross*. Wheaton, IL: Crossway, 1986.
———. *Faith Tried and Triumphant*. Grand Rapids: Baker, 1994.
Machen, J. Gresham. *Christianity and Liberalism*. Grand Rapids: Eerdmans, 1923.
Maclaren, Alexander. *Expositions of Holy Scripture*. 17 vols. Grand Rapids: Baker, 1982.
———. *Expositions of Holy Scripture*. 17 vols. New York: A. C. Armstrong & Son, 1894.
Mohler, R. Albert. "The Scandal of Biblical Illiteracy: It's Our Problem." AlbertMohler.com. October 13, 2005. https://digital.library.sbts.edu/handle/10392/1921. Accessed May 24, 2019.
Murray, Iain H. *D. Martyn Lloyd-Jones: The First Forty Years, 1899–1939*. Edinburgh: Banner of Truth, 1982.
———. *Heroes*. Edinburgh: Banner of Truth, 2014.
———. *Jonathan Edwards: A New Biography*. Edinburgh: Banner of Truth, 1987.
Packer, J. I. *Knowing God*. Downers Grove, IL: InterVarsity Press, 1978.
Paley, William. *Natural Theology*. Edited by Frederick Ferre. New York: Bobbs-Merrill, n.d.
Palmer, Benjamin Morgan. *Life and Letters of James Henley Thornwell*. Richmond, VA: Whittet and Shepperson, 1875.
Perowne, J. J. Stewart. *The Book of Psalms*. 2 vols. 1878. Reprint, Grand Rapids: Zondervan, 1976.
Piper, John. *Don't Waste Your Cancer*. Wheaton, IL: Crossway, 2011.
Plumer, William S. *Psalms*. 1867. Reprint, Edinburgh: Banner of Truth, 1975.
Prothero, Rowland E. *The Psalms in Human Life*. New York: Dutton, 1904.
Robertson, O. Palmer. *The Flow of the Psalms*. Phillipsburg, NJ: P&R Publishing, 2015.
———. *Psalms in Congregational Celebration*. Darlington, UK: Evangelical Press, 1995.
Ryken, Philip Graham. *Courage to Stand: Jeremiah's Battle Plan for Pagan Times*. Wheaton, IL: Crossway, 1998.

Ryle, J. C. *Expository Thoughts on Mark*. 1857. Reprint, Edinburgh: Banner of Truth, 1985.

Schaff, Philip. *History of the Christian Church*. 8 vols. 1858. Reprint, Peabody, MA: Hendrickson, 2002.

Smellie, Alexander. *Men of the Covenant*. 1903. Reprint, London: Banner of Truth, 1960.

Spurgeon, Charles Haddon. *The Treasury of David*. 3 vols. Peabody, MA: Hendrickson, n.d.

Stott, John R. W. *Favorite Psalms: Growing Closer to God*. Grand Rapids: Baker, 2003.

Tate, Marvin E. *Psalms 51–100*. Word Biblical Commentary 20. Waco, TX: Word, 1990.

ten Boom, Corrie. *The Hiding Place*. Grand Rapids: Baker, 1984.

Tozer, A. W. *The Knowledge of the Holy*. 1961. Reprint, San Francisco: HarperSanFrancisco, 1992.

VanGemeren, Willem A. "Psalms." In *The Expositor's Bible Commentary*, edited by Frank E. Gaebelein, 5:3–880. Grand Rapids: Zondervan, 1991.

Warfield, Benjamin B. *Faith & Life*. 1916. Reprint, Edinburgh: Banner of Truth, 1974.

Watson, Thomas. *A Body of Divinity*. Edinburgh: Banner of Truth, 1958.

Wells, David F. *God in the Wasteland: The Reality of Truth in a World of Fading Dreams*. Grand Rapids: Eerdmans, 1994.

Wilcock, Michael. *The Message of Psalms 73–150*. Downers Grove, IL: InterVarsity Press, 2001.

Willborn, C. N., ed. *Selected Writings of Benjamin Morgan Palmer*. Edinburgh: Banner of Truth, 2014.

Yancey, Philip. *Disappointment with God*. Grand Rapids: Zondervan, 1988.

Index of Scripture

EXTRABIBLICAL CITATIONS

Index of Subjects and Names

Available in the Reformed Expository Commentary Series

Old Testament

1 Samuel, by Richard D. Phillips
2 Samuel, by Richard D. Phillips
1 Kings, by Philip Graham Ryken
2 Kings, by Philip Graham Ryken
Esther & Ruth, by Iain M. Duguid
Ezra & Nehemiah, by Derek W. H. Thomas
Psalms 42–72, by Richard D. Phillips
Psalms 73–106, by Richard D. Phillips
Ecclesiastes, by Douglas Sean O'Donnell
Song of Songs, by Iain M. Duguid
Daniel, by Iain M. Duguid
Jonah & Micah, by Richard D. Phillips
Zechariah, by Richard D. Phillips
Zephaniah, Haggai, and Malachi, by Iain M. Duguid and Matthew P. Harmon

Forthcoming

Genesis, by Richard D. Phillips